GENDER IN HISTORY

Series editors:
Lynn Abrams, Cordelia Beattie, Pam Sharpe and Penny Summerfield

The expansion of research into the history of women and gender since the 1970s has changed the face of history. Using the insights of feminist theory and of historians of women, gender historians have explored the configuration in the past of gender identities and relations between the sexes. They have also investigated the history of sexuality and family relations, and analysed ideas and ideals of masculinity and femininity. Yet gender history has not abandoned the original, inspirational project of women's history: to recover and reveal the lived experience of women in the past and the present.

The series Gender in History provides a forum for these developments. Its historical coverage extends from the medieval to the modern periods, and its geographical scope encompasses not only Europe and North America but all corners of the globe. The series aims to investigate the social and cultural constructions of gender in historical sources, as well as the gendering of historical discourse itself. It embraces both detailed case studies of specific regions or periods and broader treatments of major themes. Gender in History books are designed to meet the needs of both scholars and students working in this dynamic area of historical research.

Jewish women in Europe in the Middle Ages

Manchester University Press

ALSO AVAILABLE
IN THE SERIES

Myth and materiality in a woman's world: Shetland 1800–2000   Lynn Abrams

Destined for a life of service: defining African-Jamaican womanhood, 1865–1938
Henrice Altink

Gender and housing in Soviet Russia: private life in a public space   Lynne Attwood

Love, intimacy and power: marital relationships in Scotland, 1650–1850   Katie Barclay

History, patriarchy and the challenge of feminism
(with University of Pennsylvania Press)   Judith Bennett

Gender and medical knowledge in early modern history   Susan Broomhall

'The truest form of patriotism': pacifist feminism in Britain, 1870–1902   Heloise Brown

Artisans of the body in early modern Italy: identities, families and masculinities
Sandra Cavallo

Women of the right spirit: paid organisers of the Women's Social and Political Union (WSPU) 1904–18   Krista Cowman

Masculinities in politics and war: gendering modern history
Stefan Dudink, Karen Hagemann and John Tosh (eds)

Victorians and the Virgin Mary: religion and gender in England 1830–1885
Carol Engelhardt Herringer

Living in sin: cohabiting as husband and wife in nineteenth-century England
Ginger S. Frost

Murder and morality in Victorian Britain: the story of Madeleine Smith
Eleanor Gordon and Gwyneth Nair

The military leadership of Matilda of Canossa, 1046–1115   David J. Hay

The shadow of marriage: singleness in England, 1914–60   Katherine Holden

Women police: gender, welfare and surveillance in the twentieth century   Louise Jackson

Noblewomen, aristocracy and power in the twelfth-century Anglo-Norman realm
Susan Johns

The business of everyday life: gender, practice and social politics in England, c. 1600–1900
Beverly Lemire

Women and the shaping of British Methodism: persistent preachers, 1807–1907
Jennifer Lloyd

The independent man: citizenship and gender politics in Georgian England
Matthew McCormack

The feminine public sphere: middle-class women and civic life in Scotland, c. 1870–1914
Megan Smitley

Elizabeth Wolstenholme Elmy and the Victorian feminist movement: the biography of an insurgent woman   Maureen Wright

JEWISH WOMEN IN EUROPE IN THE MIDDLE AGES
A QUIET REVOLUTION

⇌ Simha Goldin ⇌

Manchester University Press

Copyright © Simha Goldin 2011

The right of Simha Goldin to be identified as the author of this work has been asserted by him in accordance with the Copyright, Designs and Patents Act 1988.

Published by Manchester University Press
Altrincham Street, Manchester M1 7JA, UK
www.manchesteruniversitypress.co.uk

British Library Cataloguing-in-Publication Data is available

Library of Congress Cataloging-in-Publication Data is available

ISBN 978 1 5261 0660 5 *paperback*

First published by Manchester University Press in hardback 2011

This edition first published 2016

The publisher has no responsibility for the persistence or accuracy of URLs for any external or third-party internet websites referred to in this book, and does not guarantee that any content on such websites is, or will remain, accurate or appropriate.

Printed by Lightning Source

Contents

PREFACE		*page* vii
ACKNOWLEDGEMENTS		ix
MAP		x
1	Introduction	1
2	Heroines by choice or by chance: martyrs, converts, and *anusot* (forced converts)	26
3	Four differing paradigms of male attitudes to women	51
4	The family unit and the change in women's status	90
5	Marital relations, power, and social standing	121
6	Women and the *mitzvot*	169
7	Cases of some prominent Jewish women	223
8	In conclusion	236

Appendices

1	Translated samples of the original source material	243
2	The main scholars referred to	250
	GLOSSARY OF HEBREW TERMS USED	252
	BIBLIOGRAPHY	257
	INDEX	267

Preface

The Jewish society that lived amongst the Christian population in medieval Europe presents a puzzle and a challenge to any historian. How did this group of people survive the various crises of the Middle Ages? How did it relate to and cope with the majority population that held opposing beliefs and was generally hostile to it? How did it forge its own internal social character?

The historian studying the social characteristics of this society and the internal relationships and forces working within it immediately notices that matters relating to women constitute a central and critical component in the written sources of this community. Matters such as the place of women in the family, their economic status, their religious status and, of course, the tension between the theoretical religious framework and social realities are dominant themes in these sources. I had been exposed for the first time to the complexities of researching Jewish society in the course of working on my own master's thesis under the tutelage of Maurice Kriegel, in which I gained a deep familiarity with the work of Jacob Katz and in particular with the chapters dealing with the family and family ties in his book *Tradition and Crisis*. For the first time I saw a comprehensive system of research integrating the sources into a clear and coherent methodological entity. This study had its beginnings there, from a desire to throw light on this subject by an inclusive examination of the Jewish community with all its various components.[1]

The subject of this study is the relationship between men and women within the Jewish society that lived among the Christian population for a period of some 350 years. The study concentrates on Germany, northern France and England from the middle of the tenth century – from the time when we have enough Hebrew sources to enable us to undertake a social analysis of the Jewish communities – until the middle of the second half of the fourteenth century – by which time the Christian population has had enough of the Jewish communities living among them and expels them from almost all the places they were living in.

The innovators of research in Judaic studies in the middle of the nineteenth century had delved a great deal already, then, into the subject of the Jewish family, and the development of Jewish law that relates to the family from different aspects. They discovered manuscripts, set up research methods and even drew up, in general terms, the limits of the research, but it was only towards the end of the twentieth century that the essential step was taken to give this research the central place that is its due.[2] From 1999 to 2003 I organized three conferences at Tel Aviv University that discussed the question of women and society in the Middle Ages and which examined from an interdisciplinary viewpoint the complex, multi-faceted aspects of the subject. Those who participated in these conferences came from the fields of Jewish history and general history, art and literature. At that time I met Dr Patricia Skinner at the International Medieval Conference in Leeds and the idea of writing a book on the status of the Jewish woman in the Middle

Ages came into being. In 2001 Avraham Grossman's monumental book was published in Hebrew and did much to advance the state of research in these areas.[3] A year later Bitkha Har-Shefi's doctoral thesis was published and proved to be a pioneering research work on questions related to the status of the woman within the world of the *mitzvot* (commandments).[4] In 2004 Elisheva Baumgarten's book was published. This ground-breaking work concentrated on the functioning of Jewish women as mothers and their relationship with their children. Baumgarten extensively and innovatively used Jewish sources in her research of these subjects.[5]

This study, which is based on the earlier works, seeks to concentrate the discussion specifically on the social field in an attempt to understand the internal developments of the Jewish community itself. The subject of attitudes towards women and the changes in their social status constitutes an excellent case for study, since it includes the majority of factors that are examinable in the functioning of the group. Within these factors can be found the views of the leadership, economic influences, fundamental philosophies, stereotyped viewpoints, group inclinations and tendencies, internal power politics and gender struggles.

Note. The book contains a great many complex technical terms in Jewish law and culture which often defy translation. I have left them, transliterated and italicised in the body of the text, occasionally with an explanatory footnote. They are all listed, with explanations, in the Glossary of Hebrew Terms.

Notes

1 Jacob Katz, *Tradition and Crisis: Jewish Society at the End of the Middle Ages*, New York 1961, especially chapters 14, 'The family' (pp. 135–148), and 15, 'Kinship' (pp. 149–156).

2 See the extremely comprehensive bibliography in E. Baumgarten, *Mothers and Children: Jewish Family in Medieval Europe*, Princeton, NJ 2004, pp. 244–268.

3 Grossman's book was published in two editions: the Hebrew version and the greatly abridged English version. (It is difficult to understand the decision to reduce significantly the content of the book in its English version, thereby reducing, in my opinion, the immense scholarship Grossman displays in the Hebrew version.) My references are primarily to the Hebrew version of the book, but I also refer to the English version where indicated. Avraham Grossman, 'Pious and Rebellious: Jewish Women in Medieval Europe', the Zalman Shazar Center for Jewish History, Jerusalem 2001 [Hebrew], and Avraham Grossman, *Pious and Rebellious: Jewish Women in Medieval Europe*, Brandeis University Press, Waltham, MA 2004 [English].

4 Bitkha Har-Shefi, Women and Halakha in the years 1050–1350 CE; 'Between Law and Custom', Ph.D thesis to the Hebrew University in Jerusalem, Jerusalem 2002; See also H. Sondra and E. Taitz, *Written out of History: Our Jewish Foremothers*, New York 1990.

5 Elisheva Baumgarten, *Mothers and Children: Jewish Family Life in Medieval Europe*,

Acknowledgements

First and foremost I would like to thank Dr Patricia Skinner, who for a long time has insisted on the importance of undertaking this study. I am also grateful to Hanna Naveh of Tel Aviv University, who was the driving force behind the three conferences at which central questions of the methodology of the study were worked out, and to Professor Miri Rubin of Queen Mary College, London University, who was always ready to answer any question throughout the period of this study, and, of course, to Yitzhak Hen of the Ben Gurion University of the Negev, in Beer Sheva, who read the study and made many constructive comments. In 2006 I was privileged to serve as a Visiting Fellow at Clare Hall, Cambridge, England, where the last stages of the study were completed. I wish to thank the members of the college for their fine hospitality and for providing me with such excellent conditions for conducting research and writing and also for looking after my family so well. Finally, I want to express my appreciation to Ilana Kraus and to C. Michael Copeland for their help in translating and editing the book.

S.G.

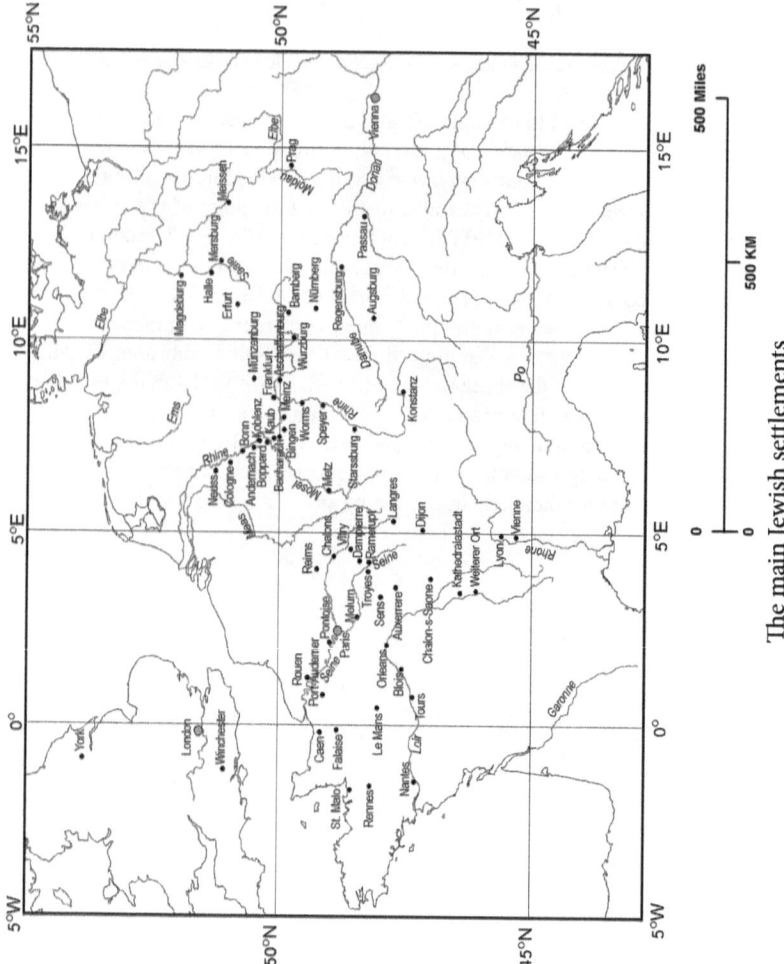

The main Jewish settlements

I

Introduction

This study started out as, and continues to be, an attempt to understand the Jewish society living among the Christian population in the Middle Ages (from 1000 to 1350): how it functioned and how it managed to survive. My research into the history, characteristics and functioning of this society led me to the realization that these questions cannot be answered without conducting an extensive analysis of the social status of the women in this population. The complexity of this question is amplified in the case of medieval Jewish Ashkenazi society in view of the numerous references of men to issues associated with women, and because of the challenge of elucidating the status of women in the light of the complete absence of any records left behind by Jewish women themselves in that era.[1] The Jewish community was fundamentally a male society, patriarchal in nature, where every facet of life manifested male superiority and control. Nevertheless, the women of this community played an important and often central role in every group and social system[2] – a matter not easily explained. This work – a study of history that relies on social historical analyses – seeks to formulate possible answers to this question, or at least to understand the events.

From previous research, I have found that the leaders of the Jewish communities in the eleventh century came to the conclusion that the Christian society in which they were living was seeking to displace them and thus win the theological struggle between the two religions. Despite its self-confidence, its convictions, and the mainly stable political situation (both in Germany and in France), the Jewish leadership assumed that the Christian society would realize this possibility. It therefore mobilized itself to meet what it perceived as a real threat. The eruption of the Crusades in Europe in the eleventh century, the dire physical blow that befell the Jewish communities of the Rhine in 1096, together with the Christian victory that followed in the Holy Land, lent a sense of urgency to this worldview. Thus a society developed that was highly committed to a cause in which the fight for every individual was imperative, and everyone – women, children, and the elderly – was mobilized to defend the ramparts.[3] This is the major characteristic of all the Jewish communities in northern Europe: they were all mobilized in the cause.

As we have said, the social framework of medieval Jewry was male-dominated. The leadership was male and it was this leadership that defined its characteristics in male terms; religious life was controlled by men and their written records are unmistakably male-dominated. These men did not look upon women as sharing equal status with their male counterparts; however, they viewed themselves as being concerned with the entire community, taking all its members – that naturally included the women – into consideration. The leaders attempted to improve the status of women so as to enlist them in the struggle to strengthen the family, the backbone of society and its prime grouping. Such improvements would immediately give rise to internal opposition, and internecine social conflict would ensue between those who opposed the change and those who supported it, with the women appearing to stand passively on the sidelines, although, in reality, they were very actively involved. Hence, in this study, we are describing a social conflict within a community, a conflict that is gender oriented, but first and foremost, is social in nature.

In an illuminating article written in 1983, Cynthia Ozick, the novelist and thinker, stressed that the status of the Jewish woman is not at all a 'theological issue but rather a sociological fact'.[4] Ozick's article is of paramount importance because it confronts every scholar in this field with the fact that even if we rely both on classic historic research methods and the gender research developed in recent years as a 'feminist methodology' in the final analysis, or more precisely, from the outset, we must deal with the social question. In effect, the entire discussion has to begin with the actual status of women in the given Jewish society, an examination of the change it undergoes, and the reasons for such change. I will argue that the social system of the medieval Jewish community did not assume that the status of women was 'theological', eternal or unchanging. Neither did the medieval Jewish community assume that there were religious ordinances whose purpose it was to perpetuate the current status of women; the opposite was true. The religious leaders believed that the *halakhah*[5] itself contained mechanisms for change and improvement. Historic research shows that in certain periods these mechanisms were set in motion as the result of historic necessity for the purpose of improving the status of women, though sometimes the opposite occurs. 'The theological argument' is put forward either to support the change or the reaction against it; and while sometimes succeeding, at the time and place we are discussing it inevitably fails.

The same mechanisms, rooted in the mores of the *Mishnah* and *Gemarah*, either produce a change that promotes the status of women or strengthens the obstacles to positive change.[6] The conflict between men and women is ongoing and does not disappear when men attempt to freeze or diminish the status of women; and when an improvement in their status does occur, women tend to want more, reinforcing the reactionary male bias. The lack of basic equality is what generates these dynamic stances. It needs to be made clear, however, that all these phenomena and the changes we are learning about reach us through the writings of men and men only.

The sources available to us were written by a relatively small group of men who filled leading positions (or by the ranks of the opposition,[7] who sought to become leaders), most of them connected through family ties. Their main occupation was that of *dayan* or judge; they sat in panels of three and passed judgment on any issue that arose within the confines of the community and the interpersonal relationships among its members. Furthermore, these talented, outstanding personalities were skilled writers whose abilities usually extended to several genres. They wrote commentaries on the Bible and Talmud, and liturgical poetry (*piyyutim*), but were mainly occupied with responding to queries sent to them from their students and colleagues.[8] Although the decisions of this male elite were based on an outlook rooted in the sacred tradition of the *Mishnah* and *Gemarah* and the literature that grew out of these texts, they themselves mirror a most interesting stage of development: they closely examined this literature, interpreted it, and compared it with the community's customs and characteristics, built up over hundreds of years, during a time when Jewish society in northern Europe was cut off from the major trends of halakhic development. The men, whose statements will be discussed in this study, saw themselves as part of this mechanism of elucidation and argument, interpretation and comprehension, and they did not necessarily rely on halakhic works. In their mind, the talmudic viewpoint was not the only one; they refused to chain themselves to it and to derive their conclusions totally from this tradition. However, when they sought to give their conclusions more weight, they did make an effort to show how extensively their deductions were derived from the Talmud, or from logical developments that came directly from the Talmud. Yet, they stressed that in their capacity as *dayanim*, they were not bound to what was written in the Talmud; but rather there were customs that had to be taken into consideration, as well as communal rulings that obligated them, not to mention precedents set by themselves and by other *dayanim*.⁹ Furthermore, these *dayanim* did not see themselves as being subject to a tradition of codification. Their method was based on the discussion and argument in the Talmud and not on legal codifications or fixed sets of rules. Their attitude towards the words of the *Geonim* was one of great admiration and respect; however, they disagreed with them and were sometimes disparaging of the principles they had set down. The immediacy of their outlook towards what was going on around them, towards political and economic forces and theological dilemmas, and towards the threats posed by missionary activities, very often determined their decisions. Their attitude towards customs was of great importance; in their minds, there was a fundamental need to take customs into consideration as one of the components of *halakhah*. These men treated all the issues they dealt with – including those related to women – in the same way, using the same methods.

In any analysis of a community caught up in a clash with its surroundings, it can be assumed that the majority population exerts an influence over the minority community; and indeed in the case of the Jewish community under discussion, the external influences imposed by the Christians living around them are obvious. The impact of Christian society was a constant not only because it aspired towards victory over the Jews and sought to convert them to Christianity; not only because the Christians considered this a challenge; and not only because of an ever-increasing intellectual curiosity among Jews with regard to Christian intellectuals, but mainly because the Jews lived among the Christians, in proximity to them, spoke the same language, lived in the same buildings, ate similar food, while nonetheless attempting to institute separation and differentiation. They cultivated another, different language, were strict about making distinctions in their foods and eating habits, and endeavoured to create their own different space.¹⁰ Hence, we must be very careful about defining these 'influences', and we must take all the other trends into consideration as well. Since the Jews of the Middle Ages were aware of the competition and of the Christian need to win the theological battle, and since they feared such a victory, they rejected Christian influence in the normal sense of the word. Nevertheless, Christian behaviour in general and Christian religious behaviour in particular, constituted a constant provocation for the Jews. They reacted to this provocation in many ways, mainly by developing contrary behaviour. In this study, comparisons will be made between the societies, but we will not be comparing the development of the status of women in Christianity with that in Judaism, not only because the starting points in the areas under discussion are very different in the two societies, but primarily because comparative research can only come after the type of study being conducted here. Comparisons will be made where they are obvious and where the parties (the Christians and the Jews) refer to them.

In order to assess the attitude towards women, we must examine at least three typical areas, key aspects of life in every society: the family, the economy, and religion. Gender studies (and feminist research) would add that in order to understand the status of women, the topic of gender as a social construct, as a tool of oppression, and as a prism for the processing of knowledge must also be examined. This study explores the manner in which the family unit is established; how the status of a woman is decided within the family and the family structure; the struggle of women against the coercive power of the men within the family, and the ability of the woman to leave her family, taking with her what she has achieved economically; her economic status; her emergence during times of social or theological crisis; and her status in the area of religion.

The Jews in northern Europe

From the tenth century and until their expulsion towards the end of the medieval period, the Jews of Europe lived mainly in communal settings in Christian towns. Two groups lived in these cities: the Christian majority and the Jewish minority. Between them there were many complex inter-relationships underpinned by a strong and constant religious tension.[11] Few records are available regarding the Jews of Europe during the Roman period and the early Middle Ages; only towards the tenth century does the extent of the information about them make it possible to conduct a historical analysis of their community, and the relations between them and the Christians.

The Carolingian kings considered the Jews a positive populating element that must be looked after and protected. In the first half of the ninth century, Emperor Louis the Pious (814–840) granted privileges to individual Jewish merchants and their families.[12] He undertook to guarantee their safety and their right to move about and trade freely, exempted them from paying various taxes, and permitted them to own pagan slaves. In all likelihood, the Jews themselves requested such imperial guarantees in order to counter Church edicts. These edicts forbade Christians from eating with Jews, entering their homes or receiving medical treatment from them; they prohibited Jews from owning pagan slaves or employing Christian servants and, especially, they forbade Jews from using the services of Christian wet nurses.[13] We owe this knowledge to the

Archbishop of Lyons, Agobard, who, in the first half of the ninth century, conducted a bitter polemic against the Emperor's defence of the Jews, and to his successor, Amulo, who crossed swords in a similar manner with Louis the Pious's heir, Charles II, the Bald.[14] For the next hundred years – throughout the eleventh century – Jews and their families continued to settle in the cities of Germany and northern France. The charters that were granted to groups of Jews during the eleventh century describe the development of these Jewish communities.

The most widely known privilege of that time was granted by the Bishop of Speyer, Rudiger, in 1084 to the Jews whom he invited to settle in his city.[15] 'When I wanted to make Speyer into a great town, I thought I would add immensely to its lustre if I would bring Jews to dwell in it.' The *Privilegium* was the result of negotiations between the Jews and the Bishop, who intended to provide them with preferential status and to be as accommodating as possible. Although the Jews were given their own neighbourhood, which was surrounded by a wall, they were not obliged to remain within its confines. It was stressed that they could conduct their business activities as they saw fit. They had 'the authorization and the right to deal in the exchange of gold and silver, and to buy and sell as they see fit in the place of their residence, outside the port, near the port, within the port, throughout the town'. The Bishop acquiesced to the Jews' request for land on which to build a synagogue and a cemetery, and granted them plots for this purpose from his own properties. This created a physical proximity between the church, where Christian rituals were performed, and the parallel Jewish sites, the synagogue and the cemetery.[16] Furthermore, the *Privilegium* granted the Jews internal judicial autonomy; thus, in most matters, the community was able to operate under to its own laws and its own judicial decisions.[17] Moreover, the Bishop allowed them to hire Christian workers and wet nurses, waived taxation on their guests, and even granted them the right to sell to Christians meat that had not been properly slaughtered according to the dictates of Jewish law. In exchange, he demanded that they join the city's security forces and participate in the defence of the city's walls.

A survey of the towns where Jewish communities developed in the eleventh century shows that Jews were active in the burgeoning commercial centres at river ports, or important crossroads. (See the map on p. x.)When the Bishop of Speyer invited the Jews to his town, they had already settled in the key economic regions of Germany, such as Mainz, Cologne, and Regensburg – important urban centres involved in river-based commercial transport, in both the Rhine and Danube valleys. Jews lived in the area which they called 'Lotharingia' where the major trade routes of the era converged. They established communities on the main route leading north from the cities of Italy, through the Mosel valley to Mainz and Trier, and from there into central France, and north to the Loire and Seine valleys. They also settled along the route that connects the Rhine valley with the Pyrenees, in the direction of Spain: Verdun, Rheims, Meaux, Paris, Orleans, Poitiers, and Bordeaux (or along the route linking Poitiers, Limoges, and Toulouse). Jewish settlements were also found in relatively small towns located at important crossroads in agricultural areas.

In the second half of the eleventh century, Troyes in northern France was an example of this type of town. At that time, it was little more than a large village. However, it was to grow significantly in the first half of the twelfth century. Its position, at the junction of the routes that connected the French areas and the commercial cities of Germany with the commonly used and safe route to Italy, ensured the city's economic development. Indeed, it was possible to predict the development of both the region and the city because already in the tenth century it was a venue for fairs. A Jewish source recounts that the Troyes community served as the principal mouthpiece in an appeal launched to raise funds among the area's communities for the redemption of captured co-religionists.[18] In other words, this was an important urban group that enjoyed privileges, despite its adherence to a different religion. And, not only did the Jews live within the Christian urban population, but there was a great deal of interaction between the two. We find that a Jew and a Christian were partners in a bakery, producing bread together, and that Jews dealt in second-hand goods, some of them apparently stolen in cahoots with the Christian underworld.[19] In Cologne, too, the Jewish community, which was already in existence in the eleventh century, developed and prospered despite occasional severe attacks. The archbishop of the city defended the Jews, even in 1096 – when forces of the First Crusade attempted to attack them – and even afterwards, until 1424 when the Jews were expelled from the city. The Jews participated in the defence of Cologne, taking up arms and making themselves responsible for defending one of the gates of the city. Throughout this period, the city had a 'Jewish neighbourhood', although the Jews also purchased houses outside their own enclave.[20]

Christianity and Judaism

At the point in time where we begin to study the Jews – about the tenth century – Europe was a Christian continent. Christianity had succeeded, during a period of several centuries, in absorbing and uprooting every religion practised both by the older inhabitants of Europe and the newcomers to the continent. Emperors and generals, missionaries and monks either forced or convinced the populace of Europe to adopt Christianity. It swallowed up all other religions, abrogated their gods, and stripped them of their rituals, implanting its doctrines into the local culture so that Christian values became fused with popular local beliefs. The westernmost area of the continent, the Iberian peninsula, was an exception. In the eighth century, Islam gained control of this region. The Christians waged a war against this enemy which came to a close only 700 years later, when they managed to expel Islam from Europe completely. At the end of the eleventh century, Christianity, full of pride and strength, invaded the Holy Land and succeeded in establishing a Christian realm there.

Throughout this entire period, the Jews were the only people living in northern Europe who did not accept Christianity. Why were they not defined as enemies, like the Muslims who had invaded Spain? Why were they not considered, as the pagan tribes had been, a group that must be coerced by any and all means into becoming Christians? To explain the existence of the Jews in Christian Europe, the Christian establishment had recourse to a quotation from Augustine (354–430). Augustine was one of the most important Church fathers, and in the Middle Ages his writings were regarded as forming the basis of Christian theology. Augustine's position as regards the Jews (found in his book *Tractaus Adversus Iudaeos*, as well as other works) is based on the concept that, by rejecting Jesus, they had made the most terrible mistake conceivable and that they are, indeed, guilty of his death. Their punishment was the destruction of the Temple in Jerusalem, their dispersion throughout the world, and the loss of their status as the Chosen People who uphold the law of God. God turned from them to the Christians, who chose to believe in Jesus. From that time on, the Christians were the 'real Children of Israel'. Because of their stubbornness and blindness, the Jews continued to adhere to their fallacious truths and beliefs, and were therefore subordinate to the Church, and had to be subservient to it.

Augustine reinforced the theological basis of this concept with the help of a verse from Psalms (59:12): 'Kill them not, lest my people forget; Scatter them by your strength and defeat them.'[21] Christianity had to suffer the presence of the Jews since they served as living proof of both the Christian religion and the truth of the holy Christian writings. The rejection of Jesus as the Messiah by the Jews, though he had been revealed to them, was the cause of their present situation. By their very state of humiliation and disgrace, the Jews actually demonstrated not only the truth upheld by the Christians, but also what happens to those who reject Jesus, or to those who might reject him in the future. The teachings of Paul must also be kept in mind (Rom. 9:27) that at the end of days, the Jews will accept the Christian revelation, which will represent the ultimate victory of Christianity.[22]

At the end of the sixth century Pope Gregory I translated this theological premise into legal instructions. From then on, Popes and leading members of the Church establishment repeated Augustine's statements and precedents in papal bulls. In this way a defensive attitude to the Jews gained sway; however, this was based entirely on the condition that the status of the Jews would be clearly inferior and that they would remain in this inferior and humiliating position. If they deviated from it, they could then be maltreated and their status could be undermined even further.

It is worth while recalling the activities of Bishop Agobard of Lyons in the ninth century and his attempts to convert the Jews to Christianity. With the help of missionaries, he tried to convince the Jews to convert, and when he had the power to do so, he endeavoured to forcibly convert their children. He made a special effort to try to convert the pagan slaves kept by the Jews, who would gain their freedom in this manner. It seems that none of Agobard's efforts met with any success. He wrote to his friends in the Emperor's court in order to prevent Evrard, the *Magister Judaeorum* (the imperial official in charge of the Jews) from taking measures against him. Evrard demanded the implementation of the Emperor's edict, which declared that a pagan servant or slave who served a Jew could not be converted to Christianity without his or her master's permission. In Agobard's opinion, such an edict was unacceptable from the Christian point of view. He even attempted to organize other bishops to oppose the authority of the Emperor in matters of Christianity, but Louis the Pious forced him to flee from Lyons to Italy.[23] The civil authorities could protect the Jews, but they were unable to eradicate or even moderate the religious tension between Jews and Christians, whether clergy or the general populace.

At the beginning of the thirteenth century, Pope Innocent III noted in his bull that protection would only be given to those who 'did not dare to conspire against the Christian belief'. In other words, he reshaped the Church's policy towards the Jews; if they persisted in deliberately refusing to accept Christianity, or sought to improve their inferior status or attempt to be masters over Christians, then they would not be entitled to the protection of the Church. Indeed, in the thirteenth century the Jewish position was undermined. But was it the Church establishment that actually determined Christian policy regarding the Jews? It is clear that the status of the Jews could only be changed if the Church had the support of the non-Church ruling authority.

It should also be kept in mind that, in medieval times, Jews and Christians lived in close proximity to one another. In the case of the Jewish–Christian joint owners of the bread-baking oven (at the end of the eleventh century), a *responsum* (an exchange of letters between a halakhic or Jewish legal authority and the person making the query) was dispatched to clarify what Jewish law (*halakhah*) relates to the Jewish partner's profit on bread baked by his Christian partner during Passover.[24] This *responsum* reveals not only the strong economic link between Jews and Christians, but also the close social ties surrounding the baking of bread. Since the bread-baking oven was one of the main focal points of life in the medieval town, joint ownership of such a facility was an indication that members of the two opposing religious groups not only lived in close proximity to one another, but also fraternized freely with one another. Similarly, the Jewish source Sefer Hasidim (Germany, beginning of the thirteenth century) recounts a story in which a Christian woman, in order to help her Jewish neighbour's son recover from an illness, offered the mother a remnant from the cross on which Jesus was crucified. So it can be seen that even though the Jews usually lived in their own neighbourhood, they were not isolated. Their homes abutted on those of their Christian neighbours and they even purchased Christian houses. Due to their economic enterprises, the Jews were very closely associated with the Christian population. The synagogue and the church were located in the same area of the town and were sometimes even next door to one another. The cemeteries were also situated near each other and religious festivals were celebrated openly for the other religious group to see.[25]

Christianity could not remain indifferent to Judaism and the Christians could not ignore the Jews dwelling in their midst. Both groups competed for the title of 'heir to the true religion'. The stronger the Christian religion considered itself to be, the more intense its 'Jewish obsession' became. It was very suspicious of the Jewish religion and its influence, as well as its ability to stimulate the curiosity of Christians. Life, therefore, was stronger than theologies and papal directives. Christians chose their own way of viewing their coexistence with the Jews. Throughout the era in question, and in direct opposition to the dictates of the Church establishment, Christian men and women worked as servants and wet nurses in Jewish households and lived together with them.

On the other hand, during the Crusades it was not papal instructions (or those of the emperors) that dictated how the Christians related to the Jews, but rather the trend of popular feeling. The launching of the campaign to wrest the tomb of Jesus from Muslim hands inevitably unleashed strong feelings towards those who were accused of his murder. This was a mission of vengeance, a war against the infidels who did not believe in Jesus, as well as a call for changing the world order to accord with the spirit of Christianity. The Jews were inexorably connected with these events.[26] The attempt by some of the participants in the First Crusade to forcibly convert the Jews is connected with this outburst of feelings, despite the fact that it contradicted the rationale of extending protection to the Jews that had been formulated by the Church. A polemic in this vein was conducted during the twelfth century between two eminent personalities in the Christian world. Bernard of Clairvaux invoked the Augustinian argument to stop Jews being harmed by Christians. On the other hand, Peter the Venerable, Abbot of Cluny, demanded the expropriation of Jewish property to finance the Crusade. He likened the Jews to Cain, who had murdered his own brother, except that they had murdered both a messiah and a god. Any Jew who did not want to convert should, he advocated, be condemned, like Cain, to a life of endless wandering.[27]

Immediately after ascending the French throne in 1180, King Philip II robbed the Jews of 15,000 marks. Two years later he expelled them from his realm, handing over their synagogues to the Church. His biographer, Rigord, enumerated the reasons for this action, thereby revealing to us the main case against the Jews, which the king's biographer saw as relevant to the public opinion of his day.[28] The elucidation starts out by declaring that every year – right before Easter or during Holy Week (the week commemorating Jesus' suffering) – the Jews attempt to kill a Christian, with the aim of inflicting a blow against Christianity and Christian values. Rigord enumerated most of the points brought up on the subject of the blood libel in the twelfth century: the connection with Satan, the secrecy, the maliciousness of an act perpetrated on the Christian holiday associated with the affliction of Jesus, the intention of harming a potential saint who could contribute to Christianity in the future.[29] Rigord explained that the condemnation of the Jews for the ritual murder of the boy, St Richard, during the reign of his father, Louis VII, had made a strong impression on Philip, who was a child himself at the time. Immediately after Richard's death, his body began to perform miracles. This incident left an indelible mark on the young Philip and, therefore, his first act as king was to imprison the Jews in their synagogue, and seize their gold and silver. This was the prelude to their expulsion from royal lands in 1182. Rigord emphasizes the conspicuous economic prosperity of the Jews in Paris in order to explain why the king expelled them from his domain. The Jews became rich from charging interest on loans, even though this practice was forbidden in the Torah. Rigord further maintained that the Jews had acquired over half the houses in Paris by means of usury. Everyone fell victim to them: city dwellers, soldiers, farmers; moreover, Jews defiled sacred Christian artefacts that had been entrusted to them as security for loans. They even attempted to convert Christians who were servants in their homes. Rigord's account demonstrates how public opinion was forged in preparation for the expulsion of the Jews and the seizure of their money.

The use of the blood libel is interesting. Starting in the twelfth century, and thereafter, the Jews were accused of killing Christian children either for revenge, for ritual purposes, or in order to use their blood. Most of the medieval Popes did not believe the blood libel story and denounced it, as did many emperors and kings. Even Louis VII, Philip's father, condemned it, but to no avail. Although the Church establishment had been attempting to keep the Jews from moneylending, their efforts did not meet with success until the thirteenth century. The attitude towards the Jews was shaped mainly by social forces in the areas in which they lived. Though the preaching of the churchmen could undoubtedly exacerbate the situation, and the kings' disposition towards the Jews, whether they extended them royal protection or expelled them, had a powerful influence on their subjects' behaviour towards the minority group, it was nevertheless the climate of the immediate Christian milieu that dictated the attitude of the populace to the Jews.[30]

The Jews were confronted with a variety of temptations aimed at their conversion. Violence was quite frequently employed against them by various groups of Christians, forcing them to decide between conversion to Christianity, and suffering, or even death. From a financial point of view, the Jews were faced with the temptation of moving from a group whose economic opportunities were being increasingly curtailed to the majority group that was eager to welcome people with economic abilities such as those possessed by the Jews. In the twelfth century, the restrictions placed upon recently converted Jews disappeared, after the Church realized that their new status ought to be a step up from their previous one.

Because the Jews were also forced to grapple with the theological temptation, it is necessary to understand the pressure brought to bear in this regard in the twelfth century. The Christians firmly believed that Jesus was the messiah whom the Jews had been waiting for. But not only had they refused to accept him, they had also betrayed him and killed him. As a result, God turned to the Christians, and since then the Jews had been paying the price for their error, as predicted in the Torah itself. As the basis for proving their convictions, the Christians cited passages

INTRODUCTION

from the Bible – in Exodus, Deuteronomy, and Prophets – which talk about what will happen to the Jews if they sin grievously against God or betray Him. The biblical citations assert that they would lose their sovereignty and become dispersed throughout the world. Forsaken and humiliated, they would have to live in the shadow of harsh gentiles, who might permit them to sojourn in their lands.

The Jews countered the Christian claims with various theological arguments, and even asserted that Christianity could not be a genuine religion because it was not even monotheistic. Even though their situation might fit the Christian descriptions, they explained that this was because the messiah had not yet come. When he did, he would deliver them from their catastrophes in the Exile and return them to the Land of Israel.[31] Nonetheless, the Christian theological arguments remained a constant challenge for the Jews, mainly because they did indeed reflect their day-to-day reality. It was difficult to ignore the fact that the Jews were dispersed throughout the world, a punishment they had been enduring for one thousand years, whereas Christianity was on the rise and growing stronger. This condition became even more difficult to bear from the beginning of the twelfth century, when it became known that the Christians had organized themselves, and had succeeded in traversing the Western world, reaching the East, conquering the Holy Land, and building a temple to their messiah on the site where the Jewish Temple had once stood. The Jewish communities had to hold their group together so that they could successfully counter the Christians on all fronts: their theological claims, the economic lure, and the direct threat of coercion and violence. Hence, we see that this community found itself in a very special set of circumstances, under the most extreme pressure, and having to mobilize all its resources and energies in order to survive.

The organization of Jewish life

But how did the Jews conduct their lives? Jewish society in the Middle Ages is unique in that its way of life followed an important, noble and complex tradition.[32] The Jewish way of life is called *halakhah* (walking) because it relates to every facet of the life cycle; literally, it is the way one needs to 'walk'. The traditions were written down, starting in the second century, in a book called the *Mishnah*. Later on, as the *Mishnah* was studied and expanded upon, the discussions dealing with the various sections of the *Mishnah* were compiled, at the end of the fourth century, in vast set of heavy, learned tomes called the *Gemarah*. The *Gemarah* together with the *Mishnah* form the Talmud that contains all the rules (not the actual laws) for organizing life, how to formulate halakhic debates, and how to make judgments. Medieval Jewry shaped its unique path on the basis of the material found in the Talmud, treating it with great reverence and calling those who study it *Talmidei Hakhamim*, or scholars. In terms of Jewish society's value system, these scholars were placed on the highest rung of the social ladder. Their knowledge of the Talmud was a key to life, since it was regarded as holding solutions for every problem that might possibly arise. The Talmud is also defined as the 'Oral Law', which complements the Torah, or 'Written Law'; thus, the Oral Law was held to be the detailed tradition and explanation of what God had handed down to His people at Mount Sinai. Hence, when the Faculty of Theology of the University of Paris decided to burn the Talmud towards the middle of the thirteenth century, the Jews felt as if their world was being destroyed and they did everything in their power to have it returned to them.

According to a basic Jewish assumption, the Talmud is the common denominator for all Jews who are living, temporarily, in dispersion, in various places throughout the world, awaiting the time when God shall see fit to return them all to their Holy Land. Until then, it is incumbent upon them to attempt to remain Jewish at all costs, no matter where they may be living, and the Talmud is the main instrument that will help them fulfil this goal. But can we conclude that European Jewry in the tenth to the thirteenth centuries conducted itself strictly according to the Talmud? The answer, naturally, is no.

The Talmud was written down and redacted in Babylonia and in the Land of Israel in the first centuries of the Common Era. The *Mishnah* was compiled in about the year 200 CE, and the redaction of the Talmud was completed by the end of the fifth century – before Christianity had become a major religion and before the advent of Islam. At that time, the Jews lived in cities and towns where they constituted the majority of the population and engaged in all types of occupations. The *Mishnah*, and the Talmud as well, reflect this state of affairs, which was not at all relevant to medieval Europe, and particularly not to the Jews living in northern France, Germany, and England. Moreover, these lands were fundamentally different in nature from the Middle East, where the Talmud was compiled. This gave rise to many problems connected with topics such as the length of the day (which affects prayers), climatic issues (which affect the celebration of the festivals), etc. Furthermore, the Jews of Europe did not engage in all occupations, but were limited to only a few, and they did not constitute the majority in the places where they lived. Hundreds of problems arose every day related to talmudic decisions that were no longer applicable. Finding no parallels to these new problems in the Talmud, it was difficult to determine the proper way of conducting oneself. What could be done at a time when the realities of life were no longer compatible with the decisions of the Talmud? The answer to this question rests on how the Talmud was interpreted.

In fact, during the Middle Ages, there were two incentives for interpreting the Talmud: scholars wanted to explain it so that it could be studied by others; and they studied it in order to find in it both moral support and practical solutions for the situations in which they found themselves. They recorded their interpretations in the margins of the Talmud's pages, in books relating to the Talmud, in prayer books that described the yearly cycle of activities in the synagogue, and in thousands of responses to queries (*responsa*) made by people who encountered problems when attempting to adapt the Talmud and the *halakhah* to everyday life. Thus, the Jewish scholars of the Middle Ages have bequeathed to us a rich source that allows us to learn about Jewish existence in that period. By seeking to interpret the Talmud so that it could be put to use in their era, they stamped their interpretations with the 'atmosphere of the times', a precious commodity for the historian. They also pointed out those places where the reality of their lives was not comparable with that of talmudic times, and where talmudic material had to be confronted and then used to help formulate the *halakhah* for their times. For the present-day scholar, this halakhic material is a source that recreates the reality of the Middle Ages, relating not only to the medieval author's present but also to his past.

These writings also reveal how Jewish society shaped its path on the basis of traditions which were not directly connected with the Talmud. During the intervening centuries between the talmudic period and tenth century, many customs had come into being and which, over time, had also acquired significance. Passed down from one generation to the next, these customs sometimes developed when the Talmud did not give an adequate explanation, or suggest what action that might be taken, and sometimes these customs even contradicted the Talmud. When the Jews came up against a new problem in the Middle Ages that was not analogous to what was fixed in the Talmud and they did not have a custom that they could utilize, they established a *takanah*. A *takanah* is a ruling that is accepted by the community, i.e., the community agrees to behave in a particular way, as defined in the *takanah*, and a new legal situation is created, which is binding and has permanent validity. Below, throughout the book, the *takanah* will be simply termed 'Ruling'.

Within this complex social and religious system, what was the position and status of Jewish women?

The status of women

In the middle of the eleventh century, in the city of Troyes, a woman named Leah launched a protest against the decision of the Jewish community on a matter of taxation. It was accepted practice for the community to tax assets, monies held by creditors, and even inventories of goods. But to meet immediate needs, the community decided to levy a tax on cultivated fields as well. Leah was incensed by the new Ruling, which she considered unfair; she declared that she could not agree with it nor would she pay the tax. She presented her arguments clearly and demonstratively. The leaders of the community, however, did not accept them. Nevertheless, they sent a detailed letter regarding the matter to a sage whom they held in high regard. His reply declared that Leah was correct. The query and the response (*responsa*) were preserved, thus we are able to hear Leah's plea from the eleventh century, albeit by means of the members of the all-male community council.[33] So how are we to understand this Jewish community? Was it accepted behaviour for a woman, a property owner, to authoritatively voice her opinion in public? What economic roles did the Jewish woman in northern France fulfil in the middle of the eleventh century and why was it so important for the community to clarify this issue before enforcing its Ruling?

At the end of the century, the Jewish communities along the Rhine endured harsh attacks by the Christians who set out to liberate the Holy Land and the grave of their Saviour from the Muslims. Those who attacked the Jews wanted them to convert to Christianity so that Europe would be transformed into a continent where Christianity alone held sway. In the main, these Jews preferred to die rather than convert to Christianity, and women constituted a large portion of those who elected to die; they even put their own children to death so that they would not grow up as Christians. Testimony to this effect is found in several sources, both in prose and in poetry, that were written during the first half of the twelfth century. One of the testimonies told of a woman named Rachel, who struggled with herself and her children in her effort to kill them and die before the Christians could subdue them.[34] Why were such women represented in the sources as more extreme than the men in their pious adherence to religion? Do we have available to us material written by men that describes what really happened to Jewish women at the end of the eleventh century?[35]

In 1241, the Frankfurt Jewish community was attacked; many Jews were killed, while some were captured and held as Christians against their will. Among those captured was a young woman who was engaged to be married to a man from Wurtzburg. The girl had been promised to him;

they were betrothed, but the wedding ceremony had not been completed. During the violent clashes between the city's Christian population and the Jewish community, the Christians captured the girl and held her hostage for several weeks, forcing her to accept Christianity. Throughout her captivity, the girl continued to declare that she was Jewish and did not succumb to material temptations. In the end, she was released and she returned to Judaism. In the meantime, the groom in question had married another woman. The sources describe the fundamental argument surrounding the issue of the young man's behaviour. The debate itself is very interesting, but one matter stands out in the discussion: the girl adhered to her beliefs in an unquestionably determined fashion and most of the men who gave their opinions expressed their revulsion with the man's behaviour.

The accounts of Leah, Rachel and the anonymous young woman from Frankfurt are some of the many examples of issues related to women that are found in the Jewish sources of the Middle Ages. These sources also provide us with information on how the Jewish community was organized and run; how Jewish communities related to one another, and their relations with the surrounding Christian society. Finally, they also give us some clear indications of the weight that women carried in this constellation.

Research on the status of women in the medieval Jewish community confronts the scholar with many problems. The female presence is very palpable in all the Jewish sources of this era, whether in chronicles, letters, halakhic and *responsa* literature, commentaries and so forth. This presence is particularly notable whether the sources deal with the public, communal sphere, or the realm of religious practice and prayer, areas in which women's activities are not equivalent to those of men. Yet, the voice of the medieval Jewish woman comes to us exclusively by means of written sources penned by men. We do not have in our possession even one source written by a woman. We read about women martyrs who die at their own hands, although it is clear that the text was written by a man. Although Jewish sources mention women who are well versed in *halakhah*, the widow of Rabbenu Tam and the murdered wife of Rabbi Eleazar of Worms did not leave historical sources from which we could learn or speculate about their ideas.[36] Even when we analyse cases that talk about customs practised by women with respect to the commandments, any revelation about the opinions of a woman comes to us through the agency or voice of a man. Thus, the study of Jewish women in the Middle Ages is limited by the manner in which men chose to transmit their images to us. Therefore, this will be a study of the Jewish society in northern France (and England) and Germany and the place of women in that society via the manner in which men shaped our understanding of this issue. The combined perceptions of men with regard to women will help us understand the interrelations between men and women, within the family and in the community structure.

But how do we determine the status of women?

The topic of the status of women in the society in which they live is extremely complex because it relates to a multitude of situations, spheres and relationships. We need to examine the legal, juridical and economic status of women and ask whether they had public or political status. These are the areas in which we discover the social forces that shaped the image of the society and its values. If women have any standing whatsoever in the economic order, or have influence in the legal and political spheres, it may be said that their position in this society is favourable. We must also examine the woman's status as wife and mother, since in the societies we are dealing with, she is perceived first and foremost as belonging to the home and family. In order to understand her status, we must analyse it within the context of the society's values. The primary values of Jewish society in this epoch centre around the preservation of Judaism, the performance of the commandments and the study of the Torah. Hence, we should examine the status of women in relation to these topics. Because these societies are basically male-oriented, we should also explore how the woman and femininity are related to on the intellectual level. In other words, how women and sex are referred to in speech, in the mythology of the group, etc. The sum total of these components will point us in the right direction and help us find an answer to the question of the status of women in this specific society.

It is not our purpose here to survey the development of women's status during the Mishnaic and talmudic periods, i.e., during 400 years of halakhic development. However, several points should be emphasized in light of the fact that these halakhic decisions formed the conceptual foundation and frame of reference for the Jews of the Middle Ages. The picture portrayed by Mishnaic and talmudic literature was that basically women lived under the authority of someone else (their fathers or husbands), therefore, their status was different from that of men. Several scholars have shown that, starting with the first and second centuries CE, as expressed in Mishnaic literature, and even more so in the third to fifth centuries, as represented in the Talmud, there was a constant improvement in the manner in which women were related to and protected.[37] Nonetheless, the basic reality did not change in principle: female children were under the authority of their fathers; married women were under the authority of their husbands. A man took a wife and brought her into his home; he could take an additional wife and he could cast his wife out at his discretion. He could do so against the woman's will, and almost any pretext was acceptable. He could break any promise or vow that his wife might make; therefore, she could not play a role in the economic or judicial system unless she happened to become a widow of means. The literature, which was written by men, extols the woman who personifies the words of the Psalm (45:14) 'all the virtues of the king's daughter are within'. The practical effect of this view was the notion that it was not proper for women to go out of the home and demonstrate a public persona. Even though the guarantees that women achieved during this period are very important – the *ketubah* guaranteed her financial welfare; the establishing of grounds for divorce safeguarded her from hopeless situations in married life; and her participation in family life, religious life, and the festivals allowed her to express her beliefs – the basic situation remained one of inequality, dependence, and weakness. While this compares the status of Jewish women with that of men in Jewish society, it does compare their status with what was prevalent in the Greek–Roman world or the Babylonian–Persian world.

The dependence of women on others is clearly set out in Mishnaic literature. The *Mishnah* (Yebamot 10a) states that a girl is financially dependent on her father. It also declares that a husband 'is entitled to whatever she may find, or make with her hands, and also has the right of invalidating her vows'. If a daughter finds something, it belongs to the father; if she works, her wages go to her father. The *Mishnah* also asserts that 'she is always under the authority of her father, until she comes under the authority of her husband through marriage'. The husband is entitled to everything that the father received, and even if a woman owns property that is hers alone, the profit derived from it belongs to the husband (and he stands to inherit the assets upon her death).[38]

During the second or first century BC, the *ketubah* was devised; it is a promissory note by the husband to his wife. This note established, in a just manner, the husband's obligations towards his wife, ensuring that she would not find herself destitute in the event of his death or their divorce. In addition, it gave the husband almost complete control in the management of his wife's assets and the profits derived from them. These factors raised the value of the wife in her husband's eyes and acted as a deterrent against his possible desire to divorce her, since this would engender financial complications and losses. The Talmud defined this relationship (Ketubot 47b): 'Maintenance was provided for a wife in return for her handiwork, her ransom in return for usufruct, and her burial in return for her *ketubah*; a husband, therefore, is entitled to usufruct.' Two of the most well known *amoraim*,[39] Abbayye and Rava, formulated the following version in the fourth century CE (Yebamot 39a; Ketubot 83:a) 'Abaye maintains that a husband's rights have the same force as his wife's: "his hand is like her hand"; Raba ... his rights are superior to hers'. A different version regarding this situation, which is frequently used, is 'whatever a woman acquires belongs to her husband' (Tbab. Gittin 77b). The fact that property belonging to a married woman was, in reality, the property of her husband, should come as no surprise. It should be remembered that this was the case throughout Europe until only about one hundred years ago, and in certain places, even later.

In addition to being economically dependent on someone else for most of their lives, women could not conduct business negotiations with men, appear in public places, or initiate lawsuits. Moreover, they were not held responsible if they caused harm to someone else; however, if they sustained injury, the responsible party was liable. Nonetheless, women could not testify in a court of law, nor, of course, serve as judges.[40] The above notwithstanding, cases in which women hold property, have confrontations with men, and bring cases to court can be found in the *Mishnah* and Talmud.[41] Though these women are certainly exceptions to the rule and do not represent the norm, this finding is important because it indicates that women did have some kind of economic capability and that there was a precedent for this type of female behaviour, which was actually found in the Talmud itself. This evidence from the Talmud could serve as the basis for a slightly different outlook towards women and problems connected with property that a man might have promised to give a woman.

In principle, men and women are equal before the law, whether in criminal or in civil matters (Tbab. Tractate Kiddushin 35b): 'What is written in the Torah relating to every punishment refers equally to both men and women, and what is written in the Torah relating to every civil law refers equally to both men and women.' However, since for most of her life a woman is dependent on others, the outcome of her actions results in a perversion of justice. As noted, she is not liable to pay damages for injuries she may cause. As mentioned in the *Mishnah, Bava Kama*, ch. 8 [4]): 'A slave or a woman who is harmed must be recompensed, but if a slave or a woman harms another, they are not liable, but payment is made later on. If the woman is divorced or the slave is freed, they are liable for payment.' In other words, even if women are, in principle, independent, and are legally accountable for what they do, as long as they are dependent on another they do not have to pay for the consequences of their actions.

INTRODUCTION

The writings of the *tanaim* and *amoraim* project the impression that the norms of their day did not look favourably upon a woman appearing in a court of law or in any sort of public place. The sages thought that a woman's dignity would be violated if she had to appear in public and that, in any event, women were not interested in doing so. Furthermore, they believed that it was necessary to create conditions that would enable women to avoid the embarrassing situation of having to appear in a public hearing in a court or any other public place where they would find themselves in the midst of a large crowd of men. From the discussion between Rabbi Meir and Rabbi Eliezer (Tractate Ketubot Tbab. 74b; Gittin Tbab. 46b, etc.), it becomes clear that both of them thought that women were indeed humiliated by appearing in court or in public. They also debated about whether the husband's feelings in this matter were relevant. In another example, the sages state their views on women's concern that they may be degraded when appearing in public for the distribution of the priestly tithe. Yet again, we discover that the talmudic literature contains cases that contradict this position; in these instances, women appear in a court of law and in public, and the opinion of the *dayanim* towards them is not negative.[42] It may be assumed that these women were well known and exceptional, and that these individual cases do not disprove the rule. Nevertheless, the main significance of this finding is the fact that these cases actually exist in talmudic literature and constitute a precedent that could be put to use in the future.

With respect to the basic values of the society, the status of women is considered important, although marginal as far as men are concerned. Unlike men, women are not obligated to perform all of the commandments, but only some of them. When we come to what was regarded as the highest value of the society, Jewish studies, women are denied the right to study the sacred texts. To support the barring of girls and women from Torah studies, the sources refer mainly to the *Midrash* on the verse from Deuteronomy (ch. 11) 'And ye shall teach them [to] your sons.'[43] The declaration of Ben Azai in tractate *Sotah* (20:a) 'A man is under the obligation to teach his daughter Torah' was forgotten, whereas it was Rabbi Eliezer's words that were remembered: 'Whoever teaches his daughter Torah teaches her obscenity' (*Mishnah Sotah* 3:4), and even the extreme emotional outcry of Rabbi Eleazar: 'It is better to burn the words of the Law than to teach them to women' (Tjer. *Sotah* 19:a, ch. 3, *halakhah* 4).

In the Middle Ages, in the communities of northern France and Germany, we find a change in the status of women which affects almost all the points discussed above. In the area of marital relations a revolution takes place when two Rulings – attributed to the tenth-century Rabbenu

Gershom Me'or Ha-Golah – establish a completely new order: a husband cannot take another wife while he remains married to his first wife, and he cannot divorce her against her will. Her agreement to the divorce is required; thus, in the language of the era: 'if she does not agree, there is no validity to the *gett*' (bill of divorce). This decision is in direct opposition to what was set down in the Talmud (in Tractate Tbab. Gittin), i.e., that the wife's agreement to the divorce is immaterial: 'The woman is cast out whether or not she agrees.' In the economic sphere, her status is changed with the help of the *ketubah* and her *nedunyah* (dowry). In later chapters we will hear about women engaged in moneylending; how they own and manage movable property and real estate; appear in courts of law and plead lawsuits in public. In other words, their financial status changes in this era from what was laid down in the *Mishnah* and Talmud and from what existed in later periods in other regions. The change in the position of the woman is also conspicuous in the values of Jewish society. Women participate in religious life in a very active manner and were prominent among the martyrs, as in the case of Rachel, mentioned above. They pray within as well as outside the synagogue; they create their own customs and even perform commandments they are not required to carry out.

The case being argued here is that the change in the status of women is the outcome of the political and social circumstances which the Jews encountered in northern France and Germany between 1000 and 1350. The pressure that the Christians brought to bear and the perceived threat that it was within the power of Christian society to convert the Jews gave rise to a different division of tasks within Jewish society. Under these circumstances, sub-groups within the society were valued differently; they were also given tasks within the social system that had not been assigned to them before. I have dealt elsewhere[44] with the children in the Jewish society of this period, and what is true with respect to children is even more applicable to women.

The nature of the Jews' financial occupations in the Middle Ages allowed women to enter the area of moneylending, mortgaging, and commerce. The male sector could bar them from these economic endeavours by invoking the commonly used technique of forbidding women from coming into contact with men who are not their husbands, a prohibition created because of sexual tension and the danger of adultery and sinful thoughts. As Baskin has pointed out, *Sefer Hasidim* (in the thirteenth century) mentions an attempt to isolate women from the male environment, which proved unsuccessful.[45] At the same time, this source also contains many confirmations of the fact that women were indeed involved in financial activities. In other words, not only did men make no attempt to keep their wives out of economic enterprises, they actually encouraged such involvement. These occupations subsequently allowed the women of the medieval era to gain entry into all the areas of communal life where they undertook a variety of tasks.

This synthesis could not have taken place unless the male mental perception of women had permitted it to happen. Women were an important factor in the financial sphere and became involved in the life of the community. During times of crisis, such as at the time of the First Crusade, which was perceived as a period of supreme test, women were the ones who were depicted as demonstrating the greatest devotion (or greater fanaticism).

In the realm of religious life, they manifest intense involvement and even though, as we have said, they are not obligated to carry out certain commandments (especially those that must be performed at a particular time) they performed them nevertheless. In addition, women are looked upon as being responsible for maintaining and transmitting the vital qualities within the family. Given this combination of considerations and circumstances, the leadership, which was entirely male, could not ignore them; consequently, women continually improved their lot. Thus, the change in the status of women may be viewed as the result of an overall social change in a Jewish society that was struggling for survival.

Notes

1 A. Grossman, *Pious and Rebellious: Jewish Women in Europe in the Middle Ages*, Jerusalem 2001 [Hebrew], p. 9; A. Grossman, *Pious and Rebellious: Jewish Women in Europe in the Middle Ages*, Waltham, MA 2004 [English], p. xiii.

2 Extensive references to women in a text whose purpose is typically didactic or ideological does not necessarily reflect an attitude of admiration towards women or a change in their status. Writers had a variety of different reasons for writing these texts in certain ways, stressing certain aspects, and choosing certain imagery for use in their discussions. As Bynum demonstrated so skilfully in her research, the new trend of the twelfth century – the monks widespread use of religious language containing female imagery – did nothing whatsoever to change the status of real women and did not reflect any change in the clerics' attitudes towards women. C. W. Bynum, *Jesus as Mother*, Berkeley and Los Angeles, CA 1984. However, in this study I intend to show that the apparent improvement in women's status as seen in the halakhic sources does in fact reflect the reality of the times.

3 S. Goldin, 'The Role of Ceremonies in the Socialization Process: The Case of Jewish Communities of Northern France and Germany in the Middle Ages', *Archives de Sciences sociales des religions* 95 (1996), pp. 163–178; S. Goldin, 'The Socialisation for Kidush ha-Shem among Medieval Jews', *Journal of Medieval History* 23 (1997), pp. 117–138; S. Goldin, 'Juifs et juifs convertis au Moyen-Age : "Es-tu encore mon frère?"', *Annales, Histoire, Sciences sociales* 54 (1999), pp. 851–874; S. Goldin, 'Jewish

Society under Pressure: The Concept of Childhood', in *Youth in the Middle Ages*, ed. P. J. Goldberg and F. Riddy, York 2004, pp. 25–43.
4   C. Ozick, 'Notes towards Finding the Right Question', in *On Being a Jewish Feminist*, ed. S. Heschel, New York 1983, pp. 120–151 (reprinted from *Lilith* magazine 6, 1979).
5   Jewish law, see the Glossary of Hebrew Terms.
6   T. Ross, *Expanding the Palace of Torah*, Waltham, MA 2004, pp. 105–107; J. Hauptman, *Rereading the Rabbis: A Woman's Voice*, Boulder, CO 1998. Hauptman, a scholar of the talmudic era, pointed out the mechanisms that developed in the *Mishnah* for correcting or improving the social status of women. She suggested that the Roman society in which the Jews lived, or other historical circumstances, interfered with or stopped these trends.
7   See the section on Hasidei Ashkenaz in Chapter 3.
8   S. Goldin, '"Companies of Disciples" and "Companies of Colleagues": Communication in Jewish Intellectual Circles', *Vox Iudaica: Communication in the Jewish Diaspora in the Pre-modern Period*, ed. S. Menache, Leiden 1996, pp. 127–139.
9   Asher ben Yehiel, *Shut haRosh* (*Responsa* of the Rosh), ed. S. Yudelov, Jerusalem 1994, no. 101 (1).
10 E. Baumgarten, *Mothers and Children: Jewish Family Life in Medieval Europe*, Princeton, NJ 2004, esp. pp. 11–12 and many examples throughout the book.
11 M. Toch, *Dunkle Jahrhunderte. Gab es ein jüdisches Frühmittelalter?* Kleine Schriften des Arye-Maimon Instituts IV, Trier 2001, p. 29; M. Toch, *The Jews in Europe, 500–1050*, ed. P. Fouracre, The New Cambridge Medieval History, vol. 1, Cambridge 2005, pp. 547–570, 872–878.
12 J. Aronius, *Regesten zur Geschichte der Juden im fränkischen und deutschen Reiche bis zum Jahre 1273*, Berlin 1902, nos 73–78, 81–83, 98, 102, 162.
13 Aronius, *Regesten zur Geschichte*, nos 26, 57, 60, 114, 115, 117, 119, 166.
14 Aronius, *Regesten zur Geschichte*, no. 108.
15 Aronius, *Regesten zur Geschichte*, no. 168.
16 S. Grayzel, *The Church and the Jews in the Eighteenth Century*, rev. edition, New York 1966, pp. 89–95, 107–109.
17 Aronius, *Regesten zur Geschichte*, no. 170, p. 73.
18 I. A. Agus, *Responsa of the Tosaphists*, New York 1954, pp. 39–42; Solomon ben Isaac (Rashi), *Responsa Rashi*, ed. I. Elfenbein, New York 1943, p. 274.
19 Solomon B. Isaac (Rashi), *Sefer ha-Ora*, ed. S. Buber, Lemberg 1905, vol. 2, no. 41.
20 *Germania Judaica*, Tübingen 1963, pp. 420 ff.
21 The accurate translation is: 'Do not kill them lest my people be unmindful; with Your power make wanderers of them; bring them low'.
22 J. Cohen, *Living Letters of the Law: Ideas of the Jews in Medieval Christianity*, Berkeley, CA 1999, pp. 19–66; S. Simonsohn, *The Apostolic See and the Jews: History*, Toronto 1991, pp. 1–12.
23 B. Blumenkranz, *Les Auteurs chrétiens latins du Moyen-Age sur les Juifs et le Judaisme*, Paris 1963, pp. 228–231; R. Bonfil 'The Cultural and Religious Traditions of French Jewry in the Ninth Century, as reflected in the Writings of Agobard of Lyons', in *Studies in Jewish Mysticism Philosophy and Ethical Literature*, Jerusalem 1986, pp. 327–348, esp. p. 328 n. 2, and J. Heill, 'Agobard, Amolo, Das Kirchengut und die Juden von Lyon', *Francia*, 25 (1998), pp. 39–76.
24 Solomon ben Isaac, *Sefer ha-Ora*, ed. S. Buber, Lemberg 1905, vol. 2, no. 41.

25 E. Baumgarten, *Mothers and Children: Jewish Family Life in Medieval Europe*, Princeton, NJ 2004; S. Bartlet, *Licoricia of Winchester: Marriage, Motherhood and Murder in the Medieval Anglo-Jewish Community*, London 2009, pp. 15–17, 36–40.
26 See Chapter 2 below, and R. Chazan, *European Jewry and the First Crusade*, Los Angeles 1987; S. Goldin, *The Ways of Jewish Martyrdom*, Turnhout 2008, pp. 4–12.
27 S. Simonsohn, *The Apostolic See and the Jews*, Toronto 1991, pp. 228–262.
28 H. Delaborde, *Oeuvres de Rigord et de Guillaume le Breton*, vol. 1, Paris 1882, pp. 12 ff.
29 J. M. McCulloh, 'Jewish Ritual Murder: William of Norwich, Thomas of Monmouth, and the early Dissemination of the Myth', *Speculum* 72:3 (July 1997), pp. 698–740; R Chazan, *The Jews of Medieval Western Christendom, 1000–1500*, Cambridge 2006, pp. 150–164, 184–185, 191–194.
30 This was also the conclusion of D. Nirenberg's book *Communities of Violence*, Princeton, NJ 1998.
31 D. Berger, *The Jewish-Christian Debate in the High Middle Ages*, Philadelphia 1979.
32 The geographical area which we are relating to is Germany and northern France, where from the beginning of the beginning of the twelfth century until the end of the thirteenth century England is in practice an extension of northern France. There was quite a measure of difference between the Jewish communities themselves and an even greater difference between the various geographical areas.
33 Meir ben Barukh, *Sheelot u-Teshuvot ha-Maharam*, Prague edition, ed. M. A. Blakh, Budapest 1895, no. 941, p. 133.
34 *The Jews and the Crusaders: The Hebrew Chronicles of the First and Second Crusades*, ed. and trans. S. Eidelberg, Madison, WI 1977, pp. 32–34.
35 *Teshuvot uPsakim, Responsa et Decisiones*, ed. E. Kupfer, Jerusalem 1973, no. 170, pp. 282–290.
36 We do not have any sources such as the story of Perpetua, Heloise, and others. The existence of educated Christian woman is much better documented in Christian sources. See for example B. D. Shaw, 'The Passion of Perpetua', *Past and Present* 139 (1993), pp. 3–45; G. Duby, *Women of the Twelfth Century*, Chicago 1997, pp. 42–66.
37 J. R. Wegner, *Chattel or Person?* New York 1988; J. Hauptman, *Rereading the Rabbis: A Woman's Voice*, Boulder, CO 1998.
38 *Mishnah Ketubbot*, ch. 4.
39 See the Glossary of Hebrew Terms.
40 J. R. Wegner, *Chattel or Person?* New York 1988.
41 S. Valler, *Women in Jewish Society in the Talmudic Period*, Tel Aviv 2000, pp. 58–71; Tbab. Tractate Bava Batra 137b, 151a–b.
42 S. Valler, *Women in Jewish Society in the Talmudic Period*, Tel Aviv 2000, pp. 105–124.
43 *Midrash Sifre*, Ekev 46, Kidushin 29b.
44 S. Goldin, 'Jewish Society under Pressure: The Concept of Childhood', in *Youth in the Middle Ages*, ed. P. J. Goldberg and F. Riddy, York 2004, pp. 25–43.
45 J. Baskin, 'From Separation to Displacement: The Problem of Women in Sefer Hasidim', *AJS Review* 19 (1994), pp. 1–18.

2

Heroines by choice or by chance: martyrs, converts and anusot (forced converts)

The events of 1096 proved to be traumatic for the Jewish communities of northern Europe, and it would seem that many of the changes in the social, economic, and marital status of Jewish women, that will be identified later on, have their origins in the catastrophe that befell the Jews of the Rhine valley. It is therefore important to look at the texts and the depictions of what happened at the time in some detail.

In November 1095 Pope Urban II presented a new idea at the Council of Clermont: an army of Christians would set out for the East, the Holy Land, with the aim of defeating the Muslims and liberating the Christian holy sites. He had hoped that, after the harvest of the following year, his representatives would take up arms to this end and lead a large company of soldiers, veterans of previous battles with the Muslims. But from the moment the idea of a Christian crusade to redeem the holy sites became public the initiators lost control over it; individuals and groups immediately enlisted for the journey to the East, answering any call to form a troop. Local preachers, minor nobles, visionaries and group organizers of all sorts began deploying forces in Europe in the name of this extraordinary idea.[1]

These groups began to set out as early as March, traversing the Rhine valley, without any system of provisions, organization or coordination. Each group had its own leaders, each with his own agenda, vision and ideals. Christian writers described these troops with a mixture of admiration and contempt, enthusiasm and criticism. On the one hand these authors depicted the piety and deep faith that motivated simple people to abandon everything and cling to the idea of redemption for the sake of Jesus. Nonetheless, their narratives did not hide the fact that, alongside the pure of heart, many negative elements had joined these crusades. Some of these people – or, according to some, all of them – thought that the campaign in which they were taking part authorized them either to convert the Jews to Christianity or to murder them, before they set out to wage war on the Muslims in the East.²

The Jews documented these events in all the usual ways. They wrote 'chronicles', and composed *piyyutim* (liturgical poems) to commemorate specific events; they produced 'memorial books' in which they listed the names of those who died during the incidents themselves, and responded to the event and its repercussions in the framework of halakhic literature.³ All of these literary or legal compositions describe the Christian anti-Jewish behaviour and the Jewish reaction to it. The intense religious aura that surrounded the Christian troops and the passion of their faith are also reflected clearly in these Jewish sources. As the Jews understood it, these feelings were the motivation behind the Christians' desire to convert Jews to Christianity. Murder, pillage, abuse, and persecution were only unleashed if the Jews denied the Christian truth and refused to be converted to Christianity. The Jews were guilty of killing and crucifying Jesus; therefore, it was only fitting that the crusade that was set out to reclaim his grave should first of all seek revenge on those who had killed him. They could only be forgiven if they accepted him and recognized him as the Messiah.

The manner in which the Christians relate to the Jews is also a reflection of the strong feeling of trepidation felt by those embarking on a long and dangerous journey to fight a war against the Muslims: they are unwilling to leave the Jews behind in Europe because they considered them a dangerous, foreign element. The Jews had to be dealt with first, they reasoned, since the Muslims are 'there' – the destination of the crusaders – while the Jews were here 'living among us'. The Jews also discerned a change in the Christian line of thinking. The Christians had now become convinced that God was on their side and, consequently, Christianity was seeking to gain control over the entire world. Hence, the Jews understood that, from this time on, they were being ordered to participate in this world as Christians and to disappear as Jews.⁴

On 3 May 1096, the vanguard of the troops that were in process of formation reached the Jewish community in the city of Speyer. According to the Jewish sources, Speyer was the first place in which an attempt to convert the Jews was made. It was here, too, that the Jewish model of behaviour was established: the Jews killed themselves and their families 'al kiddush Hashem' (in sanctification of the Name of God), before the Christians could succeed in forcibly converting them or killing them. The first person to take this action and guide others along this path was a woman. John, the Bishop of the city, sent out troops to fight against the attackers and even punished some of them severely. Thus, despite the fact that many of the Jews had already taken their own lives, the suffering of the Jews of Speyer was in fact less than in other places. Both the Christians and the Jews repeated this form of behaviour in other cities such as Worms, Mainz, Metz, Würzburg and Nuremberg. Wherever the Christians would make their explicit demand of the Jews – 'Convert or die' – the Jews would react by refusing point-blank and killing themselves. On 10 June 1096, the Christians did manage to force Jews to convert to Christianity in Regensburg.[5]

This whole offensive against the Jews lasted for three months, until the Christian soldiers left the area and set out for the Holy Land. However, these regiments of Christians never reached Palestine. The King of Hungary, Colomon, realizing that this multitude of destruction would be looking for an outlet in his territories, stopped them near Weisselburg, on the banks of the Danube. Other forces carried on the campaign, and on 15 July 1099 they captured Jerusalem, turning it into a Christian city and establishing a Christian State in the Holy Land.

These events had a formidable impact on all aspects of life for the Jews from the twelfth century onward. It was now plain that the Christians were indeed capable of carrying out their threat to convert Jews to Christianity by force, and that the community had to prepare itself for this contingency. The age-old Christian theological claim that God had abandoned the Jews and was now on the side of the Christians seemed to be corroborated by historical events and by what was happening around them. Christendom had in fact conquered the Holy Land, liberated the Holy Sepulchre, and established a Christian State in Palestine. Both physically and theologically, the situation of the Jews had become very difficult. In response, they strongly emphasized the Jewish way of dying – *mavet al kiddush haShem*, Death in Sanctification of God's Name. The Jews felt that they had triumphed over the Christians, because they made the demand to 'convert or die' an empty letter by choosing to kill themselves – both women and men – and their children. The Christians had neither gained actual converts, nor managed to kill Jews.

Mavet al kiddush haShem is the Jewish term given to this extraordinary phenomenon that was both remarkable and heartrending: men and women (or women and men) who were willing to pay with their lives so as not to forsake their religion. These are the so-called Jewish martyrs.

Despite the fact that the authors of the texts describing these actions, as well as those who formulate the messages for future generations, are all men, the role of women in these events is salient.[6] These writers emphasized the fact that the first act of self-killing was carried out in

Speyer by a woman, 'the first to kill herself *al kiddush haShem* in all the communities'.⁷ From then onwards, women are depicted as playing a central role in everything that happened, and this can be seen in several examples that describe women, whether as individuals or in groups:

> The women girded their loins with strength and slew their own sons and daughters, and then themselves ... The most gentle and tender of women slaughtered the child of her delight. They all arose, man and women alike, and slew one another. The young maidens, the brides, and the bridegrooms looked out through the windows and cried out in a great voice: 'Look and behold, O Lord, what we are doing to sanctify Thy Great Name, in order not to exchange You for a crucified scion who was despised, abominated, and held in contempt in his own generation, a bastard son conceived by a menstruating and wanton mother ... '
>
> There were also many women there who sanctified the Name of their Creator with their last breath, not giving Him up for the crucified (hanged) bastard. One of them was Mistress Rachel, the spouse of our late master, Rabbi Eleazar, who had been the colleague of Rabbi Judah, son of Rabbi Isaac; Rabbi Judah, a famed scholar, had also been slain in Sanctification of God's Name. There were other saintly women with them who also sanctified God's Name. These pure souls were brought before the churchyard, where the enemy attempted to persuade them to submit to baptism. When they arrived at the temple of their pagan cult, the women refused to enter the edifice of idolatry, rooting their feet on the threshold, unwilling to enter and inhale the odour of the offensive incense. When the errant ones saw that the women stood firm against the abomination, and, what is more, that they remained true with all their heart to the living God, they fell upon them with axes and smote them. Thus the saintly women were slain in Sanctification of God's Name.
>
> There were two other pious women: Mistress Guta, wife of our master, Rabbi Isaac, son of Rabbi Moses, who had perished in the flames in Sanctification of God's Name. These women also sanctified the Name of the Holy one, whose Oneness is on the lips of all living creatures, at the time that the martyred men were slain in the courtyard of the bishop. The women had found sanctuary in the courtyard of a burgher, and the enemy came and drove them from the house. And demanded that they defile themselves with their evil water. But the women placed their trust in the Holy One of Israel and extended their throats, and the errant ones slew them without mercy.⁸

The most outstanding quality attributed to women in the context of *mavet al kiddush haShem* is knowledge: they knew 'the will of their Creator'. According to the chronicler, women usually knew what to do. They are the first to perform the self-killing; they know that the children must also be killed; and when they saw that the group would not have enough time to perform the self-killing ceremony of *mavet al kiddush haShem*, they threw money and jewels out to the Christians in order to delay their entry into the building in which they had all gathered. In the words of the author: 'their children were slaughtered at the hands of compassionate women so as to do the will of their Creator'. Seeing the Sefer Torah being ripped apart, the women then urged the men to action; the writer again points out: 'And when the pious and pure daughters of kings saw that the Torah had been ripped apart, they wailed and cried out to their husbands ... and when the men heard the words of the pious women, their zeal was aroused.'[9] The author highlights the fact that, at one point, the Christians in Trier understood that the women were the ones who killed the children and encouraged the men to die *al kiddush haShem*. Moreover, the chronicler related, when they brought the women to the castle they separated them from the children, closed the moat, and did not allow them to ascend the wall; 'all this the women do to incite their husbands to revolt against the hanged (crucified) one'.[10]

In describing the women, distinctly masculine idioms and associations are applied. Alongside terms that usually characterize women ('pure', 'daughters of the kings', 'compassionate'), explicitly male characteristics and attributes are used for both men and women; for example: 'holy', 'pious', 'important', 'saintly'. Moreover, the portrayal of the women draw on explicitly 'male' metaphors, such as 'women girded their loins', a phrase that has a particularly male association.[11]

Texts describing *mavet al kiddush haShem*, whether prose or *piyyutim*, plainly underscored the fact that women appear alongside men and perform the same acts that they do, even engaging in battle with the Christians: 'the saintly women would throw the stones through the windows on the enemies and the enemies would throw stones at them, and they would be pelted with stones until their flesh and faces were full of many cuts, and then the women would throw insults and curse their attackers'.[12] The phrase 'many cuts' used here in reference to women is usually reserved for men wounded in battle and for the famous Ten Martyrs, who were all male heroes.[13]

In order to describe the conduct of the Jews, the authors uses mainly biblical images from sections of admonishment, prophecies of wrath or the Book of Lamentations.[14] His representations of women, however, are just the opposite of the biblical ones, thus sharpening and exaggerating their role to an even greater extent. In the section of admonishment, and in Lamentations in particular, women are used to show the abysmal depths to which the Jews would sink when God punished them: women would kill their children and even eat them in their terrible hunger. In the chronicles the same images and language are used in the opposite sense, to depict the sublime heights to which Jewish acts of martyrdom reached. 'The soft and joyous killing of the child of her happiness' is based on the admonishment section in Deuteronomy (28:56), where it is said that if the Jews do not follow the path which the Lord has set for them, they will be punished very severely. The tragedy described in Lamentations is transformed in 1096 to an event in which the Jewish mother proves the strength of her belief and her will to fight.[15]

This is seen clearly in the example of another Rachel:

> Who has seen or heard of an act like the deed of the righteous and pious young Mistress Rachel, daughter of Isaac, son of Asher, and wife of Judah? She said to her friends: 'Four children have I. Have no mercy on them either, lest the uncircumcized ones come and capture them and raise them in their mistaken beliefs. In my children, too, shall you sanctify the Holy Name of God.' One of her friends came and took the knife to slaughter her son. When the 'mother of the sons' saw the knife (the *ma'akhelet*)[16] she cried loudly and bitterly and smote her face and breast, and said: 'Where is your grace, O Lord?' With an embittered heart she [the mother] said to her companions: 'Do not slaughter Isaac before his brother Aaron, so that he Aaron will not see the death of his brother and flee.' A friend took the boy and slew him. A delightful little child he was. The mother spread her sleeves to receive the blood, according to the practice in the ancient Temple sacrificial rite (Exod. 29:18–21). The lad Aaron, upon seeing that his brother had been slaughtered, cried: 'Mother, do not slaughter me,' and fled, hiding under a box. She also had left two daughters, Bella and Madrona, modest and beautiful maidens. The maidens took the knife and sharpened it, so that it would be completely smooth. They extended their throats, and the mother sacrificed them to the Lord, God of Hosts, who commanded us not to depart from His pure doctrine, and to remain wholehearted with Him, as it is written: 'Thou shalt be wholehearted with the Lord thy God' (Deut. 18:13).
>
> When this pious woman had completed sacrificing her three children to their Creator, she raised her voice and called to her son: 'Aaron, Aaron, where are you? I will not spare you either, or have mercy on you'. She drew him out by his feet from under the box where he had hidden and slaughtered him before the Exalted and Lofty God. Then she placed them all on her arms, two children on one side and two on the other, beside her stomach, and they quivered beside her, until finally the enemy captured the chamber and found her there sitting and lamenting over them. They said to her 'Show us the money you have in your sleeves'; but when they saw the slaughtered children, they smote

and killed her upon them, and her pure soul expired. It is of her that it was said: 'The mother was dashed in pieces with her children' (Hos. 10:14).[17]

This shocking excerpt makes it clear that the roles and functions, which had up to now been the sole province of men, were transferred to (or undertaken by) women. It is the woman who decides on death and the form of death. The passage about Rachel utilizes two particularly important Jewish myths: the binding of Isaac and the sacrificial ceremonies performed at the Temple. In both these instances, men were originally the main players and filled all the roles. But women are now the protagonists in the texts written after the First Crusade. The depiction of Rachel's actions directly parallels the rite of sacrifice performed in the Temple: the bringing of the sacrifice, the ritual slaughter, the throwing of the blood, and the recitation of the prayer. In the Temple, the men of the family perform the entire ceremony, while the women remain (as spectators) in the women's gallery. Priests, who are also men, conduct the actual sacrificial rite. In the Middle Ages, this image undergoes a change. Now the person who brings the sacrifice, performs the sacrificial rite, and recites the prayer is a woman, a priestess.[18]

This element is even more prominent in passages that re-enact the binding of Isaac. In the biblical narrative (Gen. 22), Isaac's mother, Sarah, does not even figure in the story. All the characters – Abraham, his servants, and Isaac – are men. Sarah only makes an appearance after Abraham returns from the 'binding' together with his servants, and then we are informed of her death. A *midrash* written on Genesis 22 explains that Satan told her what her husband had done, and so caused her death. In a famous illustration of the binding of Isaac, Satan is shown raising Sarah aloft so that she can see what is going on, an action that brings about her death. Some medieval texts recreate the story of the sacrifice of Isaac, with a woman taking the place of Abraham (and sometimes even replacing Isaac). The story of Rachel clearly illustrates this switch of roles. Moreover, the language used to describe Abraham sacrificing Isaac is applied to Rachel, as well as to other women who kill their children, while words used in Genesis, or the related *Midrashim* dealing with Isaac, are used to depict girls. In other words, a mother is playing the role of Abraham, while girls often appear in the part of Isaac.[19] In the medieval narrative, the mother is dominant; she makes the decisions and performs the sacrifice. She takes on Abraham's task and uses his words, speaking in the style of Genesis. In the case of Rachel, more than twenty sentences embellished with *Midrashic* associations are required to portray this woman and describe her act of sacrifice, whereas the father merits only one sentence: 'And the father cried and wailed when he saw the killing of his four sons, handsome and charming, and he went and fell upon the sword in his hand and his innards burst forth and he wallowed with the others who had been killed.' Rachel and her children are not literary fabrications. Her name and her children's names are inscribed in the Memorial Book that commemorates those who died *al Kiddush haShem*: 'Madame Rachel and her four children who were slaughtered, Bela, Matrona, Aaron and Isaac.'[20]

The reason that this description of Rachel's actions arouses such strong feelings is the fact that she struggles with herself and her emotions. She is not a fanatic or a cruel mother who has no hesitations or second thoughts about sacrificing her children. She focuses her attention on them and is deeply distressed by the fact that she must kill them; she complains bitterly to God, and struggles with herself and her children so that they will die in the proper way. For this reason, her justification – 'Lest the uncircumcized ones come and capture them and raise them in their mistaken beliefs' – rings true.

The symbolic involvement of the binding of Isaac and the Temple sacrifices is crucial to the above account of Rachel and her children and indeed the male writers who describe the behaviour of women had recourse to precedents from the Apocrypha, the *Midrash*, and the Talmud describing somewhat similar behaviour.

One of the sources used in the twelfth century to justify and encourage death *al kiddush haShem* is the *Midrash* found in the Talmud (Tbab. Tractate Gittin 57b) that tells of two ships that sailed from the Land of Israel to Rome after the destruction of the Temple. The ships carried Jewish boys and girls destined to be prostitutes in Rome. The girls ask the boys if suicide at sea instead of the life of abomination that awaits them will prevent them from entering the Garden of Eden. The boys' reply is that if they take their own lives by jumping overboard they will merit entry into the Garden of Eden. The girls immediately jump into the sea and die. The boys say to themselves: we shall learn from their actions and also commit suicide. In the Middle Ages, men and women who were familiar with this story acknowledged the leading role played by women in history of martyrdom. In other words, even though the boys possessed the necessary knowledge, the girls had not only the willingness to sacrifice but also the ability to see what was the right way to act. The boys followed the girls' lead. Medieval Jewish men and women were familiar with this story and the leading role played by the women in martyrdom. Two girls from Cologne who commit suicide by jumping into the river cite the same passage to justify their action.[21]

Despite its popularity, this *Midrash* had less impact on the Jews of the Middle Ages than the story of 'the mother and her sons', a well known example of Jewish martyrdom. This incident is associated with the rule of Antiochus in the second century BCE; it first appears in II Maccabees (Chapter 7).[22] This is an example of the evolution of a story with a lesson connected to a norm of behaviour, which is transmitted as an exemplary action that should be emulated. According to the story, the emperor himself captured the woman and her seven sons. When pressed to accept the emperor's gods, each brother refused, responding with a passage from the Bible; then each one in turn was executed. The climax of the story is reached in the episode of the youngest son, who rebuffs the ruler with a lengthy response. The mother was allowed to take leave of her son. She was not executed along with her children, but died afterwards by killing herself. As scholars have already shown, this story is similar to episodes in both Roman literature – descriptions of the treatment of heroes and the course of their trials – and the Christian literature of martyrdom of that era.[23]

Three versions of the story are found in talmudic literature. In the Babylonian Talmud (Gittin 62b), the youngest son could have saved himself by means of deception, yet he not only withstands the test, but also castigates the emperor. The mother's name is not mentioned and at this stage her role is secondary to that of her youngest son. Her importance in the story is the message she pronounces, that is, what the story seeks to transmit to future generations. The mother kissed her little boy before his death, a distinctly maternal gesture, and sent him off to give a message to 'Our Forefather Abraham': 'You built one altar, and I built seven.' After that she commits suicide, and then a heavenly voice is heard: 'The mother of sons is happy'. In the second version, in *Midrash* Eikhah Rabah,[24] the mother expands on her message to Abraham: He has no cause to be proud; he built only one altar, while she built seven. Abraham's experience was only a test, whereas her trial was real, and it was repeated seven times. In the third version, in Pesiqtah Rabati, the mother is barren before she gave birth to seven sons. This motif is stressed at the end of the *Midrashic* narrative and is linked to the verses about the childless Hannah (I Samuel 1, 2:5), who gave birth to Samuel and dedicated him to the service of God. From this point on, the mother in the story is called 'Hannah'.[25]

Given this backdrop, the role of the woman should be understood in an even more specific manner. The contemporary (twelfth century) paradigm of the Jewish mother was a composite of Abraham, who was given the ultimate test of belief, and the character of Hannah, the mother who saw how her seven sons were killed because they refused to convert, with the addition of a new dimension: the willingness of the mother to kill her children with her own hands. This manifestation of the prevailing mood appears again and again in the Jewish sources of the time, where the use of the two terms 'the mother of sons is happy' and 'mothers and babes were dashed to death together' is common.[26]

The phrase 'the mother of sons is happy' is found in Psalms (113:9), which describes how God is able to completely change the circumstances of human beings. A poor person may become rich and live among the richest people of the land; a childless woman may become the mother of many children, a mother who is happy with her sons. The *Midrash* on the mother and her seven sons explains that she was barren before she gave birth to the seven boys, who were then sacrificed, and adding greater import, she is called Hannah. The verse from Psalms was directly appended to this account, becoming a permanent embellishment for stories about mothers who sacrificed their children. In Genesis (32:12), Jacob uses the expression 'mothers together with children' to express the destruction of the family (this is also the sense in Deuteronomy 22:6). The prophet Hosea adds the words 'dashed to death' to this phrase in order to accentuate the prophecy of doom hanging over Israel.[27] In the Middle Ages, these verses took on a new meaning that emphasizes the role of the Jewish mother at a time when the Jews are under pressure to convert to Christianity.

The sources that describe the Jewish experience during the First Crusade shaped the basic perception of the way Jewish society interacted with the Christian population, defined it, and related to the factors that threatened its unity. Even though scholars disagree about the historical reliability of the specific events in these sources, it is clear that death *al kiddush haShem* is perceived in subsequent generations as a norm of behaviour, which they were obligated to emulate, and that it occupied a very important place in the hierarchy of group values.[28] During the ensuing centuries, until the Jewish communities in Germany were almost completely annihilated following the period of the Black Death (the middle of the fourteenth century), the Jews were often confronted with attempts to forcibly convert them to Christianity. In response they either killed themselves or died while unwaveringly rejecting Christianity. Many examples of this are recorded: during the various crusades; in 1171 in the city of Blois in northern France; in 1190 in York, England; throughout the thirteenth century, and particularly when it was drawing to a close; and during the time of the Black Death in the fourteenth century. And throughout this period, the Jews of northern France, England, and

Germany lived under the influence of the norm of *kiddush haShem*, willing to withstand the test, as their forefathers had, if necessary.

Both men and women, and even children, were called upon to uphold this norm and refuse to submit to Christianity. Although the emphasis of the Jewish martyrological literature changes in the second half of the twelfth century and the role of women is no longer as central as it was at the beginning, they nonetheless stand alongside the men in the chronicles and *piyyutim* that describe the death of Jews, unwilling to convert to Christianity. In the Memorial Books and the infinite number of martyrs they contain, there was no change in the status of women between the end of the eleventh century, during the First Crusade, and the middle of the fourteenth century during the time of the Black Death.[29]

Rabbi Ephraim of Bonn, the author of the Book of Remembrance, compiled the most important documentation of the events that occurred in the second half of the twelfth century in the Jewish communities of France, England, and Germany. Rabbi Ephraim himself and the manner in which he relates to women will be discussed below; however, in comparison with those who wrote immediately after the First Crusade, his references to *mavet al kiddush haShem* are much less voluminous. He is more of a historian than a teacher, hence his descriptions are more dispassionate and, in contrast to the accounts of earlier writers, they do not explicitly expound the message of martyrdom.[30] Rabbi Ephraim of Bonn hardly mentions women at all and when he does it is not in the context of the family, but as widows and individuals. Those who appear in a depiction of martyrdom, die passively, and there is only one account of a woman, Gotheila of Aspenbruck, who killed herself, like the women of the First Crusade. On the other hand, Rabbi Ephraim portrays the men as being much more passive than they appeared to be in the earlier narratives. Thus, in the twelfth-century narratives about their acts of martyrdom, men and woman are again represented as behaving in a similar manner. In the *piyyut* that Rabbi Ephraim of Bonn composed commemorating an act of martyrdom (that occurred in 1171), he states that women killed themselves and their children: 'And the mothers hurried and rushed their friends to be burned. And they sacrificed their children as voluntary offerings.'[31]

All the genres of Jewish writing in the Middle Ages retain the central role of women in the acts of *mavet al kiddush haShem*, even though they were all written by men. This was true of both prose and *piyyutim*, as well as of the memorial lists that were compiled in the twelfth century and subsequently. The names of women and men alike were read aloud and memorialized in order to reinforce the message of the Jew's willingness to preserve his or her religion to the death.

To clarify the question about the extent to which the society valued women in the context of preserving the Jewish religion, it is worthwhile examining another type of source, that is, sources dealing with one of the central issues that absorbed the Jewish community in the twelfth and thirteenth centuries – how did the Jewish group relate to those who left its ranks and converted to Christianity.[32]

From the beginning of the twelfth century on, Jewish society was constantly threatened by the Christians. The Jews felt that there could be a recurrence of attacks by Christians, like those that had occurred previously, as well as attempts to force them to convert to Christianity. From this time onwards, the act of becoming a Christian was considered an extremely serious and damaging deviation, and the apostates were treated with ever increasing distain and hostility. In contrast, works composed in the twelfth century, combine depictions of the piety of women, as described in the sources associated with the First Crusade, with another trait that is regarded as being specifically feminine. Very few Jewish women convert out of choice and they remain steadfast in their adherence to Judaism, even when their husbands convert. Rabbenu Tam, the major authority of the Jews of northern France in the twelfth century brings this issue up in a halakhic discussion. A query was sent to him regarding the validity of a *gett* that mentions the name of a man who converted to Christianity (but not the new name he adopted upon his conversion). In his response, Rabbenu Tam notes, by the way, that he knew of more than twenty *getts* given to wives by husbands who had converted to Christianity, because the women had decided to remain Jewish.[33] This halakhic comment indicates that these women preferred to remain within the Jewish community and adhere to the Jewish religion, even though they knew that this could result in their becoming *agunot* (women who cannot remarry). If a woman's 'New Christian' husband refused to grant her a *gett*, then, according to Jewish law, she would not be able to remarry, and her personal and economic status would become very difficult.

This highlighting of the women's piety and their desire to remain within the fold of Judaism is very significant. In the twelfth and thirteenth-century Jewish sources, the image of the man who converts to Christianity is negative, no matter what the circumstances. Whether he converted out of conviction or was forcefully persuaded, he was considered a threat to the Jewish religion. If he succumbed to the temptations of material rewards, gluttony or sexual desires, he is treated with extreme contempt.[34] Against this backdrop, the essentially different manner in which society related to women is particularly evident. In medieval Jewish sources, it is very rare to find even a hint that there were any women who converted to

Christianity of their own free will. In most cases, if a woman did convert, it was the outcome of coercion. Women, more so than men, adhered to Judaism and were willing to make sacrifices, no matter the cost, to hold on to their religion.[35]

There are two possible but contradictory explanations of this phenomenon. Women may have been extremely fearful of leaving their religion and going over to other, unknown 'pastures', preferring familiarity and safety to a new adventure. This sort of behaviour is typical of women who stay almost exclusively within the confines of the family unit, have very little contact with external society, and know little or nothing about the rival religion. This is not at all true of Jewish women in the Middle Ages. Thus, the explanation must be sought in another direction: very few women (in relation to men) converted to Christianity voluntarily because they clung uncompromisingly to their religion. The examples extant throughout the Jewish sources make it clear that those Jewish women who were forcibly converted to Christianity tried desperately to return to their former religion, even when it was clear to them that there was no guarantee that they would be able to resume their previous lives, which they had abandoned under duress.

The manner in which men related to these women is revealed through the deliberations that took place in the Middle Ages regarding the return of married women to their Jewish husbands after they had been held in captivity by Christians. The sages attempted to study this problem from the halakhic point of view, by examining a 'similar' situation dealt with in the *Mishnah* and the *Gemarah*, a propos women who were captured or kidnapped, and subsequently released to their families and husbands. The *Mishnah* draws a distinction between two types of women taken capture. Those who were imprisoned by the 'heathens' for the sake of money, in which case it is assumed that they would not be harmed or raped, and, therefore, there is no doubt they are able to return to their husbands, are defined as *shevyot* (prisoners). In contrast, women who were captured by troops whose only purpose was to pillage and murder are called *nihbashot* (captured); in such a case it was reasonable to assume that a woman would offer herself to her captors and try to appease them sexually in order to assure her physical survival. The *Mishnah* and the *Gemarah* debate whether or not such a woman, who had been held under such circumstances and was subsequently released, could be permitted to go back to her husband.[36]

Starting in the twelfth century, most of the halakhic debates dealing with this issue developed the idea that a woman who had been captured by Christians and forced to convert against her will was not to be considered as having been defiled by the Gentiles; that is, she was designated a *shevuyah* and thus could return to live with her husband. In the opinion of the sages, the Christian authorities took care that no harm of a sexual nature should come to the Jewish women they captured. Not all the Jewish legal authorities accepted this idea so readily. A twelfth-century *dayan* (judge) was called in to adjudicate the case of a woman who had been coerced into converting to Christianity; when she was released by her Christian captors, she returned to her husband as if nothing had happened. The *dayan* apparently hesitated about whether to designate the woman a *shevuyah* or a *nihbeshet*, but in practice the woman returned to her husband without the benefit of decisions of sages.

Cases of this sort clearly revealed 'the boundaries of the *halakhah*' in the area of marital relations. Jewish society took into consideration the fact that these women had been forced to remain with Christians for a certain amount of time, and took them back. This was also the opinion in an incident recounted by Rabbi Hayim ben Rabbi Yitzhak, who described a woman of twenty who was coerced into becoming a Christian; she remained with the Christians for nine years! After her release, she married a *kohen* (a member of the priestly caste).[37] Although this case does not involve a married woman, the sages nevertheless saw no reason to place obstacles in her path by raising talmudic precedents.

Although Maharam (c. 1220–1293) was very strict regarding male converts who wanted to return to Judaism, he was lenient with respect to the women who were forcibly converted.[38] He accepted the testimony of the victims themselves and thus made it possible for them to return to their husbands, emphasizing that 'they never practised idolatry, but the priest said his abominations to the gentiles and they remained silent'. It would seem that the *halakhah* came to the aid of forcibly converted women and accepted them back into the fold of Judaism.

But was this always the case? How did the general male public relate to this problematic situation? As usual, life was far more complicated than any broad generality. In order to better understand the complexities involved, let us look at another incident. In 1241 the Jewish community of Frankfurt was very brutally attacked by Christians.[39] About 180 Jews were killed and twenty-four were forcibly converted, among them one young girl, who was engaged to be married to a young man from the city of Würzburg. After managing to escape, she discovered that her betrothed had married another woman. All the sages, except for Rabbi Isaac (known as Or Zarua) defended the young woman. Their main premise was that, in their day, the Christians safeguarded forced converts and made sure that they were not harmed or sexually molested. The only one to rule against the determination that she should be considered a *shevuyah*, was Or Zarua, who declared that there was a suspicion that she might have been willing to be defiled in order to save her life. His stand is difficult to accept unless we assume that at this time, when he held a position in the Würzburg community, he was influenced by the family of the young man involved, who objected to his marriage with the girl who had been forcibly converted.

Several major sages in the region opposed the actions of the young man in this case, apart from the statement by Rabbi Isaac Or Zarua, and we have available to us the declarations made by five of them. The most important is that of Rabbi Yehudah HaCohen of Freiburg, who declared unequivocally that an injustice was being done to the young woman. It was he who raised the question in letters sent at his initiative to 'all sages and *dayanim*'. The other letters that we have were written by two students of Rabbenu Simha – Rabbi Meshulam ben David and Rabbi Shmuel bar Avraham HaLevi. We also have the statements of Rabbi Hayim, the son of Rabbi Isaac Or Zarua, who quotes the determinations of another sage, Rabbi David ben Rabbenu Shealtiel.

These sages are ostensibly discussing a halakhic issue; however, upon closer inspection, their statements show that they are dealing with a fundamental perception of women. It is perfectly clear in the minds of these sages that, in their times, young Jewish women who are caught and forced to submit to Christianity do not give up hope. Moreover, these women do not think that they will be spared from death if they surrender themselves physically; therefore, they cannot be classified under the *mishnaic* labels of *shevuyah* or *nihbeshet*. Hence, the sages conclude that they have before them a third situation: a woman who knows that she has been captured unlawfully, who does not despair or abandon all hope of being released and who seeks throughout the time of her captivity to return to her family and to Judaism.

Rabbis Yehudah HaCohen and Meshulam ben David stressed the breach of promise given at the time of the engagement, an act, which in their opinion, is equal to the violation of the ban on bigamy. But their wrath is mainly expressed in the comparison they make between the behaviour of the boy and that of the girl. The girl remained faithful to Judaism even though she was forced to accept Christianity. She refused to marry a rich and prominent Christian, and in response to this offer declared: 'I do not desire (such an offer), since I am engaged to a Jew'. Furthermore, it was known that, throughout the time they were confined, she and other girls persistently attempted to escape from the Christians until they eventually succeeded. Indeed, several non-Jews, both men and women stated, without realizing the significance of their remarks, that the Jewish women had remained chaste and preserved their respectability. The fact that they were not forced to marry Christians and did not have sexual relations with them, coupled with the knowledge that they managed to escape their Christian captors at the end, proves that God rewarded their praiseworthy behaviour and saved them by miraculous means. Moreover, the sages noted instances in which women, who returned to Judaism after having been forced to convert to Christianity, were permitted to resume conjugal life with their husbands.

Paradoxically, the most vociferous in his opposition to the opinion of Rabbi Isaac Or Zarua was his son, Rabbi Hayim. He relies on the opinion of Rabbi David ben Rabbenu Shealtiel, which conflicts with his father's conclusions precisely in the realm of *halakhah*. At the end of his discussion, Rabbi Hayim dissociated the incident from the mishnaic precedent of the *shevuyah* or *nihbeshet*. The woman was not a *shevuyah*, since her captors had no intention of returning her; neither could she be considered a *nihbeshet*, because she was very strictly kept from becoming the victim of any act of violence, and most particularly sexual violence.

Rabbi Meshulam ben David cites the opinion of his important teacher, Rabbenu Simha, who set down the following principle: if women who were captured 'accept as true' that it is possible to free them by putting pressure on their captors or by bribing them, or if they do not even consider the option of remaining Christian, they are worthy of returning to their husbands, without any difficulty. This viewpoint overturns the *mishnaic* argument. Rabbi Meshulam even brings a precedent for his statement, an incident very similar to the one under discussion. There, because of the concern about the prohibition on bigamy, a young man was forced to divorce the woman whom he had married in order to marry the first woman to whom he had made a solemn promise of marriage. This demonstrates a new attitude towards women, beyond the halakhic perspective. This attitude is clearly manifested in the statements of Rabbi Shmuel bar Avraham haLevi. He opposes the halakhic claim brought against a young woman who was considered a *nihbeshet*, which maintained that a woman whose life was being threatened would attempt to appease (her captors) sexually in order to save herself. Rabbi Shmuel attacked this point of view with the succinct declaration: 'I do not know who permitted him to look upon the daughters of Israel as whores.'

As I have already pointed out, the language and images used by the men who describe, analyze, and either criticize or praise the actions of women are extremely significant and revealing. For example, Rabbi Yehudah haCohen portrays Jewish girls in general, and especially those who became Christians against their will, as 'daughters like cornerstones' who were tempted by the threatening edge of the sword, and all the while their hearts were directed towards God in heaven. This representation is based on an association from a verse in Psalms (144:12) that describes boys and girls: 'For our sons are like saplings, well tended in their youth; our daughters are like cornerstones, trimmed to give shape to a palace.' 'Trimmed girls' means virtuous Jewish girls, innocent and respectable in their conduct, like the walls (or pillars) of a palace.

Similarly, Yalkut Shimoni, a *Midrash* written in this period, also uses this image; both Rabbi Yehudah haCohen and Yalkut Shhimoni's use of this phrase is based on Rashi's commentary on the Talmud. Rashi makes a connection between the verse in Psalms and another verse from the Book of Zechariah (9:15): 'And be filled like a dashing bowl/ Like the corners of an altar.' Rashi explains why the dashing bowls in the Tabernacle were used in the description of the girls in Psalms – 'corners' (cornerstones). The dashing bowls in the Tabernacle (and in the Temple) were used to cast the blood on the altar. According to Rashi, a bowl filled with blood for a sacrifice may be compared to a married woman who is filled with desire solely for her husband, and waiting for him, saves herself for him alone, come what may. Rashi sees these women as the foundation, the basis upon which the walls of the palace – the Temple – stand firm.[40] Rabbi Yehudah HaCohen also composed a *piyyut* that describes what occurred in Frankfort and in it he used the expression 'daughters like cornerstones' to represent all the daughters of Israel, the women who died *al kiddush haShem*. This *piyyut* reveals that he drew no distinction between women who had died *al kiddush haShem* and those who were forced to convert to Christianity. In both cases, they are pure from the sexual standpoint. Some of them chose to die *al kiddush haShem*, whereas others were coerced into converting but even then they held on to their purity and their faith.[41]

Nevertheless, these sages' perceptions of the daughters of Israel do not absolve us from making an attempt to understand Rabbi Isaac 'Or Zarua', because an analysis of his *responsa* may enable us to identify the various attitudes to women with which he was wrestling, attitudes that were more than likely shared by a large part of the group we are studying.[42] He was wavering between two approaches. On the one hand, he was careful to point out, with great emotion, that it is absolutely forbidden to disparage the young woman. On the other hand, according to his halakhic perception, which was derived from the Talmud, there could be no alternative other than to look upon the case as one involving a *nihbeshet*. A more in-depth examination of his statements leads to the observation that, at the foundation of his halakhic perception lies a harsh attitude towards Christianity, which he views as a contaminated, immoral religion, that causes harm to women. He disagrees with the concept that the Christians protect the Jewish women they capture. On the contrary, he sees the Christians as being consumed by their desires and treating the Jewish women they forcibly convert with contempt; he also suspects that they despoil the women even before they convert them. The inner struggle that Rabbi Isaac Yitzhak Or Zarua was undergoing is revealed in the strong language he uses. He was particularly impressed with those who, under the circumstances, sacrificed their lives and died *al kiddush haShem*: 'For them our hearts mourn and we should be remorseful and grieve for the saintly persons who were killed in Frankfurt. Blessed are they and blessed is the portion of those who sanctified God, may He be praised and feared, with their bodies, they have dealt a kindness to their souls because they have found their just reward.' The phrases 'sanctified with their bodies' and 'kindness to their souls' indicate, more than anything else, Or Zarua's attitude to those who did not sanctify their bodies and did not deal kindly with their souls. What comes to the fore here are his conflicting feelings towards women who did not take the road of self-killing, as did their sisters in previous generations.

The same tension can be discerned in the letters of several sages that clearly express a particular tone: these women failed in their test. Nevertheless, the decisions they handed down enabled the women to return to and become reconnected with their families and the society. In contrast to previous declarations, which actually extolled the women who did not allow themselves to be influenced by the Christianity that was forced upon them and found a way to return to Judaism, what we see here is quite plainly a male perception that has difficulty coming to terms with this behaviour.

An explicit spokesperson for these feelings with respect to women was Rosh (Rabbenu Asher ben Yechiel), who lived at the end of the thirteenth century. As did others, he made decisions, without hesitation, that women who had managed to escape after having been coerced into accepting Christianity, could return to their husbands. Nonetheless, he strongly criticized them for not dying *al kiddush haShem*.[43] He begins his elucidation with the phrase: 'On the women who did not have the strength to serve in the king's palace.' The phrase 'to serve in the king's palace' is taken from the well known verse in the Book of Daniel (1:4): 'youths without blemish, handsome, proficient in all wisdom knowledgeable and intelligent, and capable of serving in the royal palace and teach them the writings and the language of the Chaldeans'. This verse is frequently used to express the strength of those who are willing to die *al kiddush haShem*. 'Rosh' stated that 'In all cases, a person must surrender his soul *al kiddush haShem*', and that these women must 'do penance and repentance and willingly accept suffering'. Nevertheless, because he thinks that the women converted under circumstance of extreme coercion and 'on pain of death', and because the Christians at this time did not permit the defiling of the women whom they wish to turn into Christians, his halakhic determination is that they may and should return to their husbands. To make his ruling acceptable to his audience, he tells a story, likening those who decide to convert out of fear to soldiers who hesitate to enter the battle. They retreat and desist from joining the other soldiers who are willing to give their lives. After the king's forces win the battle, they approach the sovereign seeking to rejoin his ranks; saying that they are willing to make 'minor amends' to their behaviour, but the king is only willing to receive them after they agree to make 'major amends'.

While the attitude here towards the *anusot* (new forced converts to Christianity) is not positive, Rosh does give them the chance to come back into the fold of Judaism without calling attention to their non-fulfilment of the obligation to kill themselves *al kiddush haShem* or making this an obstacle to their return. It would seem, however, that his real attitude towards these women is in fact more severe. According to him, they should have died *al kiddush haShem* rather than convert, even under duress. Yet, he, too, made the point that was in the minds of all, and particularly in the minds of all the women: it was, in fact, their conversion to Christianity that safeguarded the virtue of the women more than anything else. A woman who converted to Christianity would immediately be given protection from the sexual point of view and was not liable to be raped. It should also be borne in mind that the Jewish community, under pressure as it was, could little afford to lose members, even suspect ones.

The views of the sages, as we learn from the sources, differed and often clashed with those of the husbands. A husband's main fear was that his wife's virtue might have been jeopardized. The superlatives used by the sages to describe how faithfully the women clung to their religion, the halakhic permissions they received, and the recognition that they were worthy and upright did not make much of an impact on the men, nor did it persuade the husbands. We find sages desperately attempting to repudiate claims by certain husbands seeking to divorce their wives who had lived among the Christians. These claims were made on the basis of the ruling that 'one who transgresses the Law (the Torah), forfeits her *ketubah*'. They wanted to divorce their wives without giving them their due according to their *ketubah*, which could have very severe economic consequences for the woman. Indeed, 'Rosh', as did other sages, virulently opposed this type of claim made by some husbands, rejecting it outright, even though, as we have seen, he was disturbed by the fact that the woman had not chosen to die *al kiddush haShem*.

Yet, the men were not concerned only with financial matters. The argument for divorcing a woman without giving her what had been guaranteed in the *ketubah* on the basis of 'one who transgresses the Law' stems from Tractate Ketubot in the Talmud. There it is explained that a woman who converts to another religion may cause her husband to transgress without him being aware of it, since she could no longer be considered trustworthy. For example, she might tell her husband that she had immersed herself in the *mikvah* after she finished her menstrual cycle, without actually doing so; give him food that is not kosher, while he remains unaware of this; or fail to fulfil vows that she has made.[44] The damage that such a woman causes her family is great. Furthermore, as is noted in particular, she is likely to lose her children during childbirth as a punishment. In the Middle Ages, an era in which infant mortality during childbirth and immediately thereafter was rampant, husbands harboured extreme trepidation of all such women. Hence, it was very dangerous for a woman to spend any time in the company of Christians, willingly or unwillingly, since she was likely to be labelled 'one who transgresses the Law'.

Thus, the husband's concern is not just that his wife's virtue may have been violated or that he may not want to have her return to his home. His anxiety stems from the fact that, even if he accepts her in his home, since she did not give up her soul *al kiddush haShem*, she could endanger her unborn children. In order to overcome this problem, which was one of mentality, the sages permitting women to return to their husbands repeatedly make two extenuating circumstances very clear. First, the women had really been in danger of being killed; second, they attempted to return to Judaism immediately and persisted in these attempts throughout the time of their captivity. In these circumstances, these women could not be defined as 'those who transgress the Law', nor should the claim be made that they should have died *al kiddush haShem*. Moreover, the term *nihbeshet* and the related halakhic rules should not be applied to them. In order to substantiate these rulings, some of the sages make use of claims they never cited in discussions dealing with men. They mention that according to Tractate Sanhedrin (74a) the rule 'Allow yourself to be killed but do not commit this act' is the subject of debate between the *Amoraim*, Abbaye and Rava, and it is known that Rava refrained from meting out a punishment to someone who had worshipped pagan gods out of fear, but without actually accepting belief in these gods. At the end of the thirteenth century, Rabbi Yedidiyah bar Yisrael, whose son died *al kiddush haShem* in 1298, cited the simple and clear words that Maimonides had written a century before, that a person who has been forced to convert against his will, and who does not give up his soul, cannot be judged or punished by a human court, nor indeed by Heaven.[45] But the apprehension of the husbands and families was decidedly a more complex business.

Another issue that relates to women should be taken into account with respect to those who converted to Christianity. It was believed that the conversion to Christianity created a defect in the genetic composition of the convert, and that, even if they returned to Judaism, this defect had already changed not only their own, but also their entire family's genetic makeup. Sefer Hasidim contains several examples of this line of thinking. Since women in this period were perceived as responsible for passing hereditary traits to the children, it is understandable that thorough searches for possible family 'defects' were mainly directed at potential brides, particularly if there were *anusim* or former converts to Christianity in the family.[46] Two families, one in northern France and the other in Frankfort, went to great lengths to prevent their sons from marrying women who they felt had become defective in one way or another – either they had converted to Christianity in the past, their former husbands had been converts, or they were suspected of having some connection with the accursed religion.[47] A letter was sent to Rabbenu Tam describing a woman who had received a *gett* from her converted husband, but the *dayan* refused to certify it. Rabbenu Tam wrote: 'And you the great benefactor, the father of the woman, shall marry your daughter to someone worthy of her; do not heed the words of the malingers.' Thus, he seeks to console the father regarding the interrogations and investigations being conducted by families of potential suitors. In the case referred to in the *responsa* literature as 'the engaged of Frankfurt', the family of a prospective groom was worried that the bride, who had been living among Christians, had been converted, perhaps even by force, and that this would damage the genetic makeup of their son's family. It is difficult to conceive of another explanation for the efforts made by members of this family to achieve the sages' approval for the nullification of their son's engagement and his subsequent marriage to another young woman.[48]

The family of a convert was labelled as such and bore a stigma. The name of the convert was omitted when his son was called up to the Torah. A popular verse in the Sefer Hasidim declares that: 'A person should not say to a Jew: 'If I do this, I will not be a Jew, I will become a Gentile or a convert'; it is an evil thing to say, and even as a condition, it should not be uttered.' In the author's opinion, it harms the Jewishness of the speaker.[49] While in the eleventh century the ruling attributed to Rabbenu Gershom Me'or HaGolah 'do not remind or shame a person who abandons his faithless way of life and returns to Judaism, that in the past he would have been threatened with excommunication or banishment' was followed, by the end of the century, Rabbi Hayim, the son of Rabbi Isaac Or Zarua did not even refer to this ruling. Thus, women who had been living among Christians were forced to pay a heavy price, even though they had been held against their will and had stringently adhered to Judaism. In their case, the perception that women clung to their religion with greater tenacity and were willing to sacrifice more in order to preserve it did not improve the way men related to women who had been coerced into living among Christians, but, on the contrary, served to exacerbate it.

As I shall show in the coming chapters some of the changes affecting the status of the woman started appearing already in the eleventh century, but the process of change accelerated and was consolidated in the course of the twelfth century. I regard the challenge of Christianity as a constant threat that affected Jewish life in the course of the twelfth and thirteenth centuries. As a result of the attack on established Jewish communities at the end of the eleventh century, the readiness to take one's own life and that of family members was recognized as something correct and proper that was done by the finest of people. Consequently the phenomenon of Jewish women demonstrating their piety and their readiness to preserve their religion came to be part of their image – the way that the men saw them and it may indeed be assumed (without us having written proof) that this was also the way that they regarded themselves. This image was to have a dominant impact, in my opnirion, on all the other subjects connected with the status of Jewish women within their communities.

Notes

1 See S. Runciman, *A History of the Crusades*, Vol. 1, Cambridge 1968, pp. 265–314; J. Prawer, *Histoire du royaume latin de Jérusalem*, Paris 1969, pp. 177–208, 223–238; Erdmann, 1977; J. Riley-Smith, 'The First Crusade and the Persecution of the Jews', in *Persecution and Toleration*, SCH,21, ed. W. J. Sheils, Oxford 1984, pp. 51–72; J. Riley-Smith, *The First Crusade and the Idea of Crusading*, London 1986 (1993); R. Chazan, *European Jewry and the First Crusade*, Los Angeles 1987, pp. 38–40; J. Riley-Smith, *The First Crusader, 1096–1131*, Cambridge 1997; S. Goldin, *The Ways of Jewish Martyrdom*, Turnhout 2008, pp. 3–12.

2 S. Goldin, *The Ways of Jewish Martyrdom*, pp. 4–5, about Albert of Aachen; J. Riley-Smith, *The First Crusade and the Idea of Crusading*, pp. 31–57; J. Riley-Smith, 'The First Crusade and the Persecution'.

3 S. Salfeld, *Das Martyrlogium des Nürnberger Memorbuches*, Berlin 1938.
4 S. Eidelberg, *The Jews and the Crusaders*, pp. 99-100.
5 For the Hebrew 'Chronicles' I used the translation of Shlomo Eidelberg, *The Jews and the Crusaders: The Hebrew Chronicles of the First and Second Crusades*, Madison, WI 1977. About the manuscripts see his introduction in pp. 16-19 and A. S. Abulafia, 'The Interrelationship between the Hebrew Chronicles on the First Crusade', *Journal of Semitic Studies* 27 (1982), pp. 221-239; S. Goldin, *The Ways of Jewish Martyrdom*, Turnhout 2008, pp. 369-370.
6 S. Noble, 'The Jewish Woman in Medieval Martyrology', in *Studies in Jewish Bibliography History and Literature in honor of I. E. Kiev*, ed. C. Berlin, New York 1971, pp. 347-355; J. Aronius, *Regesten zur Geschichte der Juden im fränkischen und deutschen Reiche bis zum Jahre 1273*, Berlin 1902, p. 81. A. Grossman, *Pious and Rebellious: Jewish Women in Europe in the Middle Ages*, Jerusalem 2001 [Hebrew], pp. 346-370; A. Grossman, *Pious and Rebellious: Jewish Women in Europe in the Middle Ages*, Waltham, MA 2004 [English], pp. 198-210.
7 S. Eidelberg, *The Jews and the Crusaders*, p. 22.
8 S. Eidelberg, *The Jews and the Crusaders*, pp. 32, 42.
9 Ibid., pp. 37, 66.
10 A. Grossman, *Pious and Rebellious, Jewish Women in Europe in the Middle Ages*, Jerusalem, 2001 [Hebrew], pp. 347-349; S. Eidelberg, *The Jews and the Crusaders*, pp. 37, 66.
11 S. Eidelberg, *The Jews and the Crusaders*, p. 32. 'Gird thy sword upon thy thigh, O mighty one' (Ps. 45:4), and 'Gird up thy loins' (II Kgs 4:29); S. Goldin, *The Ways of Jewish Martyrdom*, pp. 117-119.
12 S. Eidelberg, *The Jews and the Crusaders*, p. 35 (my translation).
13 Midrasch Echa Rabbati (Lamentations Rabbah), Vilna 1899, no. 3; Midrash on Psalms (Midrasch Tehillim), ed. S. Buber, Vilna 1892 (repr. Jerusalem 1966), chapter 9.
14 On the writing of the sources see R. Chazan, *European Jewry and the First Crusade*, Los Angeles 1987; S. Goldin, *The Ways of Jewish Martyrdom*, Turnhout 2008.
15 S. Eidelberg, *The Jews and the Crusaders*, p. 32.
16 *Ma'akhelet*, the term for the knife used in the binding of Isaac (Gen. 22:10) – see Glossary of Hebrew Terms.
17 Eidelberg, *The Jews and the Crusaders*, pp. 35-36.
18 See the stories about the act of Rivka, who lies dying in a pool of her own blood; the small, young woman of Tirer; the beautiful young woman who asks to be killed. S. Eidelberg, *The Jews and the Crusaders*, pp. 50, 55, 65-67.
19 S. Eidelberg, *The Jews and the Crusaders*, pp. 36, 54.
20 S. Salfeld, *Das Martyrlogium des Nürnberger Memorbuches*, Berlin 1938, p. 12 (117). The links between the different types of source (chronicles, memorial lists, and *piyyutim*) is totally clear, though the question of their chronological order has not yet been given a full answer. The chronicles and the *piyyutim* were written in the course of the first half of the twelfth century (the Second Crusade in 1147 is not mentioned in them), whilst the memorial lists cover the period from the end of the eleventh century until after the middle of the fourteenth century.
21 S. Eidelberg, *The Jews and the Crusaders*, p. 66.
22 Starting in the first century CE, the story was adapted and embellished by contemporary elements so as to underscore the Jews' suffering during the Roman era (there is an

emperor figure in each version).
23 S. Liberman, 'The Martyrs of Caesarea', *Annuarire de l'Institut de Philologie et d'histoire orientale et slave*, 7 (1939-1944), pp. 395-446; A. Agus, *The Binding of Isaac and Messiah*, New York 1988, pp. 11-32.
24 *Midrash Eikhah Rabah*, no. 1.
25 *Midrash Pesiqtah Rabati*, no. 43.
26 S. Spiegel, *The Last Trail: On the Legends and Lore of the Command to Abraham to offer Isaac as a Sacrifice*, trans. J. Goldin, Philadelphia 1967. The story of Rachel ends with the phrase: 'Of the one it is said, "mothers and babes were dashed to death together." She and her four sons; when the saintly woman died over seven sons, it was said of her, "The mother of sons is happy."'
27 This is also the aim of the exaggerated cruelty attributed to Sennacherib.
28 S. Goldin, 'The Socialisation for *Kidush ha-Shem* among Medieval Jews', *Journal of Medieval History*, 23 (1997), pp. 117-138.
29 For a different opinion see S. L. Einbinder, 'Jewish Women Martyrs: Changing Models of Representation', *Exemplaria*, 12 (2000) pp. 105-127. A. Grossman, *Pious and Rebellious: Jewish Women in Europe in the Middle Ages*, Waltham MA 2004, pp. 209-211 [in English].
30 R. Chazan, 'Ephraim ben Jacob's Compilation of Twelfth Century Persecutions', *Jewish Quarterly Review*, 84 (1994), pp. 397-416.
31 S. L. Einbinder, 'Jewish Women Martyrs', p. 120.
32 S. Goldin, 'Juifs et juifs convertis au Moyen-Age : "Es-tu encore mon frère?"', *Annales, Histoire, Sciences Sociales*, 54 (1999), pp. 851-874.
33 Jacob ben Meir, *Sefer haYashar leRabbenu Tam: Heleq haShe'elot vehaTeshuvot (Responsa)*, ed. S. F. Rosental, Berlin 1898, nos. 25 -26, pp. 42-45; Jacob ben Meir, *Sefer haYashar leRabbenu Tam: Heleq haHidushim* (News), ed. S. S. Schlesinger, Jerusalem 1959, no. 766, pp. 448-449.
34 Goldin, 'Juifs et juifs convertis au Moyen-Age'.
35 Despite the clear tendency of the men who wrote the texts to play up the role of the women so as to emphasize this phenomenon and to drive home the lesson to the men who failed to behave properly that 'the women behave properly, but not you men ... ' it was clear that that the sources do reflect actual feminine behaviour. In the Memory Books the names of the women appear and in the *responsa* literature the descriptions are of real events in which the women played a central role.
36 Tbab. Tractate Ketubot, 26b.
37 Hayim ben Rabbi Isaac, *Responsa*, Leipzig 1860, no. 103.
38 Meir ben Barukh, *Sefer Sharei Teshuvot*, ed. M. A. Blakh, Berlin 1891, no. 80, pp. 187-188.
39 E. E. Urbach, *Ba'alei ha-Tosafot*, 4th edition, Jerusalem 1980, pp. 432-433, 526-527. The texts are in *Teshuvot uPsakim, Responsa et Decisiones*, ed. E. Kupfer, Jerusalem 1973, no. 170, pp. 282-289; Sefer Mordekhai on Qidushin no. 568, see G. J. Blidstein, 'The Personal Status of Apostate and Ransomed Women in Medieval Jewish Law' [Hebrew], *Shenaton haMishpat haIvri*, 3-4 (1976-1977), p. 83-99; Tbab. Ketubot, 26b Rashi and Tosafot there, Tosafot on Tractate Avoda Zara, 23a v.s. teda, Rashi on Avoda Zara 25b v.s. beisah, Tosafot their v.s. ica benyehu.
40 See Rashi on Pesahim 87a and in Bava Batra 75a, Midrash Psalms, ch. 145, Yalkut Shimoni on Psalms, 1973, no. 888.

41 *Sefer haDmaut* (Book of Crying), ed. S. Barnfeld, vol. III, Berlin 1926, pp. 332–335, 299–305.
42 Isaac ben Moses, *Sefer Or Zarua*, no. 747.
43 Asher ben Yehiel, *Shut haRosh*, ed. S. Yudelov Jerusalem, 1994, 32:8.
44 Tbab, Ketubot 72.
45 *Mishneh Torah*, Yesodei Torah, ch. 5, sec. 4.
46 Judah ben Samuel, *Sefer Hasidim*, ed. J. Wistinetzki, Frankfurt 1942, no. 1822, p. 465.
47 Jacob ben Meir, *Sefer haYashar leRabbenu Tam: Heleq haShe'elot vehaTeshuvot (Responsa)*, ed. S. F. Rosental, Berlin 1898, nos. 25–26, pp. 42–45; *Teshuvot uPsakim, Responsa et Decisiones*, ed. E. Kupfer, Jerusalem 1973, no. 170, pp. 282–289.
48 *Sefer Hasidim*, nos. 1821, 1163, 1330–1332, 1109, 1404, 1898, 1097; L. Finkelstein, *Jewish Self-government in the Middle Ages*, New York 1924, pp. 175 (1), 179–180.
49 *Sefer Hasidim*, nos. 2 (p. 6), 372, 406, 642, 1084, 1881, 1891, 1922.

3

Four differing paradigms of male attitudes to women

The medieval Jewish sources were written by men, who very rarely wrote about their private lives, their life histories, or even their intimate thoughts and feelings. As already noted, none of these texts were written by women, yet references to them, subjects related to them, and relationships between men and women take up a significant portion of these sources. How should we understand the mind-set of the Jewish men who authored these texts with respect to women? Can we delve more deeply into their feelings and thought processes, that is, beyond simple male misogynous perceptions and the male desire for control?

The attitude of the male sages towards their wives and towards womankind in general cannot be understood without comprehending the male conceptualization of situations where male and female were liable to come into conflict. In all the sources that discuss the nature of the human male, it is clear that the sages have a very low opinion of the ability of any man (including themselves) to withstand the temptation inherent in the sexual tension, which women, by their very essence, represent. At times their writings reveal animosity towards women – all women – and the seduction and sexuality associated with them. They usually stress the fact that men are not capable of resisting this temptation, which must, therefore, be kept at a distance and severely circumscribed. Under these circumstances, attitudes towards women are bound to be highly problematic, because this meta-halakhic point of view not only works to the woman's disadvantage, but also makes the fear of womankind stronger in unexpected situations.

In a presentation made to fellow scholars some time ago, Shulamit Valler pointed to the discussion in the Talmud in Tbab. Tractate Berakhot 61a where the writer attempts to avert situations in which, he fears, a man could become excited by a woman – by her very presence – even if she does nothing to entice him.[1] A woman taking a walk, totally unaware that a man is walking behind her, cannot be accused of trying to tempt him; and, naturally, a woman cannot be accused of attempting to weaken the moral resolve of a man who comes to pay her for something he purchased from her. Nonetheless, the recommendations in the Talmud suggest that a man should be forbidden to walk behind a woman in the street, even if she is his wife. A man should also refrain from encountering a woman while crossing a river on a bridge, and if he walks behind a woman on a river path, he forfeits his place in the world to come. The text also points out that a man who plans to give a woman money that he owes her – from his hand to hers – in order to gaze upon her, will end up in hell. This particular section of the Talmud can only be understood in light of the writer's deep sense of the male's inability to control his sexual instincts.

In the Middle Ages, Rashi, for example, commented on an unclear episode in the Talmud in order to clarify this point. The story recounts how Rabbi Aukba's desire for a certain woman was so great that he became ill. It so happened that the woman was married and in need of money. She came to ask him for a loan and was even willing to submit to his wishes. After Rabbi Aukba succeeded in conquering his desires, not only did he recover from his illness, but his face also began to shine (or a sort of light appeared to be glowing above his head). Rashi intimates that this happened because Rabbi Aukba was able to avert the destruction of a family and prevent a woman in distress from committing adultery.[2] This outlook – the fear of the woman's sexual power – had a far-reaching impact on the Jewish society that was developing in the Middle Ages, a society that glorified family life and did not preach male celibacy; a society in which women were playing an increasingly important role, both in the economic and in other spheres.

From the medieval sources we see several different 'male' paradigms. Discovering the guiding principle behind the male sage's positions is, however, problematic because most of the sources they authored are halakhic in nature and because in most of what is available to us it is rare to find texts that shed light on intimate feelings. One significant exception is Rashi (Rabbi Solomon ben Isaac) himself. Because of the wide variety of sources that have been preserved in his name, he has given us the opportunity to develop a unique understanding of his views. (A great deal of research has, of course, also been devoted exclusively to Rashi.) I have made the assumption that, in his writing, Rashi refers mainly to the married woman – the wife – whom he considers of great importance because he sees her as the mainstay of the household, the person who keeps the problematic desires of the man – the husband – in check, and the person responsible for the future generation. These are classic roles in which male society casts women everywhere.

As I pointed out in Chapter 1, medieval Jewish society in the period under discussion here is a society that mobilized all its resources in the fight for survival against an ominous, hostile Christian world. Thus, the male sages develop a different paradigm that views the woman of their era as an important and essential component of this Jewish society. In order to strengthen the society from within, they enable the development of halakhic mechanisms that improve the social status of the woman in the community. The strength of the community was the primary concern of the proponents of this paradigm and their attitude towards women derived from it. They advanced the status of women in order to consolidate the group; favoured permitting halakhic development in regard to a variety of issues; did nothing to hinder this development; and, chiefly, enabled women to enter the closed male world in the economic and religious spheres. Two sages exemplify the supporters of this view: Rabbi Eliezer bar Nathan, from the beginning of the twelfth century, and Rabbi Meir ben Barukh (the Maharam of Rothenburg), from the end of the thirteenth century.

Any society that develops this kind of male paradigm will, inevitably, generate an opposition backed by those who view the breaking down of time-honoured boundaries between men and women as a blow to male superiority, an action which they believe actually undermines the foundations of society. It is indeed possible to distinguish a paradigm that views the success of women as something negative, and sages who vehemently oppose the implications arising from the change in the status of women and the breaking of the bounds that defined their place in society. Rabbi Ephraim of Bonn is a member of this group, as is Rabbi Asher ben Yehiel at the end of the thirteenth century.

In Jewish society of the twelfth and thirteenth centuries, there was a group that called itself 'Hasidim' (which translates as 'pious', but is not to be confused with the group of the same name that developed in eighteenth-century eastern Europe) that was characterized by religious extremism, intense mysticism, and typical oppositional aim: to create an alternative rabbinic communal leadership. The members of this group have left us a singularly impressive body of literature that relates to our topic, and presents yet another paradigm for viewing women and their role in the systems of Jewish society. These four paradigms that are presented below are the outcome of research blending questions raised within the spheres of gender research and feminist theory with the research methodology of social history.

Rashi and the 'family paradigm'

Rabbi Solomon ben Isaac, better known by his acronym 'Rashi', was born in 1041 in (Troyes, Northern France) and died in 1105.³ He appeared as if out of nowhere. He never mentions either his father or his mother. Most likely his family tree did not boast remarkable Torah scholars, teachers, or high-placed halakhic leaders. In my opinion, this attribute helped mould a unique individual, who was blessed with a rare combination of traits: modesty and extreme stubbornness; great scholarship and genius; readiness to confront teachers and illustrious individuals; and a deep spirituality. He started a family at a very young age. When he was twenty, he was already married and soon became the father of three daughters. He moved from France to Germany, and studied in Mainz and Worms for about ten years. It seems that towards the end of the sixth decade of the eleventh century, when he was thirty years old, Rashi moved to Troyes in France. Several years later, he again travelled to Germany to his teachers. At that time he realized that he could not continue these sojourns on a permanent basis, and from then on he remained in northern France where he embarked on his scholarly endeavours. Twenty-five years after leaving the *yeshivahs* of Germany, Rashi received a letter containing a question addressed to him by Rabbi Nathan ben Maqir, who lived in Germany. In his response, Rashi emphasized how unhappy he was about being far away from his teachers in Germany and revealed that when he had lived there during his younger years, his life had not been easy: he had been in want of food and clothing, and there had been a 'millstone around his neck'. The phrase that he used is taken from a talmudic discussion about whether it is best to study Torah first and then get married or to do things the other way round (Tbab. Tractate Kiddushin 29b). In the Talmud, Rabbi Johanan questions the reasoning behind the idea that a man should marry before beginning to occupy himself with Torah study by asking: '[Can a man have] a grindstone around his neck and study Torah [at the same time]?' Rashi used this verse to describe his circumstances during his student years, but incorporated it in a letter written later on in life, mainly as a way to express the longing he felt for his teachers.⁴

Rashi was a very active community leader and a *dayan* (rabbinical judge), and he has bequeathed to us an extremely wide variety of sources. He was a biblical and talmudic commentator; he wrote halakhic deliberations and rulings; answered queries sent to him; prayed devoutly and wrote *piyyutim* (liturgical poems). He relied on a very broad range of literature to support his interpretations; aside from the Talmud and his own *midrashim*, he referred to several collections of *midrashim*, which he drew on for many of his innovations, frequently using them in a new and different way, changing, adding or removing material according to his own code.[5]

Because of his stature as a communal leader, his clear and sharp analyses of the conduct of medieval Jewish society, and his strong desire to take a unequivocal stand on every issue that arose around him, whether near at hand or further afield, he was the most important sage of medieval northern France and a point of reference for all those who came after him. His massive and extremely remarkable oeuvre of study and analysis of the Jewish sources was intended to introduce tools that could be used to lead the community; therefore, his commentaries, *responsa* and insights formed the basis of almost every halakhic discussion that took place in the twelfth and thirteenth centuries.

Rashi was a perspicacious leader of the small Jewish society, tempest-tossed in the sea of Christians surrounding them. He understood the Christian world, its politics, beliefs, and the dangers it posed for the Jewish community.[6] He seems to have witnessed several Christian attacks against the Jews, and he died in 1105, that is, about ten years after the severe blow that befell the Jews of Germany and the communities where he had spent his formative years. Yet, since we have no way of knowing what he wrote before or after the tragedy of 1096, we cannot identify which of his letters were written in the aftermath of that communal trauma.

As we have said, in the Middle Ages, Jewish authors did not tend to communicate autobiographical information, and did so only very rarely and in a random way; naturally, it is difficult if not impossible to draw significant conclusions about a writer's personality from such chance biographical items. Rashi had three daughters, though we only have concrete information on two of them. The eldest was named Yocheved and the epithet of 'pious' was attached to her name in two instances. 'Yocheved the pious' married her father's most outstanding student, Rabbi Meir ben Samuel, while his second daughter, Miriam, married another well-known teacher, Rabbi Judah ben Nathan.[7] Rashi's grandsons were the ones who imparted his methods and teachings and they had a strong impact on Jewish communities until the end of the twelfth century. We know nothing whatsoever about Rashi's wife. He mentions her only once in all of his voluminous writings. A Christian came to his home on the eighth day of Passover and gave his wife cakes and eggs. She did not know what to do with the cakes, so she sent someone to call him from the synagogue so that he could instruct her on the correct course of action.[8] What is the significance of this sole reference? Did he include it to serve as an example in a response to a query, or in order to hint that she did not attend synagogue on the eighth day of Passover and did not know that on the last day of the festival *Hametz* (leaven and foods containing leaven) owned by a non-Jew should be placed in a corner?

Rashi's genius is manifested in the unique way in which he incorporates or compares different types of sources, which he consulted concurrently in order to arrive at conclusions as a *dayan*, a maker of halakhic decisions, or as a communal leader. Since Rashi's legacy is made up of a variety of genres, we can track his overall viewpoint regarding the status of women and their role through this literature: his judgments on husband/wife conflicts; his biblical commentary in which he describes female characters in the Bible in light of the extensive *midrashic* literature available to him; and his commentary on the Talmud, where he seeks to adapt the thinking of the *tannaim* and *amoraim* to his epoch and make it the foundation for decision making.[9]

As a whole, Rashi's entire *oeuvre* points to the central role of the family and particularly the key position and importance of the woman as the pillar of the Jewish family. He stresses what he considers the classic female roles: restraining the husband's dark desires, creating the family and defending the home.

The medieval sages' attitudes towards women and their nature can often be deduced from the biblical or exegetical viewpoints they express on woman's first appearance in the Bible. Attitudes towards the female – both the exceptionally positive ones and those that are so negative as to be misogynist – exist side by side in the exegetical literature that relates to the beginning of the Book of Genesis, the creation of woman, and what occurred in the Garden of Eden. Examples of this abound. From the 'positive' point of view, the verse 'It is not good that the man should be alone' (Gen. 2:18) is used to explain the passage in Proverbs 'Whoso findeth a wife findeth a great good and obtaineth favour of the Lord' (Prov. 18:22); in other words, the word 'woman' is analogous to the word 'good'. The word 'his wife' in *Gematria*[10] equals the Hebrew word for 'helpmate', but while 'male' in *Gematria* is equal to the Hebrew for blessing, 'female' in *Gematria* equals the word 'damage'.

On the one hand, woman was created from the rib so that she would be 'subject to her husband like a rib'; on the other hand, God put Adam to sleep so that he would not see that the woman was created from one of his bones and be contemptuous of her. The woman is similar to Satan; but she protects the man from Satan. Regarding the words 'He built a woman' (out of the rib; Gen. 2:22) the Hebrew word used is close to the word meaning wisdom indicating that woman has more intelligence than man, as well as the potential for prophecy. At the same time, one may find totally misogynist exegesis, which describes how God chooses 'to make' the woman so that she has good attributes, yet she turns out to have only negative traits, and so on.[11]

Since Rashi casts woman in the role of defending the husband from his bestial desires, creating the family, and supporting the man in all his endeavours, he sees the female image in a positive and favourable light. He portrays the first woman, from the moment of her creation, as being married and dwells mainly on her positive attributes. He ignores the biblical exegesis that asserts that woman was created after man and from part of his body. He describes the creation of mankind as the forming of both a male side and a female side, and interprets the Hebrew word for 'rib' from which the woman was created, in the sense of 'side'. In other words, the creation of woman is really the division of the first human creation into male and female. In his commentary, Rashi underscores the partnership and cooperation between man and woman, and her ability to curb the lustful desires of her husband; hence, the man is obligated to respect his wife, and treat her with appreciation and tenderness, and must never harm her.[12]

In a different example, Rashi explains the harsh words of the curse pronounced against womankind in Genesis 3:16, prior to the expulsion from the Garden of Eden: 'and thy desire shall be to thy husband and he shall rule over thee', in the sense that sexual relations are initiated by the man and not the woman, unlike other commentators, who use this as a justification for a husband's unfettered control over his wife. In Rashi's view, a man's true nature is fundamentally problematic since he is weak and controlled by his lusts; hence, the role of the woman as restraining her husband's bestial desires within the framework of the family is critical. Thus, relations between a man and his wife must always be at an optimum and the man is the one who is primarily responsible for establishing this situation. The 'curse' on Eve relates to the woman's desire (or instinct) to have sexual relations with her husband, although the respectable wife does not demand this of her husband but waits for his initiative. That is to say, female lust is under control, and in Rashi's opinion, within the confines of marriage, it has a crucial function: containing the uncontrolled sexual desires of the man.

The married woman's desire for sexual relations with her husband serves the purpose of procreating the Jewish people and this is a focal point of Rashi's understanding of a virtuous woman, i.e., a wife. This conceptualization emerges in his commentary on the word 'mirrors' in Exodus 38:8. The women who left Egypt had mirrors they used for adorning themselves, yet they donated them for the building of the brass laver in the tabernacle. In Rashi's opinion, Moses was unhappy about this contribution because he saw the mirrors as instruments of the evil inclination; after all, women used them to prepare themselves to be seductive. But here God himself taught Moses an important lesson and pointed out the great worth of this gift: the women used the mirrors to adorn themselves in Egypt so that their husbands, slaves worked to the bone all day, would continue to desire them and continue to have sexual relations with them thus continuing to produce offspring. Rashi maintained that this was the reason why these mirrors were used to cover the basin in the Tabernacle built by Moses in the desert, and later on in the Temple. This was also the basin from which water was drawn to examine the 'rebellious wife' for the purpose of 'returning harmony to the relations between husband and wife.'[13]

Thus Rashi created a paradigm of the Jewish family. A husband, who is ruled by his sexual desires, chooses a woman to marry and enters into a contract with her. In this way three objectives are realized: sexual restraint within the boundaries of the *halakhah*; the founding of a family and the assurance that the man will have offspring; and the dedicated 'work' of the woman for the household, the family, and the husband. In order for this 'system' to function properly, the man must honour his wife 'more than his own physical being', 'love' her, and meet all her needs. The woman's function is to do her utmost to help her husband. Rashi borrows from the *midrash* the interpretation of the words uttered by God (in Genesis) while He was creating the woman: 'I will make him a helpmate' (2:18). He uses the *midrash* to interpret the strange combination of Hebrew words for 'helpmate'. The words in Hebrew are literally 'a help opposite him' which means, Rashi says, that if the man is lucky she will be a help, and if not, she will oppose him. Rashi asserts that by blaming Eve for the sin he committed – that of failing to obey the single command given to him by God, Adam, the first man, commits another sin. When he makes his wife responsible for his sin and says, 'The woman whom thou gavest to be with me,' Adam is showing ingratitude for the favour God did for him, the 'favour' of giving him the woman as a 'helper'. Rashi emphasizes the help the woman gives her husband by citing a verse from the Book of Job – 'Is not my help in me? And is wisdom driven quite from me?' (6:13) – to prove that help is connected to wisdom. He explains that when a woman does not help her husband with his immediate needs, his wisdom dissipates; he is forced to deal with the needs of his household and is unable to find the time for Torah study.[14] Rashi's other writings, especially the collection of his *responsa*, indicate that he was aware of the economic role filled by women in their homes. They ran businesses; travelled about for business purposes; and were a force to be reckoned within the economic arena, quite on a par with the men. They appeared before rabbinical courts; conducted transactions with the Christian authorities, obtained better terms than the men, etc.[15]

From Rashi's standpoint, setting up a family and having children is the most important thing in life. In his commentary on the word 'childless' in Genesis 15:2, he makes this very clear. Abraham, the great believer, is without children and fears that his material success has been his reward for belief in God. After his military victory in the War against the Kings and God's promise 'Your reward is very great' (Gen. 14), Abraham complains that he has no one to whom he can bequeath this 'reward': 'Lord God, what wilt thou give me, seeing I go childless and he that shall be possessor of my house is Eliezer of Damascus?' (Gen. 15:2). The word, which is usually translated as 'childless', also means 'forsaken', 'alone', 'solitary'. When giving his interpretation of this word, Rashi indeed describes Abraham as a man with no heir. But, quoting a similar very word meaning 'destruction' from various books of the Bible (Ps. 137:7, Hab. 3:13, Jer. 51:58 and Zeph. 2:14), Rashi maintains that a man without children is in a constant state of destruction, and (taking another similar word to 'childless', meaning 'awake' from Song. 5:2), claims that a childless man is akin to a man who has never been awakened. When called upon to explain the concept of *karet* (divine punishment by untimely death) he describes it specifically as 'walking alone (without children) and dying before one's time'. Rashi sees life without children as something tantamount to the experience of annihilation, something worse than death.[16] He contends that Sarah gives her maidservant, Hagar, to Abraham, her husband, when she finds out that she is barren because in this indirect way – by means of her husband and her servant – she will have children. He draws attention to Sarah's words: 'it may be that I may obtain children by her' (Gen. 16:2) (translated literally the Hebrew says 'that I may be built up by her') and Rashi explains that 'anyone who does not have children is not built up, but destroyed'.[17] In the end, a son was born to Abraham, and when his life was coming to a close, the biblical text says 'and the Lord had blessed Abraham in all things' (Gen. 24:1). Rashi points out that in *Gematria*, the Hebrew word meaning 'in all things' equals the Hebrew for 'son', giving us to understand that only a man who has children is fully blessed. Rashi repeats many times the words of Rachel, who is barren, to Jacob 'give me children or else I die' (Gen. 30:1), teaching us that anyone who does not have children is thought of as dead. When Rachel finally gives birth to Joseph, she says: 'God hath taken away my reproach' (Gen. 30:23), and Rashi explains that this means: I was a disgrace because of my childless state.[18]

Rashi's views might have remained theoretical exegetical concepts, but they manifested themselves in the halakhic decisions he made as a *dayan*. He believed that women had tremendous strength and, consequently, had a critical role to play in creating the home, dealing with the actions of their husbands, and bringing children into the world. Every time Rashi, serving as *dayan*, was called upon to adjudicate in the matter of a husband who acted cruelly towards his wife, causing her harm, he decided in favour of the woman. The most outstanding example of this is a response he wrote to a query he received from a woman who asked for his help. Her husband had divorced her and was attempting to prevent her from receiving what was her due under her *ketubah*.[19] The man alleged that signs of leprosy had been discerned on his wife's nose and face, along with another skin disease. He went on to say that his wife and her family had concealed these defects from him before he married her even though they had been present and despite the fact that it was well known that her family suffered from these types of diseases.[20] In his capacity as a *dayan* Rashi heard witnesses who testified that these signs had not existed when the woman married, as well as her representative, who recounted that the signs appeared on her face only later when she had started living with him. On the basis of this testimony, Rashi invalidated the claim of defects made by the husband and forced him to give her the entire worth of her *ketubah*, since he had not treated her with respect when she was his wife.

It is worth while taking a close look at what Rashi says on this point. He condemned the actions of the husband, viewing them as vile. To his way of thinking, a covenant between man and wife forms the basis of the marital relationship and he looks upon the unilateral breach of this covenant by the husband as a serious criminal act. In his *responsa*, he compared the actions of a man worthy of being considered a Jew 'of the seed of our forefather Abraham', with those of someone who does not deserve to be considered a Jew in respect to their relationship with their wives. But, Rashi argues, even non-Jews do not commit such acts against their wives. Affection between a man and wife are the key to a normal family life. ('[The Lord] has given the heart for closeness [affection] and for detachment [coldness].') A husband must invest time and energy to endear himself to his wife, an outcome that can only be achieved if he is intimate with her in the psychological, emotional sense. It is closeness between the spouses which creates endearment, and according to Rashi's way of thinking, such intimacy always produces a satisfying connection between them, and it is the husband's responsibility to make sure this happens. He also noted that when a husband treats his wife well it will stand him in good stead when he seeks to enter the Gates of Heaven.[21]

This thinking forms the basis for Rashi's attitudes that support the woman within the familial structure. He incorporates them time and again in his biblical exegesis and his decisions as a *dayan*. For example, he interprets the words of Lamech to his wives Adah and Zillah (Gen. 4:23) as an attempt to persuade them to renew marital relations with him.[22] Rashi takes the basic story from the *midrash*; however, the idea that the women were free to leave their husband who had committed murder and refrain from having sexual relations with him was an addition he made.[23]

To Rashi, marital relations, affection and love between man and wife were of primary importance. He writes about mutual love and desire between man and wife in the introduction to his commentary on the Song of Songs. Rashi saw this book as a metaphorical expression of the longing for repentance and a return to the divine spirit in the era of Exile – foreseeing that the Jewish People would be scattered throughout the Diaspora following the destruction of the Temples – and a deep, heartfelt desire to repent. He believed that this was why King Solomon chose to write the Song of Songs in a language that alludes to a woman separated from her husband, her lover, and a man who remembers his past loves but is still tied to his wife with bonds of love. In Rashi's opinion, the use of metaphoric language that portrays a man and woman separated from each another, allows the nation to understand this text and repent. Without becoming involved in theological or mystical issues, it is clear that Rashi's thinking relied on his vision of the ideal relationship between spouses, motivated by 'strong love', mutual desire and affection, and the ongoing wish to forgive and return to a shared life.[24]

This strong connection and the ideal of the marital relationship can also be seen in his interpretation of the section from Genesis that describes how Abraham takes a woman named Keturah after the death of Sarah. Rashi explains that when Sarah died, Isaac brought Hagar back to his father Abraham. From the time of her expulsion, Hagar, whose name is now Keturah, had not agreed to tie herself to any other man, and her new name was given to her because her deeds were as pleasant as incense (*keturet* in Hebrew).[25] Citing the *Midrash*, he seeks to complement the character of Abraham, who was commanded by God to obey his wife Sarah and send Hagar away. Now, after Sarah's death, he attempted to correct the situation by marrying Hagar, who had remained faithful to him over all the years. Hagar is portrayed here as a loyal and devoted woman.[26]

Rashi sees the woman as 'the source of life', 'the mother of all humanity' who bears children and ensures the continuity of the species. In his exegesis on the story of the Garden of Eden, he ignores, as I have already noted, the misogynist material available to him and purposely chooses to describe the terrible loneliness of the first man, acknowledging that he was a species unto himself, incompatible with the other species, and the only one without a mate. When God understood his plight, He created a mate for him. Rashi also sees the sin of Eve in a different light. She was lured by the words of the serpent and disobeyed the one and only command she had received from God due to the words of the serpent who told her that if they eat of the fruit of the tree, their eyes will be opened, they will be like God, the creator of worlds, and will know good and evil. The serpent had appealed to her feminine ability to create worlds, since, in the end, the most important role of woman is the continuing of the species. This is also Rashi's approach in explaining her name, Eve – Havva in Hebrew, which is derived from the word for life – and she is the giver of life. Thus he ignores and stifles the tendency to interpret her name as originating from the root *hivai*, meaning a serpent in Aramaic, the approach that saw the female figure, all females, in league with the inveigling serpent to break the commitment to God.[27]

On the other hand, it is also obvious that Rashi regards the woman who deviates from her position as the pillar of the household as a serious threat. His predisposition to defend women against male authoritarianism, along with his tendency towards 'natural' justice, does not prevent him from seeing backsliding women as extremely dangerous. Rashi views with disfavour a married woman who departs from her role, harms her husband in any way, commits adultery or creates problems in the family, and he casts her in a negative light. This disapproval is most conspicuous when he conveys precise messages to Jewish society by means of his interpretations of various talmudic narratives.[28] In some of the stories, the woman is depicted in a particularly negative light, and Rashi's explanation of this portrayal is even more clear-cut. He recounted, for example, the story of a woman who attempted to lure a man, who was escorting her, into having sexual relations, and explained that she had claimed that her baby was dead (even though it was alive) so that he would go with her to bury it, so she would have the opportunity to have relations with him. Rashi told this story so as to describe women, who deviate from the status he holds that they should have in the framework of the family, and he presents this 'bad' woman in a very explicit manner. This is also the sense in which we should understand a story he quotes from the Talmud. He cites Rabbi Meir, who put his wife Bruria to the test. Rabbi Meir convinces one of his students to seduce her and in the end she succumbs; afterwards she commits suicide, strangling herself because of what she has done. The purpose of the story, as Rashi tells it, is to show that conducting such 'tests' within the family constellation is dangerous. It is a trap that any man, even as high-ranking a sage as Rabbi Meir, could fall into; and putting a woman to the test, even a highly respected woman such as Bruria, posed a great danger.[29]

The female image that Rashi saw in his mind's eye was not a theoretical one. All the memorials written for women, which have been preserved, display expressions of affection, admiration, and praise that diverge from the normal pattern of writing. However, modern scholars might well regard the demands Rashi made on married women as a typical example of male control, or of 'gender as a social construct'. Apart from Rashi, there were others who can be included in this 'family paradigm'. Rabbi Eleazar of Worms, whose wife and daughters were killed before his eyes by Crusaders in 1196, commemorated his murdered wife in a liturgical poem in which he describes her with impassioned words of love and devotion, listing her attributes as a perfect wife who did all the household work, managed the school which he headed, and knew how to perform the Commandments. Even if the poem is an understandable over-idealization of his murdered wife and daughters, this does not diminish the realistic portrayal of daily life that it reflects.[30]

Yet, the images that emerge from the memorials and the poem of Rabbi Eleazar are not those of women who are controlled by men. These were women who had a strong position within the family and among the women of the community; they were involved in work that was generally considered the purview of men, and became leaders during times of crisis.

The negative male paradigm

Every improvement in the status of women in society gave rise to opposition from a male group. This opposition was not instinctive in its nature and it was not always rooted in blind misogyny. From a societal perspective, the male group felt that their ability to control and supervise was being undermined and their intellectual superiority cast in doubt. Starting from the second half of the twelfth century, these feelings became increasingly intense among some of the men and among the male sages as well. I will limit myself here to two illustrative examples of this behavioural paradigm.

The first is Rabbi Ephraim of Bonn, a *dayan* and a *paytan* (liturgical poet) of the second half of the twelfth century, known in particular for the history book which he wrote, *Sefer Zekhirah* (The Book of Remembrance) in which he described the terrible events that befell the Jews of

France and Germany during the twelfth century.[31] Even though he refers to women who died as martyrs, he minimizes these references significantly and his descriptions make no mention whatsoever of the major role given to women who died as martyrs during the First Crusade.[32] In an important article, Susan Einbinder attempted to extrapolate from the writings of Rabbi Ephraim of Bonn something about the change and decline in the status of women during the course of the twelfth century. In his book *Pious and Rebellious* Grossman correctly claims, conclusions cannot be drawn on the basis of one source alone.[33] Yet neither of these scholars correctly positioned Rabbi Ephraim of Bonn or the essence of what he wrote about women. As an important liturgical poet, he wrote the poem 'How doth she [the city, Jerusalem] sit solitary' for the Ninth of Av fast, where he surveyed all the tragedies that had befallen the Jewish people, including the martyrdom during the First Crusade, but he did not mention women at all.[34] What we have here is not a change in the status of women, but rather a man who thinks that the status of women had reached too high a level and that it should be limited. Indeed, he strictly limits his mention of them in his chronicle, and ignores them entirely in the abovementioned poem.

This tendency to ignore women or criticize their prominence is also demonstrated in his well known text about the 1171 blood libel of Blois (France), where he interweaves the character of the Jewish heroine Pucellina. On 26 May 1171, more than thirty Jews were burned to death in Blois, the capital of the Loire valley (the sources mention thirty, thirty-one, and thirty-two). A servant of one of the local Christian nobles saw a Jew watering his horse in the river and thought that he saw the Jew throw the body of a small child into the river. The town nobles accused all the Jews of the 'murder' and, even though there was no body, a trial by ordeal was conducted, which 'proved' that the witness had told the truth. The Count of Blois, Theobald, decided to burn all the Jews of the town at the stake, except for the children and those who agreed to convert to Christianity. Since no one agreed to convert, all of them died a martyr's death. The event had an extremely traumatic effect on medieval Jewry since the municipal authorities and the nobility, which had previously protected them, destroyed an entire community on the pyre.[35]

We have several sources for this story. It appears in a Christian chronicler's account of accusations levelled against Jews for murdering Christian boys on Passover. It is found in the correspondence of various Jews who investigated the event immediately after it started; they reported it to Rabbenu Tam, who evidently headed a group that had formed to attempt to save the Jews of Blois from death. The story is repeated in the letters sent to various towns in an effort to memorialize – by means of fasting and prayer on the day of their death, 20 Sivan – the community that had been wiped out, and its martyrs. Accounts of the story are also found in numerous liturgical poems written to commemorate the mass burning and afterwards in liturgical poems recited on the anniversary of the event. Rabbi Ephraim's version, however, contains a vivid and interesting description of the events, which goes beyond what is depicted in the other texts.[36]

This account (the last event described in the book) was written in 1197 on the basis of the letters sent from France to the Jews of Germany. Here Rabbi Ephraim presents the character of a woman, Pucellina, as an important protagonist of the story and in an indirect manner accuses her of bringing about or causing the terrible calamity. One of the letters, which were disseminated to explain the events, gives an account of the relations between Theobald, the Count of Blois and the Jewess Pucellina and describes the connection between them as an economic one (apparently an interest-bearing loan). The missive presents a picture of an intractable businesswoman who manages her affairs with stubborn determination; the Count supports her in all her activities, even the business transactions she conducts in an obstinate and firm manner with his wife and her wet nurse. The nobility of Blois took advantage of this incident to hurt her, and perhaps to divest themselves of debts they owed her as well. The Jewish texts state explicitly that those who arrested her did not tie her up as they did the other Jews; but they prevented her from gaining access to Theobald. Rabbi Ephraim of Bonn notes that when the Christian servant related the original story, he was aware of his master's quarrel with the Jewish woman known as Pucellina. Rabbi Ephraim tells us that when the Jews were arrested by Count Theobald, Madame Pucellina gave them all encouragement saying that 'she was certain of the love of the authorities who had shown her much love until now'. Yet, she did not know that the Count's wife had incited him against her, telling him not to listen to Pucellina because she loathed this Jewish woman, who was on close terms with her husband. Rabbi Ephraim also indicates that at the beginning the Jews trusted her because she was not tied up as they were. The tone of Rabbi Ephraim's words indicates that a Jewish woman, who was strong, wealthy, well connected with the Christian authorities, and aware of her power and abilities posed a danger to the community, and in the case of the Jewish community of Blois, a mortal danger. The local nobility transferred their hatred of her to all the Jews of the town. The Count, who had previously supported her, was forced to heed his wife.[37] In effect, Ephraim of Bonn, who called Pucellina *'gevartanit'* (a masculine-like, tough female), accused this woman and her arrogant, strong-willed personality of destroying the community. In the Bible, '*gevartanit*' is used to describe a very strong blow and is derived directly from the Hebrew word for a man. In exegetical tradition, the word is used to refer to women who fill male roles and are as strong as men.[38]

The letters reveal that some thirty members of the community, which numbered forty individuals, were put to death. The Christians took the small children (only the boys, it seems) in order to raise them as Christians. This correspondence also indicates that the Jews conducted vigorous lobbying activities in the court of King Louis VII; paid bribes to free the children; and attempted to prevent similar instances from occurring in the future. The memorial books have two lists that identify the martyred Jews of Blois, one with thirty-one names, the other with thirty-three. The first list includes twenty women and eleven men, and the second, nineteen women and twelve men. The family units are not clearly defined, but two families appear to be listed as such; the other men and women do not seem to be connected to one another. In both lists there are four women with children, but whose husbands are not identified – these are: Madame Pucellina and her two daughters, Madame Leah and two daughters, Madame Malka and her daughter, Madame Sara, Madame Hanna and the child she bore. In effect, the lists reveal that the martyrs of Blois were primarily women; most of those who chose death were women; among the children most of those put to death were girls. The lists include one boy (who had just been born) and five girls. The Christians may have actually taken only the boys to be raised as Christian and sent the girls to the flames.

The fact that so many women were involved in this act of martyrdom is entirely ignored in other sources, and in particular merits no mention by Rabbi Ephraim of Bonn. What remained was the image of Pucellina, who undermined the situation, and that of three men, the *Kohanim* who were not consumed by the flames. The only Jew who managed to survive the mass execution and testified to what happened was Rabbi Barukh ben David HaCohen, the brother of one of the murdered *Kohanim* (Rabbi Yehiel). Rabbi Yehiel Ha-Kohen and Rabbi Yekutiel the son of Rabbi Judah, relates that they were not consumed by the fire, and that they and another person walked out of the pyre while singing a prayer. The Christians had to kill them and then throw their bodies back into the flames, where their bodies were eventually consumed. Of the seven liturgical poems available to us that describe this event, only one dedicates a stanza to a description of the women who hastened to go to the pyre; it identifies seventeen women (out of thirty-one martyrs) and relates how they entered the Gates of Heaven going directly to 'the Hall of the King'. The only prose account that highlights the glory of the female martyrs is that of Rabbi Ovadiayhu the son of Rabbi Makir, who disseminated the testimony of the Blois community itself.[39]

Why did Ephraim ben Jacob of Bonn decide to minimize the martyrological value of the women? Why did he vilify Pucellina and blame her for failing to save herself and her fellow Jews? There are no clear-cut answers to these questions. There exists the possibility that his negative attitude to women might have been coloured by the quarrel that he and his brother had with their brother's widow. This brother had died without leaving a male heir and they wanted to gain control of his property and prevent his widow from taking possession of it. As mentioned in Chapter 5, they used the matter of *yibum* (levirate marriage) as a legal ploy. This would have enabled the widow to marry anyone of her choice, but allow them to get their hands on their brother's property, which in reality, was his widow's assets.

The second example of a male sage who sees the improvement of the woman's lot as a danger is Rabbi Asher ben Yehiel (Rosh), who is often referred to in studies dealing with a variety of different issues from this period. His line of thinking about the place of women is seen in the *responsa*, where he stresses that the reforms made for the benefit of the woman created a situation in which 'the power of the woman is greater than that of the man', an outcome, which was not the intention of those who created the rulings (an explicit reference to Rabbenu Gershom Me'or HaGolah).[40] Furthermore, he uses the same type of argument when denying the request of women who seek to free themselves from husbands who are mentally ill or have skin diseases. The *Mishnah* established clear definitions for freeing women from the bonds of marriage, he reasoned, and we cannot add or expand on these cases, not in the matter of insanity or of newly-acquired skin diseases. This was also his view with respect to a woman who claimed that her husband 'was repulsive to her'.[41]

Rabbi Asher ben Yehiel's correspondence indicates that this was his basic approach, which, he felt, was manifested in various areas of *halakhah*. In his objection to the immediate release of a 'rebellious wife', he reasoned that in earlier periods women were more modest and their claims genuine; therefore, the *Geonim* hastened to acquiesce to their demands to free them from their husbands. 'In our times', he asserted, 'the women of Israel are immodest and boastful'. This is his basic assumption, that he often attributes, gratuitously, to his teacher, Meir ben Barukh of Rothenburg (Maharam).[42] Rabbi Asher ben Yehiel opposes forcing the husband to give a *gett*[43] on the grounds that the women of his day were brazen; and, he also opposes the marriage of a woman who has buried two husbands, whom he calls a 'killer wife'. As Grossman demonstrates, in this case, Rabbi Asher ben Yehiel expands the 'prohibition' which he himself formulated, beyond what may be inferred from the Talmud, especially in creating a categorical distinction between a wife whose husbands have died and a husband whose wives have died.[44] Even when he granted women's requests, he went out of his way to point out that this did not give them a higher status that of a man. He permits women to pray in a language that is not the holy tongue (Hebrew), but not in the case of public prayer. In other words, the main prayer service, which is normally conducted in public, is in reality the purview of men, and women are dependent on them.[45]

Rabbi Asher ben Yehiel's reservations about the growing power of women were expressed indirectly, 'between the lines' of his texts. He was a forceful halakhic leader known for his widespread influence, and it was generally acknowledged that many others learned from his writings, *responsa*, and decisions. Until the end of the fourteenth century, these restrictive male attitudes were not adopted by the majority of halakhic leaders. I believe (although limitations of space prevent me from expanding on this here) that the Jewish migration to the East, the many changes the Jews experienced, and the ongoing exposure to the halakhic rulings made by the sages of Spain would bring about a shift in the status of women, and that beginning with the sixteenth century, the women of Ashkenaz would lose some of the achievements they had gained in the previous era. The lessening of the tension between Jewish communities and the external Christian society in the regions of Eastern Europe, the loss of internal communal solidarity, and the social restratification of Jewish society, and most importantly, the shift from home-based study to same-sex educational institutions, the *Heder*, led to a deceleration in the improvement in the status of women, in comparison to the pace and quality of the previous era. With all this the Ashkenazic female subgroup nevertheless still continued to show some progress in improving status vis-à-vis the male subgroup.

The Hasidic paradigm

'*Hasidei Ashkenaz*' is the label used to designate the group of people, active in Germany from the end of the twelfth and throughout the thirteenth century, who left their unique mark on medieval Jewish literature in their most important book, *Sefer Hasidim*, and other, unusual sources, which are available to us. *Sefer Hasidim* is written as a series of passages, most of them stories containing moral lessons (exempla), along with sections of philosophy, ethics, and *midrash*. This book (or at least the greater part of it) was written by Rabbi Samuel the Hasid and his son Rabbi Judah the Hasid, with the explicit aim of propagandizing their ideas among the Jewish communities of Germany.[46] Since the middle of the nineteenth century, scholars have discussed the book and these Hasidic leaders, yet much controversy still remains regarding many aspects of this subject. However, no one disputes the fact that the Hassidim of Ashkenaz were not a sub-group (or sect) within the Jewish community, but rather a distinctive oppositional group that challenged the Jewish halakhic leaders and some of their values. They were influenced by the ideas of the surrounding culture, which they processed and eventually turned into Jewish ideas.

We have information on three key figures in this group, who left a lasting impression: Rabbi Samuel the Hasid and Rabbi Judah the Hasid, who wrote *Sefer Hasidim*, and Rabbi Eleazar of Worms, who accepted some of the concepts advocated by the aforementioned writers, incorporating them into the system of early thirteenth century German rulings and *halakhot*. Their writings contain unusual and fascinating mystical views, which have left a mark on opinions found in other works written by this group. The extent of the impact made by *Hasidei Ashkenaz* and their written works is a matter of dispute; scholars are still engaged in an ongoing debate on both the degree to which their accounts reflect what actually took place in the community, and whether their works are utopian in nature or a form of biting criticism that does not really mirror the realities of the medieval communities in the thirteenth century.[47] For our purposes it is important to note that, given the oppositional and critical viewpoint of these *hasidic* writers towards the Jewish society in which they lived, many aspects of Jewish social life are reflected in a way, which cannot be observed in the various other sources available to us. Moreover, an idealized portrayal of reality provides important insights for the researcher, which, when taken together with comparisons from other sources, illuminate areas which would have otherwise remained completely obscure.

Overcoming sinful desires was one of the important tasks facing a person who aspired – by means of constant improvement – to become a *Hasid*. Desires or drives are enormously powerful; they are the internal voice that persuade a person to commit a sin. The *Hasid*'s way of life is one of overcoming the sinful inclination and striving to prevail over these drives.[48] If he fails and succumbs to his drives, he must search for a road that will lead him to repentance and atonement. Through repentance he will understand his actions and confess them; through atonement he returns to the situation in which the sin was committed, but this time he prevails over the dictates of his drive. This is the way of the *Hasid*. (*Sefer Hasidim* discusses many forms of temptation; but, for our purposes, the focus here relates to the temptation aroused by women.)

Sefer Hasidim takes an excruciatingly ambivalent and complex stand regarding women. It discusses the obligations of an ideal family life alongside sexual and erotic tension, while accepting the notion that adultery may occur at any given moment. Some scholars see *Sefer Hasidim* as an unambiguously anti-female work.[49] In my opinion, this is not the case. People who advocate extremely moral behaviour, preach modesty, and warn against any type of temptation present numerous examples in which women play a major role. Erotic attraction and the consequent sexual implications appear to be the worst sort of temptation, while the male is perceived as extremely weak, a creature incapable of withstanding this sort of temptation. In this sense, the female plays a key role, since she is capable of arousing the evil inclination in a man, in any man, something which he cannot withstand. From this standpoint, the power of the woman, by her very essence, is a central motivating force for sin in the world of a *Hasid*.

The Hasidic sources do not preach celibacy, since one of the ways a *Hasid* puts *Hasidic* ideology into practice is by establishing a family and fathering children who will follow the *Hasidic* path. A man's powerlessness in the face of temptations emanating from a woman, reaches new dimensions in the writings of *Hasidei Ashkenaz*. According to their way of thinking, the victory of sexual lust is taken for granted. They define this desire as the sexual arousal of the man and as 'the power of the love for women'. Love, too, which is perceived as an uncontrollable desire on the part of a male for a female, is discussed a great deal. Without any intention on her part, a female, by her very presence, arouses sexual desire in the male; this might be problematic in view of the fact that *Sefer Hasidim* lays great emphasis on the fact that a man is obligated to spend a significant amount of time with his wife and make her happy.[50]

Sefer Hasidim highlights three major biblical characters, who were unable to resist the emotions of love that took control of them, and the subsequent catastrophes that befell them: Samson, a symbol of heroism; David, characterized as the epitome of a *Hasid*; and Solomon, the wisest of men. These three men made mistakes with regard to women, despite the fact that they were without doubt extraordinary individuals: heroes, *Hasidim*, and wise men. The author of *Sefer Hasidim* concludes this discussion by noting that a man who is in love with a woman is likely to have adulterous relations with her; and, since sexual desire is such a strong force, he has to be very careful indeed. The structure of the male personality is such that he is unable to control his desires; therefore, the recommendation of *Hasidei Ashkenaz* is that he must build a system of impediments to distance himself from the object of his desire (for example, by avoiding marriage with someone who is not the object of his lust). Even the magical powers possessed by some of the heroes of *Sefer Hasidim* are of no avail, because the lust of a man towards a forbidden woman cannot be halted by invoking magic, and because were he to invoke magic this could also diminish his desire for his wife, towards whom he is duty-bound.[51]

The Jewish male cannot practice total abstinence from women, since one of commandments he has to fulfil is the establishment of a family – a committed (*Hasidic*) home that is part of the Jewish nation; therefore, he must cope with his lust. Hence, the relations between an unmarried man and his future wife receive a great deal of attention. The basic assumption of the *Hasidim* is that an alliance to which one of the parties does not agree should not be encouraged; the woman must agree to be married, and accept her partner without reservation. The matchmaker is enjoined to pay more attention to the requirements voiced by the young woman than to those of her parents.[52] After the marriage, the close relationship between husband and wife are emphasized; for example, the husband is admonished not to keep his activities secret from his wife and told to share his experiences with her, even if he sees a miracle. They also describe a man taking a bath with his wife.[53] The notion that the woman should not be angry during sexual relations is stressed and gives rise to a long list of suggestions to help the husband control his behaviour towards his wife. He must make sure that she has not been crossed nor made to feel coerced into having sexual intercourse. The husband should not justify his parents' criticisms of his wife lest this casts a shadow over her mood. Furthermore, a great deal of emphasis is placed on mutual feelings of love between the man and woman, and the concept of love is discussed at length. The power of love is defined as the force that binds a man and a woman; it is what influences a man to choose a certain woman, the one he desires and for whom he feels passion.[54]

Out of fear of improper behaviour by dissatisfied young women, *Hasidei Ashkenaz* come out strongly against their marrying older men without their full consent. The author of *Sefer Hasidim* calls this a type of prostitution of the young woman by her father and vigorously condemns this practice. In his commentary, he even equates a situation in which a father forces his daughter to marry an old man with the passage 'Do not prostitute thy daughter to cause her to be a whore' (Lev. 19:29). It is clear that he sees the unsatisfied desires of a woman as a potential danger, which may lead to improper conduct on her part. While she is not required to restrain her desires, the text warns against creating a situation in which a woman's unsatisfied desire may lead to adultery.[55]

The writing of *Hasidei Ashkenaz* with respect to women is also characterized by their outspoken desire to understand the nature of womankind. The starting point of their discussion is that women, just like men, are liable for sins originating from sexual desires ('Like the men are warned, so are the women'). According to them, women have sex drives that operate in similar ways to those of men. In other words, a woman has passions; she can fall so completely in love that she loses her common sense just like a man. This, then, is the basis of their approach, which advocates complete separation between the sexes, preferably starting at an early age.[56] *Hasidei Ashkenaz* did not think that women were consciously attempting to cause men to sin. They saw the power of a woman as her ability to control the thoughts and actions of a man, even when not actually in his presence, and all the more so when close by him. Hence, when in her company, he must gather all his strength to withstand the temptation and avoid thoughts of transgression and sinful behaviour.[57] *Hasidei Ashkenaz* described such extreme behaviour in a tale. Three people were discussing the piety of their fathers who tested themselves and proved their ability to overcome their desires. One son recounted that his father, who lived in extreme poverty, knew where his neighbours kept their money; he went to the spot every night but did not steal the money. The second parent did not react when humiliated by other people. The third father was deeply in love with a married woman, who loved him in return; he deliberately went to stay in her house when her husband was away, kissed and embraced her, but forced himself to refrain from having sexual relations with her.[58]

Women are viewed as being obligated to perform the Commandments (*mitzvot*) and to be responsible for their behaviour; therefore, *Sefer Hasidim* asserts that girls must be taught everything connected with performing the Commandments (the commandments relating to Sabbath and prayers are cited as examples), together with matters relating to married life and family purity so that they will not behave improperly. Although the *Hasidim* stressed the distinction between the level of knowledge required of girls and that required of boys, because basic education was provided at home, it is evident, that girls had the opportunity to be part of the educational process, whether directly or indirectly.[59]

The medieval perception that woman were responsible for transmitting physical traits is clearly articulated in *Sefer Hasidim*, whose propaganda is obviously aimed at creating a society of *Hasidim* that will be better than the existing, 'bad' Jewish society in which they live. This goal was never fulfilled: we have no information about subgroups of *Hasidim* living in the Jewish communities and even the *Hasidic* writings themselves make it clear that this was an utopian ideal. Nonetheless, much can be learned from their writings despite their tendency to propagandize. In order to create a proper and moral *Hasidic* family, a man must marry a woman who shares his values. This is half of the problem; the other half is his offspring. How can he make sure that they will be good children and that they grow up to be good young people? The proper educational approach is not the only decisive factor; consideration must also be given to 'genetic' makeup. A *Hasid* must establish a family; hence, like every other Jewish male, he needs to have normal sexual relations with his wife, even if he knows that he may have 'bad' children. King Hezekiah knew that the son he would sire would definitely turn out to be evil. Nevertheless, when he did not perform the commandment of procreation he was punished and became seriously ill. The prophet did not accept the justification King Hezekiah gave for his actions and admonished him: 'what business do you have interfering in the mysteries of the Holy One Blessed be He?' In order to circumvent this problem, the *Hasid* is advised to marry a woman who comes from a 'good home', i.e., a family known as a good *Hasidic* family. Most importantly, her brothers must be scrutinized, since any children she bears will be similar to them. This approach, which *Hasidei Ashkenaz* took from the Talmud and the medieval commentaries, justified marriage to one's niece (the daughter of one's sister).[60] Since the woman carries the genetic traits of her children, she guarantees, if her brothers are 'good', that her children will also have 'good' qualities. Hence, it seems that many men insisted on marrying their nieces, thus ensuring that their children would be similar to them. *Hasidei Ashkenaz* paid a great deal of attention to this matter, because it allowed them to guarantee, even before marriage, the establishment of a proper *Hasidic* family. Not only would the woman be suitable for the *Hasid*, but also the offspring.[61]

Some scholars see these concepts of *Hasidei Ashkenaz* as support for their argument about this group, i.e., that they tended to exclude women from public space. In reality, the texts they wrote demonstrate that the woman was definitely present in every aspect of a man's life in his home, as well as in the public sphere; indeed, there was no way to exclude women from the public arena. The fear – the power of temptation, the danger for the male – conveyed by the authors of these ideological texts points to their major position of women at the core of family and communal life, and their abilities in the public sphere. In the sections of *Sefer Hasidim* that describe how a man progresses along the *Hasidic* path, coping with the female presence, and the constant danger on account of the strong sexual desire is always aroused. A man must train himself to achieve a state whereby he does not see the faces of women even when he is attending a wedding feast and beautifully dressed women are present; when he meets a woman on the street (whether married or unmarried, Jewish or Gentile); or when he encounters women washing clothes and the hems of their dresses are raised, revealing their legs. In all these situations, he must simply close his eyes and act as if he sees nothing. The stance taken by *Sefer Hasidim* is that the man is a slave to his desires. Yet the book offers a unique, optimistic axiom; it assumes that a man, any man, who chooses the path of the *Hasidim* will be able to cope with his desires, which tempt him to be intimate with women and to engage in illicit sexual relations.[62]

The community paradigm

In many of the sources the attitude towards women stems from the male sages' conviction that the interests of the community must be given the highest priority. They adopted this approach because their primary concern was finding ways to solve problems within the Jewish community so that it would be able to withstand various crises. For example, a ruling was made, which limited to eighteen months the period of time a man was permitted to be absent from his home. This ruling, which is clearly supportive of women, is based on the communal concern that any harm that befalls a woman also harms the community. It was a mechanism instituted to circumvent the problems that arose because men would often go to distant lands to earn a livelihood and remain away from home for long periods of time. This ruling forced the husband to limit his absence from home to no more than one and a half years; moreover, he had to prove, prior to his departure, that there were no quarrels between him and his wife; that she agreed to his trip; and that he was leaving behind sufficient funds and assets to pay his debts and ensure the maintenance of his wife and children for the duration of his absence. Furthermore, the sages asserted that this amount had to include enough money to pay for teachers so that his children would be able to study. In addition, this ruling established that after his return, the husband could not set out again immediately on another long journey; instead, he had to remain at home with his wife for at least six months.[63]

In the first half of the twelfth century, Rabbi Eliezer ben Nathan (Raban) of Mainz, recognizing the intense trauma Jewish society was experiencing in the aftermath of the attacks on Jewish communities at the outset of the First Crusade, enlisted all the forces available in an emergency effort to strengthen the community. This effort was designed to prevent a theological or religious breakdown and to enable the community to continue to cope with the Christian world around them. Similar steps were also taken by his younger contemporary in northern France, Rabbenu Tam. During the later decades of the twelfth century and throughout the thirteenth century others in both regions also made the good of the group their chief priority, their major representative being Rabbi Meir ben Barukh of Rothenburg (Maharam). This sort of 'emergency action' gave a significant boost to the status of marginal groups within the community; in general, the reaction among the sages was indeed to defend women and their rights in the broadest possible sense.

Rabbi Eliezer ben Nathan was born in Mainz at the beginning of the last decade of the eleventh century, and was merely a boy when disaster overwhelmed his community during the First Crusade, in 1096. He grew up to become a halakhic leader and a representative of the first post-Crusade generation.[64] The Mainz community was rebuilt very quickly, yet anyone familiar with the writing of Rabbi Eliezer can recognize how much the disaster of 1096 affected him. He expressed the trauma of these events in the descriptions he wrote as an adult, in his chronicle, in liturgical poetry and in his commentaries on the poems of others. Scholars studying the Middle Ages disagree about the effect of the disaster that befell the Jews at the end of the eleventh century. For Rabbi Eliezer ben Nathan, there is no question. It is obvious from his religious poetry and the feelings he expressed that reflect his desire to commemorate the Jewish behaviour of giving up their lives and sanctifying the Name of God as martyrs in the face of the attempt made to coerce them to convert to Christianity.[65]

It is difficult to establish the identity of Rabbi Eliezer ben Nathan's teachers or the places where he studied; however, we do know that in his adult years he was a teacher and *dayan*, and answered many queries that were sent to him from Germany and northern France. The image that emerges from his writings is that of a leader who is clearly aware of himself, of his personality and his role. He stood at a critical crossroads of crisis and renewal. His halakhic rulings show that he was, on the one hand, a passionate defender of 'the customs of our forefathers', and on the other, he did not hesitate to innovate and publish his innovations in explicit language. In my opinion, this was the result of the aftermath of the disaster – which he and his community had experienced in the first half of the twelfth century. During periods of crisis and weak leadership, when there was a scarcity of halakhic teachers, the tendency was to rely on and sanctify customs, and to look upon them as guidelines for living in an insecure world. Rabbi Eliezer ben Nathan not only defended customs, but also endeavoured to give them halakhic form, to change their status from that of religious practices that had no authority from the Talmud, to religious observances based on the discourse of talmudic sages and their logic.[66] He was well aware of the needs of Jewish society during what he saw as a critical juncture. Our interest here is in his role as a community leader, who changed the status of women on the basis of his social and communal worldview. This is the context in which the reforms that he instituted in favour of women should be understood. As I see it, Rabbi Eliezer ben Nathan is the epitome of a leader who brings about change in the status of women, which he based on a halakhic process because his aim was to mobilize all the resources of the community to cope with a particularly difficult period and he saw women as a key factor in defences designed to protect the community, the family and the Jewish People.

In the first half of the twelfth century, following the crisis of the First Crusade, Rabbi Eliezer ben Nathan changed the status of women completely by formulating two rulings connected to marital relations, marriage and divorce; backing the societal change with halakhic arguments; and eliminating the obstacles that stood in his way. He was the first to mention both aspects of the ruling and the first to remove the enormous threat hanging over it, the commandment of procreation. He also provided the very legitimate explanation, which allowed the rulings to be put into effect and applied in practice.[67] In the problematic context of the 'rebellious wife', too, Rabbi Eliezer ben Nathan removed the main impediment that stood in the way of the husband's marrying another woman. He concluded that when men were allowed to marry more than one woman, dealing with the matter of a 'rebellious wife' had often been a long, drawn-out affair of many stages, as explained in the Talmud.[68] Today, Rabbi Eliezer explained, when the communal ordinance has established that a man can have only one wife, a long and complicated process is no longer feasible in the case of a 'rebellious wife'; instead, she must be freed immediately, that is, the husband should be forced to divorce his wife.[69]

Rabbi Eliezer ben Nathan also supported the ruling that made the amounts of money in the *ketubah* uniform, i.e., a respectable sum that would remove the possibilities of local jealousy, humiliation, or a sense of arrogance among the Jewish families in a particular community. In the same way that the ruling establishing the *ketubah* was made long ago so that men would not take their marriages lightly, the rule was now made to provide the same sum of money for the permanent amount in the *ketubah* for both the wealthy and the poor woman, Rabbi Eliezer ben Nathan took action – making sure to use *mishnaic* language – to explain the matter of the *kitzotah*[70] (the new total amount) as a permanent addition to the *ketubah* and to the dowry.[71]

Rabbi Simhah ben Samuel of Speyer was born in the fourth decade of the twelfth century and died in 1225, having reached a ripe old age, though he was blind. His importance stems from his unusual personality and from the impression he made on his colleagues, and particularly his students. He was appointed to the *Beit Din* (court) at a very young age and participated in numerous deliberations, which made him intimately familiar with the human foibles and communal shortcomings of his era. Rabbi Simhah ben Samuel of Speyer was a leader in the same category as Rabbi Eliezer ben Nathan. In comparison to Rashi or even Rabbi Eliezer ben Nathan, he left behind very little in the way of written records; however, some of the *responsa* that have been preserved indicate that he combined Rashi's outlook regarding the place and importance of women within the family unit, and his excessive concern about them, with the collectivist approach that placed the responsibility for sustaining the family system on the community as a whole.[72]

Rabbi Simhah emulated Rashi in his line of thinking, viewing the relations between husband and wife as all-encompassing, idyllic, and without flaws. Indeed he may have been the sage with the most extreme views, since he believed that if the system becomes damaged in any way, the family unit should be immediately dismantled; moreover, he was also prepared to remove any obstacle in order to free a woman from the bonds of matrimony. The rabbis hesitated to coerce a husband into divorcing his wife, i.e., to force him to grant her a *gett*, because according to the halakhic thinking, a *gett* given under coercion is problematic. There was concern that even the vaguest hint that the *gett* is not proper could lead to a child born to a woman, after she remarries, who had been given such a *gett*, being considered a *mamzer*. This would constitute a very serious social blemish for the child and prevent his/her future marriage within the community. This fear made some of the sages balk at the idea of forcing men to give their wives a *gett*. Rabbi Simhah sought to resolve this issue.[73]

One of the cases dealt with by Rabbi Simhah gives us the opportunity to learn about his thoughts on this issue. A complaint was made by the father of a woman who had been battered and humiliated. It transpired that her husband had been in the habit of beating her; he also humiliated her by apparently forcing her to go about in public without a head covering.

Rabbi Simhah wrote a sharply-worded letter to the *dayanim* in which he gave them the following instructions. First, he told them, the husband cannot behave towards his wife as he wishes (he referred to the discussion in Tbab. Tractate Baba Kamah 32b). He also pointed out that a man who beats his wife is much worse than a man who attacks another man, since a wife relies on her husband to defend her and her 'tears are common' (she often sheds tears). The innovation in Rabbi Simhah's response was that he instructed the *Beit Din* on the essence of their function. He saw this 'family' problem as a community dilemma, one which communal institutions had to make an effort to solve. He believed that it was the *Beit Din*'s duty to put a stop to such behaviour on the part of the husband. He told the court to force the husband to repent his actions and also to appoint arbitrators on their behalf to monitor the husband's behaviour and intervene and resolve all the conflicts that might arise between the spouses. If the man did not desist but continued to beat and humiliate his wife, Rabbi Simhah demanded that the *dayanim* impose a stiff fine on him, that is, the standard punishment, and that the man be be forced to follow the ruling of an adjudicator. In other words, he insisted that the most severe social pressure should be applied in this case. Rabbi Simhah also asserted that the man would be out of favour with God (i.e., he would not be allowed to enter Paradise in the world to come). In addition, he made the radically unusual suggestion of recourse to a Christian court of law to ensure that the man would be punished and beaten if he was not prepared to divorce his wife. Rabbi Simhah knew that this directive was a deviation from the restrictions of the *halakhah* as delineated by his predecessors; however, he made a point of showing his agreement with his fellow *dayanim*, with whom he consulted: in this case, a *gett* by coercion must be authorized, that is, a *gett* imposed by non-Jews.

We need to ask what motivated Rabbi Simhah to insist on such an extreme approach that invalidated all the standard, widely-accepted thinking on this issue.[74]

Grossman maintains that Rabbi Simhah was influenced by the teachings of *Hasidei Ashkenaz*, who were opposed in principle to physically injuring any human being and looked upon such behaviour as a terrible sin for which confession and atonement must be made.[75] Yet this explanation cannot account for Rabbi Simhah's habit of giving atypical advice to women in distress when their husbands refused to divorce them. He supported the ruling regarding the 'rebellious wife' originated by the school of the *Geonim*, who maintained that such women should be immediately freed from their husbands. But this was not the standard practice in his milieu; in thirteenth century Germany, where the Jews had developed other methods of dealing with the situation. Nevertheless, Rabbi Simhah strictly adhered to the approach of separating spouses as soon as it was realized that an unbridgeable gap existed between them. In such cases, he also supported the idea of coercing a man into giving his wife a *gett* and freeing the woman, and was not concerned about the fear that such a divorce, granted against the husband's wishes, might lead to the birth of a *mamzer* in the future.

This was also his attitude in the case of a *yibbum* (levir), who refused to give *Halizah*[76] to his brother's wife (to free her to marry another man) and attempted to force himself on her. The *yibbum* was evidently convinced that if he became intimate with her or had sexual relations with her, she would become his wife on the basis of these acts. The widow, who was 'of distinguished lineage and wealthy', who was in possession of her deceased husband's funds and did not want to share them with his brother, came to complain to Rabbi Simhah. He gave her some unusual advice: to spit in the face of the levir in front of witnesses and thus initiate the *Halizah* process Afterwards, he himself disqualified the brother from contracting a levirate marriage with the woman. Rabbi Simhah elucidated this line of thinking in statements made regarding another case. A young man had gone blind after becoming betrothed[77] to a woman, but the *dayanim* were reluctant to force him to divorce his fiancée. Rabbi Isaac ben Moses had written to Rabbi Simhah stating his view that it was not necessary to invoke a *gett* given under compulsion, since the woman was not an *agunah*[78] because the young man in question was able to have full sexual relations and because it was a well known fact that women loved their blind husbands. Rabbi Simhah used strong language in his criticism of this opinion. He argued that a woman, who did not know ahead of time that her husband would go blind and marries a blind man against her wishes, is like an *agunah*. He declared that 'there is no greater *igun* (enchainment) than this'. He believed that the woman's fondness for her husband is what brings about normal family life; in other words, he viewed the harmonious relationship between man and wife as the mainstay of the family.[79]

Nonetheless, Rabbi Simhah's approach also led him to be more stringent than others in certain cases. In one case, a woman told the rabbinical court that while conducting business, she had journeyed from one place to another and been raped by two escorts. After the woman lodged the complaint, the two perpetrators were arrested by the Christian authorities; however, someone saw to it that they were freed and they returned to their homes. Although the question whether or not such a woman may return to her husband, had already been debated in the Talmud, the thirteenth-century *dayanim* gave permission for such a woman to remain with her husband.[80] Rabbi Simhah, on the other hand, argued that they should not return to their husbands and recommended that the spouses be separated. Certain sages, Rabbi Eliezer ben Yoel Halevi in particular, wrote to him specially to convince him to go along with the opinions of the other sages and allow such women to remain with their husbands. Rabbi Simhah's response is not available in writing, but if we follow his halakhic decisions and take a closer look at Rabbi Eliezer ben Yoel Halevi's letters, it becomes very clear that harmony between the spouses was especially important to him. Just as he protested against husbands who abused their wives, he helped to free 'rebellious wives', and showed the widow how to free herself from her levir, he also sought to prevent an undesired wife (because she had been raped or captured) from returning to her husband.[81]

In the second half of the thirteenth century, Rabbi Meir ben Barukh of Rothenburg (Maharam) also followed this trend. His viewpoint about women and their status stemmed from his deep-seated understanding, as a leader, of the importance of community solidarity. Hence, on the one hand, his approach sought to improve and reinforce the status of women, and on the other, to place limitations on them. His fundamental line of thinking, which linked the status of women and the social question, is highlighted in a *responsum* in which he described a theoretical community where there are only *Kohanim*. In this case, he asserted, the women of the community should be 'called up' to the Torah.[82] In principle (according to Tbab. Tractate Megillah 23), women can be called up to the Torah; however, the talmudic concept of 'public dignity' precludes such a practice. If a justification were found to suspend 'public dignity', a woman could be 'called up' to the Torah.[83] In contrast, Rabbi Meir ben Barukh was upset by the fact that women served as godmothers at *brit milah* (circumcision) ceremonies, which took place in the men's section of the synagogue. In his opinion, a woman's presence in the male section of the synagogue was a major disruption to the ceremony itself.[84] His motivation was not to offend women; rather, he was concerned about the communal value of the prayer service. This was also the reason behind his opposition to the custom of adding a male child to make up the prayer quorum if a tenth adult male was unavailable. He opposed this practice in principle and did not object to the presence of children in the synagogue or at a prayer service.

In 1272, Rabbi Meir ben Barukh received a letter written by three *dayanim* from a city, which they left unnamed, but not far from Erfurt. They sought his advice either because of the difficulty in a case that awaited their final decision, or because they wished to share the heavy responsibility it entailed with other *dayanim*. They recorded the main points of the discussion in the form of minutes and sent it to other *dayanim* in the nearby city of Erfurt, and in far-off Würzburg, as well as to Rabbi Meir ben Barukh of Rothenburg.[85] A man by the name of Isaac decided to seek his fortune far away from home. He set out on 16 March 1271, and one year later, he heard that his wife had borne a child. The baby was born in 1272, one week after Purim (in the last week of February that year). Isaac quickly returned home, attempted, without success, to divorce his wife on the grounds of adultery and prevent her from obtaining the value of her *ketubah*. In other words, the child that was born would become a *mamzer* and the woman would be divested of all the funds entitled to her from her *ketubah*. At first the court refused to convene; however, in light of the pressure brought to bear by the husband, they did assemble and listen to evidence. Afterwards, they circulated the abovementioned letter in which they asked for advice from other *dayanim*. In my opinion, the court refused to convene because they were afraid of the consequences of the decision that would be made; therefore, they suggested to the husband that it would be more worthwhile to divorce his wife and give her what she was entitled to receive on the basis of her *ketubah*. But Isaac refused.[86]

Sarah, the wife, claimed that when Isaac set out on his voyage, she was already pregnant. He countered that that was impossible, since everyone knew that she had borne the child twelve months almost after he left. The *Beit Din*, when it was forced to convene and investigate, heard witnesses with different stories. Some testified that she had the baby twelve months after her husband set out on his journey. One man reported that on the eve of Shavuot (Pentecost), he was on his way to Sarah's home to say *Kiddush* for her, because he knew her husband was away from home; at that time he saw her in the company of non-Jews. The *dayanim* assumed that that was when she became pregnant, since exactly nine months separate the holidays of Shavuot and Purim. In addition, Sarah's father came to the *dayanim* to ask them if it was permissible to kill his daughter in view of her behaviour. Other evidence, which proved to be of utmost importance, indicated that seven months before the birth, someone had asked Sarah if she was pregnant; she had loudly denied it and also cursed the questioner vehemently.

It is worthwhile taking a closer look at Rabbi Meir ben Barukh of Rothenburg's answer, because it reflects the problems he had with this particular woman and his method of analysis in this case, which I believe, he considered a communal problem. On the one hand, he revealed his opinion about the woman and her behaviour at the very beginning of the *responsum*. He did not refer to her by her name (Sarah), instead he called her Gomer daughter of Diblaim, the famous prostitute who the prophet Hosea is commanded by God to take as his wife (Hosea 1:3).[87] On the other hand, he discussed at great length the matter of witnesses and fundamental halakhic questions that emerge in this case: the probable adulterous act, the divorce of the wife against her will, sexual relations with Christians. Nevertheless, the communal point of view in this *responsum*, the community's responsibility towards this particular woman, is clear, since, in the final analysis, Rabbi Meir ben Barukh of Rothenburg made it possible for her to receive the contents of her *ketubah* so that she would not be divorced without any means of support. Here he had to weigh important issues that could affect the community itself. A lesson obviously had to be taught to anyone who did not behave according to *halakhah* in marital relations. Jewish society had to condemn this type of behaviour and women especially had to know that such actions would be punished. Yet, even this kind of woman must be safeguarded within the confines of the Jewish community and every effort must be made to keep her from going over to the Christian world and to prevent a situation of *mamzerut*. Above all, an attempt had to be made to preserve the advancements achieved by the women, i.e., that they could no longer be divorced without their consent.

Rabbi Meir ben Barukh's solution was a work of art created by a community leader who attempted to solve a 'communal' problem (and he may have succeeded). He demanded that the woman be divorced, even against her will, but he also ordered the husband to pay her the sums of money owed to her on the basis of her *ketubah*. If she denied having relations with Christians or did not explain why she denied her pregnancy at first, she stood to lose even the standard amounts she would under any circumstances be entitled to receive. In this way, he intimated to the entire community – especially the women – that a female suspected of indecent behaviour would be punished, thus forcing her husband to divorce her, while giving her the funds stipulated in her *ketubah* so that she would not become destitute. As a result, he kept this woman and others like her, from going over to the Christian camp.

The community outlook also emerges in Rabbi Meir ben Barukh's attitude towards the issue of women who were assaulted by their husbands. In a patriarchal society where the male – the father or the husband – is considered superior to the female from the point of view of economic rights, religious duties, and education, a fundamentally negative attitude against a man beating a woman will not exist. The principles laid down in the Talmud limited this type of behaviour. It vehemently opposes attacks against any human being, and heavy fines and punishments are meted out to the perpetrators. But the Talmud contains no separate or specific references to assaults against women, in principle, except for a passage about a man who hurt his wife unintentionally during sexual intercourse; he had to bear the cost of the damage done to her. Based on this principle, it is obvious that if a man must pay damages when he causes unintentional harm to his wife, he is most certainly forbidden to attack, beat, or deliberately injure her. On the other hand, if his preferential status over his wife, as her protector and tutor, is acknowledged, does he have the right to give her a beating, which does not cause bodily harm, for 'educational' purposes? After all, not only superiority but also responsibility is stipulated. If a father's responsibility towards his young children permits him to give them 'positive beatings' so as to teach them, is he not allowed to beat his wife to educate her? Can a husband hit his wife if she refuses to do the work that she is obligated to do according to the stipulations of the *Mishnah* and *Gemarah*? And most importantly, can violent injury committed by a husband against his wife be used as grounds for divorce by the wife?

We have already seen that at the beginning of the thirteenth century, Rabbi Simhah of Speyer came out vociferously against husbands assaulting their wives, and strongly urged that the spouses separate immediately when such behaviour occurs. Rabbi Meir ben Barukh of Rothenburg adopted the same attitude; however, he placed much more emphasis on the aspect of propriety and possible repercussions. He also emphasized the halakhic aspect of violent behaviour and charged the communal organizations with correcting the situation. This *responsum* is reminiscent of Rabbi Simhah's, which I analyzed above, and not by chance, since Rabbi Meir ben Barukh studied under Rabbi Simhah and frequently referred to him in his texts. Nonetheless, Rabbi Simhah's solution was to separate the spouses, that is, to break up the family unit, whereas Rabbi Meir ben Barukh expanded the role of the community in this matter. His halakhic basis was the general talmudic prohibition against assaulting a friend, which obviously includes a ban against wife beating. Moreover, a husband is commanded to respect his wife, as it is said: 'a man must respect his wife more than his own body' (Tbab. Tractate Sanhedrin 76b). In addition, there is a *halakhah* that asserts that as a matter of course, the situation of a woman who marries improves and cannot deteriorate. Rabbi Meir ben Barukh of Rothenburg asserted that the community must punish anyone who injures his wife, and he tries to force him to mend his ways; if he persists in this behaviour, he may even be punished physically. He used the expression 'to cut off his hand', but we do not know if they actually meted out physical punishment, either to deter or to punish such behaviour. In any event, Rabbi Meir ben Barukh allowed a woman to sue for divorce and obtain the funds allotted to her in her *ketubah* in a case involving an abusive husband.[88] We know that in the same era, Rabbi Peretz bar Elijah of Corbeil sought to establish a ruling to deal with this type of situation. He suggested a ruling relating to complaints lodged by women, or their family members, against abusive husbands. The ruling demanded that the husband swear on pain of excommunication that he would not beat his wife again, and if he did not undertake such a commitment, the court would award the wife maintenance, which he would have to pay, as if he had left her to go on a long journey.[89] There is no doubt that the sages considered this problem a community issue.

Sometimes Rabbi Meir ben Barukh of Rothenburg considered women's behaviour as undermining the foundations of the society and the community. Although this viewpoint led to the idea of curbing the power of women, it did not cause them any fundamental harm. He believed that a rise in the number of divorces was a problem that had an impact on the robustness of the Jewish community; therefore, he made it difficult for women going through a divorce to obtain the property they were entitled to, or for a 'rebellious wife' to obtain what she believed was her due. Nonetheless, his decisions were a far cry from those of his student, Rabbi Asher ben Yehiel (Rosh), whose attitudes towards women were negative and restrictive. Rabbi Asher ben Yehiel frequently referred to his teacher, Rabbi Meir ben Barukh, to support his arguments, though he added his own interpretations.[90]

In this chapter we have examined the different approaches to femininity displayed by the men who wrote the sources we have today. We will now see these different approaches in action when these sages sought to deal with the problems presented to them by their communities.

Notes

1. S. Valler, *Women in Jewish Society in the talmudic Period*, Ramat Gan 2000, pp. 18–22; C. Ozick, 'Notes towards Finding the Right Question', in *On Being a Jewish Feminist*, ed. S. Heschel, New York 1983, pp. 140–142.
2. Rashi on Tbab. Sanhedrin 31b, L. Landau, 'Rashi's Stories in the Babylonian Talmud', *Eshel Beer-Sheva* 3 (1986), pp. 101–117.
3. A. Grossman, *The Early Sages of France*, Jerusalem 1995, pp. 122–166, 182–253; A. Grossman, *Rashi*, Jerusalem 2006, pp. 21–28.
4. Solomon B. Isaac (Rashi), *Responsa Rashi*, ed. I. Elfenbein, New York 1943, no. 14, p. 8. A. Grossman, *The Early Sages of France*, Jerusalem 1995, p. 126.
5. A. Grossman, *The Early Sages of France*, Jerusalem 1995, pp. 122–166, 182–253.

6   A. Grossman, *The Early Sages of France*, Jerusalem 1995, pp. 121–140.
7   Rashi's third daughter, Rachel, is mentioned in correspondence between the two cousins (the sons of Yocheved and Miriam) about their aunt, 'Madame Rachel', who was divorced by her husband.
8   Solomon B. Isaac (Rashi), *Responsa Rashi*, no. 114, p. 142; A. Grossman, *The Early Sages of France*, Jerusalem 1995, p. 125 n. 11.
9   A. Grossman, 'Rashi`s Teachings concerning Women', *Zion*, 70 (2005), pp. 157–190. Grossman expressed keen interest in this topic and wrote an article about it that cited a great many sources from Rashi's writings. I wish to add to this research the social perspective of Rashi as a male archetype and the attempt to explain his position towards women from a societal point of view. My outlook towards Rashi's thought processes is neither 'positive' nor 'negative' but sees them as being based on the social structure of the Jewish community with which he was familiar.
10 Gematria, the assignation of numerical values to Hebrew letters.
11 Sefer Tosafot haShalem, ed. J. Gellis, vol. I, Jerusalem 1982, pp. 67–133, esp. pp. 67, 108, 111–113. A. Grossman, 'Rashi's Teachings concerning Women', *Zion*, 70 (2005), p. 159 n. 7.
12 He ignores all the homiletical interpretations that itemize the bad qualities of the archetypal woman who was created from the rib: inferior, licentious, gossipy, etc. *Midrash Devarim Rabbah*, ed. S. Liebermann, Jerusalem 1974, 6:11.
13 Rashi on Exodus 38:8; see A. Grossman, 'Rashi's Teachings concerning Women', *Zion*, 70 (2005), p. 168.
14 Rashi on Genesis 3:12; Rashi on Avodah Zarah 5b *s.v.* Aser Nathan; Rashi on Yebamot 62b–63a, Genesis Rabbah 17:3.
15 Solomon B. Isaac (Rashi), *Responsa Rashi*, no. 240, no. 128, pp. 155–156.
16 Rashi uses an interpretation by Menahem ben Sarouq and adds an explanation in the vernacular for this term. Rashi on Genesis 17:14, 15:1, 24:1; Leviticus 20:20; Yebamot 55a, Shabbat 25b.
17 Rashi utilizes a text from *Midrash Bereshit Rabah* (2:45) but with a fundamental change; the *midrash* states: 'Anyone who does not have children it is as if he is dead, as if he is destroyed,' whereas Rashi omits the words 'as if'.
18 Genesis 16:2, 30:1, 30:23.
19 Solomon B. Isaac (Rashi), *Responsa Rashi*, no. 207, nos 232–234; Isaac ben Moses, *Sefer Or Zarua*, 2 vols, Zhitomir 1862, vol. II, Babba Kama 85.
20 According to Tbab, Ketubot 75a, hidden defects were diseases or defects of the body that could be hidden from view.
21 As Grossman, 'Rashi's Teachings concerning Women', *Zion*, 70 (2005), pp. 164–165, pointed out, Rashi added this of his own accord to the list of claims for gaining entry to heaven: negotiating in good faith, and setting aside time for Torah study. Rashi on Sota 47a, Rashi on Shabbat 31a.
22 After Lamech killed Cain and his son, his wives withdrew from him and refused to live with him or have marital relations with him. See Rashi on Genesis 4:23 (see Nedarim 90b, Midrash Tanhuma 1:11).
23 Rashi uses the words 'the women took leave of him and he placated them' and recalls the statement from the Talmud, in Tractate Nedarim, about a situation in which women distanced themselves from their husbands, claiming that 'heaven stands between us'. The *Mishnah* and *Gemarah* recommend that 'they act "by way of request"',

which means, it would seem, attempting to deal with the problem by psychological and social means.
24 Rashi's Introduction to the Song of Songs.
25 Rashi on Genesis 24:62, 25:1.
26 The female figure was also depicted in this way in the story which Rashi developed on the basis of a passage from the Talmud. In the story of the rat and the pit, the woman is a positive, loyal, and loving character, in contrast to the man, who does not display these qualities. Rashi on Tbab. Tractate Ta'anit 8a.
27 Eruvin 100b, see Ecclesiastes 2:22 and in Exodus 1:19, 'they are vigorous', and Rashi on Genesis 2:20-21.
28 Grossman, 'Rashi's Teachings concerning Women', *Zion*, 70 (2005).
29 Rashi on Kiddushin 8b. Grossman, who portrays Rashi in a positive light, explains that the sage used this story because it was the only version available to him and he merely replicated it. See Grossman, 'Rashi's Teachings concerning Women', *Zion*, 70 (2005), p. 172, and J. Dishon, 'Images of Women in Medieval Hebrew Literature', in *Women of the World: Jewish Women and Jewish Writing*, ed. J. Baskin, Detroit 1994, pp. 35-49.
30 See Chapter 7.
31 S. Goldin, *The Ways of Jewish Martyrdom*, Turnhout 2008, pp. 191-196; R. Chazan, 'Ephraim ben Jacob's Compilation of Twelfth Century Persecutions', *Jewish Quarterly Review*, 84 (1994), pp. 397-416.
32 In Sefer Zekhirah, Ephraim of Bonn refers to Madame Mina of Speyer, who in 1146 was tortured by having her ears and thumbs cut off in an effort to force her to convert to Christianity; to Madame Guthalh of Aschaffenburg, who drowned herself in a river to avoid conversion; and to a young woman who spat on the cross in church when they tried to convert her by force. He also describes the forced baptism of a woman and her three daughters and refers to the water as 'cursed [bitter] waters', which is reminiscent of the Sotah water.
33 S. L. Einbinder, 'Jewish Women Martyrs: Changing Models of Representation', *Exemplaria*, 12 (2000), pp. 105-127; A. Grossman, *Pious and Rebellious: Jewish Women in Europe in the Middle Ages*, Jerusalem, pp. 370-372 [Hebrew]; A. Grossman, 'Pious and Rebellious: Jewish Women in Europe in the Middle Ages', Waltham MA 2004, pp. 209-211 [English].
34 Ephraim of Bonn, *Sefer Zekhirah*, ed. A. Habermann, Jerusalem 1970.
35 S. L. Einbinder, 'Pucellina of Blois: Romantic Myths and Narrative Conventions', *Jewish History*, 12 (1998), pp. 29-46; S. Goldin, *The Ways of Jewish Martyrdom*, Turnhout 2008, 193-202.
36 Goldin, *The Ways of Jewish Martyrdom*, pp. 193-202 and bibliography there.
37 The daughter of Louis XVII and his first wife, Eleanor of Aquitaine.
38 Leviticus Rabba, in Midrash Rabba ch. 18, Rashi on Chronicles 2, ch. 13; Isaiah 15:5; Jeremiah 48:34; *Yalkut Shimoni*, Jerusalem 1968-1973, Isaiah no. 419.
39 S. Einbinder, *Beautiful Death*, Princeton, NJ 2002, pp. 164-166, S. Spiegel, *The Last Trail: On the Legends and Lore of the Command to Abraham to offer Isaac as a Sacrifice*, trans. J. Goldin, Philadelphia 1967.
40 Asher ben Yehiel, *Shut haRosh*, ed. S. Yudelov, Jerusalem 1994, 42:1.
41 *Teshuvot uPsakim, Responsa et Decisiones*, ed. E. Kupfer, Jerusalem 1973; no. 156, p. 243; Asher ben Yehiel, *Shut haRosh*, 43:3; Grossman, *Pious and Rebellious: Jewish Women in Europe in the Middle Ages*, pp. 425-427.

42 Asher ben Yehiel, *Shut haRosh*, 43:6.
43 See the Glossary of Hebrew Terms.
44 Asher ben Yehiel, *Shut haRosh*, 53:8; A. Grossman, *Pious and Rebellious: Jewish Women in Europe in the Middle Ages*, Jerusalem, 2001, pp. 489-490 [Hebrew]; A. Grossman, *Pious and Rebellious: Jewish Women in Europe in the Middle Ages*, Waltham, MA 2004, pp. 269-270 [English].
45 Asher ben Yehiel, *Pisqei haRosh*, Berakhot 2:2.
46 Judah ben Samuel, *Sefer Hasidim*, ed. J. Wistinetzki, Frankfurt 1942; I. Baer, 'The Religious-Social Tendency of Sefer Hasidim' [Hebrew], *Zion* 3 (1938), pp. 1-50; H. Soloveitchik, 'Three Themes in the Sefer Hasidim', *AJS Review*, 1 (1976), pp. 311-357.
47 M. Güdemann, *Sefer haTorah veHayim beArzot Askenaz beYemei haBenyim*, 3 vols, Warsaw 1897; Baer, 'The Religious-Social Tendency of Sepher Hassidim', pp. 189-194; I. Marcus *Piety and Society: The Jewish Pietists of Medieval Germany*, Leiden 1981.
48 The term 'Hasid' usually refers to men, though we do find sources using the feminine form 'Hasida' to refer to women.
49 J. Baskin, 'From Separation to Displacement: The Problem of Women in Sefer Hasidim', *AJS Review*, 19 (1994), pp. 1-18.
50 Baskin, 'From Separation to Displacement: The Problem of Women in Sefer Hasidim', p. 3, no. 6; Eleazar ben Judah of Worms, *Sefer ha-Roqeah*, Venice, 1549, nos 14, 20.
51 *Sefer Hasidim*, nos 69-71, 1090.
52 *Sefer Hasidim*, 1102-1104, 1108 (pp. 281-282), 1112 (p. 282), 1131 (p. 286).
53 *Sefer Hasidim*, nos 386, 952, 984, 1059, 1089, 1112-1114.
54 M. Harris, 'The Concept of Love in Sefer Hassidim', *Jewish Quarterly Review*, 50 (1949), pp. 13-44.
55 *Sefer Hasidim*, nos 391, 1131, 1134, 1136, 1142, 1191, 1894. S. Borchers, *Jüdisches frauenleben im Mittelalter*, Frankfurt am Main 1998, pp. 32-45; A. Grossman, *Pious and Rebellious: Jewish Women in Europe in the Middle Ages*, Jerusalem, pp. 100-103 [Hebrew]; A. Grossman, *Pious and Rebellious: Jewish Women in Europe in the Middle Ages*, Waltham, MA 2004, pp. 56-57 [English]. See esp. in Sefer Hasidim nos 1102-1105 (Sanhedrin 76a, Yebamot 4a) and Tosafot to Qiddushin 41a.
56 *Sefer Hasidim*, nos 38, 59, 60, 64, 835, 1159. For example: a young woman who falls desperately in love with the teacher who comes to her home to instruct her brothers.
57 *Sefer Hasidim*, nos 38, 59, 60, 64, 835, 835, 1159.
58 *Sefer Hasidim*, nos 69-71, 1090.
59 *Sefer Hasidim*, nos 52-53 (pp. 44-45), 1501-1502 (see in Yoma 66b), 835.
60 Tbab. Baba Kama 110a; Rashi on Tbab. Sota 12a *s.v.* leshem shamaim, Yebamot 83a, Sanhedrin 76b (see Deuteronomy 13:6, Song of Songs 8:1). In Sefer Hasidim, nos 362, 375-376, 1091-1094, 1099-1100, 1921.
61 Eleazar ben Judah of Worms, *Sefer ha-Roqeah*, no. 12, p. 27.
62 It mentions a period of repentance during which the repenter does not speak to women, places himself in the same situation, turns away from a repetition of the sin, and inflicts extreme physical punishment on him. See Sefer Hasidim in the sources in the previous notes, esp. n. 00, p. 00. Baskin's articles: J. Baskin, 'Jewish Women in the Middle Ages', in *Jewish Women in Historical Perspective*, ed. J. Baskin, Detroit 1991, pp. 94-114; Baskin, 'From Separation to Displacement'.
63 L. Finkelstein, *Jewish Self-government in the Middle Ages*, New York 1924, pp. 168-170.

64 Eliezer ben Nathan, *Sefer Ra'avan*, Jerusalem 1984, introduction; V. Aptowizer, introduction to *Sefer Ra'aviah* (Eliezer ben Yoel haLevi), Jerusalem 1938, pp. 49–57; E. Urbach, *Ba'alei ha-Tosafot*, 4th edition, Jerusalem, 1980, pp. 173–184.
65 S. Goldin, *The Ways of Jewish Martyrdom*, Turnhout 2008, pp. 110–112, 148–160.
66 Eliezer ben Nathan, *Sefer Ra'avan*, nos 8, 10, 17–19; I. Ta-Shma, *Early Franco-German Ritual and Custom*, Jerusalem 1992, pp. 32–34, 243–244.
67 See Chapter 2.
68 The woman is warned that if she does not return to her husband she will be fined and required to pay part of the value of her *ketubah*; as the process continues, other fines are imposed.
69 Eliezer ben Nathan, *Sefer Ra'avan*, p. 261; E. Westreich, *Transitions in the Legal Status of the Wife in Jewish Law*, Jerusalem 2002, pp. 91–95.
70 See the Glossary of Hebrew Terms and in Chapter 4 below.
71 Eliezer ben Nathan, *Sefer Ra'avan*, no. 87, 288–289. He was also innovating when he explained a custom: 'And [we should follow] what our forefathers did: not to protest against women who wave the lulav and recite the appropriate blessing.'
72 Aptowizer, *Introduction to Sefer Ra'avia*, pp. 412–414; Urbach, *Ba'alei ha-Tosafot*, pp. 411–420; A. Grossman, 'Woman in Rabbi Simcha of Spaier's Teaching', *Mayim MiDaliu* (2002), pp. 177–189.
73 Similarly to Rabbi Isaac in France. See for example Isaac ben Moses, *Sefer Or Zarua*, 2 vols, Zhitomir 1862, vol. I, no. 754.
74 Clearly recalling Rabbenu Hananel ben Hushiel. Isaac ben Moses, *Sefer Or Zarua*, vol. II, Baba Kama, no. 161; Meir ben Barukh, *Sheelot u-Teshuvot ha-Maharam*, Prague edition, ed. M. A. Blakh, Budapest 1895, no. 927, Sefer Hassidim, no. 1086 p. 277.
75 A. Grossman, 'Women in Rabbi Simcha of Spaier's Teaching', *Mayim MiDaliu* (2002), pp. 177–189.
76 See the Glossary of Hebrew Terms and the section 'Levirate marriage and Halizah' in Chapter 5.
77 A divorce with a *gett* was required even if the couple were only engaged to be married.
78 See the Glossary of Hebrew Terms.
79 Meir ha-Kohen, *Haggahot Maimuniuot*, Hilchot Eshot, 14:20; Isaac ben Moses, *Sefer Or Zarua*, vol. I, nos 760–761; J. Katz, 'Levirate Marriage (*Yibbum*) and *Halizah* in post-talmudic Times', *Tarbiz*, 51 (1981–1982), pp. 59–106. Tragically, it seems that Rabbi Simhah of Speyer gradually lost his sight as he grew older, until he finally became totally blind and the Torah portions had to be read aloud to him.
80 Isaac ben Moses, *Sefer Or Zarua*, vol. I, no. 615.
81 It is interesting to note that Rabbi Simhah also made sure that his daughters were knowledgeable in religious matters and even allowed women to join the quorum of the *zimun* for the grace after meals, in contrast to Tbab. Tractate Berachot 45b. Mordekhai on Berachot, no. 158.
82 When the Torah is read publicly in synagogue between three and seven men are 'called up' to recite the blessings, according to the occasion. If a *kohen* is present he is 'called up' first, but Kohanim are excluded from making the subsequent blessings, so in a community where there were only Kohanim there would be no one to make the subsequent blessings – a theoretical problem which Maharam solved theoretically.
83 Meir ben Barukh, *Sheelot u-Teshuvot ha-Maharam*, Prague edition, no. 108; Mordechai on Gittin, no. 404; A. Grossmann, *Pious and Rebellious: Jewish Women in Europe in*

the *Middle Ages*, Jerusalem 2001, p. 326 [Hebrew]; A. Grossman, *Pious and Rebellious: Jewish Women in Europe in the Middle Ages*, Waltham, MA 2004, p. 187 [English].

84 A. Grossmann, *Pious and Rebellious*, Jerusalem 2001, pp. 321–324 [Hebrew]; A. Grossman, *Pious and Rebellious*, Waltham, MA 2004, p. 190 [English].

85 One of the *dayanim* may have been a student of Rabbi Meir's. Meir ha-Kohen, Teshubot Maimuniut on Moses ben Maimon, *Mishneh Tora*, Sefer Nashim, no. 25; Meir ben Barukh, *Sheelot u-Teshuvot Maharam bar Barukh*, Lemberg 1860, no. 310; Mordechai on Yebamot, nos 121–122.

86 In this way she would not be divorced against her will, in contradiction to the ban of Rabbenu Gershom Me'or HaGolah; she would retain the money stipulated in her *ketubah* (and not end up destitute), and the question of the mamzerut would no longer be an issue.

87 Rashi interpreted this name as a reference to her profession – 'a prostitute who is used and trampled on by everyone is like a dried fig' – a sentence that in Hebrew includes variations of both the names 'Gomer' and 'Diblaim'.

88 Meir ben Barukh, *Sheelot u-Teshuvot ha-Maharam*, Prague edition, no. 81; Meir ben Barukh , *Sefer She'elot uTeshuvot*, Cremona edition, Jerusalem 1986, no. 291.

89 L. Finkelstein, *Jewish Self-government in the Middle Ages*, pp. 216–217; A. Grossman, 'Violence against Women in Medieval Mediterranean Jewish Society', in Y. Azmon (ed.), *A View into the Lives of Women in Jewish Societies*, Jerusalem 1995; Grossman, *Pious and Rebellious*, Jerusalem 2001, pp. 388–397 [Hebrew].

90 Grossman deals with this at length in his book, citing numerous substantiations. See A. Grossman, *Pious and Rebellious*, Jerusalem 200, pp. 428–446, and A. Grossman, *Pious and Rebellious*, Waltham, MA 2004, pp. 223–224 [English].

4

The family unit and the change in women's status

The status of the woman within a newly formed family unit is dependent on a number of factors, the most important of which are her economic power and her position within the marital relationship. Although these are ostensibly distinct, it is apparent that they are, in fact, inseparable. The status of a wife within the family unit is based in part on her husband's status; but also on the extent to which her husband can divorce her against her will; on whether or not he is also married to another woman; and on the strength of the wife's economic status. In this and the following chapter the legal structures underpinning women's status within the family unit are explored and examined.

Economic status

From early times, going back as far as the first century BCE, the woman's economic position upon her marriage was unquestionably poor. Before a young woman could leave her father's family and move to her husband's family, the latter had to pay a sum of money to her family; then she, as a proprietary chattel, left the domain of her father and moved to that of her husband and his family. This sum of money, called the *mohar* (bride-price), confirmed that the woman was almost completely devoid of independent legal status. Prior to her marriage she was subject to the authority of her father, and after marriage, to that of her husband. If her husband decided to divorce her, or if he died, she would return to her father's house.

Texts from the Mishnaic period contain evidence that this state of affairs had undergone a total change. This had come about for two reasons. First, the price of the *mohar* had increased and the sages were displeased with the fact that men might have to wait a long time before they could marry. In their words: 'they would get old without having married'.[1] The second reason was more complex. It was simply too easy for a husband to divorce his wife, and the sages were opposed to this, declaring that something needed to be done 'so that it will not be a light thing in his view to divorce her'.² The easy divorce was based on two factors, one legal and the other economic. From the legal point of view, the husband knew that he could divorce his wife on almost any pretext. Tractate Gittin in the Babylonian Talmud contains a discussion in which the sages debate the simplest pretext that a man can use in order to divorce his wife. In contrast to the school of *Beit Shammai* that maintained that a claim for divorce must be connected to adultery on the part of the wife, the view of the *Beit Hillel* school was that a husband is entitled to divorce his wife for any reason, even the most trivial, such as overcooking his food.³ From the economic point of view, the husband knew that his family had already paid the *mohar*, that is, the 'price' of his wife and that this money was now in the hands of her family; so he did not worry about any possible future financial damage that a divorce might bring and did not hesitate to divorce his wife if he so wished.

In order to rectify this state of affairs, a new economic legal institution called the *ketubah* was established, whose explicit advantage was that the money paid as the *mohar* became both a fixed amount and one which was frozen and held for the benefit of the woman to be paid to her only at the time of the dissolution of the family unit through divorce or the death of her spouse. From this point on, even young men or those who had no readily available funds with which to pay the prohibitively high cost of the *mohar*, could marry and start a family. On the other hand, a husband could no longer divorce his wife so easily, because this now had financial consequences in the form of the payment he would have to make to his wife upon divorcing her. Furthermore, this sum would have to come from his assets. The community leaders hoped that this payment, which husbands were now obligated to pay their wives, an amount that would be deducted from their assets, would prevent them from divorcing their wives on impulse.

The initial use of such a promissory charter is commonly dated to the end of the second century BCE. At that time the *ketubah* was a promissory note given by the husband to his wife in which he agreed that 'All my property is mortgaged to your *ketubah*.'⁴ The Mishnaic literature written up to the end of the second century CE contains extensive discussions on the *ketubah*, indicating that this new document was widely used. It was enlarged and expanded to include arrangements for all matters pertaining to the newly formed family unit and anything that had to do with the obligations the husband undertook with respect to his wife. Already in the

Mishnaic period, the *ketubah* was defined as the basis of marriage. Rabbi Meir expressed it forthrightly: 'Any man who undertakes to give a virgin less than 200 zuz or a widow less than a *maneh* [100 zuz] is committing an act of prostitution.'[5] Indeed, from that time onward, the *ketubah* became the basis for married life from the standpoint of both the husband's obligations to his wife and the economic foundation of the new family unit.

Since such an important legal document existed to provide for prospective brides, their fathers quickly availed themselves of it. From then on they could protect their daughters from the fundamental inequality that existed between husband and wife. Such an attempt is recorded in Tractate Ketubot (ch. 4 (7–12)), where along with the undertakings of a *ketubah* for his wife, the husband also commits himself to free her if she is taken captive and a ransom is demanded for her release; to take care of her if she falls ill; and to take care of her and her children within the extended family (in polygamous households). Furthermore, in the event of a divorce, he cannot claim that the expenses he incurred on his wife's account are equivalent to the sum he undertook to pay her (her *ketubah* or marriage portion) and then leave her without means of support. In addition, fathers also included the dowry (*nedunyah*) in the *ketubah* contract, that is, the sum total of the assets the woman provides to her husband. In the event that the family unit is dissolved, the property included in the dowry would revert to the woman, even if her husband had been able to benefit from part of the profits derived from these properties during the course of their marriage. If the value of the dowry was high, the husband was required to add to the fixed amount of the *ketubah* (200 zuz for a virgin; 100 zuz for a widow) a sum subsequently referred to as the '*ketubah* supplement', a sum of money stipulated in the *ketubah* which was guaranteed to the wife in order to ensure her economic independence in case of divorce or widowhood. In other words, a document was created that was a promissory note by which a man undertook to fulfil certain obligations to his wife (to provide her with food, clothing and sexual satisfaction), and in which three sums of money were recorded: the *ketubah* itself ('the main portion of the *ketubah*'); the dowry (the assets that the woman brought with her from her parents' home, which remained hers in perpetuity); and an additional sum, which a man undertook to pay in addition to the main portion of the *ketubah* (the *ketubah* supplement). With the introduction of this new institution, the economic status of women within their homes underwent a complete and total change; they were now guaranteed property and money upon becoming divorced or widowed, and were no longer compelled to return, empty-handed, to the parental home.

This contract, which gives form and structure to the new family unit, continued to develop throughout the course of Jewish history, mirroring Jewish social life in general, and the establishment of families and the status of women, in particular. During the Middle Ages, and especially in the countries with which we are concerned here, the amounts stipulated for the dowry and the *ketubah* supplement became uniform and fixed (similarly to what had occurred to the main portion of the *ketubah* itself). In other words, instead of a detailed dowry that each woman brought with her to her marriage and the *ketubah* supplement, which every groom undertook to provide his wife, a uniform and fixed sum was designated for all of these amounts. This sum was called the *kitzotah*, the term used in the Talmud to designate the fixed amount of the *ketubah* itself. And similarly, the reason given for this decision in the Middle Ages was the same as that used to establish a uniform sum for the main portion of the *ketubah*: it was so as not to humiliate any person who could not afford more.⁶ This phenomenon is especially curious given the fact that the logic behind the *ketubah* contract is to guarantee the financial status of a woman in the event of divorce or widowhood; therefore, the sum of money associated with the dowry or the supplement should correspond to the woman's financial situation and status at the time of her marriage. The advent of a permanent supplement was intended to blur the economic disparities between one family and another and between one bride and another.⁷ The large fixed sum produced by means of the contract held by the wife brought about the financial consolidation of the family's resources and prevented the division of its assets into smaller, weaker parts.

During the first half of the twelfth century, Rabbi Eliezer ben Nathan (known by his acronym, Raban) refers to the *kitzotah* in his discussion of the institution of the *ketubah* and the fixed amount of the contract (as discussed in Tbab. Ketubot 54b). The talmudic sages had questioned why the *Mishnah* found it necessary to state that the amount of the *ketubah* is 200 zuz and that whoever wants to add to that amount may do so, since this is clear and self-evident to all. Their answer was that attention must be given to ensuring that at least the main portion of the *ketubah*, which is obligatory for all, should be uniform, following the talmudic injunction, cited above, proscribing humiliation of someone who has not the means to offer more. In the opinion of Raban, the sages were applying this rule in his day (the Middle Ages) to all the amounts in the *ketubah*. As it was then, so it is now; the amendment was made for the benefit of the woman 'and our forefathers in our kingdom sense the possible humiliation and stipulated the same addition for the rich man and the poor man so as not to humiliate someone who does not have more, and the reason for these rules is to make a law and set a limit so that it will not be a light matter in his [the husband's] view to divorce [his wife]'.[8] Just as the sages had once established the *ketubah* in order to ensure that men would not treat their wives with indifference or disrespect, and stipulated the same amount – which was fixed in the *ketubah* – for both the wealthy and the poor woman, so did the sages in Rabbi Eliezer ben Nathan's time follow the same pattern. And in order to underscore this, they took pains to use the same Mishnaic language when explaining the matter of the *kitzotah*, which is presented as a permanent extra, replacing both the *ketubah* supplement and the dowry.[9]

In order to establish the halakhic logic of this matter and legitimize it, Raban made use of the discussion in Tractate Bava Metziah (104), which cites the opinion of Rabbi Yosé on the method of collecting on *ketubot* and promissory notes where the sum actually paid out exceeded the required amount. Raban compares this to the question of men who agree to record a *ketubah* supplement whose value is far greater than their brides' dowries in order to enhance their respect for their brides. In explaining his views about 'What was the common practice', i.e. to record in the women's *ketubot* £50 (the text actually refers to *litrin*, probably a local currency, translated here as 'pounds'), even if they had brought with them only £4, he relied halakhically on Tractate Ketubot (66), which states that often what is recorded in the *ketubah* and in the dowry is not in fact the sum that enters [the family unit] but a different amount. In the end, however, the amount paid out is exactly the sum total of what was brought into the marriage and not the recorded amount.[10] In addition to the halakhic aspect, Raban adds that it is also the practice among grooms to record in the *ketubah* an amount at least three times greater than that which the bride brought with her:

> the last generation hastened to create the ruling for the women of Israel, so that it should not be easy in the eyes of their husbands to divorce them, and made the rule about the *ketubah*, whether small or large, that all alike wrote an equal dowry, as well as the *ketubah* supplement, that adds the rule of equality for small and large alike, and what is collected by the poor woman is the same as that of the rich one.[11]

It was known to all that the amounts written in the *ketubah* and the *ketubah* supplement were standard formulas and the actual payments made were not revealed.

This approach remained in practice in succeeding generations in the regions under discussion here (northern France and Germany) and we learn about it from numerous instances in which the husband evidently thought to compensate his wife with less than the full amounts of the *ketubah*. These examples introduced the argument about the disparity between what the woman actually brought to the marriage and what the man recorded in the *ketubah* 'in order to enhance his wife's [reputation]'. At the end of the twelfth century, Rabbi Isaac ben Abraham discussed the case of a woman living at that time who wished to free herself from an impotent husband and the query concerned which of the amounts recorded in her *ketubah* she was willing to forfeit in order to facilitate this action. Rabbi Isaac ben Abraham decided that she should naturally receive her dowry; yet the question of the disposition of the *ketubah* supplement was still unresolved. In his decision he notes explicitly 'even though large dowries are written in *ketubah* deeds because a small sum might appear inadequate to all and sundry, the supplement recorded is what really shows [the level of] respect for the bride'.[12]

At the end of the thirteenth century, Rabbi Meir ben Barukh of Rothenburg (Maharam) discussed the matter of a rebellious wife and the question of which of the sums in her *ketubah* would remain in her possession. He noted that:

> it is well known that she did not bring such a large sum to the dowry, instead, it was out of respect that they acted as in the days of the talmudic sages, when they would add [to the amount] … and in this kingdom, it is common practice to record a uniform [amount] for the dowry so that the well-to-do will not get carried away and in order not to shame those who do not have so much, but because she is a rebellious wife, she will have nothing more than what she brought with her.[13]

Since we are dealing with small communities where social relations played a pivotal role in group cohesiveness and the ability to withstand the pressures of the external group (the Christians), the leaders chose to make decisions that reinforced social cohesion in the community. Thus they concluded that, superficially at any rate, a uniform sum should be offered to all brides, whereas specific economic decisions regarding the property brought by the woman to her new home were contained in agreements drawn up by the families prior to the wedding.

The marriage ceremony, too, underwent significant changes during the Middle Ages. In the past, the ceremony had consisted of two distinctly different parts, the *erusin* (engagement) and the *kidushin* (marriage) ceremonies, and the agreements had been signed between the families in private. After the two ceremonies were merged into one formal event, everything became public; thus a new situation was created whereby the groom read the *ketubah* to his bride in public in the presence of the entire community. Everyone could now hear about the economic status of the bride and this went against the basic feelings of the community. For this reason, the communal leaders saw to it that the amounts guaranteed to all the brides were made uniform in public, just as one thousand years earlier; the value of the statutory stipulation of the *ketubah* had been made uniform for all women.

The combination of a change in the marriage ceremony and a more exacting social attitude brought about a complete transformation in the financial status of women. They now possessed a *ketubah* that contained very large sums of money, and in the event of their widowhood they stood to inherit all of their husband's property, thus preserving the family's assets as a complete and undivided entity. The status of the widow changed totally as well. It should be pointed out again that, in order to prevent deception and fraud on the part of the husband, a development took place – starting from the Mishnaic period – whereby the *ketubah*, as a promissory note, held the highest priority as a financial commitment that a man could take upon himself, even over the rights of orphans. In other words, the payment to the widow of her *ketubah* took precedence over any money her late husband had bequeathed to his children. By virtue of this promissory note that she held, the entire sum of the financial obligation recorded in the *ketubah* was transferred to the widow immediately upon her husband's death, even if this constituted the sum total of his financial assets, and she became a very strong financial entity. If she chose not to marry, her economic status remained strong; if she remarried, the property that belonged to her (the property of her family of origin) became, in its entirety, the dowry that she would bring with her to the home of her second (or third) husband. In this way she would continue to be a strong economic force in her new family unit, both because of the financial resources that she brought with her and due to the fact that her *ketubah* contained a *kitzotah* that represented a large amount of money.

Already, in the first half of the twelfth century, Rabbi Eliezer ben Nathan was well aware of the power of the widow and turned to Tractate Ketubot (96a) for support in this issue: 'A widow who took possession of property for her upkeep or for [payment of] her *ketubah* may keep what she has taken and the sages do not have the power to take it away from her.'[14] He encountered the problem of a widow who claimed money belonging to her husband, money that was held by the husband's uncle, his father's brother. Before his death, the husband had asked his uncle to transfer this money (a substantial sum) to his father, a request which the uncle in fact carried out. Then the widow demanded the money, which her late husband had given him for safekeeping, from the uncle. Rabbi Eliezer ben Nathan wrote a lengthy response to this query, explaining why, in this case, the uncle acted appropriately in retaining the money.

Nonetheless, his explanation reflects the strength of the widow's ability to gain control over the family's property.[15]

The *responsa* literature of the Middle Ages bears witness to the power of the widow to gain control over her late husband's assets, claim them as her own, and retain them. Numerous testimonies about the attempts of orphans to gain possession of their late father's valuable property, which was in the hands of his widow, are available. Books are an example of the type of valuable property taken by widows. We are told that in one case a widow took possession of her late husband's books in order to collect her *ketubah* portion. The children of the deceased tried to prove that they had in their possession a deed predating their father's marriage to this woman which gave them ownership of the books.[16] Not unexpectedly the widow claimed that they had taken more than what they were entitled to according to the sums recorded in the *ketubah*, because the husband, on his deathbed, had given them presents that were part of his property.[17]

At the end of the thirteenth century, Rabbi Meir ben Barukh of Rothenburg also dealt with this issue. He received a query from *dayanim* (judges), who apologized in their letter for approaching him, since 'great sages have already ruled [in this matter]'. Nonetheless, they declare that, 'we have knotty legal problems here and we have need of your opinion'. The main issue was a financial dispute between an heir and a widow, who had taken control of all her husband's property and was holding on to it. The son claimed that his father had promised him £30 before he died, whereas his mother denied this, arguing that she had spent large sums of money on his education before he became thirty. The son maintained, further, that his mother had made a promise to his wife, which had been sealed with a handshake, that she, the mother, would continue to support them. The mother denied this completely. In practice, the stronger party in such a dispute is always the widowed mother, who claims that she is collecting whatever she deserves according to her *ketubah*. We even have testimony concerning a son who threatened to seek justice from the non-Jewish authorities in order to compel his mother to return funds and property that she had appropriated.[18]

The power of the widow was so great that in one case, in the city of Boppard, a widow refused to transfer part of her husband's property to his heir, even though there were witnesses to the fact that the father had bequeathed this property to his son and that the mother had agreed to the father's decision when he was still alive. Rabbi Hayim ben Isaac of Vienna came to the aid of the son, but only after the heir started a *bitul tefilah* (disruption of public prayers) protest to bring pressure on the community so that they would persuade Rabbi Hayim to make a decision in this matter.[19] It is, therefore, not surprising those men who were about to die did everything in their power to ensure that parts of their property were transferred to their heirs before their death, a measure which they hoped would guarantee the routine process of inheritance and prevent their wives from gaining complete control over all their property.

Rabbi Meir ben Barukh of Rothenburg (Maharam) cited as an example a *responsum* that he had in his possession, which was attributed to Rabbenu Gershom Me'or HaGolah (i.e., from the beginning of the eleventh century). It dealt with two partners who were both far away from home, one of whom was about to die. While on his deathbed, the dying partner hurried to give his associate a list of instructions concerning his property, in effect, a document designed to transfer his property to his children before his wife could claim it as hers.[20] Maharam also documented several cases of this nature that he himself had encountered. A man, who had married twice, had a daughter from his first marriage and two sons from his second marriage. The man became gravely ill and attempted with every means available to guarantee some property to his daughter from his first marriage. Along with a friend, he devised various schemes for transferring property to this daughter and to his sons, so that his present (second) wife would not be able to gain control of this property as well.[21] In another instance, Rabbi Meir ben Barukh describes a situation in which a concerned father, aware of the strained relations between his only son and his wife, attempted to give his son a will while still alive, since he knew that his wife, when widowed, would take control of all his property and his only son would have to 'go begging from door to door'.[22]

In the event of divorce, the husband and wife would arrive at a logical division of property so that she would be able to free herself from him and each of them could build a new family unit. The basis for this was evidently the self-same agreement, discussed in the *responsa* literature, which they had made prior to their marriage.[23] When this process was completed, it was clear that two provisions had to be made to uphold it. One was that the man could not divorce his wife easily, hence Raban quotes a ruling according to which the man cannot divorce his wife against her will (see below). Secondly, the entire proceeding was to be carried out by mutual agreement; most likely, this also led to an agreement regarding the division of the family assets. And one confirmation of this is the dearth of *responsa* dealing with property disputes between spouses during the divorce procedures.

The improvement in their economic status had profound effects on women's social standing. From the legal point of view, the situation changed dramatically because women could no longer be considered as persons with no legal standing, since they possessed (even if potentially) a great deal of property and money. It goes without saying that this new set of circumstances also reflected on their economic potential. A woman's strong economic position was achieved with the help of her *ketubah* and dowry, and as a widow she was able, in practice, to take control of the familial assets. Hence, we hear about numerous women who lent money (either for interest or on the basis of a pledge) to Christians.[24]

Again it is Raban who highlights this change for us in his response to a query sent to him in the first half of the twelfth century. The claimant gave an item to a woman as a deposit for safekeeping and when he asked for its return, the woman declared that it was no longer in her possession. The plaintiff demanded that the woman swear she no longer had the item and that she had not made use of it for her own needs, or compensate him for it. The woman's husband presents an argument based entirely on the Talmud and the status of women that it reflects. He tries to dismiss the entire matter by relying on the talmudic provision in Gittin, 'What a woman acquires belongs to her husband.'[25] Furthermore, he maintains that, since he is responsible for her, she cannot be sued, and most important, he demands that she should not have to appear in court because this would be unseemly for her. Rabbi Eliezer ben Nathan's response invalidated one by one all of the husband's claims. Though Raban's arguments derive from Mishnaic and talmudic discourses, it is noteworthy that he regards the economic status of women in his era, the twelfth century, as widely divergent from that of the talmudic period. He asserts that, 'It appears to me that there is no substance in what the husband is saying ... all the more so now, at a time when women act for themselves, run shops, deal in commerce and moneylending and banking, making and repaying pledges. And if we were to say that they may not commit themselves to undertakings and promises concerning commerce and business, others could not conduct business with them.'[26]

A careful examination of the facts revealed in both the query and the response makes it clear that women played a major role in economic life. They had become a vital element of the general economic force that could not be ignored; moreover, the tone of the response makes it quite plain that, at that time and in this place, things had changed.

Status within the family

The twelfth century witnessed fundamental changes in the status of Jewish women as far as their relationships with their husbands and within the family is concerned. Two Rulings[27] gave rise to this new state of affairs.

One Ruling stipulated that a man cannot marry more than one wife, while the second declared that a man may not divorce his wife against her will, and in the words of that era: 'If the woman does not agree, there is no validity to the *gett*' (bill of divorce).

The combination of these two rulings produced a fundamental change. Although the first Ruling instituted monogamous marriage in the Ashkenazic communities, men were already being deterred from taking a second wife because of the extra sections that had been added to the *ketubah*. At the same time, Jews living in other regions had developed different methods to prevent polygamy.[28] What was innovative about this Ruling, however, was that it prohibited polygamy from the outset and that it was universally applied. Moreover, it was merged with the second Ruling, which made the divorce dependent on the wife's acquiescence. In order to comprehend the ultimate significance of this change in the male consciousness, we must first understand the extent to which the change affected the entrenched and basic structure of Jewish society's fundamental values; second, we must clarify when the change took place; and third, we must chart the opposition to the change.

The uniqueness of these Rulings lies in the extent of their incompatibility with and divergence from talmudic-based *halakhah*, as well as the complexity of their link to other areas of *halakhah*. The attitude of the Babylonian Talmud, which shaped the Jewish mechanisms for establishing and dismantling the family unit, is exactly the opposite of the viewpoint promulgated by these Rulings. The ability of a man to marry more than one woman is a matter of *halakhah* established in the Babylonian Talmud on the basis of one of the most famous *amoraim*, Rava, who lived in the middle of the fourth century. Rava permitted polygamy on the condition that a man lives up to the responsibilities he took upon himself in the *ketubah*, that is, to provide food, shelter and clothing of an appropriate standard as well as regular sexual relations.[29] This decision on the part of Rava contradicted the opinion of Rabbi Ammi, an *amora* of Eretz Yisrael of the preceding generation, who had made an attempt to rule that a man who marries a second woman should first divorce his previous wife and pay off her marriage contract.

Here, Rava is voicing a 'male decision' that was congruent with the male's social standing in the talmudic era and with his own perception regarding the fulfilment of the commandments. A man was obligated to fulfil the commandment of procreation ('Be fruitful and multiply', Gen. 1:28)) and for this reason the *halakhah* permitted him to divorce his wife after ten years, if it transpired that she was barren. Men were even permitted to take another wife long before those ten years were up. It was also incumbent upon a man, from a religious point of view, to perpetuate his brother's name, if he died childless. In this instance, a man was supposed to marry his brother's widow (this is termed a levirate marriage, or *yibbom*, and he a levir) and the child born of this union would be named after the dead brother, thus perpetuating his name. In such cases, the fact that the living brother was married did not stand in the way of performing this commandment, since he could marry more than one woman.

Now, after the acceptance of these two Rulings, a situation was created whereby it was not always possible to fulfil the two above-mentioned 'male' commandments. A man, who was obliged to perform the commandment of procreation, could not take another wife while married to a barren spouse, and neither could a married man, obliged by the levirate marriage commandment, marry another woman (his late brother's wife) in order to fulfil his halakhic obligation. What would be the fate of these two commandments after this dramatic change? Did the Ruling have the power to invalidate and annul these explicit biblical commandments?

A study of the subject of divorce in the Babylonian Talmud makes it clear that the numerous discussions dealing with the *gett* (bill of divorce), its form, the manner in which it is given to the woman, etc., are based on the unequivocal Mishnaic assumption that 'The situation of the man who gives a divorce is different from that of the woman, for a woman is divorced with or without her consent, while a husband can divorce his wife unilaterally.'[30] Now that a husband must obtain his wife's consent to her divorce, the overall attitude towards this issue changed.

Scholars often tend to give weight to the Ruling that prohibits polygamy because they believe that it is the basis for the Jewish community's transformation from a polygamous to a monogamous society. In practice, most of the sources available to us indicate that Jewish society in Christian Europe had become unquestionably monogamous before the issuing of the Ruling. The impact of the surrounding Christian population on Jewish society in this regard is unmistakable. In those regions where the laws from the era of the Roman Empire continued to hold sway, Christians were monogamous, and the same held true for the Jewish society living in their midst. In all areas where Jews lived among Christians, they adapted their patterns of family life to the life style of their environment. Already at the end of the fourth century, Theodosius published an edict (30 December 393) that prohibited Jews from marrying 'several women at the same time'. The law dealt with both the *mos* and the *lex* of the Jews, that is, both the customs and laws associated with marriage, the rituals of the marriage ceremony, the ties of kinship between bride and groom, and even the age of marriage. The Jews adopted the principles of the Roman law where they regarded it as a practical matter, such as a monogamous way of life, but as far as in-group customs are concerned, they continued to live according to their own traditions. One generation after the promulgation of this edict, in the second half of the fifth century, a Christian observer[31] commented that the situation among his Jewish neighbours had indeed undergone a change. When Theodosius, while commenting on Paul's instructions in his first Letter to Timothy (III:12) that 'A church helper must have only one wife', he notes that 'in the past both the Greeks and the Jews would enter into marriage contracts with two, three, or even more women at one and the same time. Even now there are those who have sexual relations with concubines and with prostitutes because the imperial laws forbid bigamy.'[32]

During the centuries that followed, the Jews, like their Christian neighbours, observed a monogamous lifestyle. Passages found in Christian literature, which repeatedly mention the prohibition against polygamy, almost always relate to the practices of priests and monks who did not faithfully abide by the ways of celibacy, or those who kept concubines. A close inspection of these sources proves that family life was monogamous, as it had been since Roman times. The legislation passed during the synod of Rome in 826 is introduced with the words 'Nulli liceat uno tempore duas habere uxores uxoremve et concubinam' ('A man shall not be husband to two women, [nor] have a wife and a concubine'). In other words, the prohibition here is not only regarding two 'lawfully wedded' wives, but also two women: a wife and a concubine! This is also the tone conveyed by tenth and eleventh-century sources, and in particular the Decretum written by Burchard of Worms in 1020. Although passionately anti-polygamous in nature, Burchard's work mainly attacks the immoral practices of priests and monks, and enumerates the laws and the cases in which the Church fathers came out against unseemly behaviour, again chiefly that of clerics who kept wives even though they were supposed to be celibate, and the fondness for keeping concubines along with lawful wives. According to Burchard having a wife and a mistress at the same time was a promiscuous lifestyle, since the lay population followed a monogamous way of life.[33]

Jewish behaviour as regards this matter, that is to say, the adoption of the practice of the surrounding population, is very clear. The Jews abandoned the option of polygamy, a behaviour conspicuously divergent from that of the Christian population, especially when in any event most of them had already given up this costly and problematic preference. In contrast to this, they did not desist from their own in-group customs that were less noticeable from the outside. This sort of behaviour mechanism is familiar to us from other places. When the Jews of Spain lived under Islamic rule, polygamy was not considered a special problem; but later, when they came under Christian hegemony, this was looked upon as a serious deviation from the norm. At that time, the Jews gradually abandoned polygamy and reinforced monogamous trends already extant in their culture and law books. Writing in the second half of the fourteenth century, Rabbi Isaac bar Sheshet, expressed it bluntly: 'Anyone who marries another woman while still being married to his wife, is writing his own death warrant [i.e., will surely be condemned by the authorities], unless he is granted permission [to do so].'[34] In the sources available to us from northern France and Germany, it appears that even before the twelfth century, the Jewish family was monogamous. When the Jews commemorated the hundreds of their brethren who died during the First Crusade in 1096 in the towns in the Rhine valley, either at the hands of Christians or as martyrs in the sanctification of God's name, it is clear that all Jewish families were monogamous units.[35]

The person who brought about this change, towards the middle of the twelfth century, was Rabbi Eliezer ben Nathan (Raban), who was born in 1090 and at the age of six experienced the traumatic events first-hand, with the assaults on the Jews of his town, Mainz. Rabbi Eliezer ben Nathan transformed the status of women completely by developing the two Rulings we mentioned above – prohibiting bigamy and divorce without mutual consent. He supported this social change with halakhic explanations and set aside its inherent difficulties. He was the first to mention both aspects of the Ruling and the first to neutralize its main threat, the commandment of procreation, while providing a very legitimate explanation, which enables the Rulings to be put into practice. In addition, it was Raban who, as we have seen, makes the important economic status of women very clear.

We must, therefore, conclude that this process actually began during his lifetime and that he was its architect. Until then, the two Rulings related to women had never been mentioned, neither as Rulings, nor as a topic for study or discussion in the halakhic literature that has been preserved. The Jewish family was, as a rule, monogamous, at least this was how it was perceived by both males and females; and problems posed by exceptional circumstances were solved without referring to any Ruling whatsoever. The Rulings actually appear in the sources towards the middle of the twelfth century, under the title 'Rule of the communities' (*takanat ha-qehilot*), in other words, a Ruling that requires the attention of all

Jewish communities. But another generation went by before, towards the end of the twelfth century, this rule was ascribed to Rabbenu Gershom Me'or ha-Golah, a highly respected and authoritative figure working in the early eleventh century. That is to say, an attempt was made to establish the Ruling and provide it with a sound basis by ascribing it to a prominent and highly esteemed figure who died about three generations earlier.

However, three documents from the eleventh century dealing with problems associated with polygamy demonstrate that such an attribution was not grounded in fact. The first is a *responsum* of Rabbenu Gershom Me'or HaGolah, who died in 1028. A woman complains that her husband has married another woman. The woman was 'unyielding' and demanded her *gett* and *ketubah*.[36] In other words, she insisted that her husband divorce her and give her all the amounts he was obligated to pay her according to her *ketubah*. The man claimed that he did not want to divorce his first wife: 'I wish to act towards you according to the "law of wives" and, since you are old, I married another woman who will bear children for me, and I will give you neither a *gett* nor [your] *ketubah*.' He obviously realized that it was not common practice to marry more than one woman, otherwise he would not have presented a legal argument for his actions. Knowing that his first wife would not be able to give him any children, 'since she was old', he allowed himself to deviate from the norm and marry another woman. This man was certain that, by virtue of the commandment of procreation, which he, and not his wife, was obligated to perform, he would be able to adjust the prohibition against bigamy to suit his cause. He did not want to divorce his wife. In his argument he declares that he wished to act according to the 'laws of wives', a term defining the obligations of a husband to his wife as deduced from Exodus 21.

Furthermore, the husband did not mention that his wife was barren. It is plain that he, like other men in a similar situation, wanted to remain with her. The woman's declaration, too, makes it clear that men do not normally marry more than one woman; therefore, she feels herself free 'to be unyielding'. Since she knows what the normal practice is, she does not bring any citations to support her argument. In her opinion, it is quite obvious that the talmudic law is not valid and that a man cannot take more than one wife, even if he claims that his wife is barren or 'old' and unable to bear him children. She believes that if he does marry another woman, he must free her and return to her all the property that she brought to the marriage, in addition to paying her all the amounts recorded in her *ketubah*.

In his response, Rabbenu Gershom Me'or haGolah did not permit the man to marry another woman. Nevertheless, he declares the woman a *moredet* (rebellious wife),[37] thus allowing him to divorce her while repaying only the dowry which she brought with her to the marriage. Yet, she forfeits the main portion of the *ketubah* and the supplement, because she was declared a rebellious wife. Rabbenu Gershom Me'or haGolah maintains that, according to talmudic law and the declarations of Rava, a man may have more than one wife. However, on the basis of the statements made by the *geonim*,[38] he was cognizant of the problematic nature of this situation – a woman who refuses to have conjugal relations with her husband – and recommends that the couple be separated as quickly as possible. In this way, although Rabbenu Gershom Me'or ha-Golah permits the man to divorce his wife against her will on the basis of the concern about his being unable to perform the commandment of procreation, he makes sure that the woman leaves with part of her property.[39]

The second *responsum* makes it very clear that Rabbenu Gershom Me'or haGolah believed that the commandment of procreation, incumbent upon the male, was of utmost importance. In addition, he thought that it was the wife's function to help her husband fulfil this commandment. Nevertheless, he did not think that a man should be married to more than one woman at the same time in order to satisfy this commandment. He preferred to permit the man to divorce his wife and then marry another, with whom he could fulfil the commandment, as was his duty. Moreover, he put great stress on the talmudic law which stipulates that a man whose wife is barren may divorce her only after ten years of marriage. Rabbenu Gershom Me'or HaGolah expressed this opinion explicitly when he was called upon to solve a dispute between a husband and wife who were married for five years without producing any offspring. The woman did not have a fixed menstrual period. (She menstruated once every six weeks three times consecutively, and then four months went by without a period, and then she would menstruate again once every six weeks three times and again there would be a lapse of four months with no menstruation.) The husband concluded that he would never be able to have children with his wife and sought permission to divorce her. Rabbenu Gershom Me'or HaGolah ruled that the man could not divorce his wife before ten years had elapsed, and then he would have to pay off her marriage contract.[40] As in the previous case, this woman assumed that a man cannot have two wives; her husband, too, was not considering the possibility of taking an additional wife. The woman did not quote any Ruling to support her argument; instead, she maintained that her irregular menstrual periods were a matter of her husband's bad luck: 'Your luck is the cause.' In his discussion, Rabbenu Gershom Me'or HaGolah emphasizes that, after ten years of childless marriage, the man must be compelled to divorce his wife and give her the *ketubah* portion, because if they are not forced to separate, the husband will continue to believe that his wife might still have a child and he will not try to find another woman.⁴¹ Here we see that men were inclined to remain with their wives and not divorce them.

In France as well as in Germany, Jewish households were monogamous, because they adopted the custom of the Christians. There is no evidence of polygamous marriages, apart from one atypical case mentioned by Rashi (Rabbi Solomon ben Isaac, 1040–1105). A certain Yizhak, was seeking to inherit his late father's entire estate, yet his father had two wives. The first one was barren and after ten years, the father married another woman with whom he did have children. The father, who was survived by both his wives, declared in his will that his first wife could live out her days in his house. When she felt that her death was at hand, she realized her rights to the house in a court of law ('swore on her *ketubah*') and left it to her brother's son. The aforementioned son of the second wife claimed that the house was part of his inheritance.⁴²

Rabbi Eliezer ben Nathan (Raban), relating to the discussion between Rava and Rabbi Ammi (Yevamot 65) about the number of women it is appropriate for one man to marry and the commentary concerning Rava's statement permitting polygamy, declares simply and emphatically that: 'Now [in his day], when the 'rule of the communities' is that a man cannot marry another woman in addition to his wife nor can he divorce his wife [against her will], we do not act according to these practices.'⁴³ Rabbi Eliezer ben Nathan is the first to mention these Rulings, defining them as the 'rule of the communities', i.e., Rulings that were accepted by the communities themselves and recognized by their members. He discusses the processes that led to the instituting of the Rulings, and the fact that they were all-embracing because of the many and varied needs of the Jews living at the turn of the eleventh and twelfth centuries. He also takes pains to complete the halakhic structure of the change while breaking down the most problematic halakhic point connected with it, namely, the commandment of procreation (and the extremely powerful halakhic authority associated with it), which allowed a man to divorce his wife without her consent and to marry more than one woman so as to carry out this duty.

In order to put this change into practice and give it legitimacy, Rabbi Eliezer ben Nathan expands the talmudic discussion. The Talmud stipulated that the family unit must be dismantled after ten years of the wife's childlessness.⁴⁴ This ten-year time span was adopted on the basis of the biblical precedent: Abraham (or Abram as he was then called) took Hagar as a wife (in addition to Sarah) only 'after Abram had dwelt in the land of Canaan ten years' (Gen. 16:3). The *amoraim* (the sages of the Talmud), who calculated the time intervals in Genesis, explained that the ten years mentioned is not the total amount of time that Abraham lived with Sarah up to then, but the number of years in which the coupled dwelled in *Eretz Yisrael*. The years in which the couple lived outside *Eretz Yisrael* were not included in the calculation of the duration of Sarah's barrenness. Rabbi Eliezer ben Nathan used this discussion to support his contention that the entire matter of divorcing a childless woman is connected to *Eretz Yisrael* and is not practiced outside its boundaries; in this way, he actually negates the importance of the commandment of procreation outside of *Eretz Yisrael*. Hence, he declares, 'In our time, no one must be compelled to divorce because of the commandment of procreation.'[45]

To support this halakhic change, he adds a brilliant rhetorical explanation. According to what is written in the Talmud, after the destruction of the Temple, it would have been fitting to refrain from marrying altogether, and, naturally, to stop bringing children into the world. 'However, statutes should not be introduced unless most of the populace is willing and able to abide by them.'[46] Hence, from the point of view of our discussion, the special status given to the commandment of procreation was revoked after the destruction of the Second Temple, because, in the aftermath of this event, the Jews should have refrained from bringing children into the world. Since it is impossible to prevent the continuation of the human species completely, people continued to have children; now, however, no court of law could force someone residing outside *Eretz Yisrael* to divorce his childless wife, because procreation was no longer an obligation. It follows that no court would now permit a man to marry a second wife for that purpose. This explication provided a solid foundation for the Ruling that prohibited polygamy and non-consensual divorce, and served as a counterbalance to the commandment of procreation that had been a threat to the Ruling from the outset.

Raban went on to posit his views also in respect to other issues. When his son-in-law, Rabbi Yoel, asked him if one may extrapolate from Tbab. Tractate Yevamot (21a) – according to which a man is forced to divorce the woman he married if she is forbidden to him (because she is too close a relative, or he is a priest and so prohibited from marrying a widow) – that one can coerce a man into divorcing his childless wife Raban answers unequivocally in the negative. He points out that a man who married a woman prohibited to him transgresses against a biblical precept, and it is for this reason that the sages decided that in such cases the man must be compelled to divorce his wife. When a woman, for whatever reason, had no children it is said: 'he is not entitled to divorce her'. We cannot force a man to divorce his wife because we do not know conclusively that she is barren; perhaps the husband is unable to father children. This is the first time that an argument is put forward against divorcing a wife on the grounds of childless marriage since it may well be the fault of the man and not the woman.[47] Obviously, such a hypothetical argument could only be made if men were monogamous, since, if a man had two wives and did not have any children with either of them, it would have been almost certain that the problem was his.

Raban also dealt with the problematic issue of a 'rebellious wife' in a way that eliminated the fundamental difficulty associated with polygamy. He asserted that when polygamy was permitted, the process of dealing with a 'rebellious wife' was often protracted, going through many stages, as explained in the Talmud.[48] Now, when the 'rule of the communities' has established that a man may marry only one wife, the long and drawn-out process associated with a rebellious wife need not take place and she should be freed immediately, that is, the husband should be forced to divorce her.[49]

In order to understand the mechanisms that led to the change, we must attempt to understand why it was introduced, and why at this particular time. The reasons given by scholars are many and varied; however, what they have in common is that they are not supported by the historical sources. Eppenstein suggests that Jewish immigrants may have come to Germany from the East and that the Jews of Ashkenaz quickly instituted a Ruling. He does not, however, support his argument with any proof of such a migration. Baron puts forward the possibility that written documents from the East may have reached Ashkenaz and that the Ashkenazi Jews hastened to create this Ruling in order to curtail any impact these writings may have had. He, too, fails to bring any proof for this theory. Friedman demonstrates, quite convincingly, that the Ruling echoes a tradition from *Eretz Yisrael* from the teachings of Rabbi Ammi, but this does not explain why the Ruling was instituted at this particular time and place. Grossman suggests that it was intended to prevent Jewish travelling merchants from marrying over and over again in every place they visited. Yet again, there is no proof to support this theory and it does not explain why Jewish merchants in other locations did not develop as decisive a Ruling as this one. Falk offers the suggestion that the Ruling should be regarded as the outcome of the Christian influence, while Westreich asserts that developments within the Jewish society itself led to its institution. Yet, neither of these theories provides an explanation as to why the Ruling was enacted at this particular point in time.[50]

THE FAMILY AND THE CHANGE IN WOMEN'S STATUS

As I have shown, in order to find the explanation for the advent of this Ruling, we must look at Rabbi Eliezer ben Nathan's environment, his era and its problems, concentrating on the period in which he became recognized and respected and was active (c. 1120–1150). In other words, we are looking at the generation that rehabilitated itself very quickly after the destruction in the area of Worms, Mainz and Cologne in the wake of the First Crusade. There is no doubt that this Ruling is connected with the efforts made in this and in subsequent generations to strengthen sub-groups within the Jewish communal system, particularly those intended to bolster the status of women.

Rabbi Eliezer ben Nathan called the Ruling the 'Rule of the Communities' and formulated it plainly and succinctly: '[A man is] not permitted to marry another woman in addition to his wife, or to divorce his wife [against her will].'[51] The process by which this Ruling was established in the twelfth century involved the publication of a local communal Ruling which had earned the approval of the members of the community. But when a local ruling proved to be ineffective because people could circumvent it by moving to a different community, it became necessary to devise a Ruling that would be applied in a more universal manner and to make sure that it was jointly approved by as many communities as possible. Indeed, in a later generation, one man (whose wife was mentally deranged) moves from Ashkenaz to Provence in order to request permission to marry another woman, and another man, taking his wife with him, goes from France to Castille in order to take a second wife.[52]

Two mechanisms existed for creating general Rulings that could be enforced in a large number of communities. They could either be effected by means of ongoing and detailed correspondence between *dayanim* (judges) over a widespread geographical area, or by attaining the agreement of *dayanim* who would meet together from time to time.[53] Raban believed that Rulings dealing with marriage and family life had to be universal and generally accepted, and this was the reason why he designated the Ruling 'the rule of the communities', the term used by members of his generation, as well as by the older members of the following generation: Rabbi Eliezer ben Samuel of Metz and Rabbi Yom Tov ben Isaac of Joigny, who killed himself in York in 1190.[54] The need for the Rulings to be accepted explains why they were attributed to Rabbenu Gershom Me'or ha-Golah, which provided them with the necessary age and venerability and purged them of novelty. During the course of the twelfth century, despite Raban's determination, men strenuously opposed the change imposed by the double Ruling. As always, their main concern was the commandment of procreation, and they used it to attempt to restrict the scope of the Ruling's jurisdiction.

At the end of the twelfth century, such an attempt was made by means of the query written by Rabbi Simhah ben Samuel, who sent it to Eliezer ben Yoel haLevi of Bonn and to the 'octogenarian Rabbi Ephraim'.[55] Rabbi Simhah asks permission to waive the Ruling for a man whose wife has become mentally deranged so that he may marry another woman so that he will not die without leaving a male heir. In other words, he was asking for the Ruling to be annulled in the name of the commandment of procreation. This *responsum* implies that when the *dayanim* realized that the wife was indeed insane, they forbade the man to live with her or to have sexual relations with her. They were apparently concerned that the woman, who was not responsible for her actions, would also not be able to maintain the laws of *niddah* (connubial purity); furthermore, it was evidently impossible to have another woman supervise her in these matters on a regular basis (as suggested in the Talmud Tbab. Tractate *Niddah* 13b). Rabbi Simhah questions whether this man will be able to give his wife a *gett* and wonders whether he will not end up 'remaining with her to the end of his days without being able to perform the commandment of procreation'.

As to the *gett*, the solution is difficult and problematic, because it is questionable whether such a *gett* would be valid even without the Ruling prohibiting non-consensual divorce. The *Mishnah* had already prohibited, in principle, divorcing a mentally deranged wife (Tbab. Yevamot 112b), for two reasons. First, the dictates of the Torah must be fulfilled precisely. Since, in regard to the *gett*, which is given to the woman, it is stated in Deuteronomy (24:1) that he 'hands it to her', an insane woman is legally incapable of receiving a *gett*.[56] Second, the husband was the person responsible for the health and welfare of his wife. Even if he marries another woman, his first wife would have to remain under his care and he would be required to safeguard her interests, making sure that she was not enticed by anyone she might happen to meet and that no one took advantage of her or harmed her because of her illness. Hence, he was not entitled to divorce her. Even if a woman was not insane all the time, she could not be given a *gett* even during a temporary remission.

Rabbi Simhah claimed that this situation was logical so long as a man could marry another woman. After the Ruling prohibiting bigamy had been introduced, he asserts, a halakhic solution had to be found to free such a man so that he might marry another woman; this could be done by means of a *gett* drawn up in such a way that it would not be challenged. In order to overcome the fundamental objection to the compulsory divorce of an insane woman, he gives a broad interpretation to the opinion of Rabbi Yohanan in the Babylonian Talmud (Gittin 71b), explaining that in an 'emergency situation' of this sort, it is possible to divorce such a wife if she has a father who can care for her. To complete his argument, he defines the Ruling as a 'vow made in public', which, although generally cannot be breached, may be waived with respect to the commandment of procreation, one of the most important commandments. Moreover, those who formulated this Ruling undoubtedly did not do so with a situation such as this in mind.

In his *responsum*, Rabbi Eliezer ben Yoel haLevi (known by his acronym as the Raviah) rejected these alternatives on the spot. He pointed out that such a claim had already been made by Rabbi Samuel ben Azriel, whose case was similar (his wife was 'truly insane'). Rabbi Samuel ben Azriel attempted to have these Rulings set aside with regard to his situation because they were extremely injurious to him, since he could not marry another woman and, due to his wife's insanity, he could not divorce her. He put pressure to bear on the *dayanim* so that they would allow him to marry; but their determination was that even if he was correct, they did not want to grant his request and bring about a return to the state of affairs that prevailed prior to the institution of the Rulings. In other words, in contrast to the intention of Rabbi Simhah, who sought to alleviate – from the halakhic point of view – the distressing situation of the husband, Rabbi Eliezer ben Yoel haLevi put forward a social perspective whose substance was safeguarding the status of the woman. These Rulings are central to the defence structure available to women and could not be disobeyed. The wording of the *responsum* clearly demonstrates that the sages and *dayanim* of the Middle Ages saw themselves responsible for safeguarding the new status of women. As in Mishnaic times, when the emergence of the *ketubah* gave women new security and improved their status, so too in the twelfth century the sages made sure that the status of women would not be undermined and that men would not treat their wives with disdain and attempt to impair their status. It is clear that the sages were concerned that the arguments relating to the commandment of procreation might well be put forward by men solely as a pretext for waiving the Ruling, when in fact they also had ulterior motives.[57]

The words of Raviah: 'in regard to the Ruling of Me'or Ha-Golah, we do not have the right to grant waivers because there are so many sick and barren women and the commandment to 'be fruitful and multiply' is often not fulfilled, so that we did not recognize a dispute between them' prove that the matter of requests to take a second wife in cases of childlessness had been rendered null and void. Therefore it is obvious that the Ruling would no longer be waived in such cases under any circumstances. Rabbi Samuel ben Azriel was also well aware of this fact and this is why he practised *bitul tefilah* (disrupting prayers) and went from community to community attempting to present his case as being so completely out of the ordinary that the Ruling should be revoked for him. But the sages did not acquiesce. The above quote of Raviah from the end of the twelfth century makes it clear that the approach of his grandfather, Raban, had become solidly entrenched and the claim of loss of ability to perform the commandment of procreation had lost much of its force. It was now accepted was that the talmudic disputation in this regard related solely to *Eretz Yisrael*, and that the circumstances of the Diaspora allowed a husband to remain with his barren wife for more than ten years and that he could not be forced to leave his childless wife.[58]

In the sources dating from the end of the twelfth century, both Rabbi Eliezer ben Yoel haLevi and Rabbi Simhah ben Samuel of Speyer refer to the Ruling that prohibits a husband from divorcing his wife without her consent and taking another wife as the 'Ruling of the *gaon* Me'or Ha-Golah'. Evidently, the objections to the Ruling formulated by Raban were so deep-seated that his grandson, Raviah, realized that the authority of his grandfather was not sufficient. Like many of his generation, he was a great admirer of Rabbenu Gershom Me'or ha-Golah and referred to him in many of his *responsa*. Consequently, he transformed the 'rule of the communities' of his celebrated grandfather to 'the Ruling of the *gaon* Me'or Ha-Golah'; such a revolutionary Ruling had to be attributed an authoritative person of indisputably high standing, who had lived 150 years before, rather than his grandfather, who was only one generation removed.

The efforts to circumvent the Ruling in the name of commandments never ceased. This can plainly be seen in the fragments of Rulings available to us today. As mentioned, Raban formulated the Ruling in a straightforward manner: 'Today, however, when a rule of the communities prohibits polygamy and [non-consensual] divorce, we do not act according to this rule.' 'Now that the rule of the communities is that no man may take a second wife [along with the first one] nor divorce his wife [against her will] we do not follow these dictates.' In later sources, the Ruling proclaimed in the name of Rabbenu Gershom Me'or Ha-Golah contains mechanisms that attempt to delimit it. The first version is: 'The ban decreed by our teacher Gershom against marrying two wives may not be lifted except with the consent of 100 people from three states and even they may not consent to doing this unless they find a manifest reason for lifting the ban, with the proviso that the marriage portion of the wife should be deposited in the custody of a trustee, in cash or in pledges.' This was an attempt to make the lifting of the ban subject to the agreement of 100 sages from different regions, thus making it theoretically possible for the leadership to override the Ruling, but the practicalties of this arrangement were such as to make it unworkable. These 100 sages must come from different locations and one of the Rulings mentions, for example: 'The ban cannot be lifted unless agreement is achieved among 100 people from three different kingdoms, such as Anjou, Normandie, and Ile de France.' But even this remote and unlikely possibility is circumscribed by an explicit statement warning those 100 sages not to agree to do such a thing too easily. This is also the case with the second Ruling: 'And the ban which Rabbenu Gershom formulated prohibiting bigamy shall not be lifted unless there is a reason to do so. In this case as well the *ketubah* portion shall be deposited in cash or in pledges.' Attempts were also made to place restrictions on this Ruling and then to limit these restrictions: 'No man shall be entitled to "toss a *gett*" to his wife without receiving permission from three communities; and if such an event does transpire, the husband, the scribe, and the witnesses shall be excommunicated, as stipulated in the ban of Me'or Ha-Golah.'[59]

The above notwithstanding, by the first half of the thirteenth century, the Ruling, now known as 'the Ruling of Rabbenu Gershom Me'or Ha-Golah', took precedence over the observance of the commandment of procreation. Proof of this change of status may be found in the writings of Rabbi Isaac ben Rabbi Moses from the first half of the thirteenth century. Rabbi Isaac ben Moses was born in Vienna in about 1180 and died in the middle of the thirteenth century. He left the region of his birth and went to the western regions of Germany, driven by a burning desire to study and devour the teachings of the sages then living in Germany and France. He wandered from one sage to another, studying their teachings with great enthusiasm, and collected all that he had learned through his studies and the writings of his teachers. Later on he put all of this material into his book *Or Zarua*, adding his own thoughts and the *responsa*, which he had written during the third and fourth decades of the thirteenth century. According to this compilation, the Ruling, which here is called the 'ban (*gezerah*) of Rabbi Gershom of blessed memory', took precedence over the commandment of procreation and supplanted it. In several places, Rabbi Isaac ben Moses notes that, from the halakhic point of view, a man may take a second wife, however, due to the widespread adoption of the Ruling, this option has now been revoked altogether.[60]

In fact, he completely accepts the situation that developed in the previous generation, i.e., the primacy of the Ruling, and his commitment to it leads him to new halakhic provinces. He once encountered the problem of a woman, who after becoming engaged to a man, had second thoughts and decided that she did not want to marry him. She demanded a *gett*,⁶¹ but the man refused to give it to her. Rabbi Isaac ben Moses determined that it was, of course, impossible to force her to marry him since 'no one should live in the same household with a snake'. He asserted that, because the Ruling was valid at that time and because the man was still obligated to fulfil the commandment of procreation, he had to be forced to agree to divorce the woman. Only in this way could this man free himself of this woman and marry another woman in order to fulfil the commandment. Here, it is not the commandment that determines the direction of halakhic development, but rather the Ruling. Since the Ruling is the halakhic determinant, it supersedes other mechanisms (marrying another woman, for example); hence, the man must divorce the woman, according to her request. Rabbi Isaac ben Moses anticipated that the *Beit din* (rabbinical court) would accept this reasoning when making its determination, and indeed this judgement was the model followed by the court decisions in this case.⁶² In fact, this case set a precedent according to which the position of the woman is favoured over that of the man.

This new state of affairs troubled the next generation of sages in the second half of the thirteenth century, who attempted to reformulate the relationship between the sexes so that this new situation would not give women predominance over men. An example of a discussion on the fundamental elements of this issue can be found in the writings of Rabbi Asher ben Yehiel (Rosh), which date from the end of the thirteenth century. He had turned to the board of *dayanim* (judges) of Mainz, Oppenheim, Worms and Speyer with a question regarding the demands made by a woman with respect to her husband. The case discussed by Rosh is that of a man who, after two years of marriage, discovered that his wife was suffering from epilepsy. Since epilepsy was thought at the time to be a contagious disease, the husband asked permission to divorce his wife, and, because he was poor, he claimed that he could not provide what was promised to her in the *ketubah*. The woman protested that she had been thrown out of his house and demanded that he fulfil the obligations he undertook towards her (as she states: food, clothing, and shelter). Rosh pointed out that if something like this had occurred in the past, the man would have divorced his wife and given her the *ketubah* portion due to her; if he did not have the entire amount of the *ketubah*, he could give her what he had in hand and the rest he would have agreed to pay her according to the decision of the *Beit din*. After the introduction of the ban of Rabbenu Gershom Me'or Ha-Golah, a husband could not divorce his wife against her will, and if he was forced to live with her as her husband, it would prove that the woman was regarded as superior to the man. Furthermore, according to talmudic decisions, if the problem had rested with the husband, he would have been forced to remove his wife from his home and give her the *ketubah* portion due to her, but in a case where the problem rests with the woman, should we force the man to continue to live with her as her husband?

Here, the halakhic question is that of disability, that is to say, a situation in which one of the spouses is found to have a disability that was not known to the other partner prior to the marriage. Since the union between the spouses is based on the premise that both partners fully agreed to it, concealing a disability on the part of one of the parties means that the affirmation given by the other party was based on a fundamental flaw. In such a case, the union itself may be annulled. This problem was discussed in both the *Mishnah* and the *Gemarah*, in Tractates Kiddushin and Ketubot.[63] The conclusions were that a man may divorce a wife who has hidden a disability without paying her the *ketubah* portion, thus causing her great injury. In regard to a husband, after much deliberation and debate, it was decided that the same would apply to a man. In other words, the wife could demand a divorce and release from a union with a husband not only if he had concealed a defect, but also if such a disability emerged during the course of their marriage; the examples given were: becoming blind, having an arm amputated, contracting a skin disease and so forth.

Rosh claimed that it was not possible to tolerate a situation in which the *halakhah* has created a new reality whereby the wife of a man who conceals a defect may dismantle the union between them, whereas the husband of a woman who conceals a defect may not divorce her because a man cannot divorce his wife without her consent. According to the opinion expressed by Rosh at the end of the thirteenth century, the Ruling was meant to correct a situation, which the sages of the generation that introduced the Ruling looked upon as unsatisfactory: where men were treating their wives with disdain, and divorcing them without their consent and on any pretext. Hence, the Ruling saw to it that the power of the woman was put on an equal footing with that of the man 'in the same way that the man does not divorce unless he consents to do so, so too the woman does not leave unless she is willing to do so'. He insists, however, that it does not make sense that the Ruling was meant to put the woman in a stronger position than that of the man, and even to bring about his shirking of the commandment of procreation.[64]

Jewish men were also concerned that women would take unfair advantage of their ability to object to a divorce they were unwilling to accept. This issue came to the fore in connection with the problem of a 'woman who trespasses against the law'. According to the Talmud, a woman who causes her husband to transgress a religious commandment (that is, by serving him food that is not kosher without his knowledge, by lying about her state of *niddah* or *taharah*, etc.), or behaves in a clearly unacceptable manner (swearing, insulting her husband in front of their children, acting in a sexually promiscuous manner, beating her husband, and so forth) should be divorced. Furthermore, if such a woman was allowed to remain with her husband, but transgressed again, she could be divorced without even being paid the value of her *ketubah*.

Rabbi Meir ben Barukh of Rothenburg (Maharam) refused to include these kinds of women within the framework of the Ruling that prohibits divorcing a woman against her will. For this type of women, Rabbi Meir of Rothenburg asserts, there is no need to collect authorizations from several communities, and a husband may divorce such a woman without her consent, in contradiction to the stipulation of the Ruling, because it was inconceivable that the Ruling was created in order to defend such negative behaviour. He comes out against Rabbi Yekutiel, who thinks that, following the enactment of the Ruling, the matter of a 'woman who transgresses against the law' must be decided in a *Beit din*, and that she may be divorced without her consent only according to the definition of the Ruling, supported by an authorization of the communities.

In a detailed *responsum*, Rabbi Meir of Rothenburg (c. 1220–1293) rescinded the halakhic basis of Rabbi Yekutiel's decision. Rabbi Yekutiel had attempted to use the precedent of a case involving a woman who, it was found, did not menstruate, in the case of a 'woman who transgresses against the law'. In the same way that he ruled out non-consensual divorce in the former instance, he also vetoed it in the latter. Maharam declared that the disability of the first woman was not defined as a defect that could serve as a reason for divorce, and, naturally, it was possible that the problem emerged after the marriage, and then 'he was ruined'. A woman who 'transgresses against the law' causes her husband to transgress and she should be punished by means of a non-consensual divorce in order to make a distinction between her and other women.[65] The other examples that Maharam discusses in connection with this issue are even more extreme. In one case, a woman sent her lover to threaten her husband and the lover indeed threatened to kill him. In another instance, a woman was warned about her behaviour; promised to refrain from behaving in that manner, even making a vow in public twice, and then again a third time that she would not repeat her misconduct, but nevertheless transgressed again. With respect to these cases, Maharam affirms, it was not possible that the Ruling was made in order to defend women of this sort against non-consensual divorce, and, of course, they should not be brought before a *Beit din* for the divorce proceedings.[66]

Notes

1. Tbab. Ketubot 82b.
2. Tosefta on Tbab. Ketubot 12a, Tbab. Ketubot 32b.
3. *Mishnah* Ketubot 9:10.
4. Tbab. tractate Ketubot 82b. The Hebrew root of the word *ketubah* is 'writing'.
5. *Mishnah* Ketubot 5;1, Tbab. Ketubot 51a. *Maneh* = 100 zuz. The *maneh* was a weight in gold or silver equal to fifty holy, or 100 common, shekels. The zuz was a coin the value of a denarius.
6. Tbab. tractates Ketubot 54b, Nedarim 4b, 'The Rabbis have fixed a limit in order that the man who has no means is not put to shame.'
7. Eliezer ben Nathan, *Sefer Even haEzer, Sefer Raban*, Jerusalem 1984, p. 261a; Eliezer ben Yoel ha-Levi, *Sefer Raviah*, ed. V. Aptowizer, 4 vols, Jerusalem, 1964, vol. 4, no. 919. Meir ben Barukh, *Sheelot u-Teshuvot ha-Maharam*, Prague edition, ed. M. A. Blakh, Budapest 1895, nos. 442, 673, Meir ha-Kohen, 'Teshubot Maimuniut', in Moses ben Maimon, *Mishneh Tora*, Isut no. 6.
8. Eliezer ben Nathan, *Sefer Raban*, p. 261a.
9. *Teshubot Geonim Kadmunim*, Berlin 1608, no. 65, p. 14. Rabbi Meshulam ben Kalonymus wrote a *responsum*, dating from the middle of the eleventh century, about the custom of equating the amount of the dowry (£50) with that of the *kitzotah* (£50). He describes the case of a man who takes a poor wife; she brings to the marriage £1, and he, in order not to disgrace her (and himself) writes in the *ketubah* that the dowry is £50.
10. In talmudic language: to create a supplementary *ketubah* or to treat the *ketubah* as an ordinary debt.
11. Eliezer ben Nathan, *Sefer Raban*, pp. 200a–200b.
12. Meir ha-Kohen, *Teshubot Maimuniut*, Isut no. 6.
13. Meir ben Barukh, *Sheelot u-Teshuvot ha-Maharam*, Prague edition, no. 442.
14. Eliezer ben Nathan, *Sefer Raban*, p. 264.
15. Meir ben Barukh, *Sheelot u-Teshuvot ha-Maharam*, Prague edition, no. 870.
16. It seems that this is a fundamental issue, because the question appears in *responsa* of Eliezer ben Yoel ha-Levi, *Sefer Raviah*, no. 995, and in *Responsa of the Tosaphists*, ed. A. Agus, New York 1954, pp. 161–163 (no. 80), Sefer Mordekhai, *Bava Batra*, no. 623.
17. Meir ben Barukh, *Sheelot u-Teshuvot ha-Maharam*, Prague edition, no. 870; Meir ben Barukh, *Sheelot u-Teshuvot Maharam bar Barukh*, Lemberg edition, 1860, no. 394; Sefer Mordekhai, Ketubot no. 251.
18. Meir ben Barukh, *Sheelot u-Teshuvot ha-Maharam*, Prague edition, no. 245–247.
19. Bitul tefilah, Disruption of public prayers in order to seek redress of a wrong (mainly a judicial or moral one). See Glossary. Meir ben Barukh, Sheelot u-Teshuvot ha-Maharam, Prague edition, no. 249, 862.
20. Meir ben Barukh, *Sheelot u-Teshuvot ha-Maharam*, Prague edition, no. 861; Sefer Mordekhai Bava Batra no. 589.
21. Meir ben Barukh, *Sheelot u-Teshuvot ha-Maharam*, Prague edition, no. 875, 966; Sefer Mordekhai Bava Batra no. 629.
22. Meir ben Barukh, *Sefer Sharei Teshuvot*, ed. M. A. Blakh, Berlin 1891, p. 165, no. 46; Meir ben Barukh, *Sheelot u-Teshuvot Maharam bar Barukh*, Lemberg edition, no. 232.
23. Meir ben Barukh, *Sheelot u-Teshuvot ha-Maharam*, Prague edition, no. 285; I. Yoval, 'HaHesderim haKaspiyim shel haNissuim beAshkenaz beYemei haBenayim', in

Religion and Economy: Connections and Interactions, ed. M Ben Sasson, Jerusalem 1995, pp. 191-207.

24 Sources from England allow us to see this phenomenon clearly. See, for example, S. Bartlet, *Licoricia of Winchester: Marriage, Motherhood and Murder in the Medieval Anglo-Jewish Community*, London 2009, pp. 72-76.

25 Gittin 77a, literally 'What the woman has purchased her husband has purchased.'

26 Eliezer ben Nathan, *Sefer Raban*, pp. 83-84, no. 115.

27 See *takanot* in the Glossary of Hebrew Terms.

28 Z. W. Falk, *Jewish Matrimonial Law in the Middle Ages*, Oxford 1966, ch. 1; M. A. Friedman, *Jewish Polygamy in the Middle Ages*, Jerusalem 1986, pp. 1-29; E. Westreich, *Transitions in the Legal Status of the Wife in Jewish Law*, Jerusalem 2002, pp. 99-105.

29 Tbab. Yevamot 65a.

30 *Mishnah* Yevamot, 14.1; Tosefta Ketubot 12, Halakhah 3; Yevamot, 123b.

31 A. Linder, *The Jews in Roman Imperial Legislation*, Jerusalem 1987, Law 22, pp. 138-140.

32 A. Linder, *The Jews in Roman Imperial Legislation*, Jerusalem 1987, Law 22, pp. 138-140.

33 J. A. Brundage, *Law, Sex, and Christian Society in Medieval Europe*, Chicago 1987, pp. 176-183, 225; J. M. Wallace-Hadrill, *The Frankish Church*, Oxford 1983, pp. 403-411; Z. Falk, *Jewish Matrimonial Law in the Middle Ages*, ch. 1.

34 Isaac bar Sheshet, *Responsa of Ribash*, no. 509. Rabbi Isaac bar Sheshet was born in Barcelona in 1326, fled in 1391 to North Africa and died in Algiers in 1408.

35 S. Salfeld, *Das Martyrlogium des Nürnberger Memorbuches*, Berlin 1938, pp. 5-12, 101-119.

36 Teshuvot uPsakim, *Responsa et Decisiones*, ed. E. Kupfer, Jerusalem 1973, pp. 222-223, no. 147; Meir ben Barukh, *Sheelot u-Teshuvot ha-Maharam*, Prague edition, no. 485; Gershom ben Judah, *Teshuvot Rabbenu Gershom Me'or haGolah*, ed. S. Eidelberg, New York 1956, no. 42.

37 Woman who refuses to have conjugal relations with her husband. A subject to be discussed more fully later.

38 *Gaon* (pl. *Geonim*), formal title of the heads of the Academies in Babylonia. See the Glossary of Hebrew Terms.

39 It would appear, then, that when Rabbenu Gershom Me'or Ha-Golah wrote this *responsum*, he did not know about the two *takanot*, which later were to be represented as rulings which he himself had formulated.

40 Sefer Mordekhai, Yevamot, no. 113.

41 Tbab. tractates, Ketubot 77a; Yevamot 84 ff.

42 Solomon B. Isaac (Rashi), *Responsa Rashi*, ed. I. Elfenbein, New York 1943, pp. 97-99, no. 74.

43 Eliezer ben Nathan, *Sefer Raban*, p. 245d.

44 Tbab. tractates Ketubot 77a, Yevamot 84 ff.

45 Rabbi Eliezer ben Nathan, *Sefer Raban*, p. 245c, 'And since ten years in *Eretz Yisrael* will be appropriate for procreation, therefore if the man was ill or the woman was ill or both were imprisoned this time is not calculated, and it appears to me that therefore it is not necessary at present to use this time frame to force procreation; and the first ones (our forefathers) did not have to have recourse to it since it is said to be abrogated except in *Eretz Yisrael*.'

46 Naturally Rabbi Eliezer ben Nathan is quoting a somewhat modified version of Tbab. tractate Bava Batra 60b. 'R. Ishmael ben Elisha said: Since the day of the destruction of the Temple we should by rights bind ourselves to neither eat meat nor drink wine, only we do not lay a hardship on the community unless the majority can endure it. And from the day that an 'evil kingdom' has come into power which issues cruel decrees against us and forbids to us the observance of the Torah and the precepts and does not allow us to enter into the 'week of the son', we ought by rights to bind ourselves not to marry and beget children, and the seed of Abraham our father would come to an end of itself. However, let Israel go their way: it is better that they should err in ignorance than presumptuously.'

47 Eliezer ben Nathan, *Sefer Raban*, p. 255d, E. Westreich, *Transitions in the Legal Status of the Wife in Jewish Law*, Jerusalem 2002, pp. 106–109.

48 The woman was threatened that, if she did not return to her husband, she would be given a fine payable out of part of her *ketubah*, and every so often, an additional fine would be imposed.

49 Eliezer ben Nathan, *Sefer Raban*, p. 281c; E. Westreich, *Transitions in the Legal Status of the Wife in Jewish Law*, Jerusalem 2002, pp. 91–95.

50 A. Grossman, *Pious and Rebellious: Jewish Women in Europe in the Middle Ages*, Jerusalem 2001 [Hebrew], pp. 126–129; A. Grossman, *Pious and Rebellious: Jewish Women in Europe in the Middle Ages*, Waltham, MA 2004 [English], pp. 70–77; S. Baron, *A Social and Religious History of the Jews*, Philadelphia 1958, vol. 6, p. 137; M. A. Friedman, *Jewish Polygamy in the Middle Ages*, Jerusalem 1986, pp. 1–21; Z. Falk, *Jewish Matrimonial Law in the Middle Ages*, Oxford 1966; E. Westreich, *Transitions in the Legal Status of the Wife in Jewish Law*, Jerusalem 2002, pp. 90–96.

51 Rabbi Eliezer ben Nathan, *Sefer Raban*, 255d.

52 See the sources in E. Westreich, *Transitions in the Legal Status of the Wife in Jewish Law*, Jerusalem 2002, pp. 137, 177–178.

53 In my opinion, the first method was far more effective. See S. Goldin, '"Companies of Disciples" and "Companies of Colleagues": Communication in Jewish Intellectual Circles', *Vox Iudaica: Communication in the Jewish Diaspora in the pre-Modern period*, ed. S. Menache, Leiden 1996, pp. 127–139.

54 H. Freiman, *Seder Qidushin Wenisu'in*, Jerusalem 1945, p. 39. Scholars dealing with this subject have put forward three possible explanations that describe the origins of this Ruling: it was written by Rabbi Gershom Me'or ha-Golah himself; it was the result of internal Jewish developments, the outcome of the long-term pressure of Christian society that outlawed bigamy, and a process that began in the eleventh century – Rabbenu Gershom's era, when there were still cases of bigamy and no communal opposition in cases where there was a conflict with a commandment – and ended with the promulgation of the ban against polygamy; it was the product of internal Jewish developments alone and Rabbenu Gershom crafted the regulation. Z. Falk, *Jewish Matrimonial Law in the Middle Ages*, A. Grossman, *Pious and Rebellious: Jewish Women in Europe in the Middle Ages*, Jerusalem 2001 [Hebrew], pp. 126–133; E. Westreich, *Transitions in the Legal Status of the Wife in Jewish Law*, Jerusalem 2002, pp. 65–70.

55 Eliezer ben Yoel ha-Levi, *Sefer Raviah*, no. 921. Eliezer ben Yoel Ha-Levi lived 1140?–1220?, the 'octogenarian Rabbi Ephraim' was probably Ephraim of Bonn, who was born in 1132. See in Chapter 3.

56 See Tbab. tractate Yevamot 113b and the Tosafists there.
57 According to Aptowitzer Eliezer ben Yoel, Ha-Levi wrote this *responsum* in 1193–1196, V. Aptowizer, *Introduction to Sefer Raviah* (Eliezer ben Yoel haLevi), Jerusalem 1938, pp. 201–203; Westreich maintained that the committee's decision was made between 1165 and 1172, E. Westreich, *Transitions in the Legal Status of the Wife in Jewish Law*, Jerusalem 2002, pp. 112–119.
58 *Sefer Mordekhai* Yevamot, no. 50. E. Westreich, *Transitions in the Legal Status of the Wife in Jewish Law*, Jerusalem 2002, pp. 114–119.
59 Meir ben Barukh, *Sheelot u-Teshuvot ha-Maharam*, Prague edition, nos 822, 491, 456, 153; *Mahzor Vitry*, ed. S. Horowitz, Nuremberg 1892, p. 798, no. 976; *Sefer Kol Bo*, Lemberg 1860, p. 116.
60 Isaac ben Moses, *Sefer Or Zarua*, vol. 1, Zhitomir 1862, no. 653.
61 A *gett* was required even to break off an engagement when the couple were not yet married.
62 Meir ha-Kohen, Teshubot Maimuniut in Nasim, no. 34; Moses of Zurich, *Sefer haSemak miZurich*, ed. I. J. har-Shosanim, Jerusalem 1973, vol. 3, no. 284, pp. 452–454; Jacob ben Judah Hazan from London, *Ez Hayyim*, ed. I. Brodie, Jerusalem 1962–1964, vol. 3, no. 11.
63 *Mishnah* Kidushin, ch. 2.5; Tbab.Ketubot 77a.
64 Asher ben Yehiel, *Shut haRosh*, ed. S. Yudelov, Jerusalem 1994, no. 42.1.
65 S. Emanuel, 'New *responsum* of Meir ben Barukh', *Mayan*, 38 (1993), pp. 15–18.
66 Meir ha-Kohen Haggahot Maimuniuot on Moses ben Maimon, Mishneh Tora, Hilcot Isut, ch. 24.4; Meir ha-*Kohen*, Teshubot Maimuniut, Nasim, 16; Meir ben Barukh, *Sheelot u-Teshuvot Maharam bar Barukh*, Lemberg edition, nos 245, 393.

5

Marital relations, power, and social standing

Marital relations

In Jewish society, men enjoyed privileged status, which society, the *halakhah* and religion had given them. From Mishnaic times on (the second and third centuries CE), an obvious trend towards rectifying and improving the status of women was advanced by men, who viewed such ameliorations as benefiting the group and averting friction, injustice, opposition, rifts, and harm to its social structure. By examining the male response to the advances women attained, we can get some measure of the intensity of the battle of the sexes within Jewish society. Any strengthening in the status of the woman brought with it a male reaction. As we have seen in the new Rulings on marriage and divorce, discussed above. Thus, following every significant victory for women, we can expect to see an attempt by men to delay its implementation or to find ways of neutralizing the women's gain. The manner in which society dealt with the change, and the opposition to it, are a good window through which to observe the forces at play within the society. The absence of female Jewish sources from the Middle Ages means that an essential element is missing from this discussion; but this lacuna may be partially bridged because of the plethora of male sources on these topics, which indeed reflect the struggle for power and control between men and women within Jewish society.

In the previous chapter, we saw the change that took place in the status of women in the monogamous family and how their independent ability to determine their own fate significantly improved their status, particularly their economic status, generating new opportunities for them. As we have seen, women's position was strengthened by their being protected from divorce without their consent. But how much power did they have to initiate divorce, and how did this change over time?

In the *Mishnah*, various mechanisms were developed to prevent a man from abusing his power over a woman in divorce. For while a woman might have been divorced either with her consent or without it, a man could give a divorce when he is the only consenting party.'¹ In the previous chapter we saw that the *ketubah* was the most important of these mechanisms. Alongside the *ketubah* and in light of the man's obligations in this document, the sages developed additional mechanisms designed to provide a woman with the means of terminating the marital relationship in certain clearly defined cases, and were defined as: 'grounds for divorce on the part of the woman'. In this context, the actual ability of a woman to free herself from her husband is openly addressed in several sources. In Tractate Ketubot, in both the *Mishnah* and the *Gemarah*, a wife whose husband has become repulsive to her is permitted to seek release from her union with him under clearly defined circumstances: the man may be afflicted with boils or have a polypus; he may be malodorous because of a physical defect or due to his occupation, such as a gatherer of dogs' droppings or a copper miner or a tanner who processes skins.²

The last *Mishnah* of Tractate Nedarim (11:12) states: 'At first it was ruled that three women must be divorced and receive their *ketubah*: she who declares "I am impure for you" (meaning she had been unfaithful, but later interpreted in the *Gemarah* as having been raped while married to a *kohen*); or "Heaven is between you and me" (meaning her husband is impotent – something that, apart from herself, can be known only to heaven) and "May I be removed from Jews' (meaning she has vowed not to cohabit with any man, including her own husband, because cohabitation was unbearable for her). But subsequently, to prevent her demanding a divorce when she had simply conceived a passion for another man, that would clearly be detrimental to her husband, the Ruling was changed in the following way: if she declares, 'I am impure for you,' she must bring proof; if she who declares 'Heaven stands between us,' they should engage in prayer (that his impotence may cease), and if she declares, 'May I be removed from Jews,' the husband can annul that part of her vow that refers to him so that she can therefore still cohabit with him, whilst remaining 'removed from (other) Jews'. In this way, three situations in which a wife might cause her husband to divorce her are defined: the wife of a *kohen* (priest) who says that she has been raped; a woman who has vowed not to have sexual relations with any Jews; and a woman who has described her relationship with her husband as 'Heaven stands between us', an expression that was understood either as a declaration that her husband 'does not shoot straight as an arrow' (is impotent), or as a charge that he lacks sexual appetite altogether. According to this *Mishnah*, the rabbinical establishment initially recognized this need and even created a mechanism that enabled women to free themselves from the jurisdiction of their husbands; later on, however, they limited this power. Men began to be concerned that women would exploit this and use the availability of legally defined claims to apply them when they 'conceived a passion for another'. That is to say, they would try to discard their husbands because they wanted to attach themselves to another man and for this purpose they would make use of arguments that would enable them to do so. Thus, the situation was initially to the advantage of the women; however, a form of hostile male reaction developed which curtailed the woman's ability to use her new achievement. All of these grounds were valid and proper provided that they were really true, said the *Mishnah*; however, it went on to ask, what could be done to overcome the problem of a woman who was not in truth suffering from a condition originating with her husband, but was simply seeking to ally herself with someone else? How could such a woman be prevented from abusing the option that had been awarded her? This fear, which the *Beit Din* (rabbinical court) raised – i.e., that women might abuse what had been awarded them – weakened their ability to take advantage of what they had been granted. Thus, the *Mishnah* tells us that at first the *batei din* recognized these grounds, but later on revoked their approval and made the right of women to free themselves from their husbands contingent upon their ability to prove that they were actually suffering as they claimed to be. For example, a woman who claimed that she had been raped must bring proof of this, and if she has made a vow not to cohabit with any man, she must agree that her husband may annul this vow in so far as it relates to him, and then the problem would be solved. In the case of a woman who claimed that 'Heaven stands between us', an attempt should be made to reach a compromise in a process called, literally, 'They will act "by way of request"' (they should engage in prayer). Apparently this means making an effort to deal with impotence by psychological and social means.[3]

This was a particularly difficult situation for a woman, since if she decided on her own to leave her husband or to refrain from fulfilling her obligations towards him she could be defined as a 'rebellious wife', that is, a married woman who refuses to perform one of her wifely duties, or is no longer willing to live with her husband and to have conjugal relations with him. In order to make the rebellious wife desist from this unacceptable behaviour, she was warned that the monetary value of her *ketubah* would be reduced month by month, as would the property that she brought with her from her father's house. If she continued her 'rebellious' behaviour, she would most likely find herself without any compensation whatsoever, even when her husband finally agreed to divorce her, or when Jewish institutions forced him to do so – so that she would be free but destitute.[4] While this was a dire situation for a woman, it was not at all problematic for a man. Prior to the institution of the Ashkenazic ban on bigamy, he could marry another woman and continue to lead a normal life, whereas she would be the principal victim. It became clear that the reform that was supposed to benefit women, the grounds available to them to initiate divorce, could only be activated if male society and the *Beit Din* would allow it. And indeed, the male establishment resisted the success achieved by women and devised mechanisms that weakened their power and, in most of the Jewish communities, the male *batei din* showed no enthusiasm for empowering a woman to exercise her right to force her spouse to give her a divorce.

Another important factor in this power constellation, one related to the Middle Ages, must also be taken into account. Presenting a *gett* and divorcing a woman were predefined as male actions. Deuteronomy (24:1) states explicitly that ' ... and he writes her a bill of divorcement, hands it to her, and sends her away from his house'. Hence, from the legal point of view, it is clear that the *gett* can be valid only if the husband hands it over of his own free will. Although, from a halakhic point of view, a *Beit Din* can force a couple to divorce, because marriage comes under its jurisdiction, they usually avoided compelling a husband to give his wife a *gett*. Their concern in this matter warrants examination. In the Talmud, such a bill of divorcement is defined as 'a *gett* given under compulsion' (Tbab. Gittin 88b). The *batei din* were very uneasy about divorces of this sort because if even the slightest doubt existed that such a *gett* was inappropriate, the coercion would become invalid and the woman would not be considered as being divorced, even though she and any man she may have married later on believed that she was. The result is that a couple could marry and unwittingly bring children into the world who could be *mamzerim*.[5] This fear deterred many sages from attempting to free women with the aid of a *gett* given under compulsion. Indeed, in the Middle Ages, *dayanim* (judges) seldom compelled a husband to give his wife a *gett*. One of the central figures in the twelfth century, Rabbi Jacob ben Meir Tam (Rabbenu Tam), believed that even indirect pressure or threats may result in a *gett* given under compulsion since such actions may cause the husband to give a *gett* involuntarily. Indeed, Rabbenu Tam developed other solutions, as we shall see below. However, the fear of *mamzerut* (creating *mamzerim*) was an essential and central element in his thinking. Other *dayanim* were wary of compelling a husband to grant a *gett* mainly because of the clear and straightforward injunction in the Torah; nonetheless, they did not refrain from suggesting indirect methods of putting pressure on recalcitrant husbands. One way, for example, was to damage his social standing and to give him notice that: 'Sages have already required you to divorce [your wife] and if you do not do so, you may be called a lawbreaker'. Some *dayanim*, however, did not hesitate to force a man to divorce his wife. In their opinion, the Talmud had already defined situations in which action of this sort could be taken against a husband, for example: if he abstained from conjugal relations with his wife; if he abused her in certain ways; if he contracted a serious illness, which she could not endure, etc. Rabbi Yitzhak, the nephew of Rabbenu Tam, obviously upheld this position, which is also recorded elsewhere in the writings of other Tosafists.[6] Although they stressed that 'clear proof' was required, when such evidence existed, they did not hesitate to make a determination permitting the use of coercion and pressure on a husband in order to obtain his consent to a divorce.[7]

On the other hand, women did not hesitate to attempt to free themselves from their marriage on any grounds, despite the problem of the *gett* given under compulsion. An extreme, though typical, example from the end of the twelfth or early thirteenth century tells the story of a man by the name of Shlomo, son of Reb Hananel, whose wife asked for a divorce because her husband was a *petzua daka*.[8] Apparently the *Beit Din* tended to agree with the request made by the woman and her family; consequently, the husband took the desperate step of *bitul tefilah*.[9] His petition ultimately reached Rabbi Eliezer ben Yoel haLevi (Raviah, c. 1140–1225). In his argument, the man recounts that he was sick, could barely walk, and needed a cane because his legs would not carry him. After more than a year had passed and he continued to suffer from this illness, he hired a horse and a guide and hastened to Barcelona, a distance of more than 1,000 km (600 miles), to see the famous Jewish doctor Rabbi Sheshet. The doctor examined him and stated that a worm had penetrated the tip of his penis and was causing injury to the groin area. This was the cause of the illness and the limitations he was experiencing. The doctor told him that he could be cured, but that the treatment could make him impotent. Using a scalpel, he made an incision and succeeded in curing the problem. After the operation Shlomo was able to walk normally, but due to the incision, the extremity of his urethra was damaged and he could only urinate upward. Nonetheless, he declared that he desired his wife as any other man; it seems that he sought to prevent the *Beit Din* from compelling him to divorce his wife and asked them to permit him to return and live with her as in the past. Rabbi Eliezer ben Yoel haLevi examined him and indeed testified that the incision and no other injury was the cause of the problem. Shlomo son of Reb Hananel continued to live with his wife and she even bore him a son, whom they named Eliezer in honour of the rabbi.[10]

First and foremost, this incident, with its happy ending, shows us that women could petition to be divorced from their husbands because the all-male rabbinical courts supported claims of this sort when they were based on precedents linked to the *Mishnah* and the *Gemarah*. Even though the courts were comprised of men, and even though they could invoke the approach advocated by Rabbenu Tam against the use, in principle, of the *gett* given under compulsion, women could still continue to exercise the right that had been granted to them to try to sever the bonds of marriage by means of one of the grounds for divorce. But the new situation created in Ashkenaz, in which a man was not entitled to marry more than one woman and his wife must agree to be divorced, created an intolerable situation from the male point of view. As Rabbi Asher ben Jehiel (Rosh) stated at the end of the thirteenth century, 'The status of the woman is liable to compete with and prevail over the status of the man.' If we add women's economic power to this picture, it is easy to see why the men were fighting to salvage their damaged superiority.

To examine the battle of the sexes in this sphere and to follow the male struggle against the power of women in the family unit, we will examine three types of women: first, the woman who attempts to free herself of a husband while retaining what she has achieved and the property she has acquired during the marriage by claiming that he is impotent; second, the childless widow who attempts to free herself from the extended family of her dead husband (the *yevamah*[11]); and third, the woman who finds her husband repulsive and decides to withhold the enjoyment of sexual relations from him or to desist from the work she has undertaken to do for him.

Impotence

The basis for the debate engaged in by the medieval sages on the power of women to seek divorce on grounds of impotence is the fascinating discussion in the Talmud on this topic in both the Tractates Yevamot and Nedarim.[12] These discussions, as well as how this subject was developed in the Middle Ages, reflect the internal male conflict over their status *vis-à-vis* the improving status of women. Tractate Yevamot (65a–65b) deals with a woman who lodges a complaint that she and her husband have no children and that the fault is his, because he does not 'shoot straight as an arrow', a euphemism for impotence. The *amora* Rabbi Ammi points out that only a woman can know if her husband 'shoots straight' or not;

therefore they believed her and compelled her husband to divorce her and pay her the amount of her *ketubah*. But, since it is the man, but not the woman, who is obligated by the commandment to 'be fruitful and multiply' (Gen. 1:28), we need to ask why the rabbis gave consideration to the woman on the subject of bearing children. The answer is that the woman making the complaint has 'submitted a special plea'. Her line of reasoning is that even though she is not obligated by the commandment herself, she needs children who will support her in her old age: 'Does not a woman like myself,' she asks, 'require a staff in her hand and a hoe for digging her grave?' That is, children to maintain her during her lifetime and provide for her burial when she dies. Thanks to this argument she is able to demand to be freed of her impotent husband so that she can marry someone who will give her children. This discussion reveals that a social mechanism was established to release women from situations that became unpleasant or intolerable; it provided them with support and allowed them to be divorced, taking with them the property they brought to the marriage as well as the financial obligations undertaken for their benefit by their husbands. Thus it is the woman who determined, with the help of the *Beit Din*, that the man was impotent and that she can be divorced.

The response of the 'opposition' appears in Tractate Nedarim, where opinions are divided. There are those who believe a woman claiming that her husband is impotent, because they make the assumption that she would not lie and would not be 'brazen in the presence of her husband'. However there are also those who bring up the concern that just because she knows that she is the only one affected by the situation, there is a risk that she might lie; therefore, she should not be believed and she is most likely making a false accusation. The sages did not follow Rabbi Ammi, who believed the woman without reservation. Neither did they permit her husband to take another wife in an effort to prove that he was not sterile. Rather, they asked her to wait until the end of the ten-year period in the hope that she might become pregnant, as if laying the blame for their childlessness on her and not on her husband.[13]

In the Middle Ages an interesting development related to this issue took place. At the end of the twelfth century, Rabbi Isaac ben Abraham (Rizba) established that a wife must be believed and that a husband may be compelled to divorce her, but only if she is satisfied with a *gett* and does not demand her *ketubah*. He had been deliberating for some time concerning a man whose wife petitioned the *Beit Din* seeking a divorce from her husband on the grounds that he was impotent, a fact she had come to realize during the course of three years. To state her claim, she used such expressions as: '[He] cannot come unto her,' 'He needs to bring salvation to his home and cannot,' 'His strength has been taken from him.' At first, the husband denied the problem; however, in the end he acknowledged his disability. Then it became obvious that the dispute was not just over the question of whether she should be released by means of a *gett*, but whether she should be given everything promised to her in her *ketubah*, including the supplements. Rabbi Isaac ben Abraham makes it clear that only the woman who bases her claim on the need for children in her old age and does not demand her *ketubah* can be believed.[14]

Although Rabbi Isaac ben Abraham's judgement releases the wife from her impotent husband, it leaves the major portion of the property owed her, the *ketubah* supplement, in her husband's hands. Rabbi Isaac ben Abraham feels that his decision is weak. If the man disagrees with his wife regarding his impotence and blames her for it, he has a basis for arguing about the *ketubah* amounts; but if he admits that he is impotent, why should she not receive all the property that she brought with her and to which she is entitled upon her divorce? According to the decision in the *Mishnah*, a man who takes an oath to abstain from sexual relations with his wife must divorce her immediately. Rabbi Isaac ben Abraham's response is extremely important. He distinguishes between a man who 'cannot become hard', in which case he must, according to law, release his wife with her *ketubah*, and the man who does not succeed in having conjugal relations because the 'woman's womb is too narrow'. Unhesitatingly, he asks the *dayanim* to compel the husband to divorce his wife and to give her her *ketubah* only when he admits that he 'cannot become hard'. But if the man claims that the reason why he cannot have full intercourse with his wife is her 'narrow womb', the judgement should not be that he is obliged to free her. Then Rabbi Isaac turns to the woman and asks her to wait for more than three years, to find a doctor for herself and her husband, and not be in a hurry. Thus Rabbi Isaac ben Abraham gives the man a prerogative that he did not have in the past – to remain married to his wife – and instructs the *Beit Din* on the way to handle such cases. He candidly explains that he arrived at this conclusion on the basis of his own personal experience 'and I was also this way, at first, with my wife for two years'. Such things happen and there is no reason to break up the marriage immediately. As to the impotent man who does admit to this condition, he decides that, he must indeed be compelled to divorce his wife, and she has to be given her *ketubah* and her *nedunyah* (dowry), but not the *ketubah* supplement. He denied the wife the generous financial supplement recorded in her *ketubah* because she had claimed that her husband was completely impotent and that she had never engaged in sexual intercourse. It was his opinion that a man grants his wife a *ketubah* supplement on account of 'enjoyment of sexual pleasures', in other words, his sexual gratification. If this does not transpire, the husband does not have to give the supplement at the time of the divorce. But a man, who achieves sexual pleasure from any sort of relations, even though the result is not the birth of children, has to pay the supplement.

Rabbi Isaac ben Abraham's economic objective is clear. Unlike other sages, he determined that a woman who claims that her husband is impotent needs to be believed; however, the outcome was that she received her actual *ketubah* and dowry only, and not the supplement. If she persisted in demanding the entire amount, she would be suspected of fabricating the story about her husband's impotence and attempting to leave him because she had become attracted to someone else.[15] Rabbi Isaac was concerned about the economic capacity of the husband's extended family. Hence, the wife could be released, but she had to leave behind significant assets. He even underscored that with respect to dowries containing written promises of amounts larger than what was actually handed over (which, as we have seen, was the practice in order to avoid embarrassment to the brides), the woman should only be given what she brought with her in reality, because if she were given more, it would be as if she had been handed the supplement, which, he believed, she should not receive. From that time on, Rabbi Isaac ben Abraham was the 'male voice' that set the tone.

His opinions are an indication of his general tendency to be uneasy about the power of women and their economic strength. In a letter he wrote to his brother (Rabbi Samson of Sens), he comes out against Rabbi Samson's position that a widow should be able to gain control of her husband's possessions following his death. In Rabbi Isaac's opinion, although the discussion in the Palestinian Talmud allows for such an outcome, it gives even more power to women, particularly those who come from wealthy homes. 'In this way you do not make it possible for anyone to live' (where 'anyone' referred to 'anyone who wasn't a woman'!) Rabbi Isaac uses the same generalities to describe all widows, both 'rich ladies who control the wealth of their husbands' and those who 'are not wealthy ladies, but if the home contains many possessions or silver and gold, they will take everything.'[16]

From then on, despite the view that, in principal, a wife should be separated from her husband when there is proof of some sort that he is actually impotent and unable to give her children to support her in her old age, the *dayanim* hesitated at every stage of the inquiry into the women's claims about their husbands' impotence. They hesitated on the question of establishing impotence, on compelling the husband to grant a *gett*, and with respect to the property the woman could take with her when the divorce was finally authorized.[17] One example of this can be seen in a *responsum* of Rabbi Eliezer ben Yoel haLevi (Raviah) dating from the beginning of the thirteenth century. Two *dayanim* (Nathan ben Isaac and Eliezer ben Simon) sought his advice about a particularly problematic case, which had already been brought before the gentile court system and *batei din*; both had been unable to hand down a legal decision.[18] The dispute was between a husband and wife who had been living together for more than fifteen years without having children. The woman claimed that she had to get a divorce from her husband because he would certainly not have any children. The expressions that she used in order to describe the situation were: 'No woman exists with whom he can succeed'; 'he has no understanding about being with a woman'; 'a woman will never be able to have a family with him'; 'seed will never be seen from him because his "arm" is malformed, defective and has a finger missing'.

The husband did not agree to release her despite the fact that more than ten years had passed and he was obligated to do so in keeping with the Ruling concerning barrenness. Furthermore, it was virtually crystal-clear that the blame rested with the husband because he showed signs of being a eunuch, he had no hint of facial hair, and his voice was effeminate. The letter was sent to Raviah by the *dayanim*, who asked him to render an opinion on several questions. First, they asked his advice about how to separate the couple since the wife rightly claimed that she needed children to support her in her old age and if she continued to live with this husband, she would never have children. From the tone of the query, it is obvious that the husband did not have the means to pay all the amounts to which his wife was entitled according to her *ketubah* and its supplements. Second, they asked Raviah to consider whether or not a physical examination of the husband was necessary since this would cause him embarrassment and might turn what until then had been a rumour into an established fact.

Raviah determined that everything should be done to convince the man to give his wife a *gett*; but that was the extent of his recommendation, he did not rule that the husband should be compelled to do so. Even though the tone of his statement clearly indicated that he was convinced by the frank testimony of the woman, his conclusion remained nothing more than a recommendation. He was not willing to compel the husband to grant a divorce. Raviah also made an effort to preserve the husband's good name and did not propose that he undergo a thorough examination that would humiliate him in the eyes of the male society around him. He was concerned about the man; even though it was obvious to Raviah that the man's problems were no secret in his community, where it was known that the wife's childlessness was not the outcome of her infertility but due to some deficiency in her husband. Thus we see that at the beginning of the thirteenth century, the *Beit Din* shows a great deal of empathy towards a woman whose husband is considered impotent, however, it does not put the full potential of its legal power to use in support of her request to be released from this man.[19]

Despite this conclusion and even though the male tendency reflected in the *responsa* literature is to deny women the supplement and to give them only the sums of the *ketubah* and the dowry, it seems that women tended to take action by claiming grounds for divorce related to impotence; in addition, they apparently enjoyed substantial financial success. This trend can be seen throughout the thirteenth century and is reflected in the sources of that era. At the end of the century, Rabbi Meir ben Barukh of Rothenburg (Maharam) expressed, in some of his *responsa*, great annoyance with the degree of impertinence and freedom displayed by the women of his day. He described what he meant in the following generalization: 'During times such as these in which the women are bold and impudent, they should not be believed'. Maharam thought that the women of his era were taking advantage of the power given to them in previous generations and that they were fabricating stories about their husbands' impotence whether it was necessary or not. In a *responsum* in which he was involved, a woman claimed that her husband had an erection problem, saying that it 'would lean against its house and would not stand up'. However, Maharam heard that this particular man already had children. He therefore cast doubt on the woman's intentions stressing that in this case, the best course to follow was the one suggested by the *Mishnah*, i.e., to act 'by way of request', which here means to seek a compromise between the couple without resorting to the issuing of a *gett* by compulsion from the *Beit Din*. Maharam also thought that impotence was often a type of illness that could be cured; therefore, there was no reason for the wife to rush to demand a divorce, and, of course, the dangerous route of a *gett* given under compulsion should not, he believed, be undertaken.[20] Situations of temporary impotence were not uncommon in that era, as contemporary literature, as well as other sources, bears out. Since marriage at that time paired two very young people, whose knowledge about what should take place between them was not very great, cases of sex phobia (fear of engaging in sexual intercourse) have come down to us. Because such cases were fairly numerous, they constituted an economic threat since young families would break up and most of the assets that were considered joint family property by the husband and his family would fall into the hands of the wife. Consequently, the *dayanim* usually ruled that in such a situation, an attempt should be made to rectify the problem; but if this proved unsuccessful, they would convince the husband to grant his wife a divorce, giving her only her *ketubah* and the dowry that was actually provided, but not the entire supplement or the promised sums of money and property.

Such a situation is described in the *responsum* of Rabbi Hayim Paltiel of Germany dating from the end of the thirteenth century in which he attempts to calm turmoil in the community.[21] The case in question dealt with a woman who requested a divorce from her husband because, in her opinion, he was impotent. ('He does not have the might of men,' she said). She also wanted to involve the communal institutions in order to have him seized physically because he refused to grant her a *gett* or appear for a hearing, and he was threatening to run away and marry another woman, a second wife.[22] It turned out that the man had had sexual relations with his wife once, on the first night of their marriage; consequently, Rabbi Hayim Paltiel concluded, there was a medical problem and the man should try to find a cure for his illness so as to recover and return to his former state. In this way Rabbi Hayim Paltiel recognized that in a marriage, a woman's enjoyment is derived from the pleasure of 'a husband who 'shoots straight as an arrow' and if her husband refuses to have normal marital relations with her, she lacks such pleasure. Since this couple had sexual relations at least once, according to the wife's testimony, Rabbi Hayim Paltiel was uneasy about forcing the husband to grant divorce lest it lead to a *gett* given under compulsion, with its problematic validity. Moreover, he was concerned that if their union remains intact and they do not have sexual relations, which are appropriate in marriage, there is an obvious risk that the man could turn to a life of sin while remaining married to his wife. This twofold concern led Rabbi Paltiel to recommend that the man be asked to take an oath to the effect that, by a certain date, he would not run away, but would seek a cure; should he still be unable to find proper treatment (a lasting cure) by then, an attempt would be made to convince him to divorce his wife voluntarily. Rabbi Paltiel made it clear that he would not agree to compel the husband to divorce his wife in any event. Indeed, this statement contains a veiled message for the wife: if she wants to be released, she must be willing to give up something so that her husband will agree.[23]

The difficulty the sages had with the notion of deciding unreservedly in favour of the woman was not just the result of their desire to balance the economic competition between men and women, which they saw as unfavourable to men subsequent to the changes in their obligations in the *ketubah* and the constraints placed on their abilities in matters of marriage and divorce. Neither was it solely the outcome of their concern about issuing a *gett* that might not be valid and consequently put the new family that the wife might establish, after the divorce, into jeopardy. Men who suffered from permanent or temporary impotence believed in the superstition or fear that they had come under a spell or been bewitched, a common belief in the thirteenth century. An argument of this sort, which is based on popular beliefs and perceptions about women and their powers (which I later discuss at length), required a different sort of approach. It could have been argued that such a man, since he does not carry on normal sexual relations with his wife, was obligated to release her immediately because the Ruling is similar to that for a man who took an oath to abstain from relations with his wife. Indeed, already in Mishnaic times, a husband was obliged to release his wife immediately in such circumstances.

In a case brought before Maharam at the end of the thirteenth century, a woman demanded that her husband grant her a divorce because he was impotent and had not had sexual relations with her at all for two years. The husband admitted that this was true but maintained that a spell had been cast on him and, bound by this spell, he could not go near his wife. Maharam did rule that the man had to divorce his wife; however, he qualified his argument by saying that the man should not be compelled to give his wife a *gett*, rather he should be convinced to do so. The rabbi added that he could even be threatened with firm language such as: 'the sages have required you to present a *gett* to your wife and if you refuse to do so, you can be called a criminal that is, labelled in society as a person who is in breach of the court'. Maharam took pains to explain that this situation was not analogous to that of a husband who journeys from place to place and does not have sexual relations with his wife (and therefore he may be forced to grant a divorce) because in this case he claimed that an external factor, witchcraft, prevented him from engaging in normal conjugal relations. Immediately thereafter, Maharam ruled that the woman whose husband claimed to be under the influence of witchcraft deserved the *ketubah* and the dowry, but under no circumstances the supplements. Like the other sages who sought to ensure that the family property of the husband remained in his hands, Maharam was also careful to state that if there were witnesses who could testify to the woman's actual dowry, and she would receive only what she in fact brought to the marriage and not the expanded, fictitious dowry that had been recorded in the *ketubah* deed.

On the other hand, Maharam ruled that abstaining from sexual relations with one's wife was totally unacceptable behaviour and if the man persisted in his refusal he would be labelled a 'rebellious husband'; a fine would be levied on him and the sums accrued would be added to the woman's *ketubah* to serve as an incentive for him to release her sooner. Maharam was very uneasy about the situation and stated 'He must remedy the matter because for two years there has been no ploughing and no harvesting and the situation is completely unacceptable, and he ties her down and keeps her from conjugal relations in vain, and if he does not want to divorce her as instructed by the sages, let more assets be added to her *ketubah*.'[24]

At the close of this era, the end of the thirteenth century, the ultimate summary of this issue was made by Rabbi Hayim ben Isaac, the son of Isaac ben Moshe (Or Zarua). At that time men suspected that women were only interested in gaining control over property and assets, and that they believed their problems to be more important than the *halakhah*. This male perception was so severely judgemental of women and the formidable economic status they had earned that Rabbi Hayim had no choice but to conclude that a woman who had been living with her husband for fifteen years without any offspring must be looked upon with suspicion even though – when her husband sought to divorce her – she was willing to give up her *ketubah* and claimed that she only wanted children to take care of her in her old age. Rabbi Hayim felt that he had no choice but to equate this woman with a 'rebellious wife'. In the end he ruled that the husband should divorce his wife under the definition of 'rebellious wife' and thus deny her all the property that she had, which was promised to her in her *ketubah*, aside from her estate.[25] In other words, from the halakhic point of view, at the end of the thirteenth century, the definition of a 'rebellious wife' provided the opportunity to punish such women, to restrict them, and prevent them from obtaining material benefits.

Levirate marriage and *halizah*

Another arena in which the battle of the sexes was fought and men attempted to enhance their economic status was the levirate marriage (*yibbum*) and *halizah* (the ceremony freeing a man from marrying his childless brother's widow).[26] The Torah (Deut. 25:5–10) states that if a married brother dies without offspring, his younger brother must marry his widow and that the first issue of their marriage should be named after the dead brother. This process is called a levirate marriage. If the surviving brother refuses to fulfil his obligation, he has to take part in a rite of humiliation. In a public ceremony, called *halizah*, the widow takes off his shoe, spits in his face, and pronounces a derogatory nickname that is added to his family's name. Following this ceremony, the widow is free to marry someone else. In the Bible it is clear that the perpetuating of the memory of the dead brother by means of a levirate marriage is the suggested and preferred option for both the dead brother's family and the widow. The *halizah* ceremony was only established in case the levir refused to perpetuate his dead brother's memory. There is no doubt that this stems from attitudes towards social status in which the extended family, or clan, is at the top of the list of priorities, whereas the brother's widow is very close to the bottom. In certain cases and in certain eras, the arrangement of a levirate marriage saved women from starvation and a total lack of social standing; on the other hand, it is obvious that the fewer ties the widow had to her dead husband's family, the more autonomous she would be in society.

The issue of freeing the woman from the bonds of a levirate marriage was already addressed in the *Mishnah*. In Tractate Bekhorot 1:7, the *tannaim* asked which commandment was preferable, levirate marriage or *halizah*. This signalled the beginning of an ongoing struggle between those attempting to release women and rank them as equal contenders with men in the social sphere, and those that sought to control them, to imprison them in the structure of the extended family, and neutralize their power. This debate came about because of an objection put forward by a *tanna* of the mid-second century named Abba Saul, who questioned the necessity of the levirate marriage (Tbab. Yevamot 39b) in light of an insightful and interesting reading of the biblical text.[27] Sexual relations with a brother's wife are considered a violation of the ban of incest, the most severe biblical prohibition (Lev. 18:16). How can this ban be disregarded and transformed overnight into a commandment?[28]

This debate stems from an awareness that even if it is permissible to marry the wife of one's brother immediately after his death, this permission derives solely from the need to perform the commandment itself, i.e., to 'perform the levir's duty', that is, 'to establish a name in Israel for his brother' (Deut. 25:5, 7). Thus, if the levir does not marry his brother's widow solely for the sake of the commandment, but out of other interests, then he is instantly labelled a sinner who is committing the most serious crime of incest. If he marries because he finds the woman attractive or sexually desirable, or because he anticipates financial gain from the levirate marriage, or for any other ulterior motive, he has transgressed and failed to observe the commandment; and now, after marrying his brother's widow, he is deeply embroiled in one of the most serious sins in the Torah (in the words of Abba Saul: 'it is as if he has infringed the law of incest; and I am even inclined to think that the child [of such a union] is a *mamzer*'. Abba Saul's conclusion gave rise to the outlook that, in order to avoid sin, *halizah* might be preferable to levirate marriage, and that the woman should be freed as soon as possible. The *amoraim* of the Babylonian Talmud attempted to veil this unexpected change of direction, which undermined their basic assumptions, and summarized the debate in the statement of the *amora*, Rami bar Hama in the name of Rabbi Isaac: 'It was re-enacted that the precept of the levirate marriage is preferable to that of *halizah*'; in other words, there is nothing here to get concerned about because levirate marriage is the main commandment.[29]

From this point on, there were two options the sages could follow, each of them with a legitimate source in a different tractate of the Talmud, one in Yevamot and the other in Ketubot. They represented two fundamental positions in regard to the release of the widow and her special situation in relation to the family of her deceased husband: (a) bound by levirate marriage and having to remain within the husband's extended family, or (b) freed by *halizah* and able to marry anyone. The explanations written by the men detail their opinions on this subject and reflect the male point of view on the status of women in a particular group and at a specific period of time. This can provide us with the methodological criteria for ascertaining key questions relating to the status of women and their power, and the degree to which men controlled the status of women and society altogether. We know, for example, that in the Geonic period in Babylonia, two schools of thought were formed and their decisions differed from one another. The Pumbedita Yeshivah continued to adhere to the attitude of the *amora* Samuel, who believed that *halizah* was paramount, whereas the prevailing school of thought at the Sura Yeshivah believed that levirate marriage took precedence. They did not manage to reach an agreed, enforceable decision.[30]

If we look at the issue of levirate marriage and *halizah* in relation to the status of women in Germany and northern France, the result is a fascinating picture of struggles and transformations taking place over a period of three centuries, which reflects the changing attitude towards women. Already during the eleventh century, we find sources from Germany and northern France that refer to this tension. If both the man and the woman agreed to it, the levirate marriage would be performed. It was also acknowledged that a woman should not be compelled to agree to a levirate marriage if she did not wish to do so. Nonetheless, the male perception derived from the Torah, where the decision about *halizah* was made exclusively at the man's discretion, and he could not be forced into it involuntarily. Indeed, if the *Beit Din* attempted to intervene, it was feared that *halizah* performed under duress would be considered improper and that it would lead to serious repercussions for the widow and the associations she might form in the future. Consequently, the attitude developed that gave preference to releasing the woman by means of *halizah*; at the same time, however, this gave halakhic legitimacy to, and increased, the man's ability to extort and intimidate the woman. On the other hand, the economic position of women became stronger as time went on in the wake of the two conspicuous changes discussed in the previous chapter: the prohibition against polygamy and the transformation of the *ketubah* into a document that incorporated almost all of the family property. These changes, which were finalized during the twelfth century, led to a situation in which men feared the growing economic strength of women to such an extent that they began to see them as a 'political' threat. In Germany they attempted to utilize the levirate marriage to tip the scales in their favour; the stronger the woman's status became, the more eager the men became to restore to themselves the property that was being taken, as they perceived it, from their families.

Traces of this tension can be seen in the letters of Rabbi Judah HaCohen dating from eleventh-century Germany that deal with cases of levirate marriage on which he was deliberating. In one instance, the fiancé of a young girl (she was apparently very young, around twelve years old) died before the wedding. Her father seized control of the property that was promised to his daughter in her *ketubah* in order to put pressure on the levir, the brother of the deceased, to grant *halizah* so that she would be free. The levir, in turn, attempted to extort large sums of money from the girl's family. In another case a levir who took an oath that he would not give *halizah* to his brother's widow.[31] Rabbi Judah haCohen was aware of the Ashkenazic practice of preferring *halizah*, unless both sides agreed to levirate marriage, and understood that the young woman could not be compelled to live with a man (the levir) she did not desire. In explaining the grounds for his decision, he quoted a saying from the Talmud connected with another topic (Tbab. Tractate Ketubot 61a) and linked it convincingly to the issue at hand: 'food should not be given to a person who refuses to accept it', 'it is given for life and not for misery'. His conclusion was that, if a man vows that he will not grant *halizah*, he will be judged in the same way as a person who vows to transgress against a commandment (Tbab. Tractate Shavuot 29a): he will receive lashings until he changes his mind. Nonetheless, Rabbi HaCohen did not conclude that every levir can be forced into freeing his brother's widow.

Rabbi Judah haCohen's reluctance was characteristic of the male way of thinking: he identified the problem but hesitated to take a harsh stand against a man. The problem of a widow bound to a levir who did not agree to release her from this obligation was extremely disturbing for Rabbi Judah haCohen until he made the effort to find a legitimate justification for her release on the basis of an incident from Tbab. Tractate Ketubot, 77a. Here two brothers who were tanners are discussed. After one of them died, it was found that his widow was entitled to refuse the levir because of his profession, despite the fact that this had also been the occupation of her deceased husband. On the basis of this case, Rabbi Judah haCohen inferred that just as the occupation of the levir could be used as an argument by a woman to reject him as a husband through levirate marriage, so, too, she was entitled to turn down such a marriage with any man she did not desire; moreover, her refusal could not be used to label her as a 'rebellious woman'. Yet, Rabbi Judah haCohen did not allow himself to rescind or even dwell on the right of a man to refuse to grant *halizah*. His decision was to rectify this problematic situation by advising the woman and the *Beit Din* to attempt to mislead the levir into agreeing to the *halizah*. The essence of the deception is not clear, and neither is the way this levir might be duped, when the only thing he sought was financial gain. In the final analysis, as Rabbi Judah haCohen himself acknowledged, the process of releasing the woman involves her giving up large amounts of money and property that belong to her on the strength of her *ketubah*. As already pointed out, Rabbi Judah haCohen understood, identified, and defined the problem very well. He was cognizant of women's increasingly strong position and realized that she could not be coerced in this matter. In fact, he also feared that attempting to compel women to agree, unwillingly, to a levirate marriage might force them to turn for help to the Christians and even lead them to convert to Christianity in order to free themselves from an undesirable husband.[32] Nevertheless, he employed the familiar method of the direct approach based on talmudic law; reinforced the male position at the expense of the slight improvement he provided for the woman's situation; and suggested to the *Beit Din* a way of helping her, in a manner that would most likely cost her a great deal in economic assets.

Levirate marriage is viewed primarily as an economic issue. The extended family is fighting for the resources of the family unit. It sees levirate marriage as a vehicle that legitimately allows them to retain their hold over their deceased son's assets, which were given to his wife in the *ketubah*, while preventing the widow from gaining control over property they consider their own. We have available to us testimony concerning three brothers: Levi, who was dying; Reuben, who lived in the same city; and Simon, who lived farther away in another city.[33] Before his death, Levi instructed Reuben not to upset his wife and not to steal from her. After Levi's death, Reuben took control of his dead brother's property, turned his widow out of her house, and did not even pay for her maintenance. Reuben's wife outdid her husband by appropriating the clothing that belonged to the dead brother's wife. Naturally, the widow turned to the community organization (and to the court), which immediately called upon Reuben to appear before them. His response to her complaint is very instructive. From his perspective, levirate marriage would delay the *halizah* for a year or two and, as he understood it, all of his deceased brother's property belonged to him as the future levir. The *Beit Din* turned to Simon, the more distant brother, and attempted to persuade him to grant *halizah* to the widow and thus release her. Simon replied that he was prepared to do so, on condition that the community forces Reuben to transfer to him the property of their deceased brother. In his view as well, the property of his dead brother reverts to the person who grants *halizah* and frees the widow from levirate marriage. The solution was to persuade the widow sign on a deed to make over the property to one of her late husband's brothers on the basis of her *Ketubah* and in this way convince them to grant her *halizah*. In other words, in order to be released from levirate marriage, she had to give up most of her property.

A generation later, Rashi (Rabbi Solomon ben Isaac), in northern France, tried to rectify this problematic situation. He, too, was a product of his surroundings and its halakhic principles, and so he also thought that when both partners agreed and so desired, they could fulfil the important commandment of levirate marriage.[34] Nonetheless, he decided to take action against the extortion perpetrated by levirs, which caused the widow, in effect, to forfeit her *ketubah*, along with funds and property to which she was entitled. His solution was to establish that when the levir and the widow did not agree to the marriage, the *Beit Din* would compel the man to grant *halizah*. In this way extortion of the widow could be avoided. Like other sages, Rashi, too, derived the legitimacy for his decision from the grounds for divorce that may be brought by women. He compared the situation of a widow waiting for levirate marriage to that of a woman who finds herself married to 'a man who is afflicted with boils' (*Mishnah* Ketubot 87:10) – in other words, a woman who has grounds for demanding, with the support of the *Beit Din*, her release from marriage due to the severe skin disease afflicting her husband with whom she can no longer cohabit. Although in this case the levir is not precisely married to the woman in the same way as that unfortunate diseased man, he is, in reality, preventing her from marrying someone else and in principle, she is bound to him as a woman is bound to her husband. In Rashi's opinion, when the *amora* Rav in Tbab. Tractate Yevamot 39b states that if the levir is 'afflicted with boils', the woman cannot be compelled to marry him, he is not referring to a man who is actually suffering from such a condition, but rather to any reason she may have for being apprehensive about living with this particular man. Rashi's solution was truly revolutionary since it gave the woman the ability to be released from a levir on the basis of her desires.[35] It is not surprising that almost everyone came out against his opinion, opposing it categorically.

Nevertheless, it remained a theoretical signpost that, for development, awaited the arrival of his grandson, Rabbenu Tam,[36] who was active from the middle of the twelfth century until the early 1170s. His point of view was that the levir and the widow should not even have any contact with one another and that the only course open to them was *halizah*. Since no alternative existed, the levir had no reason to extort the widow; he had to grant *halizah*. Moreover, he had no leverage for attempting to obtain her *ketubah* or parts thereof. In effect, Rabbenu Tam enabled the widow to free herself from the bond of the levirate marriage process with all her property intact; yet, if she actually wanted to marry her husband's brother, she could no longer do so. Rabbenu Tam's Ruling was based, as was his usual practice, on far-reaching and daring interpretations of talmudic sources. He interpreted a statement made by *amoraim* that levirate marriage should not be forced on the partners but it had to be explained to people who had come for the purpose of performing *halizah* that this alternative existed, to mean that even those who wanted a levirate marriage should be forced to accept *halizah*.

From this he inferred that even those who wanted levirate marriage must be induced to accept *halizah*.[37] This constituted a fundamental and revolutionary change in the status of women, which manifested itself in two ways. Not only did they acquire even more economic strength, but the change also reinforced the prevailing public sentiment that women were free entities neither dependent on nor restricted by the male environment.

The attitude towards Rabbenu Tam's Ruling was interesting. On the one hand opposition to his proposal/Ruling was almost universal because he had, in effect, cancelled the commandment of levirate marriage. On the other hand, his suggestion completely solved the problem facing the community with regard to these widows and arranged the relationships within the new family unit in the best possible way. As in other similar cases (such as the cancellation of the commandment of procreation by Raban), this allowed the community's religious authorities to solve internal family problems without becoming involved in the family wrangling. This reform, which underscores the negative aspects of marrying one's brother's widow, could now be attributed to Rabbenu Tam and began to filter slowly through the restrictions of family relationships and marriage in northern France during subsequent generations.

In Germany, however, they opted for the Ashkenazic Ruling and rejected the opinion of Rabbenu Tam, with the men exploiting the weapon of levirate marriage to reclaim a substantial portion of the family assets, which had been transferred to the widow. An excellent example of this process is found in an incident that took place during the 1250s or 1260s in Germany. Rabbi Kalonymus died without sons and his two brothers, Rabbi Ephraim and Rabbi Hillel, wanted to marry his widow, Origia.[38] Because the families were wealthy, distinguished, and part of the circle of scholars who documented the dispute, many details relating to this case are available to us. Members of Rabbi Kalonymus's family joined forces to safeguard the family assets and prevent them from being transferred to the widow's family. The brothers insisted on their biblical right to marry their brother's widow even though both of them were already married, and according to the Ruling prohibiting polygamy, they were barred from any form of marriage with her. Furthermore, Origia was an older woman who had not borne any children and more than likely would not be able to do so in the future. Thus, the biblical injunction to preserve the deceased brother's memory by naming the infant son after him would not be fulfilled in this case.

Their legal argument was their right to the husband's – their brother's – inheritance. They simply wanted to keep for themselves that part of their brother's legacy which was in his widow's *ketubah*, and even determined her portion: 'land, books and money equal to 100 zekukim'. The widow was demanding that they be forced to grant her *halizah* so she could remarry; the brothers were refusing to do so claiming that, because they were levirs, they could prevent her from obtaining *halizah* and being able to remarry. A special *Beit Din* was set up, composed of representatives from three prominent *batei din*, which decided in favour of the brothers. The reasons for their determination are not available to us; however, it appears that the *Beit Din* accepted the halakhic argument that the deceased's brothers, who were entitled to perform levirate marriage according to the Torah and the commandment of levirate marriage, should not be compelled to grant *halizah*. The claims concerning the advanced age of the widow and the fact that both brothers were already married bore no weight, it seems. Raviah, who cited this case in his writings, noted that the male side of this dispute was closely associated with his own family and stated explicitly that his father, Rabbi Yoel (who was also Rabbi Ephraim's teacher and blood relative) was pressed upon to attend this sitting of the *Beit Din*. He also made the point that the widow Origia accepted the decision of the *Beit Din* because of its halakhic aspect, without attempting to use her influence with the Christian authorities to affect the decision of this distinguished *Beit Din*. We do not know what Origia thought about the brothers' fight to obtain their part of her inheritance, but we do know that she did not ask for assistance from her relations. Thus, a situation was created whereby the men agreed to free the widow if the funds to which she was entitled (as a widow) were transferred to them. This was not a simple malicious and totally callous act, but rather an act of male defiance against a key reform that had created economically powerful widows. We know that Origia, the widow in question, then married an important gentleman, who held an influential position, Rabbi Elyakim Parness, and did not have any children.

The male (or family) economic position prevailed in this case because it relied on the halakhic viewpoint that gave the men legitimate support. The obligatory reliance on the Torah and the indisputable opinions of the *amoraim*, together with the men's desire to continue to hold onto the family assets in the face of women's ever-increasing power, kept the sages from attempting to deal with the communal problems that emerged when the position of the women was so severely trammelled. The sages and *dayanim* were uneasy about these cases because of the clear injustice to the woman and because of the pressures created in the community when, on the one hand, woman's economic power was increasing, and on the other, attempts were being made to curb this trend. This unease is reflected in the writings of Rabbi Simhah ben Samuel of Speyer (second half of the twelfth and beginning of the thirteenth century). He supported the halakhic concept that, in principle, the levir cannot be forced to grant *halizah* against his will, because levirate marriage is a commandment laid down in the Torah; therefore, he opposed Rashi's stand on this issue. At the same time, he was unable to condone the extortionist behaviour of the levirs, which came very close to being in direct contravention to the accepted standards of morality. In one instance, he learned that the levir of a wealthy woman was attempting both to employ extortion and to force her into levirate marriage, as well. The levir might have thought that by forcing himself on the widow and having conjugal relations with her he would make her his wife against her will and acquire her assets. Rabbi Simha advised the woman to spit in the levir's face (and to do so in front of the witnesses, apparently) and in this manner the rabbi disqualified the man from contracting a levirate marriage with her.[39]

It is important to understand the way these *dayanim* thought. They had a strong desire to help women when they believed there would be some social or communal benefit. They were not afraid of improving the status of women even at the expense of explicitly male interests. However, they could not relax the halakhic principles they espoused, which had been instilled in them and which they viewed as the sole formative element in the Jewish way of life. This tension was a decided source of mental turmoil for them. Their ambivalence is reflected in some of the texts that comprise the Sefer Hasidim.[40] On the one hand, the author vigorously reinforces the severe prohibition that exists against tormenting widows and promotes the idea that they should be granted *halizah* and freed as quickly as possible from their difficult situation. This source also tells the story of a man who did not grant *halizah* to his brother's widow; he contracted a disease in his legs, but immediately after hastening to give her *halizah* and freeing her, he recovered from the illness. On the other hand, levirate marriage was considered an everyday occurrence, in view of the fact that the assets held by the widow were still considered the property of the dead brother. Thus, the author of Sefer Hasidim wrote that if it is known that the widow received much more than her *ketubah* from her husband, it was considered legitimate to put pressure on her to transfer to the brothers what she received as 'wealth far in excess of her *ketubah*'. Nevertheless, looking at the advice given by the author, he tended to prefer *halizah* to levirate marriage. For example, he recommended *halizah* in the case of a man who, on his deathbed, instructed his brother to contract a levirate marriage with his wife, even though she had already been widowed twice before. If a father and mother put pressure on a brother to enter a levirate marriage, *Sefer Hasidim* counselled him to grant *halizah* instead. If parents put pressure on a levir to harass his brother's widow so that they could acquire their son's property, it is incumbent on him to give *halizah*. If a levir comes to a sage and explains to him that because his brother's widow is generally a nuisance he is not giving her *halizah*, thus preventing her from marrying and causing trouble for someone else, the sage explains 'you should do your duty (and grant *halizah*) and let other men act with caution where she is concerned'.[41]

An example of such a situation can be found in the work of Rabbi Eliezer ben Samuel of Metz, author of the book *Sefer Yere'im*, who lived in France at the end of the twelfth century (d. 1198).[42] He was one of the main advocates of the Ruling banning polygamy, although he was greatly disturbed by a married man's inability to fulfil the commandment of levirate marriage or *halizah* set down in the Torah. He believed that both the commandment and the Ruling had to be upheld; consequently, he devised a process that fulfilled both requirements. When levirate marriage is required and the levir is married, the Ruling will be annulled. The man can potentially marry his brother's widow and remain married to his wife; however, he will grant *halizah* to the widow. After the ceremony, the Ruling will become valid again.

Though this pronouncement by Rabbi Eliezer of Metz appears to be theoretical in nature, it can teach us a great deal about the relations between men and women in the medieval Jewish community. The change could not contradict the *halakhah* and certainly not what was written in the Torah concerning the commandments. This was a burning issue for the men. This was why the change was so problematic and those instituting it so daring and revolutionary; it was also the reason why the public did not always accept their changes. In northern France as well, Rabbenu Tam's change was not universally put into practice, his charisma and authority notwithstanding. The fundamental change instituted by Rabbenu Tam took effect in France in the same way as the other changes we mentioned, that is, slowly and in the course of at least two generations. Even during his era, we know of a query sent to him about a man from Troyes who was married when his brother died without offspring, and then his own wife died. In the question he addressed to Rabbenu Tam, the man asked whether he should perform levirate marriage or *halizah*. In other words, the average person did not understand Rabbenu Tam's Ruling.[43] Moreover, two generations later, at the beginning of the thirteenth century, the most important leader in northern France, Rabbi Jehiel of Paris, wrote about a levir who did not relate to the teachings of Rabbenu Tam or the decisions of the *Beit Din*, and refused to grant *halizah* to his brother's widow, although he was married and 'chains her down because he has his eyes on [her] wealth'. Rabbi Yehiel consulted with Rabbi Nethanel of Chinon because he wanted to excommunicate the man in order to force him to comply. Rabbi Nethanel turned to another sage, Rabbi Isaac ben Todros, who passed judgement in the name of Rabbenu Tam, stating that in this case the levir must be compelled to give *halizah* and should not be given any financial reward. In northern France, these problems even continued into the era of the author of the *Sefer Mitzvot Katan*, that appeared in 1277 (SemaK), who argued that a man who ties down his brother's widow should be excommunicated in order to persuade him to grant her *halizah*.[44]

Throughout the centuries, the sages in France attempted to free these women, but without success. In Germany, matters remained as they had been. Although the pronouncements of the sages reflected the influence of Rabbenu Tam, a survey of the *responsa* literature reveals that the men did not easily renounce their economic power and continued their extortionist behaviour. This situation generated countless problems that had to be debated. Even attempts to sever ties between a widow and a married levir did not always succeed, undermining the communities' system of Rulings. Towards the middle of the thirteenth century, Rabbi Isaac of Vienna wrote a lengthy and methodical summary of everything he knew on the subject of levirate marriage and *halizah*, an interesting work that straddled both sides of the fence. Rabbi Isaac ben Moses of Vienna, an admiring student of the sages of northern France, already knew about the reforms instituted in the previous two generations and cited their decisions; however, he qualified each of his own judgements with the levir's ability to acquire the property of his brother's widow. He knew about the opinions of Rashi (and of Rabbi Judah ben Nathan), who ruled that the levir must be forced to give *halizah* and release the widow; yet he pointed out that Rabbi Judah ben Nathan thought it preferable to deceive the potential husband rather than compel him to comply by means of the *Beit Din*. He was familiar with the opinions of Rabbenu Tam, whom he admired as a leader whose halakhic decisions served as guidelines. He knew that Rabbenu Tam forbade any contact whatsoever between the levir and his brother's widow, even if they both agreed to a levirate marriage, and even if it was obvious that the levir was marrying out of a desire to perform the commandment (such as a case where he had a wealthier or more attractive fiancée and still preferred his brother's widow).

Nonetheless, Rabbi Isaac of Vienna stripped Rabbenu Tam's reforms of their real essence by giving weight to two reservations. First, he restates the arguments of those who opposed what Rabbenu Tam was saying, first and foremost Rabbi Isaac ben Samuel, who disagreed with Rabbenu Tam's opinion and revoked it. Second, he claimed that Rabbenu Tam, like other sages, meant that the levir should be convinced with words only, that is, persuasion should be used, not coercion by means of the *Beit Din*. In order to prevent extortion, Rabbi Isaac ben Moses explained that if the levir is married, he is prohibited from demanding anything of his brother's widow and he must be forced to grant *halizah*. To support his contention, he cites Rabbi Isaac haLavan (a student of Rabbenu Tam's), who based himself on the Talmud, Tbab. Tractate Ketubot 2a that anyone harmed by a Ruling made by the sages is in an analogous position to a person injured by a Torah-based decision, and it is not necessary to compensate him. This is reasonable with regard to a married levir; but what is proper for an unmarried levir? Neither Rabbi Isaac of Vienna nor Rabbi Isaac haLavan reached the same conclusion as their revered teacher, Rabbenu Tam.[45]

A debate between *dayanim* in the second half of the thirteenth century also illustrated this tendency in Germany. They discussed a query submitted by the father of a bride. Immediately prior to the wedding ceremony, the prospective bridegroom's brother died and the father in question sought the help of the *Beit Din* to force the bridegroom to give *halizah* to his brother's widow before he married his daughter. This question appears to be hypothetical, because it is clear that the young man can only marry one woman and indeed the groom expressed his intention to marry his bride at the appointed time and as arranged. Yet, the tone of the father's request implied that he was concerned about the question: which association was the stronger, the one that derives from the commandment of the levirate marriage or the ban against polygamy? The father was genuinely troubled by the connection that bound his prospective son-in-law and wanted to make sure that his daughter was marrying someone who had no previous attachments. This line of thinking confirms the extreme importance that people continued to attach to levirate marriage, a connection that was fundamentally derived from a commandment in the Torah, and proves that they had not yet assimilated the changes (the anti-bigamy Ruling and consensual divorce) which continued to trouble them several generations after their introduction. Rabbi Avigdor ben Elijah haCohen (d. 1275) determined that because in his day people think along the lines of Abba Saul, i.e., that potential levirs are not motivated by the obligation to perform the commandment, and since the generation is not sincere and not relating properly to the stipulations of the Torah, the connection between a man and his brother's widow, to whom he may grant *halizah*, is not as strong as the association formed with his betrothed.[46]

Whereas in northern France the view was formed that levirate marriage should never be performed and *halizah* was the only option, in Germany levirate marriage continued to be thought of as normal practice throughout the thirteenth century.[47] Up to the end of that century, French authors referred to this distinction, bringing this point up repeatedly in their writings. For example, Rabbi Perez ben Elijah of Corbeil (d. c. 1295) wrote: 'In those places it is common practice to perform *halizah* and not levirate marriage, but in Ashkenaz, the practice is to perform levirate marriage.' The French rabbi, Isaac ben Elijah, wrote to Rabbi Hayim ben Isaac, the son of Isaac ben Moshe (Or Zarua) of Germany: 'We have not become accustomed to this halakhic law because it has not been our practice to perform levirate marriage at all in France.' Similarly, Rabbi Hayim himself stated: 'In France they do not allow the performance of the levirate marriage at all.'[48]

Towards the end of the thirteenth century, Rabbi Meir haCohen, a student of Maharam, depicted the opposing camps. The one that included Rashi, Rabbi Azriel the son of Rabbi Nathan (a contemporary of Rashi), Raban of Mainz, Rabbenu Tam, and Rabbi Yossi bar Oshaya haLevi believed that halizah was the ideal solution, whereas the opposing camp, which included Samuel ben Meir (Rashbam), Raviah of Bonn, Isaac ben Asher haLevi (Riba), and Rabbi Simhah ben Samuel of Speyer, believed that levirate marriage was preferable over *halizah*, and all that this implies.

In the end, during the thirteenth century, the German communities solved the problem in the same way as they dealt with many other issues involving changes that had to gain public acceptance and cooperation: they created a Ruling. We have available to us fragments of Rulings dealing with this topic, which allow us to reconstruct the essence of the Ruling and the attempts made to implement it. According to sources we have, Rabbi David ben Kalonymus of Minzburg had already formulated the Ruling that standardized this question towards the end of the twelfth century, in 1196. Rabbi David was active at the turn of the century and was instrumental in developing the Rulings (he is signed on Rulings in 1220). It was also known that he was the teacher of Rabbi Samson ben Abraham of Sens, a student of Rabbenu Tam; consequently, he knew about the reform instituted in France. We know that the Ruling was disseminated among the German rabbis whose signatures appear on it – Raviah of Bonn, Eleazar ben Judah of Worms, Simhah ben Samuel of Speyer, etc. – and that it was revised and given further reinforcement at the end of the thirteenth century by Maharam of Rothenburg. The reason for the creation of the Ruling was apparently knowledge about the French method established by Rabbenu Tam, which developed at the end of the twelfth century in northern France. In view of the growing number of problems and the powerful impact that the legal decisions of Rabbenu Tam of France had in Germany at the end of the twelfth and beginning of the thirteenth centuries, it became necessary to regulate the matter in the German sector as well. The Ruling formulated by Rabbi David was actually intended to promote the German method of leaving the property in the hands of the levirs as a recommendation of the *Beit Din*.[49]

The Ruling is comprised of two sections, one dealing with a widow and the other with a woman, whose fiancé had died, in respect to levirate marriage. The Ruling addresses the problem which the men considered to be critical, that is, the danger that their family's assets could be transferred to another family together with their brother's widow, and it gave his family (the remaining brothers) the halakhic means to regain this property for their extended family. The Ruling created a new reality based on an interesting compromise between the two parties. It stated unequivocally that the solution to this situation was *halizah* and not levirate marriage. In other words, the community decided that the levir should be kept away from his brother's widow and in this way they solved the complex problem using the 'French' method. The extended family was thus prevented from exploiting the opportunity to extort the widow with threats of *aginut* (the condition of a woman who may not remarry since she lacks a *gett* of divorce)[50] until she gave them the property transferred to her by virtue of her *ketubah*, which she was entitled to take with her when she set up a new family in the future. The Ruling established that, under threat of excommunication, the levir must grant *halizah* and release the widow within three months; this meant that an arrangement regarding the division of dead brother's property had to be made. According to the Ruling, the authority for making such an arrangement was given to the *Beit Din*, but the assets defined by the *halakhah* as belonging to the wife (*nikhsei melog*) would always remain in the hands of the woman and were not subject to discussion or argument.

The Ruling instructed the local *Beit Din* by alluding to the case of the daughters of Zelophehad (Num. 27) where it is written: 'No inheritance of the Israelites may pass over from one tribe to another'. The daughters of Zelophehad were women who did in fact receive an inheritance, although only on condition that they marry men from the same tribe. This is more than a hint to the *Beit Din* that, in regard to the property of the now disbanded family, preference should be given to the man's extended family, just as in the case of the daughters of Zelophehad, where the property of the tribe was preserved according to the ownership rights of the male heirs. Nevertheless, since the Ruling views the power of the *Beit Din* as a central component in the communal arrangements, it can only recommend a course of action to it. The *Beit Din* and its *dayanim* have to make the decisions.

From the halakhic standpoint, the most conspicuous point in the Ruling is the fact that its authors were no longer concerned that *halizah* given under compulsion might be a future threat the widow gaining release. They had come to the conclusion that the levir could be compelled to grant *halizah* to his dead brother's widow. Thus they fully accepted the trend that had been initiated in France by Rashi at the end of the eleventh century and then resolutely continued by his grandson, Rabbenu Tam, in the second half of the twelfth century. The sages understood that their decision did not conform in full with what had been developed in the Talmud: levirate marriage is a commandment; in theory there was no way to compel someone to grant *halizah*; and the fear existed that such coercion might bring about an unsuitable *halizah* and generate a problematic halakhic situation for the widow if she married again. Nevertheless, at the end of the thirteenth century, even Maharam agreed that the most damaging aspect of this problem was the behaviour of men who, because of their greed for money, created situations in which Jewish women become *agunot*. To Maharam this was an insufferable state of affairs and so, in the end, he supported the Ruling, did not oppose attempts by the *Beit Din* to compel *halizah*, and declared that the recalcitrant levir 'should be flogged until he gives in', etc. As a consequence, at the beginning of the fourteenth century, circumstances in Germany were similar to those in northern France, that is to say *halizah* was favoured by all concerned. When Rabbi Asher ben Yehiel (Rosh) went to Spain at the beginning of the fourteenth century, he spoke out against what he observed there, saying that in Ashkenaz and France the practice is that no levirate marriage is performed at all, even if both parties wish to do so. Nonetheless, the families evidently did not find it easy to accept this decision, and from the letters of *dayanim* in fourteenth and fifteenth-century Germany, it appears that this Ruling had to be repeatedly reinforced. The most complicated example appears in the writings of Rabbi Joseph ben Solomon Colon (Maharik) in fifteenth-century Italy. He sought to put pressure on a levir of this type and have him excommunicated. The man refused to grant *halizah* to his brother's widow because he wanted to extort a large sum of money from her and, in order to evade the decisions and Rulings of his community in Germany, he simply went to a different city and ignored the demands of his community. As a consequence, he turned the woman into an *agunah*. Rabbi Joseph Colon wrote that, in addition to the ban he placed on the man, he requested that the *Beit Din* in his city compel the man, in other words, that it should free the woman. In the end, the sages came to the conclusion that a forced *gett*, that is to say one given under compulsion, the practice which they feared more than anything else, was the right thing to do.[51]

The rebellious wife

From the standpoint of the male world, the case of a 'rebellious wife' is the most problematic. It involves a woman who is seeking the right to influence the family unit and even break it up on the basis of her will, without having to rely on a man and his decisions. We have seen that the male world was forced to authorize a *gett* given under compulsion in cases of impotence or levirate marriage. But men found it difficult to approve the break-up of a family unit when a woman sought to do so because of her own emotional state, and naturally, by labelling her a 'rebellious wife', they challenged her request with the usual pretexts that limit the power of the women within the family and in the economic sphere.

The source of the term 'rebellious wife' (or 'rebellious husband' for a man) is the *Mishnah* and *Gemarah* where it is used to describe a married woman or married man who refuse to fulfil the obligations which they undertook when setting up the family unit. In the *Mishnah* and *Gemarah*, the problem is solved in the following manner: in the case of a 'rebellious wife' who refuses to carry on normal marital relations with her husband or to carry out one of the tasks that she is obligated to perform, sums of money to which she is entitled are deducted from her *ketubah* and after that, she is divorced; for the 'rebellious husband', the punishment is the reverse; the amount of money he has to pay his wife according to her *ketubah* is gradually increased and in the end, the *Beit Din* forces him to grant her a divorce.[52] A closer examination reveals that the sages distinguished between two types of rebellious wives: (1) those who do not provide a specific reason, or as the Talmud defines it '[One] who says, 'I like him but wish to torment him' (Tbab. Tractate Ketubot 63b); that is, a woman who wants to remain with her husband but intends to cause him pain and distress; (2) those who claim 'He is repulsive to me', that is, a situation whereby, for whatever reason, a wife cannot have normal sexual relations with her husband or continue to live with him.[53]

On the basis of the discussions related to rebellious women in the *Mishnah* and the *Gemarah*, it appears that, despite the threat and the punishment, women did indeed choose this path in order to free themselves from husbands to whom they were bound. At first, a woman's *ketubah* was actually reduced by seven denarii every week until the entire amount of the *ketubah* was exhausted, and then she was divorced by her husband. At a later stage, the practice changed. The *Beit Din* gave the woman a warning and for a period of four weeks in succession she was declared a 'rebellious wife' in the synagogue. If she did not recant, they warned her again and then she lost her entire *ketubah* and was divorced. In an attempt to prevent these 'rebellions', the *amoraim* increased the woman's punishment by postponing the awarding of her *gett* for twelve months so that she could not marry again during that time; in addition, the husband was not required to provide for her maintenance throughout that twelve-month period. This punishment acted as a deterrent because it prevented women from remarrying for one year.[54]

Underlying the decision about punishing these women was typically male, paternalistic logic that sought to put the woman back in her place performing her duties. This was done by threatening, and carrying out, the confiscation of property and financial assets to which she was entitled at a gradually higher rate until all her property was wiped out and she was left with no assets; afterwards, she was also divorced by her husband. A threat of this sort was effective against a woman who says that she is interested in tormenting her husband and the sages used this method in an effort to persuade such women to get back on the right path. 'Male logic' was also behind the discussions in the *Mishnah* and *Gemarah* about whether or not to return property to a woman who decides to change her mind after part of her property has been confiscated. 'Male logic' can also be seen in the demand, advanced in various ways, for extra punishments for this type of woman, because she was suspected of 'becoming attracted to another' or seeking to extort money from her husband, since he knew that she would be refraining from doing certain tasks and having sexual intercourse with him for a long time.

None of these pretexts is relevant in relation to a woman who seeks to free herself from her husband on the grounds that he 'is repulsive to her'. According to some of the men (Rashi, for example), by presenting this claim, the woman already knows that she is giving up her *ketubah*, so why not free such women immediately, they asked. Why do they also have to endure the long procedure of warnings, delay, deductions from their *ketubah* and the punishment of waiting twelve months to receive a *gett*? The only possible answer is that the male viewpoint here is characteristically paternalistic. The men thought that they knew what was best not only for themselves and the community, but also for the woman herself. Consequently, they wanted her to go through the same process even when she claimed for objective reasons that her husband was repulsive to her and she was not willing to continue living with him under any circumstances. This extreme paternalistic approach is reflected in the Talmud, in the words of the *amora* Mar Zutra, who believed that economic pressure should be brought to bear on every 'rebellious wife'. He apparently thought that this type of woman did not know what she wanted or the extent to which she was putting herself in danger when she attempted to gain release from her husband in this manner. However, among the *amoraim*, he is quite alone in this paternalistic attitude.

A significant change with respect to the issue of the 'rebellious wife' occurred in 651 in Babylonia and its satellite communities with the formulation of the 'rebellious wife Ruling', which meant in practice that a woman could demand a *gett* from her husband and that he would have to release her immediately. In other words, the *Beit Din* could compel the husband to divorce his wife without delay. The husband would also be obligated to give her her *ketubah* and her dowry, including inalienable assets (*tzon barzel*) and her estate (*melog*) property;⁵⁵ however, he would not have to give her any supplement to the *ketubah* nor any presents she received while they were married. In the tenth century, Sherira ben Hanina Gaon (*c.* 906–1006), also of Babylonia, described this change and the reason for it. He believed that there was a danger that women would turn to the Muslim authorities to force their husbands to grant them a divorce. Such a *gett* given under compulsion was very problematic and could, as we have indicated above, have extremely severe repercussions, and might make the future children of the woman (if she married again later on) *mamzerim*. In order to prevent such a scenario, the *Geonim* created a Ruling (called *takanat ha-Geonim*) so that from that time forward, a woman could demand a divorce and her husband would have to release her immediately and even give her her *ketubah* and her assets specified therein.⁵⁶ From an historical point of view, the explanation and justification for the creation of this Ruling, that Sherira Gaon came up with some 300 years after its introduction, should be treated with some scepticism. What is certain, however, is that delaying the provision of a *gett* for twelve months, or even longer, and the forfeiting of the supplemental amounts in the *ketubah*, constituted a fatal blow to women, who found themselves in an intolerable situation, without any means of support from either their husband's family or from their parents. This risk gave rise to the concern that women would turn to a life of sin, a view adopted by later generations.

In Germany the *takanat ha-Geonim* was recognized and applied up to the twelfth century. In three *responsa*, Rabbenu Gershom Me'or HaGolah (who died in 1028) indicated that, in his day, the practice was to follow the *takanat ha-Geonim*, in other words, the man divorced his 'rebellious wife' immediately. It is important to pay attention to the fact that he made it clear that the reason for this stance was that 'the women of Israel should not turn to a life of sin', a possible allusion to the possibility that these women might convert if they were not shown goodwill and freed from the bonds of a marriage intolerable to them. He discussed the case of a woman whose husband contracted a skin disease; after five years she claimed that she could no longer live with him and she requested a divorce on the grounds that 'I can suffer him no longer.' Rabbenu Gershom instructed that she should be divorced without delay, even if this meant compelling her husband to give her a *gett*, because he was afraid that the woman might turn to a path of sin if they delayed granting her her *ketubah* or a *gett*. The explanation given by Rabbenu Gershom was simple. He believed that the talmudic precept and *takanat ha-Geonim* should be followed in this case: the woman should be released promptly, even if it meant forcing the husband to give her a *gett*, an action which must not be delayed for a year.[57]

Rabbenu Gershom Me'or HaGolah enabled the woman to be divorced, though he did require her to pay a high price for her release. Since he harboured the suspicion that if women learn about this option they will take undue advantage of it, he allowed them to have their *ketubot*, but without the supplements. He expressed his concern that 'The floodgates will be opened and women everywhere will deceive and marry, and then before you know it, they will say that they cannot suffer their husbands and their *ketubot* will be paid, they will marry again and after a year or a month they will do this again, and the [situation] will become irreparable.'[58] In this way, he believed, he could prevent women from exploiting this situation. It should be remembered that, in effect, Rabbenu Gershom's Ruling in the case of a woman who claimed that 'he is repulsive to me', which also involved the forfeiture of part of the amount to which she was entitled, was the outcome of the ever-present fear that 'she is attracted to another man'. As we have seen in Chapter 4, in Rabbenu Gershom's day, it was theoretically possible to have more than one wife. This was why he thought that the *takanat ha-Geonim* was a suitable solution; it was preferable for the man to divorce the woman rather than have her lapse into a life of sin because she lacked the means to support herself for twelve months. Rabbenu Gershom deprived these women of part of their *ketubot*, certainly the supplements, and maybe even the main portion of the *ketubah*, but not the dowry. 'Life of sin', the concept he mentioned with trepidation, may be understood as either prostitution, since in this situation, a woman would have to rely on someone to maintain her, or the fear that she might convert to Christianity.[59]

In northern France they adopted a similar approach. In Rashi's commentary on the Talmud that deals with the issue in Tbab. Tractate Ketubot 63b, his basic line of reasoning is that a woman who claims 'he is repulsive to me' is willing to relinquish her *ketubah* and for this reason, the husband may immediately grant her a divorce. With regard to the talmudic problem of the 'rebellious wife' who declares 'I wish to torment him,' he states that she should be coerced by reducing her *ketubah*; but if she states 'He is repulsive to me, but I desire not the man and not the *ketubah* as it is,' she is not forced to wait, but is given a *gett* and leaves her husband's house without her *ketubah*. On the other hand, Rashi did not imply that the man may, or must be compelled to grant a divorce. This was clearly stressed by his grandsons and students in the twelfth and thirteenth centuries. They made the assumption that if Rashi had thought that it would be necessary to compel the husband to grant a divorce, he would have stated so explicitly.[60]

In the twelfth century, the marital relationship underwent a fundamental change and, of course, the worldview of the sages at that time also changed. After establishing the Rulings that favoured women (the prohibition of bigamy and the institution of consensual divorce) the legislators of the Rulings felt that it was now necessary to restrict women. The decision regarding immediate divorce made in the Geonic period was no longer applicable in Ashkenaz. The *Geonim* did not consider divorce under compulsion a major problem because a man who released his wife quickly and without difficulty could easily have been married to another woman. In Ashkenaz, from that time forward, a man could not have more than one wife, and how could she be allowed to control his destiny? In essence, the 'rebellious wife' who declared that she wanted to cause her husband distress was actually saying that she is refraining from doing her wifely duties and from sexual intercourse for the length of time it takes for him to agree to divorce her. It is not surprising that this was looked upon as arrogance, impertinence, brazen and even immoral behaviour on her part. The male world had given her the position of a wife in a monogamous family and forced the husband to obtain her acquiescence to divorce, whereas the woman was taking advantage of this situation to coerce him into complying with her wishes and to extort property from him. Hence, it is understandable that the two leaders in Germany and northern France, who spearheaded the reforms that improved the status of women, were also the ones who favoured the idea of dealing very harshly with the 'rebellious wife'.

Raban of Germany, who was the architect of the Rulings prohibiting bigamy and non-consensual divorce, fought vigorously against the possibility that a married woman could, after all the reforms that had been made to bolster her status, attempt to rid herself of her husband or cause him distress by abstaining from sexual relations with him. Rabbi Eliezer declared that it was necessary to take extreme measures in regard to such women, openly indicating that this outlook stemmed from the new situation in his generation whereby women know that if they behave according to the definition of 'rebellious wife', their husbands cannot take another wife. By abstaining from sexual relations, they were, he maintained, exploiting the new situation that the leadership had created for them. Raban stressed that it was intolerable for a woman to be able to benefit simultaneously from her ability to put pressure on her husband due to the ban against his taking another wife and her right to force him to give her a divorce. Therefore, he said, such women must be denied what they gained by means of the new Ruling. The solution he offered was to threaten to allow the husband to marry another woman, making the woman an *agunah* for one year. This plan of action was meant to teach other women a lesson and deter them from behaving in the same manner.[61]

In northern France at that time (the first half of the twelfth century), Rabbenu Tam made a similar decision.[62] We can learn about Rabbenu Tam's overall point of view on all its levels, because we have available to us his commentary on the relevant sections of the Talmud, as well as his response to a query about a concrete incident in one of the communities.[63] He strenuously opposed the option of compelling divorce on the husband. In his commentary on the Talmud he stressed first of all that the Talmud established that the husband grants divorce exclusively at his discretion. Second, according to talmudic precedents, a woman can make a claim in a *Beit Din* only in regard to situations enumerated in the Talmud; moreover, only another court is entitled to examine the proofs she was required to bring before them to compel the husband to grant a divorce. As regards all other cases, the *Beit Din* had no authority to compel a man to grant a *gett*. The reason for these assertions was that the woman is suspected of 'being attracted to another man'. Indeed, Rabbenu Tam's statements clearly indicated his fear that women would try to deceive their husbands and exploit the situation to obtain a divorce and their *ketubah*. He derived his justification for this suspicious attitude towards such women from the Talmud, which states that the *dayanim* (the judges) should not tend to agree in advance even with a woman who claims that 'Heaven stands between us' ('He is impotent') or 'I cannot live with him any more', because she is suspected of being attracted to another man. He also sought to avert situations in which a woman who claims 'he is repulsive to me' could turn to the local authorities in order to annul both the marital and economic relations between her and her husband. The aim of such a woman, he believed, was to harass her husband, to withhold sexual relations from him for a long time, and to force him to pay her as much as possible when, in the end, he divorced her.

Rabbenu Tam's testimony about an actual case gives us a clearer idea and emphasizes another factor underlying his thoughts on this subject. He discussed a debate he had with his brother, Rabbi Samuel ben Meir (Rashbam), and with a group of *dayanim* from Paris, who tended to support the idea of a *Beit Din* compelling divorce on husbands in cases of 'rebellious wives'.[64] In his opinion, a man should not be compelled to grant divorce. He was afraid that if the wife accepted such a *gett*, the children produced from a new union contracted later on would be *mamzerim*. This was also the basis of his protest to his brother: 'Heaven forbid that our rabbis should create *mamzerim* among the Jewish nation.' He also opposed the *takanat ha-Geonim* because it did not delay the granting of a *gett* for a 'rebellious wife' and forced the husband to give it immediately, asserting that the *Geonim* did not have the authority to establish such a procedure. Rabbenu Tam's argument is based on the new situation whereby the husband cannot marry another woman. He implied that the 'rebellious wife' was ostensibly willing to be released from the marriage at the cost of sums of money subtracted from her *ketubah*, although in reality she wanted to torment her husband and in order to achieve this goal she was prepared to keep him 'tied up' for twelve months, during which time he could not marry another woman. The new situation created this opportunity for her. Since the husband could not marry another woman, the 'rebellious wife' could prevent him from engaging in normal sexual relations until he divorced her. Such a woman, Rabbenu Tam maintained, was not worthy of being 'rewarded' by having her husband forced by the *Beit Din* to grant her divorce, particularly in view of his conviction that forcing the husband to grant divorce was forbidden because of the possibility that it might lead to producing *mamzerim*.

The fear of creating *mamzerim* led him to oppose any suggestion made by the sages of the Paris *Beit Din*. A man cannot be forced into awarding a *gett*; indirect coercion is also forbidden, as is 'persuasion' by gentiles; all of these methods produce a *gett* given under compulsion, transforming the children born from the woman's subsequent marriage into *mamzerim*. In Rabbenu Tam's view, the problem of *mamzerim* was so critical that it superseded all others. Since he dealt with two cases which are available to us, we know that this was not just a theoretical opinion. One dealt with a man who married the daughter of Rabbi Samuel of Chappes; the *Beit Din* ruled that he had to divorce her, whereas Rabbenu Tam revoked the sentence and bribed the husband 'in money and in kind' until he agreed to divorce his wife. Although this contradicts his general belief that indirect coercion is forbidden, it seems that in handing down judgements in specific cases, he sometimes contradicted his own principles. Similarly, in the other case, Rabbenu Tam decided to enlist everyone in the husband's surroundings to agree to put social pressure on him, separating and isolating him from the community in a sort of excommunication until he agreed, 'voluntarily', to divorce his wife: 'they should not speak with him, transact business with him, or invite him to their homes for a meal or a drink, and if he gets sick, they should not care for him or even visit him'. His *responsum* confirmed his opinion that a husband whose wife declares 'He is repulsive to me' has to divorce her, as proven by the situation he initiated whereby the husband would have to divorce his wife because of tremendous pressure exerted by the entire community; nevertheless, the authorization of a *gett* given under compulsion filled Rabbenu Tam with trepidation due to his fear of *mamzerut*. This approach served as his guiding light to such an extent that he made the following crucial statement: 'It is better to let her remain an *agunah* than to make her sons the objects of gossip.' In other words, it is preferable for the community and for the woman that she remains an *agunah* (unmarriable) rather than entering a situation in which her children might be considered *mamzerim*.

Rabbi Isaac (Ri), Rabbenu Tam's nephew (his sister's son) took a different approach. He also had a guiding principle: the power of the *Beit Din* to impose its opinions even in cases involving married couples. Ri challenged the response of Rabbenu Gershom Me'or HaGolah regarding a woman who asked for a divorce five years after her husband contracted a skin disease. Ri opposed not only Rabbenu Gershom, who deliberated on how to rule in the case of this 'rebellious wife', but also his uncle (without actually naming him) because he (Rabbi Isaac) focused on the authority of the *Beit Din* to impose divorce and a *gett* in this case. Citing several *halakhot* from the Talmud in which the *Beit Din* compels the husband to divorce his wife against his will, Ri asserted that in this case the wife was blameless and tried to live with her husband. In his opinion, it was impossible to avoid imposing a *gett* by compulsion on the husband, since she was not the guilty party; furthermore, she was entitled to receive her *ketubah*. He also upheld the *takanat ha-Geonim* in respect of its propagating prompt divorce, since in this way it would be possible to avoid the long delay prior to the granting of the *gett* (twelve months) and to circumvent the risk that 'young Jewish women will embark on a life of sin, whether through prostitution or conversion'.[65] In effect, Ri was saying that the problem of the 'rebellious wife' can be resolved by using the solution that exists for the woman who declares that 'he is repulsive to me', and in this way he was again offering an effective and halakhic solution.

Yet Ri's opinion was not accepted. The *responsa* literature abounds with discussions on the subject of the 'rebellious wife' that took place throughout the thirteenth century. Most of them do not look upon the woman who claims 'He is repulsive to me' as anything other than a wife who refuses to live with her husband but nonetheless seeks to obtain his money. The leadership formed an almost solid front against these women to prevent them from getting hold of family assets of any kind even if such property was defined as their possessions or property they had brought with them at the outset of their married life. In other words, the sages were attempting to restore the men to the superior economic position they had previously enjoyed, while at the same time punishing the 'rebellious' women. Indeed, any case we might choose to examine will illustrate that this especially resolute male reaction was due to the very powerful status of women, from both the economic standpoint and as regards their position within the family, and because, in reality, they had achieved their objectives. This male behaviour was the outcome of the increase in both the economic power of women and their apparent desire to free themselves from husbands whom they found objectionable. If the sanctions against a 'rebellious wife' consisted of fines or the withholding of some of the amounts of their *ketubot*, women may have been able to tolerate such penalties in view of the reasonable economic circumstances under which they began married life. This was particularly true of a widow who remarried. The threat made by Raban – to allow the husband to marry another woman when his wife 'rebels' – was not effective because the sages were very reluctant to use it, and it is reasonable to assume that women understood this and did not allow it to dissuade them from pursing their goals. And even though from the twelfth century on, Rabbenu Tam's fear about 'creating *mamzerim*' was also taken into account, it was not a major consideration among the sages.

The subject of 'rebellious wives' is frequently addressed in German sources dating from the middle of the thirteenth century. The main protest voiced by the male writers was against the economic power and various advances achieved by women, as borne out, they believed, by the growing number of 'rebellious wife' cases. The conviction that this was a main characteristic of female behaviour was so widely accepted that an important scholar even used it in the title of his book on the subject of women in Jewish society.[66] Let us examine, in this light, a few of the prominent cases in the *responsa* literature of the thirteenth century through the eyes of the most prominent halakhic authorities. Fortunately, several *responsa* dealing with this issue, which were written by the most influential halakhic authorities of that generation have survived. We have available to us several *responsa* written by Rabbi Meir ben Barukh (Maharam) himself, as well as those written by his students, Rabbis Hayim ben Isaac, the son of Isaac ben Moshe (Or Zarua) and Asher ben Yehiel (Rosh). Rabbi Hayim tells us that his opinions are drawn from the teachings of his mentor, Maharam, and from his own father who died in 1250. Rosh's opinions are also based on what he learned from his eminent teacher, Maharam, what he learned on his own, and what he felt he could contribute after his travels to Spain, at the beginning of the fourteenth century, where it was customary for the Jews to marry more than one wife and to divorce 'rebellious wives' according to the *takanat ha-Geonim*.

The first example is a direct query from *dayanim* in the community of Regensburg, who describes a problem and request/suggest a way to resolve it.[67] Although written in an agitated and unclear style, it demonstrates that even then, at the end of the thirteenth century, they did not know what to do or how to pass judgment in cases dealing with 'rebellious wives'. This illustrates the power of the woman as well as the authorities' inability to make decisions that contradict women.

The writer described the *dayanim* dealing with this problem as 'orphans and the sons of orphans', who did not know how to pass judgement: Should they follow the precepts of the *Mishnah* and *Gemarah*, or make their own 'academic' decision? Nonetheless, all of their questions related to the attempt to curb the financial powers of the 'rebellious wife' and sought to clarify how and to what extent it would be possible to restore to the husband the property that the wife was entitled to take with her, or how to fine her on account of the amounts connected with her estate or her inalienable assets, payments that the husband deducted from her *ketubah*, property that she brought with her in her *ketubah*, etc. (As in every case discussed in these sources, the opposite situation was also described in which it was the man who had 'rebelled'; this was done in the name of fairness and in order to understand how much a man would be obligated to pay his wife.) The interesting point is that the writers did not dare reverse the Ruling of Rabbenu Gershom Me'or HaGolah with respect to the 'rebellious wife', as, they recalled, had been the suggestion of Rabanat the beginning of the twelfth century. The implication was that the women were threatening to turn to the Christians. The sources did not make it clear whether they were simply intending to seek assistance from the Christian authorities against their husbands or were contemplating conversion to Christianity; but what is certain is that, whatever their intention, it deterred the men. Yet, the sources also provided a different explanation related to the nature of the men. It was obvious to the writers that the men should not be given such a powerful weapon as the revocation of Rabbenu Gershom's Ruling, because they would not consider it a sanction designed to bring about a woman's backing down from her 'rebellion', but instead they would take advantage of the situation to avenge themselves by preventing her from remarrying. They would categorically refuse to grant her a *gett* and she would find herself an unwillingly married woman and an *agunah* in her own home with her husband married to another. The colourful phrase used by the petitioner 'give him a bone between his teeth', shows that although he felt that the husband's position *vis-à-vis* his 'rebellious wife' deserved to be reinforced, the author of the query could not consent to cause the wife hardship by reinstating the situation that had prevailed prior to the ban on polygamy. He summed up the petition by asking that the *dayanim* be permitted to determine which of the amounts that comprise the wife's assets should remain with the husband.

The response (written by Rabbi Meir ben Barukh himself, or in which, at the very least, his opinions are included) reveals that his moral inclination was to separate the spouses so that the wife would not be rewarded for her transgressions, and on the other hand the husband would not be permitted to marry another woman while still being married to her. Maharam strenuously opposed this last possibility because he was against a man having two wives, or even seeming to have two wives, 'that one is his wife and that one is his mistress' (Tbab. Tractate Ketubot 62b), a phrase that illustrates more than anything else the importance which the sages of his era attached to the institution of the family, its sanctioned structure, and the status of women within it. He was also concerned that this sort of treatment would lead Jewish women to embark on a path of sin.

Maharam's response is on two levels, one expresses his theoretical views and the other is the actual Ruling. This duality is often found in the sources dealing with the 'rebellious wife'. On the theoretical level, Maharam stressed that the woman should be punished in some way in order to teach all women a lesson; for this reason he rejected the idea of compelling the man to grant a divorce, which he regarded as allowing 'the guilty party to profit from [her] sin'. Nonetheless, he believed that the spouses should be separated and suggested that the man grant his wife a conditional divorce at this time subject to her relinquishing certain funds; after that, he would immediately be allowed to marry another woman. Maharam recommended that the *gett* should not be given hastily in order to punish the wife, and so that other women would learn a lesson, would appreciate their husbands, and not rebel against them.

On the second level, when Maharam addressed a specific case, his Ruling was different. The man claimed that his wife left home suddenly during her pregnancy and moved to her parent's home, remaining there after the birth of the child. The woman claimed (through her legal guardian) that the husband would beat her, even when she was in *niddah*, causing her great 'suffering and humiliation' and now she declared that 'he is repulsive to me'. In other words, she was using this claim to repulse her husband's attempt to represent her as a 'rebellious wife' and weaken her position. Maharam's resolution was unusual in that it justified both sides and thus obviated the need for the intervention of the *Beit Din*; in fact, he attempted to force the couple to compromise and solve their problem by themselves. In the woman's favour, he declared the rule that 'we cannot force her to live with a snake' but he was not prepared to compel the husband to grant a *gett*, because he feared that it would be a *gett* given under compulsion. Thus, Maharam stated explicitly that the couple should decide for themselves and since he ruled out the intervention of the *Beit Din*, he relied on a solution that would develop from the relationship between the spouses. (As we shall see later on, he often used this method.) In contrast to this resolution, Maharam adopted a far more stringent attitude towards a 'rebellious wife' when he found out that she had been attempting to deceive her husband and break away from his authority while holding on to a large portion of [his] property, or that relatives had given her advice on how to break up the family unit while retaining her husbands' property.[68]

Rabbi Asher ben Yehiel (Rosh), Maharam's student, was the main figure in shaping the attitude towards women with respect to this issue.[69] We have already seen that, in regard to various topics, his attitude towards women was based on his belief that in the wake of the important change attributed to Rabbenu Gershom Me'or HaGolah, which he regarded as the ultimate change, there was every reason to fear that women would become superior to men. Rosh wrote some of his works in Spain; after going there and surveying the situation, he compared it to what was then accepted in Ashkenaz and made Rulings and decisions on this basis. With respect to the issue under discussion, he had to make a great effort to put across his views because in Spain, where he was living at the beginning of the fourteenth century, the *takanat ha-Geonim*, the Geonic tradition and methods dealing with the 'rebellious wife' held sway. They enabled the rebellious woman to be divorced from her husband by means of a *gett* given under compulsion and even took into consideration the writings of Maimonides, who maintained that the husband should be forced to divorce his wife if she claims that she finds him repulsive and cannot have sexual relations with him.

Rosh's basic argument was that the decisions of the *Geonim* and Maimonides were based on assumptions that were appropriate for a different time and different women; they were made as 'provisional or *ad hoc* ordinances or Rulings', temporary in nature, due to the fear that the woman might turn to non-Jewish authorities or embark on a path of sin. For this reason, he believed, they agreed that the *Beit Din* could compel divorce. To counteract this view, he cited the resolute stance taken by Rabbenu Tam against divorce under compulsion, which leads to *mamzerut*. Furthermore, he asserted that the women of his day were 'immodest', their only aim being to free themselves from the male authority of their husbands or to form a relationship with another man.

Rosh's use of the term 'immodest' should be understood as referring to a woman who possesses property, is assured of her superior and powerful status, and strives to achieve her objectives in a male world and with the all-male *Beit Din*. In essence, he tried to expound that if the approach that advocates the release of a 'rebellious wife' gains broad acceptance, this will turn into a plague and all women will act in this manner: 'They will no longer behave as the children of our Father Abraham, living under the authority of their husbands, but will turn their attentions to other men and rebel against their husbands.' The women of his day: 'follow their capricious desires'; 'find other men attractive and more desirable than the husbands of their youth'. On the other hand, he described his fellow males as 'loving the wives of their youth'. To bolster his claim, he cited the approach of his eminent teacher, Maharam, noting in particular that sage's suspicions relating to a 'rebellious wife', that is to say, she planned her 'rebellion' in order to gain control of funds. This was why Maharam tried to find out if someone had given the woman advice about how to behave and which sums to demand. If he discovered that someone had indeed counselled her, Maharam did not authorize these sums of money to be handed over to her because he suspected, according to Rosh, that 'she was attracted to another man'. Although Maharam was conscientious about making sure that the 'rebellious wife' received everything that she had brought to the family unit, he did not agree to compel the husband to grant a divorce and also demanded a thorough investigation of any woman who claimed that her husband 'was repulsive to her' before he would believe that she was telling the truth. Nevertheless, wherever Rosh described what actually transpired, we see that in the end, the women obtained their release and their money. He concluded the discussion about this issue by saying that: 'it is appropriate to rely on your custom at the present time to force [the husband] to give a *gett* in a timely manner'. This lends further support to my contention that women almost always won the cases that were heard in the *Beit Din*.

The more we examine later sources attributed to Maharam's actions in cases of 'rebellious wives' brought before him, the more we find his students citing the ever-increasing strictness he adopted as this behaviour became more widespread. According to his students, towards the end of his life (the last decade of the thirteenth century) he fought this trend mainly by forbidding the woman from receiving property from the family unit she was in the process of dissolving, even assets from the dowry that she had brought with her from her parents' home, her estate, which would remain in the hands of her husband – a severe, almost unprecedented punishment.[70]

Rabbi Hayim ben Isaac, the son of Isaac ben Moshe (Or Zarua) provided a precise and cogent picture of reality at the end of the thirteenth and beginning of the fourteenth centuries. In one instance he proved that, in reality, it was possible to compel a husband to grant a *gett*. Let us take, for example, the case of a man by the name of Naphtali, who had married his daughter to a man, who, it turned out, did not have sexual relations with his wife for a period of three years. With the aid of Christians, Rabbi Naphtali got hold of the man and along with the Christian authorities, put pressure on the son-in-law and threatened him. The husband agreed to grant his wife a divorce on payment of a certain sum of money (£44); however, he hastened to make a public announcement that this was a *gett* given under compulsion. The *dayanim* decided that, since the husband had taken the money, his public announcement was invalid.[71] This meant that, if a woman had justifiable grounds (impotence) and the husband avoided having marital relations with her, it was appropriate to deal with him in this manner, even if he announced that he had been forced into granting the divorce.

As with other issues dealt with in this chapter, attempts were also made to formulate Rulings to solve the problem of the 'rebellious wife'. Rabbi Hayim ben Isaac recounted that, at the end of the thirteenth century, Maharam had received a request from Rabbi Yedidyah of Speyer, in the name of the three communities (Speyer, Worms, and Mainz), to create a Ruling according to which a 'rebellious wife' would leave the family unit without any property whatsoever, even what she had brought with her from her father's house.[72] If Maharam went along with this (as Rabbi Hayim implied he did), his conclusions about 'rebellious wives' had indeed become more severe, since we have seen that, in sources attributed to him, he had defended their right to the property that they brought with them to their new family. According to Rabbi Hayim, the reason for such an extreme stand was that, at the end of his era, Maharam decided that in view of the fact that women frequently utilized the weapon of the 'rebellious wife', it was necessary to put a stop to this behaviour, which brought harm to the men and to the community. Subsequently, decisions related to this matter became more and more radical as they were dealt with by succeeding generations of his students, up to the time of the fifteenth-century rabbi, Jacob ben Moses (Maharil). Each one declared that they were carrying on the tradition of Maharam; each one was more strict with regard to the property that a 'rebellious wife' was not permitted to remove from her husband's domain; and each one attempted to establish this arrangement in the form of a Ruling that would deal more strictly with a 'rebellious wife' and take away her right to any of the property to which she was entitled. One of Maharam's students wrote that if it is found that someone else (her mother, for example) convinced the woman to 'rebel', she would be punished by having her husband take possession of all of her property and 'throwing the *gett* in her face'. He even stated that a Ruling to this effect was created in Bamberg.[73]

It seems clear that towards the end of the thirteenth century, women understood that they could be divorced from their husbands if they so desired by invoking the claim that 'he is repulsive to me' or by behaving as a 'rebellious wife'. The men tried to put a stop to this trend by attempting to regain control of the property that the women sought to obtain. The result was a battle between the sexes on the economic plane in which the men were the victors, as their accounts would have us believe. On the other hand, the sources make it clear that women took such steps more and more frequently, and that the *dayanim* hesitated to take a stand that would undermine the rights that the women had achieved thus far. The threat that a husband could be allowed to marry another woman without divorcing the first was not effective, and in the end, the inclination to divorce these women without giving them the property they were entitled to was not put into practice. Indeed, aside from the reference I found in connection with the Bamberg community, none of the sources contains a Ruling that dispossesses the woman of the property she was promised in her *ketubah*, a fact which illustrates the formidable status of women at this time.

Notes

1. Tbab. tractate Yevamot 113b.
2. Tbab. tractate Ketubot 75a–77a.
3. Tbab. tractate Nedarim 90b–91a (see *Mishnah* Nedarim, ch. 11:12); Tpal Nedarim 42d.
4. Tbab. tractate Ketubot 54b, 63a; Tbab. tractate Shabbat 52a.
5. A *mamzer* is a child born from a union prohibited under pain of death, or *karet*.
6. Tosafot on Ketubot 70, 70a, 77a; Rosh on Yevamot, ch. 6 (11).
7. See Chapter 2 and Glossary of Hebrew Terms on *bitul tefilah*. Disrupting prayers in the congregation and holding the worshippers hostage while explaining his problem.
8. This term is used in Deut. 23:2 to describe a man who has a defect in his sexual organs: 'No one whose testes are crushed [*petzua daka*] or whose member is cut off shall be admitted into the congregation of the Lord.'
9. See the Glossary of Hebrew Terms.
10. V. Aptowizer, *Introduction to Sefer Raaviah* (Eliezer ben Yoel haLevi), Jerusalem 1938, pp. 209–211, No. 983; J. Shatzmiller, 'Doctors and Medical Practices in Germany around the Year 1200: The Evidence of Sefer Hasidim', *Journal of Jewish Studies* 33 (1983), pp. 149–164, 583–593; J. Shatzmiller, *Jews, Medicine and Medieval Society*, Berkeley, CA 1994, p. 57 n. 1 (p. 172).

11 See the Glossary of Hebrew Terms.
12 S. Shiloh, 'Impotence as a Ground for Divorce', *Fifth World Congress of Jewish Studies*, Jerusalem 1969, vol. 3, pp. 353–367.
13 Tbab. tractate Nedarim 91a, 'for there is a presumption that a wife would not be so brazen to her husband's face as to advance a claim that he knows is false'. Tbab. tractate Yevamot 65a and Tosafot Yevamot 65a *s.v.* sbeno u vena.
14 Meir ha-Kohen, Teshubot Maimuniut, in Moses ben Maimon, *Mishneh Tora*, Isut no. 6. He reinforced this determination with halakhic proof from Tbab. tractate Yevamot 117a, which talks about a woman who declares that her husband died and that she was free to remarry. In this case, the Talmud established that if she also demands payment of her *ketubah*, she should be distrusted because she may have an interest in another man.
15 Tosafot on Nedarim 91a, Tosafot on Yevamot 65b, Rosh on Ketubot 1:18; 5:6.
16 Meir ben Barukh, *Sheelot u-Teshuvot ha-Maharam*, Prague edition, ed. M. A. Blakh, Budapest 1895, nos 319, 870; Meir ben Barukh, *Sheelot u-Teshuvot Maharam bar Barukh*, Lemberg edition, 1860, no. 394; Rosh on Ketubot 11:2, Sefer Mordekhai on Ketubot 251, Meir ha-Kohen, *Teshubot Maimuniut* to Moses ben Maimon, *Mishneh Tora*, Isut 26.
17 Isaac ben Moses, *Sefer Or Zarua*, Zhitomir 1862, vol. 1, no. 652.
18 See also S. Bartlet, *Licoricia of Winchester: Marriage, Motherhood and Murder in the Medieval Anglo-Jewish Community*, London 2009, pp. 55–57.
19 Isaac ben Moses, *Sefer Or Zarua*, Zhitomir 1862, vol. 1, no. 652; Meir ben Barukh, *Sefer She'elot uTeshuvot*, Crimona edition, Jerusalem 1986, no. 271; A. Grossman, *Pious and Rebellious: Jewish Women in Europe in the Middle Ages*, Jerusalem 2001 [Hebrew], pp. 68–87.
20 Meir ben Barukh, *Sefer She'elot uTeshuvot*, Crimona edition, Jerusalem 1986, no. 271.
21 Rabbi Hayim Paltiel lived at the end of the thirteenth and the beginning of the fourteenth centuries.
22 Meir ben Barukh, *Sheelot u-Teshuvot Maharam bar Barukh*, Lemberg edition, 1860, no. 136.
23 Meir ben Barukh, *Sheelot u-Teshuvot ha-Maharam*, Prague edition, ed. M. A. Blakh, Budapest 1895, no.94 ; Asher ben Yehiel, *Shut haRosh*, ed. S. Yudelov, Jerusalem 1994, no. 43 (2, 5, 12).
24 A. Agus, (ed.) *Responsa of the Tosaphists*, New York 1954, no. 75.
25 Hayim ben Rabbi Yitzhak, *Responsa*, Leipzig 1860, no. 69.
26 J. Katz, 'Levirate Marriage (*Yibbum*) and *halizah* in Post-talmudic Times', *Tarbiz* 51 (1981–1982), pp. 59–106; L. M. Epstein, *Marriage Laws in the Bible and the Talmud*, Cambridge, MA 1942, pp. 81–91, 123–126.
27 L. M. Epstein, *Marriage Laws in the Bible and the Talmud*, Cambridge, MA 1942, pp. 81–82.
28 A partial answer to this problem has been provided by the Mekhilta Bahodesh 7, p. 229, which points out that the two prohibitions were presented together in the Torah; consequently, the fear that anyone who enters a levirate marriage with his brother' s wife is committing incest is unfounded.
29 Tbab. Yevamot 39b.
30 J. Katz, 'Levirate Marriage (*Yibbum*) and *Halizah* in Post-talmudic Times', *Tarbiz* 51 (1981–1982), p. 63 nn. 14–18.

31 *Teshuvot uPsakim, Responsa et Decisiones.* ed. E. Kupfer, Jerusalem 1973, nos 141 (pp. 212–213), 143 (pp. 217–218); Isaac ben Moses, *Sefer Or Zarua*, Zhitomir 1862, vol. 1, no. 676; about Rabbi Judah haCohen see A. Grossman, *The Early Sages of Ashkenaz* [Hebrew], Jerusalem 1981, pp. 175–210.

32 Isaac ben Moses, *Sefer Or Zarua*, Zhitomir 1862, vol. 1, no. 676, 'any women would get in touch with a pagan and rebel'.

33 Meir ben Barukh, *Sheelot u-Teshuvot ha-Maharam*, Prague edition, ed. M. A. Blakh, Budapest 1895, no. 881; A. Grossman, *Pious and Rebellious: Jewish Women in Europe in the Middle Ages*, Jerusalem 2001 [Hebrew], p. 161 n. 153.

34 Tosafot on Yevamot 39b *s.v.* vei nicah.

35 Rashi on Yevamot 39b *s.v.* Amar Rav; Isaac ben Moses, *Sefer Or Zarua*, Zhitomir 1862, vol. 1, no. 638; Meir ha-Kohen, *Haggahot Maimuniut*, Hilcot Yibbum ve halizah 1.

36 J. Katz, 'Levirate Marriage (*Yibbum*) and Halizah in Post-talmudic Times', *Tarbiz* 51 (1981–1982), pp. 70–71, Rashi on Yevamot 39b *s.v.* Amar Rav.

37 Tosafot on Yevamot 39; Tosafot on Ketubot 64a; Isaac ben Moses, *Sefer Or Zarua*, Zhitomir 1862, vol. 2, no. 638, Sefer Mordekhai on Yevamot, ch. 4 (31); Rosh on Yevamot, ch. 4 (17); Moses of Coucy, *Semag. Sefer Mizvot Gadol*, Venice 1807, Ashe no. 52; Meir ha-Kohen, *Teshubot Maimuniut*, Isut 32; J. Katz, 'Levirate Marriage (*Yibbum*) and Halizah in Post-talmudic Times', *Tarbiz* 51 (1981–1982), pp. 59–106.

38 V. Aptowizer, *Introduction to Sefer Raaviah*, Jerusalem 1938, no. 973, p. 203; A. Grossman, *Pious and Rebellious: Jewish Women in Europe in the Middle Ages*, Jerusalem 2001 [Hebrew], pp. 163–165; Sefer Mordekhai on Yevamot 4:31.

39 J. Katz, 'Levirate Marriage(*Yibbum*) and Halizah in Post-talmudic Times', *Tarbiz* 51 (1981–1982), p. 73; A. Grossman, *Pious and Rebellious: Jewish Women in Europe in the Middle Ages*, Jerusalem 2001 [Hebrew], p. 164; Rosh on Yevamot ch. 14 (11).

40 On Sefer Hasidim see I. G. Marcus, *Piety and Society: The Jewish Pietists of Medieval Germany*, Leiden 1981.

41 Judah ben Samuel, *Sefer Hasidim*, ed. J. Wistinetzki, Frankfurt 1942, nos 721–723, p. 284.

42 *Responsa et Decisiones*, p. 214; Sefer Mordekhai on Yevamot, no. 57.

43 Meir ben Barukh, *Sheelot u-Teshuvot ha-Maharam*, Prague edition, ed. M. A. Blakh, Budapest 1895, no. 466.

44 Joseph ben Solomon Colon (Maharik), *Responsa Maharik*, Warsaw 1884, No. 102.

45 Isaac ben Moses, *Sefer Or Zarua*, Zhitomir 1862, vol. 1, nos 619, 638; Isaac ben Jacob haLavan ('white') (twelfth century) was a tosafist of Bohemia, the author of *tosafot* on *ketubot* and *yoma*, known also to have compiled various *piyyutim*. He was also known as Isaac of Bohemia or Isaac of Regensburg. He was a brother of the well known traveller Pethahiah of Regensburg. Isaac lived in Germany and in France, where he studied under Isaac ben Asher ha-Levi and under Rabbenu Tam.

46 Sefer Mordekhai on Ketubot, no. 291. Avigdor ben Elijah haCohen (*c.* 1200–1275), talmudic scholar in Italy and Austria, was born in Italy and studied under Eleazar ben Samuel of Verona, Isaac of Verona and later Simha ben Samuel of Speyer. For a number of years lived in northern Italy, in Ferrara, in Mantua and in Verona. For a time he lived in Halle, Germany, from where he conducted halakhic correspondence with Hezekiah ben Jacob of Magdeburg concerning a deed of divorce. On the death of Isaac ben Moses (Or Zaruah) of Vienna, Avigdor was invited to succeed him at Vienna. For about twenty-five years he was the central rabbinic figure in Austria,

and transplanted the talmudic scholarship of Italo-German Jewry to Austria, which eventually became the most important centre of Ashkenazi Jewry. He was one of the teachers of Meir ben Barukh of Rothenburg.

47 Meir ben Barukh, *Sheelot u-Teshuvot Maharam bar Barukh*, Lemberg edition, no. 384.
48 Kol Bo, No. 78; Hayim ben Rabbi Yitzhak, *Responsa*, Leipzig 1860, nos 146, 50.
49 See for example Meir ben Barukh, *Sheelot u-Teshuvot ha-Maharam*, Prague edition, ed. M. A. Blakh, Budapest 1895, no. 866; J. Katz, 'Levirate Marriage (*Yibbum*) and Halizah in Post-talmudic Times', *Tarbiz* 51 (1981-1982), pp. 84-85; L. Finkelstein, *Jewish Self-government in the Middle Ages*, New York 1924, pp. 229-230; Moses Parnas, *Sefer HaParnas*, Vilna 1897, nos 358-359; Yam shel Slomo Yevamot, ch. 4 (18); Moses ben Isaac Mintz, *She`elot uTeshuvot Rabbenu Moshe Mintz*, ed. J. S. Domb, Jerusalem 1991, p. 18b.
50 An agunah refers to a married woman who for whatsoever reason is separated from her husband and cannot remarry because it is unknown whether he is still alive. Here the term is also applied to a 'levirate widow' if she cannot obtain *halizah* from the levir.
51 J. Katz, 'Levirate Marriage (*Yibbum*) and *Halizah* in Post-talmudic Times', *Tarbiz* 51 (1981-1982), p. 84; see E. E. Urbach, 'The *Responsa* of R. Asher b. Yehiel in Manuscrips and Printed Editions', *Shenaton Ha-Mishpat Ha-Ivri* 2 (1975) pp. 1-154; Joseph ben Solomon Colon (Maharik), *Responsa Maharik*, Warsaw 1884, no. 102.
52 *Mishnah* Ketubot, ch. 5, *Mishnah* 5: 'The following are the kinds of work which a woman must perform for her husband: grinding corn, baking bread, washing clothes, cooking, suckling her child, making ready his bed and working in wool.' *Mishnah* Ketubot, ch. 5, *Mishnah* 7: 'If a wife rebels against her husband, her *ketubah* may be reduced by seven denarii a week. R. Judah said seven tropaics. For how long may the reduction continue to be made? Until [a sum] corresponding to her *ketubah* [has accumulated].... Similarly, if a husband rebels against his wife, an addition of three denarii a week is made to her *ketubah*. R. Judah said three tropaics.'
53 Tbab. tractate *Ketubah* 63b.
54 Tbab. tractate Ketubot 63a-63b.
55 *Tzon barzel*, property, is appraised before the marriage, with its value entered into the *ketubah*. The husband accepts responsibility to repay the full value of this property in the event that he dies or they are divorced.
56 M. Schapiro, 'Divorce on Grounds of Revulsion', *Dinei Israel* 2(1970), pp. 124-130.
57 Gershom ben Judah, *Teshuvot Rabbenu Gershom Me'or haGolah*, ed. S. Eidelberg, New York 1956, nos 40-42; Meir ben Barukh, *Sheelot u-Teshuvot ha-Maharam*, Prague edition, ed. M. A. Blakh, Budapest 1895, nos 261, 865, 250.
58 Gershom ben Judah, *Teshuvot Rabbenu Gershom Me'or haGolah*, ed. S. Eidelberg, New York 1956, nos 40-42.
59 In this context, it should be recalled that Rabbenu Gershom' s son converted to Christianity and died a Christian. A. Grossman, *The Early Sages of Ashkenaz*, Jerusalem 1981, pp. 112-113; S. Goldin, 'Juifs et juifs convertis au Moyen-Age : "Es-tu encore mon frère?"', *Annales, Histoire, Sciences sociales* 54 (1999), pp. 851-874.
60 Meir ben Barukh, *Sheelot u-Teshuvot ha-Maharam*, Prague edition, ed. M. A. Blakh, Budapest 1895, no. 946.
61 Eliezer ben Nathan, *Sefer Even haEzer, Sefer Ra`avan*, Jerusalem 1984, p. 261b. Evidently, this group of sages was also mentioned by Isaac Or Zaru'a in vol. 1, no 476.
62 A. Grossman, *Pious and Rebellious: Jewish Women in Europe in the Middle Ages*,

Jerusalem 2001 [Hebrew], pp. 438–450, shows that the same process happened elsewhere in Italy and Spain.

63 Tosafot to Tbab. tractate Ketubot, 63b s.v. Aval; Jacob ben Meir, *Sefer haYashar leRabbenu Tam: Heleq haShe'elot vehaTeshuvot (Responsa)*, ed. S. F. Rosental, Berlin 1898, no. 24; Jacob ben Meir, *Sefer haYashar leRabbenu Tam: Heleq haHidushim* (News), ed. S. S. Schlesinger, Jerusalem 1959, no. 4 pp. 15–16.

64 Evidently, this group of sages was also mentioned by Isaac Or Zaru'a in vol. 1 no 476.

65 Meir ben Barukh, *Sheelot u-Teshuvot ha-Maharam*, Prague edition, ed. M. A. Blakh, Budapest 1895, no. 262.

66 A. Grossman, *Pious and Rebellious: Jewish Women in Europe in the Middle Ages*, Jerusalem 2001 [Hebrew].

67 Meir ben Barukh, *Sheelot u-Teshuvot ha-Maharam*, Prague edition, ed. M. A. Blakh, Budapest 1895, no. 546.

68 Sefer Mordekhai on Ketubot no. 187; Jacob ben Moses Mulin, *Shut Maharil heHadashot* (new *Responsa*), ed. Y. Satz, Jerusalem 1977, no. 23; Jacob ben Moses Mulin, *Shut Maharil heHadashot* (new *Responsa*), ed. Y. Satz, Jerusalem 1979, no. 197.

69 Asher ben Yehiel, *Shut haRosh*, ed. S. Yudelov, Jerusalem 1994, 43:8.

70 A. Grossman, *Pious and Rebellious: Jewish Women in Europe in the Middle Ages*, Jerusalem, 2001 [Hebrew], p. 445 n. 142.

71 Hayim ben Rabbi Yitzhak, *Responsa*, Leipzig 1860, no. 126.

72 Hayim ben Rabbi Yitzhak, *Responsa*, Leipzig 1860, no. 69.

73 Meir haKoen, *Haggahot Maimuniut* to Moses ben Maimon, *Mishneh Tora*, Ishut, ch. 14 (30).

6

Women and the mitzvot

The highest level of Jewish religious expression is the performance of the *mitzvot* – the divine Commandments. In addition to those *mitzvot* that are understood, recognized, and defined as *halakhah* (Jewish Law), there also developed a wealth of customs (*minhagim*) that underwent changes over the course of time. *Halakhah*-based Commandments are found in or derived directly from the Torah (the Pentateuch or Written Law) or from the Talmud (Rabbinic or Oral Law). On the other hand *minhag* was based on ancient tradition, new modes of behaviour, geographic surroundings and changing circumstances, so that, in theory, these customs were seen by the rabbis as carrying less weight than the divinely ordained Commandments.

Women were not required to perform all the Commandments, yet their desire to perform and fully experience the *mitzvot* extended to almost all areas of *halakhah*. Their involvement was particularly noticeable in those areas that made medieval Jewish Ashkenazic culture unique, that is, the grey area between *minhag* and *halakhah*.[1] In my opinion, most Jews, both men and women, who wished to live a Jewish lifestyle in the fullest sense of the word saw no essential difference between the halakhic *mitzvot* and those based on *minhag*. Such distinctions were the concern of scholars and sages, teachers and leaders, all of whom were men. The fact that nearly all the material available to us today was written by a circle of learned men explains why it contains so many scholarly debates over distinctions between *halakhah* and *minhag* with respect to the observance of *mitzvot*, the exact manner in which they are to be performed, and the rules that govern them. Men and women who maintained the *halakhah* out of the genuine and simple conviction that this was the way to worship God did so without paying attention to these distinctions, even if they were aware of them. The religious conduct of women was marked by their desire to participate in the religious experience itself;

thus they saw no difference between carrying out a *minhag* or a clear-cut *halakhah*. Women considered the performance of any religious act which, in their eyes, made them part of the public religious experience, an essential part of the world of *mitzvot*. Very few learned men sanctioned this behaviour. They knew that, in principle, a distinction had to be made between *halakhah* and *minhag*, and that the women's behaviour undermined the male mind-set that many special Commandments were designated for men only.

Yet, men traditionally perceived the female spirit as being ardently devoted to religion, which was supported by the biblical tradition that the women had refused to take part in the creation of the golden calf in the desert. Aaron the High Priest had directed the people to go and bring the gold jewellery of the women, and of sons and daughters, for building the golden calf. The women, because of their spiritual devotion to God, refused to take part in this sin, which was defined as a specifically male failure. According to the text, the men were the ones who brought the jewellery to Aaron (Exod. 32:2–3), and the tradition of the medieval commentators on the Bible preserved the women's unequivocal refusal to fulfil their husbands' demands, asking them: 'You want to make a sculpture or molten image, which does not have the power of salvation?'[2] Here the medieval sages make their point by using an extremely significant expression 'sculpture or molten image'. This expression is associated with the public pledge made by the people of Israel on entering the Land of Israel to remain loyal to God: 'Cursed be anyone who makes a sculpture or molten image, abhorred by the Lord, a craftsman's handiwork, and sets it up in secret. And all the people shall respond, and say Amen' (Deut. 27:15).[3] This led to the sages granting the first day of every month (*Rosh Hodesh*) to women as a holiday and day of rest, on which they were forbidden to work.

In the synagogues of the Middle Ages, the cantor (*chazan*) would announce, on the Sabbath preceding *Rosh Hodesh*, the precise time on which the first day of the new month would be ushered in during the approaching week.[4] This was the way people knew when the new moon would first be sighted, when to recite the special *Rosh Hodesh* prayers and when the monthly holiday for the women would begin.[5]

By the beginning of the twelfth century, there appears to be more writing on the issue of women and Commandments than in the past. In principle, women, just like men, are obligated to perform most of the Commandments; however, there are *mitzvot* which they are not required to perform at all and others that are specifically intended for them. Yet men, the sages, shaped the realm of these *mitzvot*, gave them meaning, and instructed the women in their performance. Nonetheless, the twelfth-century debates and deliberations of the sages frequently reflect the pressure brought to bear by women seeking to influence the manner in which certain *mitzvot* were carried out, to raise the observance of customs to the level of the *mitzvot* themselves, and even to permit the performance by women of Commandments that women were not obligated to perform. The self-confidence of women had grown as the result of the developments we described in the previous chapters. Women were taking an increasingly active part in the economic activities of the community, they could express themselves on the public level and during the attempts of forced conversion by the Christians, and they confirmed the high status they had attained. Thus, what men wrote about the realm of Commandments reflected not only the pressure brought to bear by the women, who sought to fill their religious world with substance through greater participation in the world of *mitzvot*, but also what some of the writers felt about these women. These authors believed that the women were attempting to lay the groundwork for their entry into areas looked upon as a distinctive male domain, and widen the breaches that allowed them to participate in male rituals, and create their own rites to express their religious devotion.

The main difficulty facing the researcher attempting to draw conclusions regarding women in the Middle Ages, particularly as regards their religion's feelings, their approach to the world of *mitzvot* and the observance of *mitzvot*, is, of course, the total absence of writing by women. All my conclusions are based on male writing that depicts women's activities through the eyes of men and the male understanding of the observance of the *mitzvot* by women, their religious devotion, their understanding or lack of understanding of the world of *mitzvot*. The description through men's eyes might even be sufficient. However, in my opinion, one can attempt to reach a higher level of understanding. From the male writing and from the male description of the actions of women one may deduce a special feminine quality in the performance of certain *mitzvot* by women, their special attitude to these *mitzvot*. Since the *mitzvot* in Judaism are practical commandments, there is considerable importance to what the men describe the women as doing when they observe the *mitzvot*, as well as their understanding of what the women mean in their performance of the *mitzvah*. I reached the conclusion that Jewish men in the twelfth and thirteenth centuries were aware that the women did have a special approach in their observance of the *mitzvot*, and that they are able, to a large extent, to describe it.

Thus though no written record authored by women exists in connection with *mitzvot* and *minhag*, we are dealing here with a very rare instance when the voice of women does come through to us and can be accessed, since when male sages write about the processes involved in the proper observance of the Commandments, they frequently refer to women's actions in this regard. The sages sometimes authorized women's practices in advance, more often after the fact, and frequently rejected them out of hand. If we pay particular attention as we trace the male voice heard in the discussions about these issues, we can, for the first time, describe the manner in which women were perceived to relate to the *mitzvot* and to belief.

In this chapter I trace the course of this debate. In the first part I relate to those Commandments that the sages define as inherently 'male': such as those concerned exclusively with men and the actions they must carry out, or those defined as having to be performed at a specific time of the day and from which, because of this proviso, women were exempt. In the Middle Ages, women did not accept this male categorization of *mitzvot*. They found ways to observe those *mitzvot* they considered important, near and dear to their hearts, or part of their world, despite male disapproval, and thus established a distinct female model.

In the second part of the chapter, I describe how the sages attempted to dictate to women the manner of their observance of *mitzvot* set aside for women alone. The male sages interpreted what they determined as being strictly female Commandments in line with their objective of keeping control over the observance of the Commandments in general. The male perspective, for instance, could not tolerate the attitude that the lighting of the candles on Sabbath eve that was traditionally performed by women was the ceremony which actually ushers in the holy day. Hence, they defined both the ceremony and the start of the Sabbath differently. Nonetheless, alongside the male outlook, a female viewpoint and practice developed in which the women considered themselves as inaugurating the Sabbath day. The male sages also defined – within the confines of the *halakhah* – all the rules associated with *niddah* (menstruation). Here, too, the women developed their own special concepts, evolving a distinctively female perspective concerning this time of the month, which affected their conception of the *mitzva* and its regulations, as well as its performance, including all the pertinent fine points.

I will show that during the Middle Ages (and, I believe, in every era), women found a way of their own to relate to the world of *mitzvot* and keep the Commandments. They created a model they considered appropriate to them, one that stemmed from their deep religious devotion (a trait which the men also viewed as feminine). This model contradicts male conceptualization, that was based on their prior immanent perception of femaleness. The aim of this chapter is not just to describe the performance of the *mitzvot* by women, but also to portray the manner in which they defined and differentiated their femininity by means of the Commandments.

Synagogue and prayer

In the Middle Ages, Jewish community life was centred around the synagogue. It was the place where rites were performed, prayer services and major ceremonies were held; it is where group socialization took place, and the image of the community took shape. The entire family – men, women, and children – came to the synagogue to participate together in these moving and inspiring ceremonies and events.[6]

Though the sages defined the synagogue as a 'place for everyone', they made it clear that the prayer service is to be carried out by men in a space defined as 'male'. The women had to come to terms with this approach and clarify their place in prayer, a *mitzva* of paramount importance in the Jewish world. Women did evidently find a way to express themselves as women in prayer, even overcoming the seemingly impossible obstacle of literacy, so as to be able to read in Hebrew the various passages recited on festivals and Sabbaths.[7]

But what was the status and weight of women within the constellation of prayer and the observance of the *mitzvot* connected with prayer? According to the early definition that appears in the *Mishnah* and *Gemarah*, women are required to participate in prayer: 'Women, slaves, and minors are exempt from reciting the *Shema* (one of the basic prayers) and from putting on *tefillin* (phylacteries), but they are subject to the obligations of prayer, of fixing *mezuzot* to doorposts and of reciting grace after meals'. Prayers are recited at fixed times, three times a day. According to the view defined in the *Talmud*, prayer is in essence a *mitzva* related to a 'plea for mercy', a frequently dealt with motif among medieval scholars.[8]

The picture reflected by the various genres of medieval sources is that during the Middle Ages, women made an effort to observe the Commandment of prayer, insisted on taking part in this religious experience, and frequently participated in ceremonies held in the synagogue – the community's central institution. They strictly adhered to the proper recitation of the prayers, attended synagogue frequently – on weekdays as well as the Sabbath and festivals – and identified with the institution and its functions.[9] For example, in the thirteenth century a woman who is involved in a family dispute over a house and property makes it clear that she does not wish to leave her community not only because her home is there and all of her relations live there, but also because she had a strong connection to the synagogue and her standing there was an important component of her identity within the community.[10] Similarly, Maharam declared, at the end of the thirteenth century, that women were required to pay for the maintenance of the synagogue since they were acknowledged to be active participants in its activities and as members of the institution itself.[11] So much did the male sages take the presence of women at all prayer services for granted that, as a matter of course, they pointed out that women need to check themselves to see if they are bleeding in the evening 'before going to evening prayers' – a fact that shows that the men were well aware that women attended prayer services every evening. Rabbi Eliezer ben Samuel Halevi dictated in his will in the middle of the fourteenth century that his children – both his daughters and his sons – should pray.[12]

Rabbi Eleazar of Worms wrote a moving poem in memory of his wife, Dolce, in which he recounts her many wonderful qualities, among them her participation in daily prayers. Written in the aftermath of his witnessing the cruel murder of his beloved wife by Crusaders of the Third Crusade, it was only natural that he would want to point out her fine character and piety. In one section of the poem, Rabbi Eliezer considers the prayer of Hannah (1 Sam.), who asks God to give her a son, and explains the connection between Hannah's words and the *amidah* prayer (the core prayer of every service, recited three times a day). According to his interpretation, it was as if the prayer of a woman, Hannah, had created the *amidah* prayer. This was how close he envisaged the connection between women and daily prayer.[13] Nonetheless, men considered themselves as taking preference over women in all matters related to prayer and the synagogue, basing themselves mainly on their superior knowledge of the language of prayer.

A more negative view is found in *Sefer Hasidim* which contains several stories that regard it as normal to find women among those attending synagogue services. The stories describe serious mistakes made by women, who, the writers believe, do not understand the importance of their presence there. Nonetheless, they make it clear that women routinely attended prayer services during the week while continuing to shoulder the burden of their regular tasks. So that, for example, to perform maternal duties they were often obliged to leave the synagogue before services ended, rather than waiting until their actual conclusion.[14]

Most of the talmudic sources dealing with study, reading, and familiarity with the Talmud refer to boys, and it is clear that the sages did not think that girls needed to be taught the sacred language or given instruction in talmudic study and knowledge, which was the main, if not the only subject imparted to children. As regards women, the sources repeated most often are the more extreme texts that assert that study is an exclusively male concern and that the Talmud should not be taught to women.[15] We see here the explicit connection between literacy and prayer made by male teachers. Women's exclusion from learning implies that they would not be well versed in the language of prayer in the synagogue. There are those who state that prayers may be recited in any language one knows, and that it is not necessary to pray in the sacred tongue. This argument emerges in an interesting discussion on whether and to what extent women may participate in the grace after meals.[16]

According to the Talmud, three men who eat a meal together, must recite the grace after meals together (as a group), whereas ten men who eat together, not only recite the grace together as a group but must include the name of the Lord as part of the grace. The Talmud permits women to say this prayer to themselves. The sages of the Middle Ages note that women do not understand the sacred tongue so that therefore there is a problem with their prayer, since, to pray properly, one must understand the language. There were also those who claimed that since circumcision is referred to in the grace after meals (God is thanked in the grace, *inter alia*, for 'your covenant that is sealed in our flesh'), women may not say this prayer.[17]

Nevertheless, it is clear from the sources that in certain families, the daughters were taught to understand the prayers and women were also allowed to be part of the *zimun* (the reciting of the grace together as a group), sometimes even joining the quorum of ten men in the recitation of this prayer.[18] These women were well versed in prayers and in the world of *mitzvot*, and possessed the self-confidence that stemmed from knowledge and membership in a learned and distinguished family. This situation could exist because at that time (and up to the fourteenth century) there were still no organized communal institutions offering instruction to all children up to the age of ten. Research indicates that children of this age group were generally educated at home, where the father would hire a tutor for his son or sons, and create a 'home classroom' by bringing in other boys, primarily relatives but evidently neighbours as well. Under these conditions, girls could also participate in the learning process, in one way or another; when they were at home, they listened to the lessons and evidently took part in them, too.[19] In the families of the rabbinic leaders and the teachers themselves, the fathers made sure that their daughters learned the holy tongue and acquired the ability to study just like the boys. A Ruling made in the second half of the twelfth century stated that a man who leaves his home for an extended period of time for the purpose of making a living (he was permitted to stay away for up to eighteen months) must prove that he has left behind enough money to support his wife and children, and pay the fees of the tutors for his sons and daughters.[20]

An important section of *Sefer Hasidim* states that girls must be taught many things, stressing the necessity of instructing them in the Commandments and the laws of the Sabbath. In addition, the father is warned to be sure to keep an eye on the man who teaches his daughters.[21] Thus in the twelfth and thirteenth centuries an educated stratum of women, who were literate, able to read the prayers, draw conclusions from the halakhic material and led the entire female population was created in France and Germany. Consequently we find epithets such as 'the woman who leads prayers for women', 'the helmswoman', etc.[22]

This in itself provoked a reaction and during the thirteenth century, we see attempts by men to push women to the periphery of the group's main institution. This stemmed from these men's disapproval of the women's increasing power within the community, and led certain men to attempt to reinforce what they saw as the superior position afforded to them by the *halakhah* in various areas. This was expressed in terms of spatial distinctions,

The men enjoyed a superior status in the male section of the synagogue, where the prayer services actually took place. Because the sexes are separated within the synagogue, they had to make sure that women were not present within its male space during prayers. The male section was indeed a male space which women were barred from entering during prayers themselves; however, they could not be excluded from the entire range of ceremonies held there during services. When the *shofar* was blown on Rosh Hashanah (the Jewish new year), or when a sermon was given in the men's section, women would join the men and then a partition had to be set up inside the male section so that the women could, though still separate from the men, could hear what they needed to.[23] The rite of lifting the Torah and displaying it to the congregants following its reading was another ritual zealously maintained by the women, who would come forward to observe and join in. They would leave their places expressly in order to gather around the entrance and windows to see the Torah scroll being lifted.[24]

When a circumcision ceremony took place in the 'male section' of the synagogue, women often participated in role of godmother to the newborn boy. At the end of the thirteenth century, Maharam made a vain attempt to put a stop to this practice. He described a woman of distinction who had been given the honour of being the child's godmother; adorned in her finest garments and jewels, she sat in the 'male section' throughout the circumcision procedure. During this extremely moving ceremony, which takes place in the synagogue, the participants (men) ceremonially accept the eight-day-old male infant by means of a ritual that will qualify him to join the ranks of Jewish men. According to Maharam, women were allowed to serve as godmothers in most places but not in the men's section of the synagogue, but despite his protests against this practice over a long period of time, no one paid attention to what he had to say on this matter, and the practice persisted.[25]

As a result of this male behaviour, the women created a space for themselves in the synagogue: the 'women's synagogue'. It is unclear whether this was a reaction by the women to their rejection from the male section or a custom which began with the Jewish settlement in Europe at the beginning of the eleventh century to which men then responded. From the perspective of the written sources and archaeological research, it is clear that, from the thirteenth century, special rooms for women existed within the general space of the synagogue; it may, therefore, be assumed that this was a female reaction to being excluded by the men from the centre of activity. From the architectural point of view, it is clear that the women's synagogue was built as an addition which only sometimes actually adjoined the central building where the men worshipped, with the connection between them consisting of narrow apertures through which the women could hear something, or see the Torah being held aloft.[26]

Although women were confined to this space it was not exclusively theirs. We have seen that on *Yom Kippur* (the Day of Atonement), Maharam would not even return to his home, instead he would remain in the synagogue for the entire fast, all night and all day. At night, he would sleep in the 'women's synagogue' after the women had gone home. In other words, this space was considered part of the synagogue and adjoined the main building.[27] Separate activities took place in the 'women's synagogue', for example, the reciting of the Book of Lamentations on 9 Av (the fast commemorating the destruction of both Temples) or other activities of a social nature. At the end of the fourteenth and beginning of the fifteenth centuries, sages noted that in cases where women had to confess or atone for their actions, they were required to present themselves before their female friends in the 'women's synagogue' and make their confession.[28] The educated women undertook the task of conducting the prayer services; they knew the language, were familiar with the customs and laws, and led the women's prayers. Rabbi Eleazar of Worms pointed out that his wife, Dolce, was one of these women. We also have similar evidence from tombstones and memorial books, about Urania of Worms, who was 'the important young woman who sang *piyyutim* aloud for women', and about Richenza, 'who leads the prayers for women'.[29]

Commandments that women were not required to perform

We have seen that women sought to participate in all events related to festivals and the Sabbath, whether in the context of family or public celebrations; and in most cases, no reason could be found to prevent this. Women are obligated to fast on *Yom Kippur*, just like men. They are bound by the Commandments of the Sabbath; they light the Sabbath candles; participate in the rites of *kiddush* and *havdalah*; take part in the main ceremony of Passover, the Seder; and they must listen to the reading of the Book of Esther on the Purim festival, etc. However, there are many Commandments from which women are exempt, and their desire to perform these despite not being required to do so was frowned upon by the male community.

In general, whenever a Commandment is performed, it is preceded by the recitation of a benediction that begins with the words: 'Blessed art Thou, O Lord, our God, King of the Universe, who has sanctified us with His Commandments and commanded us to … ' According to the Talmud, some of the *mitzvot* have to be performed at a specific time of the day and women are exempt from performing these Commandments, since it is assumed that women may have to attend to their children at these times. Since women are not required to fulfil these Commandments, they cannot recite a blessing that contains the words 'who has sanctified us with His Commandments and *commanded us* to … '. Despite this clear and simple delimitation, the medieval sources make it plain that the women of northern France and Germany performed such Commandments and also recited the accompanying benediction. A man who recites 'who sanctified us and commanded us to … ' knows that he is required to fulfil the *mitzva*. A woman who says the same words, on the other hand, has no similar support; moreover, she knows that the sacred sources of the Talmud state explicitly that 'all time-bound *mitzvot* – men are obligated by them and women are exempt' (Tractate Kiddushin 33b–35a). If they recite a blessing superfluously they also run the risk of taking the name of the Lord in vain.

Nevertheless, women felt the need to fulfil these *mitzvot* and realized that if the accompanying benediction was not recited there would be no value in their performance. Sitting in a *sukkah* is such a Commandment but we nevertheless find women who perform this Commandment and recite the related *brakha* (benediction), because it symbolizes their participation in a major family event. Another such 'male' Commandment is the waving of the palm branch with the other three 'species', which is considered the central ceremony of the Festival of Tabernacles, but we find that women also perform this rite, and recite the accompanying benediction. We also hear about their desire to participate in the ceremony of the sounding of the ram's horn on the New Year, regarded as the major symbolic rite of that festival.

They therefore relied on the knowledge that women in preceding generations had recited the associated blessings. This was how they expressed their desire to be part of the world of *mitzvot*. It was primarily the power of custom.

The male point of view

In general, the sages tended to authorize the women's practices. They nevertheless conducted an extensive halakhic discourse to clarify for themselves the issues surrounding the custom and its status, allowing us to examine the male point of view on the matters in question. The major discussion on *mitzvot* derives from a section of a *Mishnah* in Tractate Kiddushin where the differences between men and woman in regard to the performance of Commandments are defined. One of the definitions maintains that men are obligated to perform all those *mitzvot* which have to be performed at a specific time of the day, whereas women are exempt from them. Yet even in the Talmud the *amoraim* already made clear that this rule is not always watertight; they cite the opinion of Rabbi Johanan, who asserts that one cannot use this ruling to draw conclusions on how to behave in real life. Examples are given of Commandments that have set times which women are indeed obligated to carry out and, on the other hand, women are not required to perform some of the *mitzvot* that are not time-bound.[30]

In performing *mitzvot* that are required to be done at a specific time, the Jewish women of the Middle Ages were actually following a tradition already mentioned in Mishnaic literature of two women who performed time-bound Commandments. These were 'Jonah's wife', who took part in a pilgrimage festival (walked, as the men did, to Jerusalem) and 'Michal bat Kushi', who wore phylacteries while praying, and the sages did not try to prevent either of them from performing these male precepts. Some of those who tried to understand the sages' reaction claimed that these Commandments (pilgrimage and *tefillin*) are not defined as having a time attached to them. Others explained the matter differently, citing the opinion of Rabbi Yosé, who held that if women are interested in performing a Commandment, they should be allowed to do so. Rabbi Yosé supported his opinion by relying on a precedent from the Second Temple Era. When an offering was brought to the Temple, the men would, as part of the sacrificial process, lay their hands upon it and bless it (*semikhah*). The women, who were located in a different part of the Temple, were excluded from the sacrificial process, including the *semikhah*, since it was derived in its entirety from the Torah (Lev. 1): 'If *any man* of you bring an offering ... ' Rabbi Yosé relates what participants in ceremonies at the Second Temple recounted: if the women so desired, the sacrifice would be brought to them in the women's section so that they could lay their hands on it (perform *semikhah*) as the men did. Rabbi Yosé described this action as providing the women with a 'pleasant experience'. This concept, which is not halakhic, describes the experiential, spiritual state of the women, and effectively highlights their desire to be closer to the action of the sacrificial process and experience something of the male religious world. This sentiment was used in the attempt to explain why the sages did not object to the women's behaviour – that of Michal bat Kushi, who prays wearing phylacteries and Jonah's wife, who seeks to participate in the experience of the pilgrimage.[31]

In the Middle Ages, the issue was discussed from the special perspective of the period. First, it becomes clear that in the eleventh century, women were already participating fully in the experience of the Sukkot (Tabernacles) Festival; they waved the four species, sat in the *sukkah*, and also recited the appropriate benedictions. The source recounts that some men did indeed object to this behaviour; the point is made, however, that 'a woman must not be prevented from reciting the benediction over the *lulav* and the *sukkah*' and goes on to declare 'since she performs this *mitzva*, she must say the blessing'. The author even bases his opinion on Tbab. Tractate Megillah (23a) where it states that in principle women may also be called up to the Torah and recite the blessing, but solely because this practice was regarded as being undignified for a woman to appear among a group of men, it is not actually implemented.[32]

At the end of the eleventh century, Rashi attacked the accepted opinion of his predecessors. He believed that women who perform Commandments they were not commanded to perform, contravene two fundamental and stringent rules. First, when they say the blessing containing the words 'who sanctified us with His Commandments' when they were not so commanded, they are making a *brakha levatalah* – a worthless blessing – and, in so doing they are violating one of the prohibitions of the Ten Commandments 'Thou shalt not take the name of the

Lord thy God in vain' (Exod. 20). Secondly, they are also contravening another prohibition – the prohibition against adding to the 613 *mitzvot* of the Torah. Rashi's statements clearly stem from his belief that the women were seeking to change the fundamental nature of the *status quo*, which rests on a clear understanding of statements in the sacred texts that differentiate between men and women with regard to the performance of the *mitzvot*: certain Commandments are allocated to both men and women, whereas some are given only to women and others, only to men. Rashi believed that any attempt to deviate from these rules and this structure is dangerous. Yet Rashi does not rely merely on one argument derived from talmudic logic, since he knew that there were those, including his own masters, who were willing to permit the benediction itself; finding support for this in the words of Rabbi Yosé of the Talmud and the 'pleasant experience' for the women. Rashi challenged the actions of the women on the basis of another principle, the prohibition against adding *mitzvot* which one was not commanded to do. In this way, he defines the aspirations of the women as a desire to change the divine order.[33]

Yet Rashi's opinion was not heeded. At the beginning of the twelfth century, the halakhic leadership in Germany and France supported the women's aspiration and even obligated their observance. In Germany, Raban permitted women to participate in the performance of the *mitzvot* and recite the accompanying blessing. Although he made it clear that he was requiring the performance of a custom that already existed in the previous generation – according to which the rabbinic leadership did not prevent women from performing Commandments which they were not required to perform. His halakhic analysis also makes it clear that he thought these *mizvot* should be performed by women, and looked favourably upon the connection which the women felt to the world of *mitzvot*. 'And [we should follow] what our forefathers did: not to protest against women who wave the *lulav* and recite the blessing, and also the blessing for sitting in the *sukkah*.'[34]

In France, the opinion asserted by Rashi's grandson, Rabbenu Tam, which corresponded with that of Raban, and opposed that of his grandfather. Rabbenu Tam, in the middle of the twelfth century, authorized women's performance of these *mitzvot* not only on the 'pleasant experience' grounds. He emphasized that in his opinion, if the *Mishnah* stated that Michal put on phylacteries, it meant that she had to make the appropriate benedictions as well. Rabbenu Tam found legitimacy for his opinion by referring to the case of Rabbi Joseph the Blind in the Talmud. Rabbi Joseph stubbornly insisted on performing all the Commandments despite his disability and despite his knowledge of Rabbi Judah's ruling, which absolved the blind from performing any of the *mitzvot*.

Here another important question is raised: which has greater value – a *mitzva* of a person fulfilling a Commandment that he has no obligation to perform, or of someone who does have the obligation? Rabbi Joseph the Blind felt extremely frustrated and disappointed to learn that the sages had decided that the latter were looked on more favourably than the former. He then discovered that Rabbi Judah had not actually said that a blind person is exempt from the *mitzvot* but rather that he must perform them. This discovery made him so happy that he held a celebration for all the sages.[35] This incident, though interesting in itself, served Rabbenu Tam as justification for his decision regarding those who volunteer to perform the Commandments. On the basis of Rabbi Joseph's ardour to perform the Commandments, he authorized women who sought to perform *mitzvot* they were not commanded to fulfil to observe them and to recite the accompanying benedictions, thus rejecting the halakhic dangers that Rashi had envisaged.[36]

Rabbenu Tam rigorously reinforced women's devotion to the performance of *mitzvot* and supported it unreservedly. This may be seen in the language of two *responsa* written in answer to two women's queries that related to fasting, a ritual which women observed very strictly. One woman who had just given birth asked whether she was required to fast, while the other woman wanted to know if she was required to fast on the fast of Esther (a fast day preceding the festival of Purim), since she had to appear before the authorities on that day. Rabbenu Tam said that they were required to fast, emphasizing the importance of their performing the Commandments, and his students in northern France and Germany upheld his approach.[37]

Rabbi Jacob of Marvege's (twelfth to thirteenth centuries) statements on this topic offer a fascinating insight into the male view of this question. Rabbi Jacob employed an interesting literary technique in which he claimed to receive answers to difficult halakhic questions 'from heaven'.[38] The questions he asked were: Are women permitted to make the blessing that is said over waving the four species? Is the person who blows the *shofar* for a group of women permitted to make the blessing for them as well? And are these benedictions not considered *brakhot levatalah* (worthless blessings), therefore taking the name of God in vain? The answer is interesting because of its structure: a combination of passages from the Bible (without any accompanying explanation), halakhic statements, *Midrash*, and halakhic determinations. The first passage is the instruction God gives to Abraham, who is displeased by Sarah's desire to cast Hagar out along with his son Ishmael. God says to him: 'In all that

Sarah hath said unto thee, hearken unto her voice' (Gen. 21:12). In other words, God orders Abraham to obey his wife.[39] The second verse is taken from the prologue to the receiving of the Torah at Mount Sinai (Deut. 5:27). 'Go, and say to them, "Return to your tents". This passage stresses the use of the plural that is both masculine and feminine, an allusion to the normal, mutual relationship that exists between the spouses. The third verse describes the apex of the Israelites' purification process in the time of Nehemiah, when the Jews returned from the First Exile and the men separated from their gentile wives and made a new covenant with God (Neh. 9). After that, there is a reference to a halakhic passage, from Tbab. Tractate Shabbat 23a. This asserts that the Commandments regarding the reading of the Scroll of Esther on Purim and the kindling of the Hanukah lights are binding upon women even though they are Commandments that have set times, because women participated in the miracles, just like the men. The text also emphasizes the connection between the *lulav* and women by using the symbol itself; the uniqueness of the *lulav* is that every palm tree contains only one *lulav*. This is an allusion to the belief that women do not have an evil inclination but only one instinct, the good inclination, in contrast to men, who have both good and bad inclinations. (It may also be an allusion to the female prophetess Devorah, who sat under a palm tree.)[40] Each of the verses that Rabbi Jacob of Marvege quotes indicates in a different way the importance of women performing Commandments that others regard as being the sole preserve of the men.

Similarly, God's Commandment with respect to the *shofar* is twofold. It derives from the fact that, when hearing the reverberation of the sound of *shofar*, men and women accept God's sovereignty upon themselves, while at the same time the sound of the *shofar* invokes the memory of the Patriarchs within God Himself, and for their sakes He has mercy on the Jewish people. Hence, it is only fitting that this ceremony should encompass both men and women.

The female point of view

Ta-Shma, one the most eminent contemporary scholars on the relationship between *minhag* (custom) and *halakhah* (law), states that the issue of women performing *mitzvot* which they are not required to do, while insisting on reciting the accompanying blessing – even though this is in absolute contradiction to legal logic – is an excellent example of the complex interaction between custom and law. It is hard to imagine a more blatant contradiction to the dictates of logic than the reciting a blessing which states ' … you have commanded us to … ' when you have not been so commanded at all. Halakhic scholars view this type of conflict as part of the debate surrounding the validity of custom and the nature of *halakhah*.[41] Ta-Shma sees this example as an important component of the discussion about the essence of custom, its validity and the willingness of the religious leadership to recognize it as a binding part of *halakhah*. Can custom make a place for itself within the core of *halakhah* and define itself as an essential part of *halakhah*? Can a certain custom be defined as *halakhah*, thus putting an end to the controversy surrounding its validity? Those who disagree do so because they do not want to see customs achieving the status of law; therefore, they attempt to keep the custom in a somewhat inferior position to that of the *halakhah* itself. Those who encourage women to perform *mitzvot* which they are not required to do, while saying the accompanying blessing, are in effect using the example of the women's desire to perform Commandments to give full halakhic authorization to a custom and grant it equal footing with halakhic law. Even though women are exempt from a *mitzva*, if the practice was to perform it, they were permitted to do so. This seems to demonstrate that custom is as strong and valid as *halakhah*.

Ta-Shma astutely points out the essential distinction between North Africa and Spain, on the one hand, and Ashkenaz on the other, in regard to customs. He argues that part of the Jewish world which maintained an almost direct connection with the *Geonim* (North Africa and Spain) adopted the approach of the Babylonian Talmud, i.e., that *halakhah* takes precedence over custom. They therefore gave preferential status to *halakhah* while custom was relegated to second place. The Ashkenazic areas, that came less under the influence of the Babylonian Talmud and the *Geonim* for a significant amount of time, bolstered the status of custom to a great extent and continued to follow this practice until they again became connected to the world of the Babylonian Talmud, during the eleventh century.

Women were strict about performing those *mitzvot* which they considered important but their selectivity in doing so indicates that they did not attempt to make any fundamental change in the religious-social order. They did not abandon their desire to participate in religious experience, no matter what the male point of view. It is understandable that women adopted and clung to customs that they found important to them to the point where the sages were unable (or unwilling) to sever the link between the women and their customs.

For example, women evidently did not insist on performing the *mitzvot* of phylacteries (Deut. 6:8) or wearing fringes (Num. 15:38), as women, we find, did in the *Mishnah*. However, it is clear that they wanted to participate in the general religious experience, whether through their involvement in their family's celebrations – the Commandment of sitting in the *sukkah*, for example – or in connection with the spiritual experience of the 'day of judgement', by hearing the sounding of the *shofar*.

The medieval sources reveal that women who were ill or had just given birth did not come to the synagogue on Rosh Hashanah (the Festival of the New Year). Such women felt disconsolate about the fact that they could not be part of what they considered the main ritual of the holiday. The solution was that they blew the *shofar* for themselves and incited the appropriate blessings, or asked a man to blow the *shofar* for them. But a man who came to the home of a housebound woman would already have recited the blessings and blown the *shofar* in the synagogue; therefore, the question was asked whether his repetition of the ritual would be considered a *brakha levatalah*.[42] The sages' concern lest the *shofar* blower might be taking the name of God in vain before sounding the *shofar* for his wife who was sick or recuperating from a birth, unquestionably led to circumstances in which women learned how to blow the *shofar* and it was not rare to find them sounding it and saying the accompanying prayers, as we learn from Rabbi Simhah of Speyer in the thirteenth century.[43] In a later era, Rabbi Jacob ben Moses Moellin, known as Maharil, asserted that it is a *mitzva* to sound the *shofar* for a woman who has just given birth and the fact that the person performing this act does so after finishing the prayers (in the synagogue) does not bother him. The opposite is the case; he sees this as a mark of appreciation for the new mother. In the morning, he asserted, the entire world is judged while the *shofar* is being sounded and now the woman is standing before the seat of judgement all alone. In order to circumvent the issue of the *brakha levatolah* for the *shofar* blower, he suggests that the woman should recite the benediction herself.[44] It appears that, starting with the end of the thirteenth century, the male sages recognized the women's need for almost complete participation in the world of the Commandments, and they even required this commitment on their part.

Women and their special Commandments

In the Middle Ages, one of the most frequently quoted passages on the relationship between women and the Commandments assigned to them is the *Mishnah* in Tractate Shabbat: 'For three sins women die in childbirth: because they were not careful to observe the laws of family purity (Lev. 15:19), to separate the *hallah* (set aside some of the dough when baking bread, Num. 15: 19–21) and in kindling of the Sabbath lights (Tbab. Tractate Shabbat 25b).' This warning places a dual responsibility on women. This warning linked the undoubtedly high rate of death in childbirth in the Middle Ages to religious shortcomings, a tactic visible in Christian sources as well.[45] The serious of the penalty stemmed from the fact that women were entrusted with three important and fundamental Commandments. The first of these, *Niddah* (the laws of family purity) affects the structure of family life and normal sexual relations, since its purpose is to separate and restrict intimacy between husband and wife. The second Commandment, *Hallah*, is a vestige from the period of the Temple, when a small portion of any dough that was baked had to be set aside for the priest (Num. 15:20). In the Diaspora it was not given to the priest but burnt and no food could be consumed if this action was not taken. The observance of this Commandment encompassed the task of the management of food preparation for the household, which was entrusted to women.[46] The third *mitzva*, the kindling of the *Shabbat* candles, ushered in the *Shabbat*, at the proper time before the *Shabbat* begins, as the sun set. That is, it created the boundary between secular time and the holiness of the Sabbath, the most important day of the Jewish week. Even though unmarried women or adolescent girls might keep these Commandments, it was made clear that only married woman were obligated to perform them. These three *mitzvot* Commandments that were entrusted to every married woman reflect the whole pattern of family life.

The male community understood the importance of the *mitzvot* that had been assigned to women, but were puzzled about why they were specifically designated for women only. The typical male response was to create a direct link between the three Commandments given to woman and the catastrophe caused by a woman – the one that took place in the Garden of Eden. Consequently, the men defined the Commandments as an attempt to allow women to correct the imperfect world for which they were responsible.

The Jewish viewpoint regarded Eve's sin to be the convincing of Adam to disobey the only Commandment given in the Garden of Eden (not to eat of the fruit of the tree of knowledge), an action which brought about man's expulsion from Paradise and his sentencing to a punishment that changed his original essence. This concept differs fundamentally from the Christian viewpoint that asserts that Eve sinned by tempting Adam and committing, together with him, the sexual act, for which there is no forgiveness.[47] According to the Jewish way of thinking, the days of the first man were not limited like those of mortals and he might have lived in the Garden of Eden for all eternity. Adam was the crowning glory of creation in that his essence was Divine. His blood was considered to be the blood of God, his spirit part of God's spirit, which illuminated the newly created world; and his body was perfect and pure, without blemish. The image used to describe the first human being is *hallah*, the complete bread, the symbol of perfect creation. By her actions, the woman caused Adam's blood to be spilled and his divine light to be extinguished; he was now mortal. From the moment he was expelled from the Garden of Eden, he began to anticipate his death. Moreover, the woman also caused creation to become impure.[48] *Midrashim* dating from the beginning of the Middle Ages absolve the first man of all guilt and ignore the express words of God in regard to Adam's failure (Gen. 3:17). Hence, the reason why women were given special *mitzvot* is that these Commandments remind every woman of the sin of Eve and allow every woman to atone for it and improve the world. The woman is responsible for the *mitzva* of *Niddah* because she caused the blood of Adam to be spilled; she is responsible for setting aside *Hallah* because she damaged his essence (immortality); and she kindles the lights because she extinguished the soul of Adam, which is compared to a candle. If she does not strictly observe these rules, her punishment will be death in childbirth.[49]

Of the three *mitzvot*, the Commandment of kindling the lights was given a very high ethical standing in the Middle Ages, more than it is given in the *Mishnah* dealing with divine punishment during childbirth. It became equated with the two *mitzvot* whose non-observance carried a punishment of *karet* (divine punishment by untimely death). This type of punishment was considered suitable for a woman who is not careful about matters of *niddah*, an action punishable by *karet*, or the problematic matter of setting aside *hallah*, where non-compliance was considered dangerous on account of the possible punishment from Heaven that also applied to other prohibitions related to the subject of *hallah*. Now, the kindling of the Sabbath candles lights was given comparable status. Medieval sages might have wanted to emphasize the point that lighting them late might constitute a desecration of the Sabbath, since kindling on the Sabbath itself was forbidden. In any event, it is clear that the lighting of candles by women was elevated and given the highest importance.

Kindling the Sabbath lights[50]

The talmudic discussion that deals with the kindling of Sabbath lights establishes two things: (1) that this act is 'obligatory' and may therefore be performed without a benediction; and (2) that the lights are kindled in honour of the Shabbat and that this is connected to the *mitzva* of enjoying the Sabbath. The lighting of the candles makes it possible to eat the

Sabbath evening meal after dark with the candles illuminating the table, allowing the meal and the Sabbath to be enjoyed. Midrash Tanhumah explains that the words of Isaiah, '... call the Sabbath a delight' (Isa. 58:13), mean that the Sabbath lights are kindled because 'if you sit in the dark, it is not a delight'.[51] In other words, the kindling of the lights both symbolized the arrival of the Sabbath and also served to illuminate the Sabbath meal later on. Defining the beginning of the Sabbath as prior to sunset, the onset of darkness, was suitable for the Land of Israel and Babylonia but completely unsuitable for northern Europe. There, according to this definition, Sabbaths during the summer would have to begin very late in the evening, so it was the practice to bring the onset of the Sabbath forward and celebrate it by lighting the candles or conducting the prayer service. We find that when the Sabbath was ushered in early in northern France, England, or Germany, the meal would be eaten during daylight hours so there was no real need for candlelight to give the meal the atmosphere of 'delight'.[52]

This being the case, the purpose of the lighting of the candles became, almost exclusively, the marking of the time of 'bringing in' the holy Sabbath, and that being the case the entrusting of the women with so important a function became decidedly controversial.

The male point of view

As we saw from the earlier discussion of certain Commandments such as sitting in a *sukkah* or hearing the blowing of the *shofar*, the 'male' view of the *mitzva* and a 'female' perception of it, though coexisting simultaneously, were often very different. From the talmudic definition, the importance of kindling the lights may be understood as relating primarily to the need to mark the time of the commencement of the Sabbath; furthermore, the medieval scholars knew that, according to ancient tradition, women were entrusted with kindling the lights. The men went out of their way to find a different method for defining the exact time when the sanctity of the Sabbath begins so that the woman would not be the one who, in practice, brings this aspect of the Sabbath into the home. The halakhic teachers made the point that it is not the act of lighting the candles that ushers in the Sabbath, but rather the evening prayer service and later on, the ritual of reciting the *kiddush* over the wine at the Sabbath meal. This way, the men would control the ceremonies that marked the commencement, as well as the end of the Sabbath. They greeted the Sabbath with prayers and *kiddush*, and took leave of the day with prayers and the *havdalah* ceremony. At the beginning of the eleventh century, Rabbi Isaac ben Rabbi Judah put this very simply. From his standpoint, the sanctity of the commencement of the Sabbath begins at the moment he, the man, recites the blessing – 'blessed be He who makes the Sabbath holy' – during evening prayers. In other words, for him, the sanctity of the Sabbath begins then during the prayer service, even if the lights are kindled beforehand. This was an opinion mentioned by the *Geonim* in Babylonia, and the Jews of northern France and Germany knew about it and discussed it in their books. Often, the two occasions could be coordinated, as described in sources dating from the early twelfth century: the husband would take the children to the synagogue for *minhah* (the afternoon prayers); the wife would stay at home and prepare herself to kindle the Sabbath lights; after the men finished the *minhah* service, they would send the children home and the children would announce to their mothers that it was time to light the candles. Here, all the members of the family took part in welcoming the Sabbath.[53]

When Rabbi Isaac ben Moses (Or Zarua) analyses the halakhic situation in the first half of the thirteenth century, he acknowledges that, according to what is written in the Talmud, evening prayers are indeed the time when the Sabbath commences; however, he cannot ignore the kindling of the Sabbath lights, so he turns to 'our ancient forefathers' who established the observance. He names Sherira Gaon, who is mentioned in *Sefer ha-Miktso'ot*, as the person who taught or learned about this from his masters. The story that supports this *halakhah* describes a Friday afternoon so cloudy and dark that people believed that the Sabbath was approaching. They quickly went to kindle the lights even before they had recited the *Minhah* prayers. After the clouds dispersed, the sages declared that anyone who had already lit the candles had taken the Sabbath upon themselves and could do no more work. Rabbi Isaac ben Moses (Or Zarua) expressed justified astonishment over the story,[54] but nevertheless declared that in the thirteenth century it was not possible for them to disagree with the earlier sages. From the continuation of the discussion, it is clear that he knew of this practice in his day and did not want to undermine it. He introduced the opinion of his teacher, Rabbi Isaac ben Rabbi Mordechai, who had stated that what may be thought of as the commencement of the Sabbath, it is the prayer in the synagogue that defines the beginning of the holy day even for those not present in the synagogue, so that the entire community may receive the Sabbath at the same time. Or Zarua may have been trying to reinforce the custom of kindling the lights as the ritual that marks the beginning of the Sabbath for fear that challenging this would also undermine the understanding that prayer in the synagogue is what ushers in the Sabbath, in practice, for everyone.[55]

The female point of view

From the female point of view, the woman is the one who receives the holy day when she lights the candles; and the start of evening prayers does not signal the beginning of the Sabbath. This is a new, different, and interesting viewpoint. What we have here is not merely the act of kindling, but the creation of a female ritual of candle lighting, reciting a blessing, and ushering in the festive day. We have available to us sources that contain excellent descriptions of the struggle associated with the act of kindling combined with a blessing, as well as the aspirations of the women in this regard and I will discuss some of these medieval sources below. The women viewed the Commandment as one meant especially for them and upheld it with all their might; they fought to make the *mitzva* and the ritual doubly important in spite of male opposition. From this standpoint, the sources portray the profound significance of the women's struggle.

Though the Talmud does not require a benediction over the kindling of the Sabbath candles, a blessing had already been defined for this ritual during the geonic period, and it was the practice to recite this blessing in northern France and Germany as well.[56] In the second half of the twelfth century, Rabbenu Tam, who lived in northern France, learned about corrections being instituted by one of the important sages, Rabbi Meshullam ben Nathan of Melun, mainly in regard to customs that had been accepted despite their lack of talmudic basis. In one instance, Rabbi Meshullam ben Nathan asserted that it was not necessary to recite a blessing on kindling of the lights. With all his well known fervour, Rabbenu Tam launched into an attack on Rabbi Meshullam's assertion and coincidentally describes the extent to which this custom had become standard practice among the women.[57]

Rabbenu Tam defines the Commandment as 'the obligation to observe the *mitzva* of enjoying the Sabbath day' and calls it a 'glorification' and a 'sanctification' of the day. If anyone attempts to abrogate the obligation to recite the blessing it is as if she is desecrating the Temple, he declares. The *aggadic* literature, he continued, gave this *mitzva* to women so they could rectify the damage done to Adam 'when the light of the world was put out'. This is indeed the custom and they practice it with great devotion and they are more knowledgeable about it than are the men. They light the candles first and at the correct time extinguish them;[58] then they kindle the lights again and recite the blessing in a whisper. Rabbenu Tam asserted that the action of the women is right and proper since '[Jewish women] are prophetesses and if not prophetesses themselves, then they are daughters of prophetesses'. This is not just a custom, Rabbenu Tam went on to declare, but also an obvious *halakhah* since the important book *Halakhot Gedolot*, states explicitly that on a Sabbath eve that occurs during the holiday of Hanukah, the Hanukah candles are lit first and only afterwards, the Sabbath candles. The implication is that kindling the lights by the woman is what ushers in the Sabbath, since the Hanukah candles may not be lit afterwards, once the Sabbath has been accepted. He also acknowledges that the entire process of kindling must be accompanied by a blessing. This was a custom and an act performed by women, and it was clear to the men that they would not relinquish their control over it. Thus, despite their continued hesitant efforts to cast doubt on the requirement of a blessing recited by women to usher in the Sabbath, most of them accepted the conclusions of Rabbenu Tam and insisted that both the custom and the blessing be performed by the women. Even those who did not require the blessing in principle, authorized the custom of the women by stressing that they were following the practices of Rabbenu Tam.[59]

Halakhic scholars, including those who acknowledged that it was the woman's responsibility to kindle the lights and usher in the Sabbath, thought that the blessing should be recited while the candles were being lit. As with every *mitzva*, where a blessing is recited this is done immediately prior to the performance of the *mitzva*. Raviah, in the book he wrote at the beginning of the thirteenth century, provides an explicit description of the manner in which the kindling should be carried out. After accepting Rabbenu Tam's opinion on the importance of the blessing, Raviah asserted that two candles should be lit and instructed the women to recite the blessing after lighting the first candle and before lighting the second one. In this way, in my opinion, he wanted the women to understand categorically that it was not they who were inaugurating the Sabbath, since they would never be allowed to light the second candle once the Sabbath had actually been inaugurated – since the lighting of fire itself is a desecration of the Sabbath.[60]

But the women had a different practice. We hear of Rabbenu Tam's sister, Hannah, who taught the women to begin reciting the blessing only after they had lit all the candles. Hannah understood that the benediction is the act that signifies the arrival of the Sabbath because during the summer in northern France and Germany, the lights are kindled when it is still daylight, before the day has waned. If the women have the power to determine when the Sabbath begins and are responsible for the ritual that marks its onset, they may only recite the blessing after all the candles have been lit, since, as we have said, it is forbidden to kindle lights on the Sabbath day once they had recited the blessing. Notwithstanding the halakhic logic contained in the instructions provided by the men, the women accepted the female reasoning put forward by Hannah. Even though the sages' writings made it clear that the blessing should be recited between the lighting of the first and second candle, the women persisted in reciting the blessing only after they had kindled both (or all, if there were more than two) the lights.[61]

The halakhic leaders asserted strongly the need to light the candles early, since they did not know exactly when the Sabbath started, and the longer the day, the more difficult it was to determine the exact time for kindling the Sabbath Eve lights. They feared that if a mistake was made and the lights were kindled too late, the Sabbath would be desecrated; and it was doubtful whether they wanted to rely on the women in this matter. Evidence of this can be seen in the custom mentioned earlier of sending the children home from the synagogue after the *Minhah* service to announce the exact time for lighting the candles to the women, who had remained in the house. The women were faced with another problem. Since, during the summer, the candles were kindled while it was still light outside; the men were no longer as stringent as they had been about eating in a place where the candles were burning, a practice laid down in the Talmud. At the outset the candles related to the idea of having light during the meal. Now when the meal was eaten during daylight, people could dine in the courtyard or in a place which was open and well lit.[62] The women understood this action on the part of the men as an expression of their desire to take over the prestigious act of introducing the holy day and thus lower their status. The women were, therefore, very strict about where the meal was taken; at the same time, they set about expanding the ritual and making sure that it had a sound basis. They took care to light the candles while it was still broad daylight so as not to kindle the lights during the Sabbath by mistake. When they were told the exact time for lighting the candles, they extinguished the lights and relit them, and only afterwards would they recite the blessing and thus usher in the Sabbath.[63] To improve the practice, they came up with the idea of spreading their hands, after lighting the candles, to hide their light from sight. When they put down their hands, they would see the light and could then say the blessing over it.[64] The literature of the period also contains evidence that women would say a *tehinnah* (a supplemental prayer of supplication) while lighting the Sabbath candles. The spreading out of the hands could very well be to hide the light of the candles while closing or covering the eyes with the hands for the *tehinnah* prayer. We first hear about women's recitation of *tehinnot* during the thirteenth century from Rabbi Jonah Girondi of Provence, who studied in the *yeshivot* of France during the first half of the thirteenth century. He gives us the typical wording of these *tehinnot:* 'Let it be Thy will that my children be lights in the world of Torah and *mitzvot* and the fear of God.'[65]

Thus the understanding developed in the consciousness of women that they were the ones who initiated the rituals of the Sabbath and sanctified the holy day. As I have noted, the men did not abandon their own different attitude, according to which they were the ones who ushered in (and concluded) the Sabbath rituals; however, it appears that during the twelfth and thirteenth centuries, they accepted and internalized the fact that this important role was the women's purview. This is the only way we can understand how authorization was given to women also for the ritual of kindling the lights on the festivals, in addition to the Sabbath. The ceremony of lighting candles on the festivals was not essential; moreover, it appears to me that the creation of this additional ritual in which the woman also fulfils the primary and central role could only have come about because of the existence of the Sabbath Eve rite.[66]

Niddah (menstruation and family purity)

The male point of view

From time immemorial, the male world has perceived the woman's monthly menses as something incomprehensible, a very dangerous and problematic time.[67] The woman loses blood for several consecutive days; then the situation is rectified and it appears as if the bleeding never took place. Men generally related to menstruating women with a mixture of anxiety, fear and admiration, which stemmed from the presence of the blood, symbolizing both the end of life and the power of renewed life. It was clear to the men that these female processes were related to obscure ancient secrets in the woman's personality, secrets in which they as men had no part. They regarded this cyclical power of renewal with absolute amazement.[68] Medieval Jewish sources discuss this matter at length and in great detail. The discussions took place on many levels, three of which are essential to our discussion here. On the first level, the theological one, we see that the male theory considered the period of *niddah* something which 'atones' for the actions of Eve, those which resulted in the spilling of male blood and the mortality of mankind.

The second level, the family level, asserts that the entire subject of *niddah* is related to conduct within the family unit and the relations between husband and wife. In the Middle Ages, the monthly *niddah* period and menstrual cycle were looked upon as a time of renewal for the woman and a critical component of relations between spouses. This is based on the opinion of Rabbi Meir in the *Mishnah*, who states the basis for normal relations between a man and his wife. In his view, people become dissatisfied with one another in the routine course of life, but the cyclicality of the menstrual period in the woman creates a cyclical period of separation and abstinence of the woman from the man. This renews the psychological desire and erotic tension between them, and recreates, every month, the psychological situation of the arousal and passion that exists between a bridegroom and his bride on their wedding night. The man yearns for his wife and at the end of the menstrual period, 'she is as enticing to him as on the day she went under the huppah (i.e. the day she was married under the wedding canopy)'. The cyclicality of the menses is also symbolized by the renewal of the moon, and the tension between its monthly disappearance and the anticipation of its return. Here, then, the woman is viewed as renewing herself each month, preserving the man's desire for her, and the sexual tension in the relationship between the spouses, the bond that creates the family.[69]

The third level is connected to the system of laws regarding ritual purity (*teharah*) and impurity (*tumah*); based on ancient and fundamental concepts in the Jewish religion, which provide the source of a fascinating view of the Jewish male attitude towards women. In Leviticus, God calls upon His people to keep the ritual purity of the entire encampment and in particular the area of the Tabernacle as a zone of special ritual cleanliness (Lev. 15:31).[70] After the Temple was built in Jerusalem, this divine Commandment was transferred to it. Everything required purifying and sanctifying: the Temple itself, its surroundings, the people who served in it, the vessels belonging to it, the sacrifices made there and eaten by the priests and the people. *Tumah* was considered the supreme enemy of proper conditions in the Temple; therefore, a system of rules was made to overcome and repel *tumah*, and achieve a state of ritual purity. In addition, situations of fundamental physical impurity were defined, such as inter-menstrual bleeding in a woman, a man's nocturnal emissions or urethral secretions, skin diseases such as leprosy, and birth and death.

Periods of ritual impurity resulting from proximity to a corpse or the act of touching a dead body were delineated. For women, the period of *niddah* (menstruation) and a certain amount of time following childbirth were defined as periods of ritual impurity. A system of 'avoidance' (and restrictions) was also set up to keep the *tameh* (impure person) away from those who might become ritually impure through contact with him or her. Rules were set down to define the conduct of the *tameh*, when the impurity took effect, and the rituals that had to be performed to terminate the state of ritual impurity and return to a state of purity. Definitions of the states of impurity were widened to include both the physical and physiological situation of a man or woman who became ritually impure from disease, proximity to a corpse, etc.) and the actions required by the *tameh* and those who might come into contact with him or her. A system of rules and regulations was set up to deal with separating and keeping away from the *tameh*, in addition to rules designed to prevent contact between the *tameh* and a person who was not *tameh*. During her menses, the woman in *niddah* is ritually impure and therefore unable to enter the area of the Temple or eat the meat of the burnt offerings. During this period, which lasts seven days, she is also not allowed to come into physical contact with her husband and so sexual relations are totally prohibited at this time. The punishment for sexual intercourse during *niddah* is *karet* (the divine death sentence) and there is one opinion that actually defines the children born of such relations as *mamzerim* (bastards).[71]

After the destruction of the Second Temple, it was clear that preserving the laws of *tumah* and *teharah* were no longer necessary or practicable. The main reason for the state of ritual purity had ceased to exist with the destruction of the Temple, which also meant that the rites of purity – all of which were connected with the Temple and carried out there – could no longer be performed. Almost all the rules of *tumah* were rescinded. *Niddah* was the only matter associated with ritual impurity that was not revoked or minimized; all the laws of separation and abstinence were preserved and their application was even expanded. In the Temple era, a woman in *niddah* would have to spend seven days separated from her family, after which she would bring a sacrifice. After the destruction of the Temple, burnt offerings could no longer be made nor was it necessary to isolate a woman from her family out of concern that her impurity would affect food. Nonetheless, the affirmation of the impurity of menstruating women was preserved, while immersion in a *mikvah* (ritual bath) replaced the offering of sacrifices. *Niddah* was no longer thought of as a public matter that concerned the Temple. Instead it became centred around the household and family, and the rules that were made governed married women and their husbands.

The changes and additions regarding women in *niddah* formulated by the male sages and set down in the *Mishnah* and later on in the *Gemarah* (Tbab. Tractates Berakhot 31a and Niddah 61a) derive from the biblical discussion concerning a person who has involuntary secretions (the *zav* (m.) and *zavah* (f.)). A *niddah*'s period of impurity is seven days: starting from the day that she begins to bleed until the end of the seventh day. On the night after the seventh day, she immerses herself in the *mikvah*, so long as she is no longer bleeding. The *zavah*, in contrast, is a woman who bleeds after her days of *niddah*. Such women must examine themselves to establish that they have not been bleeding for seven consecutive days; and they may then immerse themselves during the seventh day, not at night. In the Talmud, hundreds of years after the destruction of the Temple, the laws of the *zavah* and those of the *niddah* were combined. As a result, every *niddah* considers herself a *zavah* when calculating the days and immerses herself as a *niddah* at night. The reason for this combination was that what defines a woman as *niddah* or *zavah* is the timing of the bleeding. A woman with a regular menstrual period has no problem, but when there is an irregularity, it is difficult to know when a woman is *niddah*, that is, bleeding at the beginning of the cycle, and when she is *zavah*, i.e., bleeding between cycles.

Thus, seven days (that are called *libun*, 'days of whitening') were added to the days of bleeding (at least five), an addition taken from the biblical discussion about a man or woman who has a discharge from their sexual organ. The woman's process of purification in the *mikvah* was also borrowed from that of the *zav* described in the Bible (Lev. 15).[72] The *amoraim* in the Talmud were aware that the greater stringencies of the laws of *tumah* related to the *zavah* had encroached on and indeed had been transferred to matters of *niddah*. Rabbi Zera praised women who see a drop of blood and insist on applying the prohibitions of *zavah* from the Pentateuch to them, incorporating these prohibitions within the sphere of *niddah*.[73]

The *Mishnah* and *Gemarah* already contained arguments about the essence of the separation between a husband and wife during *niddah*. The Talmud contains two references to the matter of avoiding physical contact. Tbab. Tractate Shabbat 13a–b describes the strict ban against eating at the same table and sleeping in the same bed. Tbab. Tractate Sotah 61a describes the avoidance of activities that the woman does for her husband (defined as a type of service activity) which she cannot do when in *niddah*. It was stated, in the name of Rabbi Huna, that the *niddah* must refrain from pouring for her husband, making his bed, and washing his face, hands and feet.[74] In order to prevent intimacy and sexual relations between husband and wife, the sages had to establish boundaries and limitations. They placed a great deal of emphasis on the additional seven days of abstinence, the *libun* days, when a woman who has stopped menstruating checks herself again and again, until she immerses herself and resumes normal sexual relations.[75] The *Tannaim*, and afterwards the *Amoraim*, suggested an alternative system of purification rituals to mark the termination of the period of *niddah* in order to fill the vacuum created by the absence of the burnt offerings made in the Temple. For the men, the purification ceremony (*taharah*) served as an announcement that the woman had been freed from the state of *tumah* which she had gone through. For the women, who were participating in a purification ritual that continued to develop throughout the ages, the rite was also an affirmation of renewed intimacy with God.[76]

The attitude towards *niddah* and the woman in *niddah* was dealt with extensively in all the writings of the medieval sages of northern France and Germany. They were called upon to discuss this issue, clarify the *halakhah* related to it, indicate the related prohibitions, and analyse the customs associated with it.[77] From the standpoint of definitions, the situation remained as it had been in the previous era: from the moment the woman sees blood, she separates herself from her husband and starts to count the days. When she sees no more blood, she changes into clean clothes and checks herself for seven more days, which are called the *libun* days. After the seven *libun* days are over, she goes, at nightfall, to the *mikvah* to immerse herself and then returns home so that she and her husband may renew marital relations.[78]

Because matters related to *niddah* have been treated extensively in the sources written by male authors and because of the special nature of these Ashkenazi sources that relate to the customs of women – which these scholars felt obliged to consider – it has been possible to reconstruct (a) what the men thought about the proper way of performing the *mitzva*; (b) the way women conducted themselves; and sometimes (c) what the women themselves felt.[79]

The talmudic sages made a clear distinction between the laws of separation and abstention between a husband and wife during the period of *niddah*, and matters of *tumah*, which they associated with matters related to the Temple. Their statements indicate their concern that physical proximity between husband and wife during *niddah* might become a trigger for intimacies on the part of the aroused and passionate man which would eventually lead him to have sexual relations with her during *niddah*, an act that could produce *mamzerim* (bastards) and be punished by *karet*. The male leadership was deeply concerned about the fact that men were unable to abstain from sexual relations for such a long period of time; they feared that some men would attempt to have forbidden sexual relations, whereas others might be overcome by their instincts and abandon the prohibitions and the separation. This perspective was based on the psychological notion termed a 'pattern of sinful behaviour': an individual who is so used to engaging in a certain permissible activity that he continues in the same pattern even when that act is forbidden. Such a pattern is particularly true in respect to marital relations. Consequently, various prohibitions were delineated in order to provide a sound and well defined basis for the woman's separation from and avoidance of her husband during *niddah*. In keeping with this attitude, the seven additional days, the *libun* days, were defined as days on which the selfsame prohibitions applied.

The halakhic sages were also aware of what women felt about this subject and often related to these feelings in their writings. They noticed that during *niddah* women saw themselves as unclean or contaminated because they were bleeding, and as a consequence, they were extremely conscientious about avoiding actions that might bring the *tumah* into the sphere of the family or society. The sages assumed that these feelings on the part of the women stemmed from their inability to grasp the distinction between the rules of separation during *niddah*, which relate to that specific situation, and the laws governing the vessels and food that can take on *tumah*, which relate to the Temple. Hence, they frequently underscored this 'feminine' lack of understanding. Even though women did not conduct themselves according to *halakhah* as understood by male scholars – and what they, these scholars, had learned from texts available to them since the days of the Talmud – they realized that the women would continue their practices no matter what they might say. Thus, the religious leadership was satisfied by the fact that the customs followed by the women and the punctiliousness they showed when they saw the blood of the *niddah* had became integrated with the additional prohibitions, which were intended to prevent the 'pattern of sinful behaviour' and keep their husbands from making intimate advances towards them.

The essence of the male attitude is already apparent in the first half of the twelfth century in northern France, when Rashi's students reconstructed his opinions and writings on this subject, and Raban of Germany expands on this topic in his book.[80] Rashi considered a good and intimate relationship between husband and wife to be an important ideal and an essential requirement for family life. His opinion, which can be found in many places, was that the relationship between husband and wife should be one of affection, or *milei de-hibah*, as he termed it. A husband is required to show his affection for his wife and he should do this though subtle words and delicate gestures of warmth and of love. In Rashi's view, when the spouses touch one another, pour for each other, pass food to one another, they increase mutual feelings of affection and create an intimate closeness and normal routine all of their own. In contrast, during *niddah* there must be clear separation between the man and woman, and the system of *milei de-hibah* must be suspended completely. His assumption was that if the state of *milei de-hibah* continued, the man would not be able to control himself and refrain from making advances towards his wife despite the prohibition. Rashi believed that by his very nature, the male could not control his instincts, a conviction he found extremely unsettling. It appears that in this regard, he did not trust himself either; his students reported that he would even refrain from handing a key to his wife when she was in *niddah*.[81] Thus, Rashi relates to all the restrictions discussed in the Talmud as measures that avoid the state of 'closeness and affection', which lead to habits of intimacy between a man and his wife. Rashi, who was concerned about 'the pattern of sinful behaviour', recommended that men should keep conversations with their wives to a minimum and even suggested that women should not wear makeup or jewellery when in *niddah*.

According to Rashi's statements, the sages were also stringent with regard to the *tumah* of vessels and clothing. They adopted a strict approach with respect to women's actions in this sphere, notwithstanding the fact that the utensils touched by a woman during *niddah* were not ritually impure, since, following the destruction of the Temple, *tumah* was no longer a matter of halakhic concern. The sages designated special vessels, clothes, head scarves, sheets and pillows for the use of the *niddah* (menstruating woman); they did not touch their wives, sit on their chairs, etc. However, a clear ambivalence can be detected in Rashi's words on this subject. On the one hand, Rashi generally encouraged such measures, in particular the meticulous behaviour of women during their period of *niddah*, especially their avoidance of synagogue attendance. On the other, Rashi saw this as excessively strict conduct that stemmed from the women's lack of knowledge. He knew that the custom is based on a misconception. Women, he believed, relate to the synagogue as the Temple and consequently refrain from attending synagogue when they are in *niddah*. Women (in *niddah*) had been forbidden to enter the Temple because of its sanctity and the level of ritual purity (*taharah*) maintained there. Since the Temple was destroyed and it is no longer possible to offer sacrifices to achieve a state of ritual purity, there is no reason to be strict about such matters of *taharah*; in the end, everyone is impure in one way or another. Moreover, the underlying concept of the rabbinic leadership was to try to avoid equating the Temple with the synagogue, which had become the community's main public platform and the hub of its social life. This is the reason for Rashi's assertion about the synagogue: 'If it is not the Temple, then everyone, man and woman, may enter there.' On the other hand, Rashi encourages the women's behaviour of avoiding going to synagogue when in *niddah*, when he says: 'In any event, it is a place of *taharah*, and it is good that they [the women] do what they do.' He praises the women's determination to exclude the *niddah* from the synagogue, a consequence of the feeling of being impure. Rashi was well aware of this feeling and understood the custom; however, he called attention to the fact that it was a custom, one which he may even have thought to be of ancient origin.[82] With his same ambivalence he commended the practice as an ancient custom, and at the same time disparaged it as being 'only a custom'.

In the first half of the twelfth century, Raban (of Mainz) pointed out how strict the women of his day were about keeping the laws of *niddah*: they rigorously adhered to counting seven days from seeing blood, and even if they saw no more blood they nevertheless zealously maintained their distance from their husbands. They would avoid doing those tasks, which the Talmud explicitly defined as jobs that a woman should not do for her husband when she is in *niddah*; nor would they cook or bake for their spouses during their *niddah* period. As a Talmud scholar, Raban knew that there were *amoraim* who favoured limiting the scope of these prohibitions and recommended methods that would allow women to perform these tasks. The *amoraim* suggested that a woman in *niddah* could make her husband's bed (but – said the *amora* Rabba – not in front of him); that she could serve him a drink or pour it for him, but only while incorporating in the action some sort of symbolic change, such as pouring with her left hand instead of her right (the *amora* Shmuel) or placing his cup beside him but not actually handing it to him (the *amoraim* Abbaye, Rava, and Rav Papa). The medieval sages regarded these practices as habits of affection and intimacy (*darkhei hibah u-kirvah*) and looked upon them as subtle elements in the close and intimate relationship that exists between a husband and wife, which in their opinion, should be suspended the minute the woman discovers that she is in *niddah*.

Raban stated that in his day, women abstained from these signs of intimacy and affection and were afraid of their repercussions. Being a typical halakhic scholar, he pointed out the distinction between the proscriptions established because of *tumah* and the stipulations made in relation to the laws of separation. Nonetheless, he was aware that in his day, and in his milieu, women did not pay attention to such distinctions; they were very stringent and applied the laws of *tumah* to themselves. As previously noted, he believed that this stringency was not the result of their study of the minutiae of the laws of *niddah*, but rather from the strong sense of *tumah* and contamination which they felt when in *niddah*. The rules of separation that the women practiced and their uneasiness about intimacies and signs of affection, their husbands' lack of self-control and attempts to be intimate, led them, as he saw it, to be more extreme in their behaviour and even more meticulous than necessary by abstaining from the tasks which the Talmud permitted women during *niddah*. The example that he brings is the custom of women in his area to abstain from cooking and baking when in *niddah* (in contradiction to Tbab. Tractate Berakhot 27).[83] In other words, both Rashi and Raban insisted on supporting the practices maintained by the women, because they conformed to the religious outlook they used to judge the behaviour of men.

During the twelfth and thirteenth centuries the questions raised by Rashi and Raban continued to be discussed by all the sages of northern France and Germany; moreover, their approach continued to be supported because the stringencies conformed with the leadership's point of view. The strictness of men who desisted entirely from touching their wives for any reason during the time when they were in *niddah* and even refrained from handing to, or accepting food or other objects from them was seen as exaggerated, albeit positive, meticulousness. In other words, the male sages who made a point of noting that these actions on the part of the husbands were merely customs – and customs of setting boundaries – demanded their implementation essentially because they provided basic support for the separation between man and woman. The leadership preferred the continued preservation of these customs because they feared a situation in which men would try to become intimate with their wives during their time of *niddah*. Hence, all the stringencies and exaggerated meticulousness received their blessing: 'And those who are strict in taking care not to hand anything from their hand into hers are commended.'[84]

Another discussion is related to eating. The sages attempted to understand the essence of the prohibitions in regard to eating and how they were applied, because they wanted to have precise definitions of the proscriptions. Was it forbidden to eat from the same plate? Was it forbidden to eat together at the same table or should the boundaries be marked as they were when meat and milk dishes were served on the same table? The debates reflect the sages' perception of joint meals as a time when a type of physical and psychological intimacy exists between the spouses, an effect of their family and marital relations. Raban asserts that during the days of *niddah* it is very important to avoid the intimacy that arises from eating together; however, he also pointed out that the husband must return to the state of intimacy at the table on the last day before his wife immerses herself, since this is when it becomes transformed from 'a pattern of sinful behaviour to a pattern of *mitzva*'. He realized that the man must begin to be more intimate with his wife again towards the end of the *niddah* period. His grandson, Raviah, thought that taking meals together even when the woman was in *niddah* did not present a problem, and this seems to be what actually took place (i.e., that man and wife ate together). Nevertheless, he, as well as others, recommended marking the table in such a way that the man would not forget that his wife was in a state of *niddah* and try to be more intimate with her.[85]

Many scholars have put forward the assumption that in this era (starting in the twelfth century) the halakhic leadership was influenced by a book called *Beraitah de-Masekhet de-Niddah* (which was written in the fifth century or later in Palestine or Babylonia).[86] The attitude presented in this book looks upon women in *niddah* as posing a danger and threat to themselves as well as those around them, and this line of thought may explain the origins of the halakhic stringencies, regarding the customs of separation practised in regard to women in *niddah*. This text restricts the woman in *niddah* in various areas. It removes her from the home, the synagogue and society, and rejects anything she touches, even the dirt upon which she treads. Several medieval sources mention this *beraitah* by name and even discuss customs that bring its assertions to mind. I would submit that although this source was indeed familiar to medieval scholars since a copy of it exists in one of their books, *Ma'asei Geonim* (The Deeds of the Geonim), it was not the book that guided them in their approach to the subject of *niddah*.

Rabbi Isaac ben Moses (Or Zarua), at the beginning of the thirteenth century, was the only one who discussed the idea that the customs of separation arose out of concern regarding the danger surrounding the woman in *niddah*. He brought up this theory in the context of a question about spouses eating meals together, but immediately rejected it. His statements referred to what he had learned from his teachers (Raviah and Rabbi Eliezer of Metz): all the customs derived from practices related to *tumah* and transferred to the sphere of *niddah* are valuable stringencies; nevertheless, they stem from a belief in a weak male psyche and not from any degree of danger relating to the female. He gives as his main example the action of his teacher, Rabbi Eliezer of Metz, who would drink from his wife's cup in public when she was in *niddah*, although he would not accept it from her hand. In this way he demonstrated that there is *tumah*, which derives from the condition of *niddah*; therefore, objects should not be taken from the hand of a woman in *niddah*. On the other hand, the food she eats or prepares or the dishes she touches should not be prohibited because there is no longer any *tumah* connected to vessels and, of course, there is no danger associated with her condition. Rabbi Isaac ben Moses stressed that the stringencies constitute an antidote to a 'pattern of sinful behaviour' and any stringency that may be introduced should be introduced. His writings contain numerous examples of what we already know from others: Women took the lead in instituting and applying the stringencies and restrictions during *niddah*. Although Rabbi Isaac ben Moses defines these stringencies as trivial, baseless and unnecessary, he still sings their praises. He recounts that women did not enter the synagogue when they are in *niddah* and that some of them did not touch books during this time. Still others do not pray aloud when other women are standing nearby so that those women would not utter 'amen' in response. The uttering of the word 'amen' was regarded as a holy act whose source could not be someone who was ritually impure.[87]

The female point of view

Women were very strict about distancing themselves from men immediately after seeing a drop of blood and beginning to count the days of *niddah*. The sources, which were written by men, make it very clear that during this time, matters of *niddah* (especially those related to immersion) were entirely under the jurisdiction of women. This differs fundamentally from the statements of the *amoraim* during the talmudic period, who considered themselves experts in this area and made certain that if there was the slightest concern, doubt, or uncertainty, women had to appear before them and accept their rulings in these very female matters.[88] In the Middle Ages, the woman was responsible for everything that happened to her body: she was responsible for finding the blood, counting the days, and keeping the clean days. 'A man must rely on his wife, whether she has told him that she is unclean or clean.'[89] As we have seen, the records available to us (compiled by men) describe separation in the context of the relevant talmudic passages and understand female behaviour as stemming from the plain *halakhah* indicated in the talmudic text. The female attitude towards the situation was different. During *niddah* women looked upon themselves as unclean or contaminated due to their bleeding; therefore, they were very strict about this period and avoided doing anything that could bring their *tumah* into the family circle or society. The strictness of the women was what created the separation favoured by the male religious leadership.

From the sources we learn that it was actually the women who emphasized the matter of *tumah* and their feelings about it. Their understanding of *halakhah* was that so long as the woman saw blood, she had to avoid contact with men and matters of sanctity. This is clearly indicated by the extreme customs, recorded in sources dating from the end of the eleventh century and thereafter, which the woman applied to themselves. The prohibition against going to synagogue during *niddah*; touching sacred books; and refraining from praying aloud when they were in *niddah* out of fear that another woman might hear her prayer and utter 'amen', plainly contradict what is written in the Talmud: that a woman in *niddah* may set aside *hallah*, i.e., perform a sacred act that is accompanied by a blessing.[90] All of these customs were connected to the personal feelings of women in *niddah*. They were not concerned so much by the fear that a man might come close to them as by the thought that they were *teme'ot* (ritually impure).

As I have noted, the halakhic leaders did not understand this behaviour and interpreted it in a different way. The illustration involving Rashi, which I mentioned, is an excellent example of this. Rashi showed empathy towards the independent thinking of women and their customs, but he did not understand it correctly. He assumed that his female contemporaries understood the sanctity of the synagogue to be the same as that of the Temple, and that this was their reason for avoiding synagogue attendance. From the prospect of his halakhic world, he could understand their feelings. This is a typical example of the male method of analysis, which attempted to understand female thinking with male tools. All that needed to be done, thought Rashi, was to explain to the women that there was no reason for their actions; indeed, if the synagogue was like the Temple, then even their immersion would not have any effect. The mechanism of *taharah* in the Temple no longer existed and everyone is like a corpse (i.e., *tameh*, impure). This was the reasoning behind his opinion that the women could enter the synagogue. But the female line of reasoning was completely different. The women felt that they were unclean (*teme'ot*) throughout the time that they were bleeding; therefore they absented themselves from events, rituals, and places related to sanctity, such as the synagogue, and refrained from reciting blessings aloud for fear that their companions might respond by saying 'amen'.[91]

The women's line of reasoning created a special, circumscribed female world. The Commandment had been given to them, and men had no part in it. Women moulded it to fit their understanding and feelings. Rashi could claim that the synagogue was not the Temple; however, the popular view established it as such in a deep, psychological sense. During the ordeal of the Crusades, the Jews, particularly the women, thought of the synagogue as the Temple in Jerusalem, where burnt offerings were made. They defended the synagogue and were prepared to die in it as if it was the destroyed Temple itself. The twelfth-century sources, which describe, in poetry and prose, what went on in the synagogues – the self-killing and the killing of the children – called attention to the way the Jews of the time created a strong link between the synagogue and the Temple in Jerusalem. These sources pointed out that time and again the women were at the forefront of the radical action.⁹² Refraining from synagogue attendance or refusing to recite the prayers aloud when in *niddah* may be considered a distinctively female act, especially in view of their deep attachment to the rituals and prayers, and as manifestations of their religious piety.

Niddah: the customs of the women

The women's behaviour in relation to *niddah* led to an extremely serious problem, from the male point of view. The women, who accepted the need for severe prohibitions when they were bleeding, were less concerned in the days following that stage, the seven days of *libun*. From their perspective, the prohibitions and separation behaviour were the result of their condition during *niddah*, the menstrual period. When this phase terminated, although sexual relations were still forbidden for seven days, there was no longer any reason for all of the other stringencies and separations. Evidently, the women would thoroughly cleanse themselves after they saw no more blood; they would change their clothing and behave as normal, outside of conjugal relations, which they would resume at the end of the seven days and the ceremonial immersion that marked the end of this period. Rabbenu Tam noticed that different women had different customs and whereas some immersed themselves only once at the end of the first seven days, many immersed twice, once at the end of the first seven days and again when the days of *libun* were over. He seems to have accepted both practices and generally went along with the decisions made by the women themselves and accepted the different customs of the women without reservation.⁹³ The halakhic leadership, that showed great stringency with respect to the ban against intimacy between husband and wife during both the days of *niddah* and the days of *libun*, opposed the independent conduct of the women; their main concern was that the husband would not be able to control his instincts when his wife was near him.

The reasoning of the sages that the prohibitions of *niddah* should also continue throughout the days of *libun* relied on a talmudic story that they would repeat time and again. The lesson of this story was meant to convince the men and the women that they should carefully abide by the rules of avoiding intimacy – which they had been instructed to follow – during the days of *libun* as well:

> A young Torah scholar, who studied diligently and tirelessly and was often in the company of true sages, died prematurely. His wife complained about the death of the young and righteous scholar before the men and before God. She visited many synagogues clutching her

husband's phylacteries, the regular use of which in prayer serves as a talisman for a long life, as it says in the prayers 'for [the words of Thy Law and Thy Commandments] are our life, and the length of our days'. 'Why,' the wife protested, 'did my husband, who studied the Torah so devoutly and learned with great scholars, die so young?' She made the scholars uneasy with her questions about the untimely death of her saintly husband and they did not know how to respond to her. One day the prophet Elijah visited her and when he heard her questions he asked her how her husband had behaved when she was in niddah. She replied that he did not touch her, even with his little finger. Elijah then asked her how her husband had behaved during the days of libun. She told him that they would eat together, drink together and sleep together in the same bed. Elijah the Prophet justified the death of the young man and praised God for not showing any preferential treatment towards the learned student because he had transgressed against a prohibition of the Torah. He explained that the passage 'and thou shalt not approach unto a woman to uncover her nakedness, as long as she is put apart for her uncleanness' (Lev. 18:19) as the verse that relates to the seven days of *libun*.[94]

This story is very clearly didactic. With a woman as its protagonist, it seems to be directed towards women, and even if directed towards men, it is so that they can persuade their wives that the prohibitions of the period of *niddah* should be strictly observed during the days of *libun* as well.

This is the context in which the sages conducted the debate about the essence of the days of *libun* and its proscriptions. In their writings, Rashi's students asserted that, to all intents and purposes, the seven days of *libun* were part of the *niddah* period, i.e., days considered unclean and contaminated exactly like those on which the woman actually sees blood. Rashi was even disturbed by the name *libun*, a term (meaning 'whitening') that implies cleanliness. He argued that the *halakhah* clearly defines the days of *libun* in exactly the same way as it delineates the days on which the woman sees blood. He described the custom of women in his area: on the days when they saw blood, the women would wear unattractive clothing; when this period was over, they changed their dress and desisted from the customs of separation, aside from actual sexual relations. Rashi praised this conduct, which was initiated by women 'demeaning themselves in the eyes of their husbands so as not to cause any transgression'; however he rejected outright any degree of renewed intimacy between husband and wife immediately after the inception of the days of *libun*. Rashi vociferously opposed this female custom of relaxing the rules of separation during the days of *libun* because his perception of 'the male psyche', led him to believe that without the rules of separation, the husband would not be able to control himself and abstain from intimacies with his wife. In keeping with the talmudic story, he emphasized that all the proscriptions, which applied to the period of *niddah*, also applied to the days of *libun* in order to create 'a fence, a safeguard and avoid transgression'. Rashi gave the issue this much weight because he feared that the moment restrictions were relaxed, the couple would be tempted to transgress by having conjugal relations, which were only permitted after the woman immersed herself in the *mikveh* at the end of the days of *libun*.[95]

The sages debated these issues throughout the twelfth and thirteenth centuries. The quantity, the detail and persistence of the writings on this subject might even be interpreted by some as verging on the prurient. At the end of the twelfth century, Raviah attempted to formulate a substantive resolution on this matter. He cited Rashi and the strong words of Rabbi Ephraim of Regensburg who irately hinted at all sorts of concessions made by various sages in regard to the days of *libun*. Like Rashi, Rabbi Ephraim of Regensburg saw the source of the problem as the man's desire to have conjugal relations with his wife before he was permitted to do so. He, too, stressed that the solution was to continue avoiding intimacy during the days of *libun*, as in the period of *niddah*, since the punishment for sexual relations during *niddah* was *karet*. Even though Raviah agreed in principle with this strict interpretation, it was apparent from what he said that, in his days, he was neither able, or inclined to fight against some of the concessions practiced by couples during the days of *libun*: gestures and touching, eating and drinking together, etc.[96] More than 100 years after Rashi's statement, Rabbi Eleazar of Worms analyses the male temperament and states that, from a psychological point of view, a man's lust actually increases when he knows that his wife is forbidden to him and she is not bleeding.[97] This problematic situation, which had already been identified at the end of the eleventh and the beginning of the twelfth centuries in both northern France and Germany, remained in the forefront of the sages' discussions throughout the centuries that followed. Nonetheless, their writings in this regard suggest that in spite of their enormous effort to require strict adherence to the laws of separation between a man and woman during the days of *libun*, they did not succeed. It was the women who, despite the reinstatement of intimacies with their husbands and normal household functioning, did not resume normal conjugal relations until they had immersed themselves in the *mikveh* again, at the end of the seven 'clean' *libun* days.

From our male sources we learn how the men interpreted the women's actions. They understood that the women were also the ones who, in effect, determined the manner of immersion, where it took place, and even its duration. The women introduced a collection of customs, not all of them consistent with the *halakhah* as set down in the Talmud, which became the norms followed for generations. The male halakhic leadership approved these customs, almost always immediately, because they had no other choice. The feeling of *tumah* that took hold of the women during their time of *niddah* manifested itself in the desire to remove all physical obstructions during immersion. According to the *halakhah*, no object can be allowed to obstruct the immersion; the water must reach every part of the woman's body. The women interpreted this law in the most wide-ranging manner, and took great care over matters that the men considered to be unnecessary embellishments. In the eleventh century, the sources mention a woman by the name of Lady Baila, the sister of Rabbi Isaac, the son of Rabbi Menahem of Orleans, who taught the women around her that the teeth must be thoroughly cleaned before immersion.[98] This custom, which was regarded as obligatory by the women, was looked upon as superfluous by the male halakhic leaders; nonetheless, they did not hesitate to authorize it. In contrast, another custom established by women contradicted, in the opinion of the sages, a clear *halakhah*. According to this *halakhah*, dirt must be removed from fingernails before immersion, so that it does not become an obstruction between the water and the body. The women's tendency to be stringent in these matters gave rise to their practice of not only cleaning the fingernails, but also trimming them entirely before immersion. This female strictness was looked upon with disfavour in the male world because women would also trim their nails before immersion on the intermediate days of the Sukkot (Tabernacles) and Passover festivals, when it was traditional to refrain from doing so. Here again, the female custom contradicted the *halakhah*, as interpreted by men, who defined it as a foolishness stemming from a lack of understanding. Similarly, the sources pointed out that women went to extremes when, instead of just washing their hair before immersion, as instructed by the Talmud, they would thoroughly scrub their entire bodies. Yet, despite their fundamental disinclination, the male halakhic leaders authorized the women's customs because they realized that the women would continue these practices, come what may. In reality, the women's customs were the determining factor, and they conducted themselves accordingly, no matter what the sages said.[99]

The time of immersion defined in the Talmud is the seventh day of the days of *libun*, after sunset, which in fact is already the following day according to the Jewish calendar. The halakhic scholars, who were aware of the fact that women washed and prepared themselves prior to the actual immersion, assumed that these preparations would also take place after sunset and before immersion. Women in Ashkenaz thought otherwise. Because they were very stringent about this bathing, and because they took great care to ensure that they immersed themselves after dark, they advanced the time of their preparations to daylight hours. According to female logic, it was preferable to carry out their meticulous preparations while there was still light. Some of the male sages opposed this and referred to the women's lack of understanding in regard to the issue, since the pre-*mikvah* washing and the immersion were supposed to take place at the same time. Other scholars did comprehend the logic underlying the women's practice in this matter and sanctioned it, thus, in effect, instituting a norm by which any determination about customs related to *niddah* followed the standards and practices set by the women. The significance of agreeing with the female customs is that on the eve of the Sabbath and of the festivals an entire day would intervene between the preparatory washing and the immersion. Rabbi Isaac, one of the prominent sages of northern France in the second half of the twelfth century, simply asked the women about their custom and accepted their decision to wash on Friday. In the end, the other male halakhic decision-makers agreed with the custom on condition that the delay would not extend for more than one day (twenty-four hours). When the Sabbath occurred on a day preceding a festival, or when there was a two-day festival, the halakhic arbiters insisted that the washing should take place right before the immersion, at sunset.

Because a proper *mikvah* was not always available, women would immerse themselves in rivers. This type of immersion could be problematic from the halakhic point of view because, according the laws governing *mikvaot*, a proper *mikvah* is one in which the amount of water it contains is more than what might be added to it. This determination disqualifies rivers as *mikvaot* during the winter and when it is raining. Nevertheless, women in Ashkenaz would immerse themselves in rivers, and in winter as well, when there was no doubt that the amount of additional water exceeded the amount contained in the river beforehand. The sages endorsed this practice after the fact, since a *mikvah* did not exist in every town, though almost every settlement was located near a river.

In the middle of the twelfth century, Rabbenu Tam in northern France and Raban in Germany approved the riverbank immersion sites used as *mikvaot* by women. Rabbi Tam devised a devious way of overcoming the abovementioned talmudic restriction on *mikvaot*. He argued that the amount of water descending from the heavens into a river is always dependent on the amount of water already in the river; and this way he authorized the use of rivers for immersion, using a 'scientific method'.

Even those who pointed out that when it was raining the amount of water in the rivers unquestionably disallowed immersion couched their statements in weak language. In effect it was obvious that women continued to immerse themselves in rivers all the time, unless there was a *mikvah* in the city. Raban sanctioned immersions even if they were carried out in facilities where the water was channelled through pipes, an arrangement prohibited by the *halakhah*. He wrote that if the custom of the women was to immerse themselves in these places, they were entitled to do so; even if it was prohibited, they would continue to use them and would not heed those who sought to put a stop to their behaviour. It was better, he wrote, that they should act incorrectly than transgress deliberately.[100] Because of the cold, the women would rinse themselves in hot water after immersion; but the sages also opposed this action. Their argument was based on the halakhic concept that it was immersion in a *mikvah* only that purifies the woman and signifies the conclusion of her period of *niddah* and this could not be adulterated with any other form of immersion. The halakhic leaders felt that it was important to emphasize this in order to 'educate' women towards greater awareness about immersion. Here, too, the male line of reasoning relied on a talmudic discussion, that deals with those places where the *mikvah* was not particularly clean. There, after getting out of the *mikvah*, the women would pour water on themselves to clean off. According to the Talmud, this was forbidden because, in the sages' opinion, there was a risk that the women would not differentiate between the types of water. It was important for them to understand that only the water in the *mikvah* and not any other water could purify them (Tbab. Tractate Shabbat 14a). The male attitude was based on their own view of reality. The men assumed that because some women preceded immersion with vigorous scrubbing and some washed in warm water after immersion in order to warm up, the women did not really understand the seriousness and importance of the immersion ritual and that female understanding was deficient and required reinforcement. The men were convinced that if the practice was solely to immerse themselves, then women would understand that it was immersion alone which brought them from a state of *niddah* to a state of *taharah* and the resumption of normal family relations.

In the Middle Ages, all the male sages pondered this problem fearing that the women would not differentiate between the bathing processes, especially since, in the end, they sanctioned the women's practices. The method which the men used to authorize these actions was to make it clear that the prohibition in the Talmud derived from the laws of *tumah*, and the talmudic concern that women might not be properly purified (*tehorot*) to eat the priestly tithe (*terumah*), as stipulated by the laws governing the Temple. In the Middle Ages, they were dealing with the laws of conjugal separation only; therefore, it was possible to authorize the women's practices. We see that the men did not trust the halakhic instinct of the women or their ability to distinguish between immersion and the rinsing that followed it. The halakhic argument enabled them to accept the conduct of the women, and in effect to sanction it, since it was obvious that the women would persist in their actions anyway. From the women's point of view, it was clear that they were indeed distinguishing between immersion and additional washing. This is an example of a male stance that assumes that it is impossible to rely on female self-awareness or a deep female understanding of the significance of *mitzvot*. This paternalistic attitude stems from the notion that women are not only removed from halakhic sources deserving of analysis, but are also incapable of accepting halakhic knowledge because of the way they think. Hence, the halakhic leaders were put off by the behaviour of the women and did not examine it thoroughly. From the outset, they assumed that the women's practices derived from a mistake on their part, the outcome of a lack of knowledge and a lack of understanding. The women, on the other hand, were well aware of the value of immersion, but they had no qualms about washing before the ritual – in order to make themselves completely clean – or afterwards (in warm water), to help them warm up. They were well aware of the value of immersion alone as the action which separated the state of *niddah*, in which they had been, from their new state of purity.[101]

According to the Talmud, it was clear that the woman needed to immerse herself in the *mikvah* on the night of the seventh day of the days of *libun*, and that this act would make it possible for her and her husband to renew conjugal relations. It goes without saying that without immersion the man could not ask for or demand the renewal of sexual relations. The sources made it clear that normal sexual relations in keeping with the *halakhah* ensured fecundity and 'good' (i.e., healthy) children for the couple. Nevertheless, these same sources clearly indicate that the time of immersion was also determined by the women. They would delay immersion for all sorts of reasons, for example, when the appointed day was cold (since it was forbidden to heat the water of the *mikvah*) or when their husbands were out of town. Even in this case the male sages accepted the rules of the women, relying on the daring statement of Rabbenu Tam that 'immersion at the appointed time is not a Commandment'. Thus Rabbi Tam again sanctioned the custom of women to determine the time of immersion. Various sages asserted that it was the man's role to convince his wife to immerse herself on time; but if she did not do so, he would simply have to wait until she went to the *mikvah*. They suggested using words of mollification, noting that every woman should be treated in a manner suitable to her, while taking local and family customs into consideration. 'This [situation] depends solely on mollification, because all women are not the same [in temperament]; some receive more affection from their husbands [than others]; and it is not proper to ask one's wife to deviate from the customs of her neighbours: daughters follow their mothers and each city has its own customs.'[102]

The women's highly developed consciousness about the essence of *taharah* in the immersion process is also apparent in the discussion on the blessing recited in relation to the ritual of immersion. A blessing exists in connection with almost every Commandment and should be recited so as to coincide with the performance of the *mitzva*, which is subject of the blessing. According to this halakhic reasoning, the woman should recite the blessing for immersion while immersing, and this is what the male sages demanded. Women in Ashkenaz decided to recite the blessing after they immersed themselves. Up to the moment of immersion, they felt impure; therefore, they felt ready to recite the blessing only after they had completed the immersion. From the perspective of halakhic intuition, the timing of the recitation of the blessing may be compared to that for the blessing made by converts, who recite the blessing after they immerse themselves in the *mikvah*, since prior to performing this act, they were not Jews. In this context, the women considered the process of switching (from one state to another) during the ritual of immersion as the essential motif; therefore, they insisted on pronouncing the blessing only after, but not during immersion. This is another female extension of the Commandment of *niddah*.[103]

The difference between the male halakhic perspective and the women's instinctive point of view can also be seen in another issue, the question of sexual abstinence after the birth of a child.[104] The practice was for women to delay immersion for a long time after the birth of a child, thus postponing the renewal of normal conjugal relations. The Torah states that after giving birth a woman is *teme'ah* (like a *niddah*) for seven days after the birth of a boy and for two weeks after the birth of a girl. From the standpoint of the *tumah* associated with sanctity and the Temple, the woman continues to be *teme'ah* for thirty-three more days, in the case of a male child, and sixty-six more days in the case of a female (in addition to the seven or fourteen days, respectively) (Lev. 12:2–5). This period (up to forty or eighty days) is called the time of the *dam hatohar* ('pure blood'). The discussions in the Talmud made it clear that after the initial period (seven days after a boy and fourteen after a girl) the woman must immerse herself as a *niddah* and then she is permitted to have sexual relations with her husband, even if she sees blood up to forty or eighty days.

The argument about whether or not normal conjugal relations may take place during this time went on throughout the Middle Ages and in every region. It dealt with the fundamental question of whether it is at all possible to have sexual relations with a women who has seen blood; should she behave as a *niddah* every time she bleeds (i.e., count the days of *niddah* and immerse herself) or wait until the end of the period before immersing, which would mean that her husband must abstain from sexual relations until the period is over. Scholars who have studied this issue tend to view it as an example of different customs originating from different places; they attempt to clarify the origins of these customs, what was done in each locale, and which customs had the greatest impact.[105] A perusal of the sources related to the centres of northern France and Germany (as well as Italy) indicates that the decision was to follow the rulings of the debate in the Babylonian Talmud, that is, conjugal relations may be renewed after the initial period of *niddah* and after immersion (seven days after the birth of a boy and two weeks after a girl). The halakhic leaders in northern France, and later on their colleagues in Germany, rescind the opinion that blood seen during the period of the *damei hatohar* should be considered as *niddah* blood and do not require the woman (and the man) to observe the prohibitions of separation associated with *niddah*. In other words, according to male reasoning, the couple should resume normal marital relations as soon as possible. The discussion in the sources reveals that, in practice, the women did not immerse themselves until the end of the *damei hatohar* period (sixty or eighty days) thus dictating to the men conduct based on the female view of the *halakhah*. The way they saw it, as long as there was any concern that blood might be seen after the birth of a child, they would refrain from immersing. Furthermore, they applied their concerns in this regard to the entire period; thus they did not follow the *halakhah*, which instructed them to immerse themselves after seven or fourteen days and then resume normal conjugal relations.

The sources written before the end of the thirteenth century reveal that in some places it was customary to immerse only at the end of the period (after sixty or eighty days), but that this practice was considered unusual, extreme, and even 'ascetic'. The natural tendency of the men was to authorize the resumption of sexual activity as quickly as possible. Moreover, since they could rely on sources in the Babylonian Talmud that prescribed such action, halakhic scholars in northern France authorized it. Zimmer correctly recognizes the distinction between the rabbinic religious leadership, which sanctioned the act of maintaining normal sexual relations throughout the period, and the general public, whom Maharam calls 'the people in the fields'. In my opinion, the opposition of 'the people in the fields' does not stem from the desire to implement extreme stringencies; rather, it is the voice of the female halakhic instinct. The female outlook was that the period of abstinence from sexual relations should continue throughout the entire period following the birth of a child, a time when a woman could suddenly begin to bleed. In this, as in other instances in the sources written in the thirteenth century and thereafter, we see that the women are the ones who determine the time of immersion, as well as the length of the time a couple will abstain from conjugal relations after the birth of a child.

Rabbi Isaac ben Moses relates that in the thirteenth century Rabbi Elijah of Paris was concerned about this matter and attempted to find out what Rabbenu Tam (who died in 1171) actually thought about it by asking one of his students.[106] At the end of the fourteenth century, Rabbi Shalom of Neustadt noted that Rabbi Isaac ben Moses had already stated, in the thirteenth century, that women would immerse only at the end of the sixty or eighty-day period. In the fourteenth century Rabbi Alexander Zuslin HaCohen – who lived in Worms, Cologne, and Frankfurt, and died as a martyr in 1348 – essentially confirms this in his book *Sefer ha-Agudah*. 'Women, who have just given birth, usually wait to immerse themselves because they are worried that they will forget the counting of the days of *niddah*.' This is of course an excuse. Women did not forget about counting of the days of *niddah*. They decided that, because they would often bleed during this time, it would be best to immerse themselves only at the end of the period, that is, after eighty days.[107] Starting with the fifteenth century, this becomes the main trend for all women.[108]

The differences between the male perspective (based on the halakhic discussion in the Talmud) – which seeks to keep the spouses apart during the period of *niddah* and bring them back together to resume normal married life and regular sexual activity immediately after this period ends – and the female view of *niddah* – as the time when a woman focuses on dealing with her body, a time when she practices the customs and rules of separation, engages in or abstains from sexual relations according to her ideas and feelings – are therefore also clearly visible in relation to this other issue: the period of abstinence between husband and wife after the birth of a child.

Notes

1 I. Ta-Shma, *Early Franco-German Ritual and Custom*, Jerusalem 1992, pp. 13–105; D. Sperber, *Customs of Israel*, vol. 1, Jerusalem 1989, pp. 9–30; B. Har-Shefi, 'Women and Halakha in the Years 1050-1350 ce: Between Law and Custom', Ph.D. thesis to the Hebrew University in Jerusalem, Jerusalem 2002, pp. 9–24.
2 Exodus 32:2-3; *Pirke deRabi Eliezer*, ed. Hayim M. Horowitz, Jerusalem 1973, ch. 44; Rashi on Megila 22a *s.v.* Rashei hodshecem; Tosafot on Rosh ha-Shanah 23a *s.v.* Mishom; Tosafot on Hagiga 18a *s.v.* Rosh Hodesh; Eleazar ben Judah of Worms, *Sefer ha-Roqeah*, Venice 1549, no. 228 pp. 53–54; Zidkiya ben Abraham, *Sefer Shibolei haLeqet haShalem*, ed. Shlomo Buber, Vilna 1886, nos 169 (p. 135), 235 (p. 218); Meir ben Barukh, *Sefer Minhagim deBei Maharam ben Barukh meRotenburg*, ed. I. Elfenbein, New York 1938, p. 17.
3 The medieval commentary stressed the words 'sculpture or molten image' in contrast to the midrashic source, which uses 'filth and abomination', since the former recalls the prohibition in the Ten Commandments against 'any sculpture image' (Exod. 20:3).
4 Rashi had already initiated this tradition in the eleventh century, in the name of his own venerable teacher. *Mahzor Vitry*, ed. S. Horowitz, Nuremberg 1892, p. 173; *Sefer Shibolei haLeqet haShalem* 170 (p. 135); *Sefer Kol Bo*, Lemberg 1860, no. 43.
5 Women would also refrain from work on Saturday evening after the conclusion of the Sabbath, on the first and eighth day of Hanukah – during the time when the Hanukah candles were burning; on the evenings during the counting of the Omer (the seven weeks between Passover and Pentecost; Tisha b'Av (the fast day commemorating the destruction of both the Temples); the intermediate days of holidays and on Rosh Hodesh. *Mahzor Vitry*, ed. S. Horowitz, Nuremberg 1892, no. 201; Isaac ben Moses, *Sefer Or Zarua*, 2 vols, Zhitomir 1862, vol. 2:93, p. 48; *Sefer Shibolei haLeqet haShalem*, no. 184 (p. 142); Sefer Minhagim deBei Maharam ben Barukh, p. 17.
6 S. Goldin, 'The Role of Ceremonies in the Socialization Process: The Case of Jewish Communities of Northern France and Germany in the Middle Ages', *Archives de sciences sociales des religions* 95 (1996), pp. 163–178; *Sefer Tosafot haShalem*, ed. J. Gellis, vol. 1, Jerusalem 1982, p. 156; B. Har-Shefi, 'Women and Halakha in the Years 1050–1350 CE: Between Law and Custom', Ph.D. thesis to the Hebrew University in Jerusalem, Jerusalem 2002, pp. 158–166.
7 The question of the extent that it was necessary to know how to read in order to participate in the prayer service in the Midle Ages is a question involving the whole nature of the service and the involvement of the congregation (both men and women) in prayers together with the *hazan* (cantor) or the prayer leader. I will be dealing with this subject fully elsewhere. What may be said here is that lieracy was indeed necessary in order to be able to read in Hebrew the various passages on the different festivals.
8 *Mishnah*, Berakhot 3:3; Talmud Berakhot 20a-b.
9 Examples include a widow who attends synagogue on Sabbath eve, women who remain in the synagogue throughout the day of Yom Kippur, Sukkot and the Sabbath. Solomon B. Isaac (Rashi), *Siddur Rashi*, ed. J. Freimann and S. Buber, Berlin 1911, p. 269, no. 31; Solomon B. Isaac (Rashi), *Responsa Rashi*, ed. I. Elfenbein, New York 1943, p. 177, no. 155; A. Agus, *Responsa of the Tosaphists* (Teshuvot Balei ha-Toshafot), New York 1954, p. 73; Meir ha-Kohen, *Haggahot Maimuniuot* on Moses ben Maimon,

Mishneh Tora, Shabbat ch. 22, no. 80; A. Grossman, *Pious and Rebellious: Jewish Women in Europe in the Middle Ages*, Jerusalem 2001, pp. 312–321.

10 It is her 'place of prayer and *minyan*'. Meir ben Barukh, *Responsa, Rulings, and Customs*, ed. I. Z. Cahana, vol. 2. Jerusalem 1960, p. 64.

11 Meir ben Barukh, *Sefer Sharei Teshuvot*, ed. M. A. Blakh, Berlin 1891, p. 320, no. 875.

12 Issac ben Joseph of Corbeil, *Sefer Amudei Gola hanikra Semak*, Jerusalem 1979, no. 293; I. Abrahams, *Hebrew Ethical Wills*, Philadelphia 1976, pp. 207–209.

13 Eleazar ben Judah of Worms, *Shirat Ha-Roke'ah*, ed. I. Meiseles, Jerusalem 1993, pp. 228–229, Eleazar ben Judah of Worms, *Sefer ha-Roqeah*, Venice 1549, no. 326, p. 222; Mishna Sota 3:4, *Midrash Sifre on Devarim* (Sefre on Deuteronomy), ed. L. Finkelstein, Berlin 1939, 46:19 (p.104); R. Biale, *Women and Jewish Law*, New York 1984, pp. 29–43.

14 Judah ben Samuel, *Sefer Hasidim*, ed. J. Wistinetzki, Frankfurt 1942, nos 464–465, 468 (pp. 132–133), 781.

15 Rashi on Megila 21b *s.v.* venavi; *Sefer Hasidim*, nos 11, pp. 7–9, 1190, p. 389; Isaac ben Moses, *Sefer Or Zarua*, Zhitomir 1862, vol. 2, p. 118.

16 Tosafot on Berachot 45b, Isaac ben Moses, *Sefer Or Zarua*, Zhitomir 1862, vol. 1, no. 184, p. 58; Meir ben Barukh, *Responsa, Rulings, and Customs*, ed. I. Z. Cahana, vol. 1, Jerusalem 1957, pp. 76–77, 187.

17 Tosafot on Berachot 45b *s.v.* shani; Meir ha-Kohen *Haggahot Maimuniuot* on Moses ben Maimon, *Mishneh Tora*, Berachot 5:5; Isaac ben Moses, *Sefer Or Zarua*, Zhitomir 1862, vol. 1, no. 186, p. 58.

18 Solomon B. Isaac (Rashi), *Responsa* Rashi, ed. I. Elfenbein, New York 1943, p. 250; Eliezer ben Yoel ha-Levi, *Sefer Ra'aviah*, ed. V. Aptowizer, Jerusalem 1964, vol. 1, p. 210; L. Elias Bar-Levav, 'Our Women have a lovely Custom: Halakhic Divisions in Accordance with Women's Practice in the Middle Ages', *Massekhet* 6 (2007), pp. 47–85.

19 E. Kanarfogel, *Jewish Education and Society in the Hugh Middle Ages*, Detroit 1992, pp. 18–19.

20 L. Finkelstein, *Jewish Self-government in the Middle Ages*, New York 1924, pp. 168–169.

21 *Sefer Hasidim*, nos 835 (p. 211), 1201 (p. 362); *Sefer Hasidim*, Margaliot no. 313, p. 245; A. Grossman, *Pious and Rebellious: Jewish Women in Europe in the Middle Ages*, Jerusalem 2001 [Hebrew], pp. 296–297; A. Grossman, *Pious and Rebellious: Jewish Women in Europe in the Middle Ages*, Waltham MA, 2004 [English], pp. 167–168.

22 S. Salfeld, *Martyrlogium des Nürnberger Memorbuches*, Berlin 1938, p. 36; J. Lewyson, *Nephashut Zadikim*, Frankfurt 1855, pp. 85–86.

23 Mordechai ben Hillel, *Sefer Mordechai*, on Shabbat no. 311; Jacob Weil, *She'elot u Teshuvot Maharil Weil*, ed. Y. Satz, Jerusalem 1988, no. 12, pp. 8–9.

24 Nathan ben Yehuda, *Sefer haMachkim*, ed. M. Fridman, Jerusalem 1968, p. 15: 'And this is the source of the practice whereby the women crowd around to see the scroll and are forced to stand during the reading of the Torah.' The man who describes the reaction of women during the First Crusade as they see the Torah scroll being desecrated and trampled upon by the Christians, who tore it and cast it into ashes and mud, stresses their responses: 'Look, see, the Holy Torah, the delight of our eyes, to which we used to bow in the synagogue, honouring it.' *The Jews and the Crusaders, the Hebrew Chronicles of the First and Second Crusades*, ed. and trans. S. Eidelberg, Madison, WI 1977, p. 37.

25 Simon ben Zadoc, *Sefer Thazbeth*, Jerusalem 1951, no. 397; *Sefer Minhagim deBei Maharam ben Barukh meRotenburg*, p. 80; *She'elot u Teshuvot Maharil Weil*, no. 32; Meir ben Barukh, *Responsa, Rulings, and Customs*, ed. I. Z. Cahana, Jerusalem 1957–1962, vol. 2, pp. 155–156. E. Baumgarten, *Mothers and Children: Jewish Family Life in Medieval Europe*, Princeton 2004, pp. 70–76.

26 It was men, of course, who took the initiative and donated the money to extend the synagogues, and we have no knowledge of women acting to recreate a 'women's synagogue'. One can assume that the extension expressed the will of the community as a whole to give women a special place in the synagogue, whether to oust them from the male section or whether because of their special devotion to prayer. R. Krautheimer, *Mittelalerliche Synagogen*, Berlin 1927, pp. 111, 132–134, 151–154. B. Har-Shefi, 'Women and Halakha in the years 1050–1350 CE; Between Law and Custom', Ph.D. thesis, Hebrew University in Jerusalem, Jerusalem 2002, pp. 178–179. M. Porsche, 'Speyer: The Medieval Synagogue', in *The Jews of Europe in the Middle Ages, Tenth to Fifteenth Centuries*, ed. C. Cluse, Turnhout 2004, pp. 421–434.

27 Meir ha-Kohen, *Haggahot Maimuniuot* on Moses ben Maimon, *Mishneh Tora*, end of Shvitat haAshor *s.v.* kol nidrei; *Sefer Minhagim Tirana*, Yom Kipur 158; Meir ben Barukh, *Responsa, Rulings, and Customs*, ed. I. Z. Cahana, Jerusalem 1957–1962, vol. 1, no. 555–556, vol. 2, no. 156, p. 149; Tosafot, Rosh haShana 27b *s.v.* veshama kol shofar.

28 *Kol Bo*, no. 62; She'elot u Teshuvot Maharil Weil, no. 12. The communities mentioned in this regard are Ulm, Augsburg, and Pappenheim.

29 J. Lewyson, *Nephashut Zadikim*, Frankfurt 1855, p. 85; S. Salfeld, *Das Martyrlogium des Nuremberger Memorbuches*, Berlin 1938, pp. 36, 299, 411; Eleazar ben Yehudah of Worms, *Shirat Ha-Roke'ah*, Venice 1549, pp. 228–229.

30 Time-bound commandments which women are obligated to carry out: eating *matzot* on Passover; rejoicing on the pilgrimage festivals; participation in *hakhel*. Examples of commandments (*mitzvot*) that are not time-bound and women are not required to perform: Torah study, *peru u-revu* (procreation), and the redeeming of the firstborn. Tractate Kidushin Tbab. 33b–35a; Tractate Eruvin Tbab. 27a.

31 *Mishnah*, Menahot 9:8; Kidushin 1:8; Babylonian Talmud, Erubin 96b, Hagiga 16b.

32 *Mahzor Vitry*, ed. S. Horowitz, Nuremberg 1892, pp. 193, 413–414; Solomon B. Isaac (Rashi), *Siddur Rashi*, no. 267 p. 127; Solomon B. Isaac (Rashi), *Sefer ha-Pardes*, ed. H. L. Ehrenreich, Budapest 1924, p. 223; Isaac ben Moses, *Sefer Or Zarua*, Zhitomir 1862, vol. 2, no. 266, p. 123; I. Ta-Shma, *Ritual, Custom and reality in Franco-Germany, 1000–1350*, Jerusalem 1996, pp. 262–279; B. Har-Shefi, 'Women and Halakha in the Years 1050–1350 CE: Between Law and Custom', Ph.D. thesis to the Hebrew University in Jerusalem, Jerusalem 2002, pp. 214–226.

33 *Mahzor Vitry*, ed. S. Horowitz, Nuremberg 1892, p. 414; Rashi on Rosh haShana 33a.

34 Eliezer ben Nathan, *Sefer Even haEzer, Sefer Raban*, Jerusalem 1984, no. 87.

35 Bava Kama 87a.

36 Jacob ben Meir, *Sefer haYashar leRabbenu Tam: Heleq haShe'elot vehaTeshuvot (Responsa)*, ed. S. F. Rosental, Berlin 1898, no. 64; Tosafot on Rosh haShana 33a *s.v.* Ha; Tosafot on Eruvin 96a–96b *s.v.* dilma.

37 *Mahzor Vitry*, ed. S. Horowitz, Nuremberg 1892, pp. 210, 327; Meir ha-Kohen, *Haggahot Maimuniuot*, Hilcut Shofar 2:1; Tosafot on Rosh haShana 33a *s.v.* Ha; Meir ben Barukh, *Responsa, Rulings, and Customs*, ed. I. Z. Cahana, Jerusalem 1957–1962,

vol 1, no. 24, p. 141; and the same approach in *Sefer Hasidim*, no. 1482, pp. 456, 942, pp. 231–232.
38 Jacob of Marvege, *Shelot u-Teshuvot min haShamayim*, Jerusalem, no. 1, p. 43.
39 The Talmud points out that Sarah was one of seven women prophetesses.
40 Judges 4:4; *Berakhot* 57a.
41 I. Ta-Shma, *Ritual, Custom and Reality in Franco-Germany, 1000–1350*, Jerusalem 1996, pp. 262–279.
42 Eliezer ben Nathan, *Sefer Raban*, Jerusalem 1984, p. 177c; Eleazar ben Judah of Worms, *Sefer ha-Roqeah*, ed. I. Meiseles, Jerusalem 1993, no. 128.
43 Eliezer ben Samuel of Metz, *Sefer Yere'im*, Vilna 1901, no. 419; Meir ha-Kohen *Haggahot Maimuniuot* to Moses ben Maimon, *Mishneh Torah*, Hilkhot Tzitzit 3:40, Hilcot Shofar 2:1.
44 Jacob ben Moses Mulin, *Shut Maharil heHadashot* (new *Responsa*), ed. Y. Satz, Jerusalem 1977, pp. 293–294.
45 D. Herlihy and C. Klapisch-Zuber, *Tuscans and their Families: A Study of the Florentine Catasto of 1427*, New Haven, CT 1985, p. 277; E. Baumgarten, *Mothers and Children: Jewish Family Life in Medieval Europe*, Princeton, NJ 2004, pp. 109–110, 174–177; I. Loudon, *Death in Childbirth: An International Study of Maternal Care and Maternal Mortality, 1800–1950*, Oxford 1992. The subject was studied scientifically for the first time only in the eighteenth century.
46 *Mishnah* Halla 2:7.
47 J. Dalarun 'The Clerical Gaze', in *A History of Women: Silences of the Middle Ages*, ed. C. Klapisch-Zuber, Cambridge, MA 1992, pp. (esp.) 19–24, 15–42; J. Y. Gregg, *Devils, Women and Jews*, New York 1997, pp. 87–100; J. Cadden, *Meaning of Sex Difference in the Middle Ages*, Cambridge 1995, pp. 74–77, 190–194.
48 The passage cited most frequently in this regard is based on a statement by the second-century *tanna* Rabbi Joshuah, who describes in a harsh and cruel manner the differences between men and women, portraying the woman as the source of evil. *Midrash Bereshit Rabba*, Jerusalem 1965, 17:8.
49 Avot de-Rabbi Nathan, New York and Jerusalem 1997, version B, no. 9, p. 25; *Midrash Tanhuma*, ed. S. Buber, Jerusalem 1997, Noach 1.
50 Important studies have been written about this topic; here it will be examined solely from the standpoint of the attempt by women to influence the household, religious space, and female space, which interfaces but does not supplant male space. I. Ta-Shma, *Early Franco-German Ritual and Custom*, Jerusalem 1992, pp. 109–135; Y. D. Gilat, *Studies in the Development of the Halakha*, Jerusalem 1992, pp. 334–344.
51 Tanhuma, Noach 1.
52 Y. D. Gilat, *Studies in the Development of the Halakha*, Jerusalem 1992, pp. 331–342; in the Middle Ages, Eliezer ben Nathan, *Sefer Raban*, Jerusalem 1984, p. 122; Meir ben Barukh, *Responsa, Rulings, and Customs*, ed. I. Z. Cahana, Jerusalem 1957–1962, vol. 1, no. 215, p. 209.
53 Eliezer ben Nathan, *Sefer Raban*, ed. I. Z. Cahana, Jerusalem 1957–1962, no. 342; Isaac ben Moses, *Sefer Or Zarua*, Zhitomir 1862, vol. 2 no. 11 (Hilkhot Shabbat).
54 Which is surprisingly similar to the story about the people who become confused and recite the evening prayers too early (Berakhot 27b).
55 Isaac ben Moses, *Sefer Or Zarua*, Zhitomir 1862, no. 16; *Sefer ha-Miktso'ot*, no. 3, pp. 2–3.

56 N. Wider, *The Formation of Jewish Liturgy in the East and the West*, 2 vols, Jerusalem 1998, vol. 1, pp. 323–351.
57 Rabbi Jacob ben Meir Tam, *Sefer haYashar leRabbenu Tam: Heleq haShe'elot vehaTeshunot (Responsa)*, ed. S. F. Rosental, Berlin 1898, 45 (4), 47, 48 (6); Tosafot Shabbat 25b *s.v.* Hova.
58 Before reciting a blessing that includes the name of God, it was necessary first to check that the candles would actually light, otherwise there was a danger of saying a *brakha levatolah*, i.e. taking God's name in vain.
59 Eliezer ben Yoel ha-Levi, *Sefer Ra'aviah*, ed. V. Aptowizer, Jerusalem 1964, vol. 1, no. 199, pp. 263–264; Hayim ben Rabbi Yitzhak, *Responsa*, Leipzig 1860, no. 115; Issac ben Joseph of Corbeil, *Sefer Amudei Gola hanikra Semak*, Jerusalem 1979, no. 279; Eliezer ben Samuel of Metz, Sefer Yere'im, Vilna, 1901, no. 429; Kul-Bo, no. 31.
60 Eliezer ben Yoel ha-Levi, *Sefer Ra'aviah*, ed. V. Aptowizer, Jerusalem 1964, vol. 1, no. 199, p. 266; Isaac ben Moses, *Sefer Or Zarua*, Zhitomir 1862, vol. 2, p. 114; Mordekhai on Shabbat 293; Alexander Susslein, *Ha-Aguddah*, Cracow 1571, Shabbat no. 45, p. 15. Zidkia ben Abraham, Shibolei ha-Leqet, no. 59 p. 46.
61 A. Grossman, *Pious and Rebellious: Jewish Women in Europe in the Middle Ages*, Jerusalem 2001 [Hebrew], p. 339 n. 109.
62 Meir ben Barukh, *Responsa, Rulings, and Customs*, ed. I. Z. Cahana, Jerusalem 1957–1962, vol 1, no. 215, p. 209; Y. D. Gilat, *Studies in the Development of the Halakha*, Jerusalem 1992, pp. 331–342.
63 See note 60.
64 We actually only learn about this custom in the fifteenth century; but the book *Shibolei HaLeket* (no. 59, p. 272), which was written in the second half of the thirteenth century by Rabbi Zidkiya, quotes a passage from the Geonim that mentions women 'stretching out their hands' after the blessing.
65 I. Ta-Shma, *Early Franco-German Ritual and Custom*, Jerusalem 1992, pp. 136–141.
66 B. Har-Shefi, 'Women and Halakha in the years 1050–1350 CE: Between Law and Custom', Ph.D. thesis to the Hebrew University in Jerusalem, Jerusalem 2002, pp. 25–39.
67 E. Marienberg, *Niddah : lorsque les juifs conceptualisent la menstruation*, Paris 2003, pp. 43–72.
68 T. Buckley and A. Gottlieb, 'A Critical Appraisal of Theories of Menstrual Symbolism', in *Blood Magic: The Anthropology of Menstruation*, ed. T. Buckley and A. Gottlieb, Berkeley, CA 1988; M. Douglass, *Purity and Danger: An Analysis of Concepts of Pollution and Taboo*, London 1966; M. Douglass, *Implicit Meanings*, London 1975, pp. 60–72, 276–318.
69 Solomon B. Isaac (Rashi), *Sefer ha-Ora*, ed. S. Buber, Lemberg 1905, vol. 2, p. 176; *Mahzor Vitry*, ed. S. Horowitz, Nuremberg 1892, no. 499; Isaac ben Moses, *Sefer Or Zarua*, Zhitomir 1862, vol. 1, no. 360; vol. 2 no. 454; Meir ben Barukh, *Sheelot u-Teshuvot ha-Maharam*, Prague edition, ed. M. A. Blakh, Budapest 1895, no. 14; Zidkiya ben Abraham, *Sefer Shibolei haLeqet haShalem*, ed. Shlomo Buber, Vilna 1886, no. 169; *Yalkut Simoni, Tazria* no. 547.
70 'Keep the people of Israel separate from their impurity, lest they die in their impurity by defiling My Tabernacle that is their midst.'
71 *Mishnah* Yebamot 4:13, Tosefta Yebamot 6:9; Tbab. Yebamot 49a. H. Eilberg-Schwartz, *The Savage in Judaism*, Bloomington, IN 1990; R. Biale, *Women and Jewish*

Law, New York 1984, pp. 147–174; L. Hoffman, *Covenant of Blood: Circumcision and Gender in Rabbinic Judaism*, Chicago 1996; L. A. Cook, 'Body Language: Women's Rituals of Purification in the Bible and Mishna', in *Women and Water: Menstruation in Jewish Life and Law*, ed. R. R. Wasserfall, Hanover, NH and London 1999, pp. 40–59; T. Meacham, 'An Abbreviated History of the Development of the Jewish Menstrual Laws', in *Women and Water: Menstruation in Jewish Life and Law*, ed. R. R. Wasserfall, Hanover, NH and London 1999, pp. 23–39; E. Marienberg, *Niddah : lorsque les juifs conceptualisent la menstruation*, Paris 2003, pp. 159 ff.

72 S. J. Cohen 'Purity, Piety, and Polemic: Medieval Rabbinic Denunciations of "Incorrect" Purification Practices', in *Women and Water: Menstruation in Jewish Life and Law*, ed. R. R. Wasserfall, Hanover, NH and London 1999, pp. 82–100; I. Ta-Shma, *Ritual, Custom and Reality in Franco-Germany, 1000–1350*, Jerusalem 1992.

73 Tbab. Berakhot 31a; Rashi on Berakhot 31a *s.v.* Yushevet; Megila 28b; Niddah 66a.

74 Tbab. Ketubot 61a; T. Meacham, 'An Abbreviated History of the Development of the Jewish Menstrual Laws', in *Women and Water: Menstruation in Jewish Life and Law*, ed. R. R. Wasserfall, Hanover, NH and London 1999.

75 S. J. Cohen 'Purity and Piety: The Separation of Menstruants from the Sancta', in *Daughters of the King: Women and Synagogue*, ed. S. Grossman and R. Haut, Philadelphia 1992, pp. 103–116; D. Biale, *Women and Jewish Law*, New York 1984, pp. 163–174.

76 S. Geller, 'Blood Cult: Towards a Literary Theology of the Priestly Work of the Pentateuch', *Prooftext* 12 (1992), 97–124; L. A. Cook, 'Body Language: Women's Rituals of Purification in the Bible and Mishna', in *Women and Water: Menstruation in Jewish Life and Law*, ed. R. R. Wasserfall, Hanover, NH and London 1999, pp. 40–59.

77 *Mahzor Vitry*, ed. S. Horowitz, Nuremberg 1892, no. 499, pp. 606–609; Solomon B. Isaac (Rashi), *Sefer ha-Pardes*, ed. H. L. Ehrenreich, Budapest 1924, p. 4; Solomon B. Isaac (Rashi), *Sefer ha-Ora*, ed. S. Buber, Lemberg 1905, vol. 2, pp. 165–176; Eliezer ben Nathan, *Sefer Raban*, Jerusalem 1984, nos 319, 333–335; Jacob ben Meir, *Sefer haYashar leRabbenu Tam: Heleq haShe'elot vehaTeshunot (Responsa)*, ed. S. F. Rosental, Berlin 1898, nos 58 (2), 59 (2); Jacob ben Meir, *Sefer haYashar leRabbenu Tam: Heleq haHidushim* (News), ed. S. S. Schlesinger, Jerusalem 1959, no. 180; Eliezer ben Yoel ha-Levi, *Sefer Ra'aviah*, ed. V. Aptowizer, Jerusalem, 1964, vol. 1, nos 173, 191–192; Tosafot, Tbab. Ketubot 61a *s.v.* mahlafta.

78 The *halakhah* as at present codified is that sexual intercourse (and any other intimacies which may lead to it) is forbidden from the time the woman expects her menses until seven clean days (i.e. days on which no blood whatsoever is seen) have elapsed. For this purpose a minimum of five days is fixed for the menses themselves. Thus the minimum period of separation is twelve days. In the evening of the seventh day without sign of blood the woman immerses herself in a *mikveh* and normal marital relations are resumed until the next menses are expected. I. Ta Shma, 'Niddah', *Encyclopedia Judaica*, vol. 12 pp. 1141–1148.

79 S. J. D. Cohen 'Purity, Piety, and Polemic: Medieval Rabbinic Denunciations of "Incorrect" Purification Practices', in *Women and Water: Menstruation in Jewish Life and Law*, ed. R. R. Wasserfall, Hanover, NH and London 1999, pp. 83, 96–97.

80 See the sources cited in note 77 by Solomon B. Isaac and Eliezer ben Nathan, I. Ta-Shma *Ritual, Custom and Reality in Franco-Germany, 1000–1350*, Jerusalem 1992, pp. 283–287.

81 *Mahzor Vitry*, ed. S. Horowitz, Nuremberg 1892, no. 499, p. 608; Solomon B. Isaac (Rashi), *Sefer ha-Pardes*, ed. H. L. Ehrenreich, Budapest 1924, p. 6; Solomon B. Isaac (Rashi), *Sefer ha-Ora*, ed. S. Buber, Lemberg 1905, vol. 2, pp. 170.

82 *Mahzor Vitry*, ed. S. Horowitz, Nuremberg 1892, no. 498 pp. 604–616; J. R. Woolf, 'Medieval Models of Purity and Sanctity: Ashkenazic Women in the Synagogue', Purity and Holiness: The Heritage of Leviticus (ed. M.J.H.M. Poorthuis and J. Schwartz), Leiden: Brill, 2000, pp. 276–278. E. Baumgarten, Mothers and Children, Jewish Family in Medieval Europe, Princeton 2004, p.78.

83 Eliezer ben Nathan, Sefer Raban, Jerusalem 1984, nos 319, 335.

84 Barukh ben Issac, Sefer ha-Terumah, Jerusalem 1979, no. 69; Isaac ben Moses, Sefer Or Zarua, Zhitomir 1862, no. 360 p. 96. Moses of Coucy, Semag. Sefer Mitzvot Gadol (Venice, 1807), lav, no. 111; Eliezer ben Yoel ha-Levi, *Sefer Ra`aviah*, ed. V. Aptowizer, Jerusalem 1964, vol. 1 no. 173 p. 195; E. E. Urbach, Ba'alei ha-Tosafot, 4th ed. Jerusalem, 1980, p. 37.

85 *Mahzor Vitry*, ed. S. Horowitz, Nuremberg 1892, pp. 605–606; Solomon B. Isaac (Rashi), *Sefer ha-Ora*, ed. S. Buber, Lemberg 1905, vol. 2 no. 1 p. 167; Solomon B. Isaac (Rashi), *Sefer ha-Pardes*, ed. H. L. Ehrenreich, Budapest 1924p. 3; Eliezer ben Nathan, Sefer Raban, Jerusalem 1984, no. 319; Eliezer ben Yoel ha-Levi, *Sefer Ra`aviah*, ed. V. Aptowizer, Jerusalem, 1964, vol. 1 no. 173 pp. 192–193; no. 192 p. 220; Eleazar ben Judah of Worms, Sefer ha-Roqeah, no. 176, 195; Or Zarua, vol. 1 no. 462 p. 133; Moses of Coucy, Semag. Sefer Mizvot Gadol, lav, no. 111; Mordekhai on Shabbat no. 238; Meir ha-Kohen, *Haggahot Maimuniuot*, Hilchot Yisurei Biaha 11:30.

86 Y. Dinari, 'The Impurity Customs of the Menstruate Woman: Sources and Development', Tarbiz 49 (1980), pp. 302–324; Y. Dinari, 'The Profanation of the Holy by the Menstruant Woman and "Takanat Ezra"' [Hebrew], Te'uda 3 (1983), pp. 17–37; S. Cohen, 'Purity and Piety: The Separation of Menstruants from the Sancta', in *Daugters of the King: Women and Synagogue*, ed. S. Grossman and R. Haut, Philadelphia 1992, pp. 103–116; E. Marienberg, *Niddah: lorsque les juifs conceptualisent la menstruation*, Paris 2003, pp. 110–111, 245–265, 293–301. The sources are: Issac ben Meir of Duren, *Sefer Sha`arei Dura*, Lublin 1599, no. 29; *Mahzor Vitry*, ed. S. Horowitz, Nuremberg 1892, p. 606.

87 Isaac ben Moses, *Sefer Or Zarua*, Zhitomir 1862, vol. 1, no. 360, p. 96; Eliezer ben Samuel of Metz, *Sefer Yere'im*, Vilna 1901, vol. 1, no. 26, pp. 47–48; Eliezer ben Yoel ha-Levi, *Sefer Ra`aviah*, ed. V. Aptowizer, Jerusalem, 1964, vol. 1, no. 173, p. 194; Eleazar ben Judah of Worms, *Sefer Roqeah*, Venice 1549, no. 317, p. 200; Meir ha-Kohen, *Haggahot Maimuniuot*, Hilchot Yisurei Biaha 11:30; Alexander Susslein, *Ha-Aguddah*, Cracow 1571, Shabbat no. 19, pp. 6–7; Kol Bo no. 85.

88 J. Hauptman, *Rereading the Rabbis: A Woman's Voice*, Boulder, CO 1998; pp. 158 ff.; C. E. Fonrobert, 'Yalta's Ruse: Resistance against Rabbinic Menstrual Authority in Talmudic Literature', in *Women and Water: Menstruation in Jewish Life and Law*, ed. R. R. Wasserfall, Hanover, NH and London 1999, pp. 60–81.

89 Isaac ben Moses, *Sefer Or Zarua*, Zhitomir 1862, vol. 1, no. 340, p. 90.

90 Bekhorot 27a. Isaac ben Moses, *Sefer Or Zarua*, Zhitomir 1862, vol. 1, no. 340, p. 90.

91 *Mahzor Vitry*, ed. S. Horowitz, Nuremberg 1892, no. 498; Eliezer ben Yoel ha-Levi, *Sefer Ra`aviah*, ed. V. Aptowizer, Jerusalem, 1964, vol. 1, no. 68; Isaac ben Moses, *Sefer Or Zarua*, Zhitomir 1862, vol. 1, no. 360.

92 J. R. Woolf, 'Medieval Models of Purity and Sanctity: Ashkenazic Women in the

Synagogue', in *Purity and Holiness: The Heritage of Leviticus*, ed. M. J. H. M. Poorthuis and J. Schwartz, Leiden 2000, pp. 276-278.
93   Jacob ben Meir Tam, *Sefer ha-Yashar (Responsa)*, no. 58 (2), 59 (2), p. 134; Jacob ben Meir Tam, *Sefer ha-Yashar (News)*, no. 180, p. 126; Tosafot on Shabbat 13b *s.v.* bimei.
94   Shabbat 13a-b; Tosafot on Shabbat 13b *s.v.* bimei; *Mahzor Vitry*, ed. S. Horowitz, Nuremberg 1892, no. 499; Eliezer ben Nathan, *Sefer Raban*, Jerusalem 1984, no. 335; Jacob b. Meir Tam, *Sefer ha-Yashar (Responsa)*, no. 58; Eliezer ben Yoel ha-Levi, *Sefer Ra'aviah*, ed. V. Aptowizer, Jerusalem, 1964, vol. 1, no. 173, p. 192.
95   Solomon B. Isaac (Rashi), *Sefer ha-Ora*, ed. S. Buber, Lemberg 1905, vol. 2, no. 1, p. 167; Solomon B. Isaac (Rashi), *Sefer ha-Pardes*, ed. H. L. Ehrenreich, Budapest 1924, p. 4; *Mahazor Vitry*, ed. S. Horowitz, Nuremberg 1892, no. 499, pp. 605-608; Tosafot to Ketubbot 61a *s.v.* mahalafta.
96   Eliezer ben Yoel ha-Levi, *Sefer Ra'aviah*, ed. V. Aptowizer, Jerusalem 1964, vol. 1, no. 171, p. 192, nos 191-192.
97   Eleazar ben Judah of Worms, *Sefer ha-Roqeah*, Venice 1549, no. 176.
98   *Mahazor Vitry*, ed. S. Horowitz, Nuremberg 1892, pp. 609-611; Solomon B. Isaac (Rashi), *Sefer ha-Ora*, ed. S. Buber, Lemberg 1905, vol. 2, p. 173.
99   Eliezer ben Nathan, *Sefer Raban*, Jerusalem 1984, no. 326; Tosafot to Niddah 66b *s.v.* im; Isaac ben Moses, *Sefer Or Zarua*, Zhitomir 1862, vol. 1, no. 363 (11), p. 99.
100 Tosafot to Shabbat Tbab. 65b *s.v.* Deamar Shmuel; Eliezer ben Nathan, *Sefer Raban*, Jerusalem 1984, no. 25 (23ab); Meir ben Barukh, *Responsa, Rulings, and Customs*, ed. I. Z. Cahana, Jerusalem 1957-1962, vol. 2, no. 106, pp. 96-97; Asher ben Yehiel, *Shut haRosh*, ed. S. Yudelov, Jerusalem 1994, no. 31:11.
101 Eliezer ben Yoel ha-Levi, *Sefer Ra'aviah*, ed. V. Aptowizer, Jerusalem, 1964, vol. 3, no. 750; Eleazar ben Judah of Worms, *Sefer ha-Roqeah*, ed. I. Z. Cahana, Jerusalem 1957-1962, no. 196; Isaac ben Moses, *Sefer Or Zarua*, Zhitomir 1862, vol. 1, no. 338, p. 88; Meir ben Barukh, *Responsa, Rulings, and Customs*, ed. I. Z. Cahana, Jerusalem 1957-1962, vol. 2, no. 110, p. 103.
102 Tosafot to Ketubbot 61a *s.v.* micalfa; Zidkiya ben Abraham, *Sefer Shibolei haLeqet haShalem*, ed. Shlomo Buber, Vilna 1886, vol. 2, no. 80, p. 165; Meir ben Barukh *Responsa, Rulings, and Customs*, ed. I. Z. Cahana, Jerusalem 1957-1962, vol. 2, no. 161, p. 240.
103 Eliezer ben Nathan attempted to make the women's actions compatible with the talmudic text, whereas Rabbi Jacob ben Meir Tam was adamantly against it. Eliezer ben Nathan, *Sefer Raban*, Jerusalem 1984, no. 328, and Peshachim at the beginning (Pesachim 7b); *Mahzor Vitry*, ed. S. Horowitz, Nuremberg 1892, no. 328 pp. 591-592; Jacob ben Meir Tam, *Sefer haYashar leRabbenu Tam: Heleq haHidushim* (News), ed. S. S. Schlesinger, Jerusalem 1959, no. 406, p. 243.
104 E. Zimmer, *Society and Its Customs*, Jerusalem 1996, pp. 220-239; E. Baumgarten, *Mothers and Children, Jewish Family in Medieval Europe*, Princeton 2004, pp. 78-79.
105 E. Zimmer, *Society and its Customs*, Jerusalem 1996, pp. 223-224.
106 Isaac ben Moses, *Sefer Or Zarua*, Zhitomir 1862, vol. 1, no. 339.
107 *Sefer ha-Agudah*, Niddah no. 18, p. 70a, Peshachim no. 13, p. 166b.
108 E. Zimmer, *Society and its Customs*, Jerusalem 1996, pp. 236-239.

7

Cases of some prominent Jewish women

In the Middle Ages the status of women in the Jewish community underwent a real and fundamental change.¹ The sources reflected this change in the economic milieu in which women functioned, and as I have shown in every chapter of this book, this transformation spilled over into other areas of daily life, a fact which the male halakhic leadership also acknowledged and internalized. At the beginning of the thirteenth century, Rabbi Isaac ben Moses suggested that men no longer caution their wives against 'concealment'. According to the Talmud, one of the prior conditions for defining a woman as an adulteress is that she has been warned by her husband beforehand not to conceal herself with anyone; in other words, he suspects that she has been outside the area where he can keep an eye on her. This precondition was set down in an era when a woman was always at home, in a place where her husband could see her, so that if she disappeared from view, he might naturally suspect her of being in contact with someone else. Rabbi Isaac ben Moses explained to men that they must abandon this means of control because in his experience, wives do not remain within sight of their husbands; thus, if a man gives his wife such a warning, he is in effect suspecting her of adultery since she often 'disappears' from view. In reality, Rabbi Isaac ben Moses was acknowledging what Rashi had already asserted at the end of the eleventh century: women are occupied with economic matters outside the home, and these activities cannot come under the category of 'concealment'.²

Rashi had already recognized that women conducted business within the community and with Christians, and in his opinion this did not present a problem. When he was a young man he received a query that involved a monetary dispute within an extended family where women played a central role. Both the elderly mother of the family and her daughter-in-law (the wife of her son who had disappeared) managed businesses, made loans to representatives of the Christian authorities, negotiated on collateral, received vineyards and land as pledges. The daughter-in-law sued her errant husband's brother; she brought deeds and documents to court, and presented her case in an appropriate manner. She bought and sold, mortgaged and redeemed property, dealt in wine. The mother of the two men was also a businesswoman who negotiated with the governor over the properties and the fees owed to her. She evidently obtained better conditions from the governor than her son had managed to get. Rashi did not see anything unusual in this situation. In other words, a new type of woman had appeared on the scene: she was confident of her abilities, conducted business with men, sometimes Christian men, came and went as necessary, but took great care to observe the *halakhot*.[3]

Because the authors of the Hasidei Ashkenaz texts put such excessive emphasis on matters of modesty, on averting situations that would give rise to temptation in the male, and prohibited men and women who were not married from being alone together in a closed room, they often described situations of this sort and searched for solutions to this problem. Their writings indicate the extent to which this behaviour was common (though it is also often the case that Hasidei Ashkenaz bring examples that teach us more about their ideas than about real life). The descriptions of the Christian houses and towns illustrate just how crowded conditions were in the home and on the street, and how closely neighbours lived to one another. The picture they paint underlines the fact that men, women and children lived together in few rooms and that in the streets Jewish and Christian men and women mingled with one another. They make it clear that women of this era were involved in every facet of life and in every area of Jewish community life, in the synagogue, and at home, as well as in commerce. Their presence could not be ignored whether they were doing the laundry, conducting business, or participating in festivals and celebrations. They were free to come and go, to walk in the city streets, to travel on roads, often on their own. One of the sages admonished a woman who was arguing with a gentile about the amount of a loan when she expressed her willingness to swear before him. In other words, the woman negotiated with the non-Jew, argued with him, and finally convinced him. 'My wife controls the money,' one of the men confessed.[4]

In his research among the Christian sources William Jordan found this type of Jewish woman, who is involved in the economic life of the community, comes and goes as she pleases, is self-possessed and self-confident. In northern France, Jewish women lent money at interest to French women and to men as well. The economic activities of Jewish women in northern France and Germany centred on small loans, made on the basis of pledges, to Christian women, who used the money to finance their routine household expenses.[5] The best sources for our topic are those preserved in the Royal Archives of England, which contain a large quantity of information about the economic affairs of Jews, a significant part of it conducted by this new type of woman. The English sources preserved the deeds of the courts of England (sales and commercial contracts, betrothal agreements, marriage and divorce papers).[6]

The Jews of England, who lived mainly in the large cities, the economic crossroads of the country, loaned money at interest on the basis of pledges that guaranteed the return of the money.[7] They constituted one of the main sources of income for the king by their annual payment to the royal coffers of the tallage – a special tax imposed on the Jews of England; as well as fines on routine business transactions – fees for licences, travel, going in and out of England, marriages; and gifts (presents to the king) offered when they addressed a request to him (£100) and thus are very visible.[8]

The sources preserve the names of many Jewish women, who have achieved a place in the annals of history.[9] The figure who embodied the new type of woman more than anyone else, and one who can shed light on the activities of other women, is Licoricia of Winchester. She is first mentioned in the sources as the widow of Abraham of Canterbury. Not only was her name preserved in the chronicles due to her business and economic successes, but also, and extraordinarily, her son was named after her. As a rule, men were listed under the names of their fathers, however her son was known as Lumbard son of Licoricia.[10] Licoricia appeared in the historic arena as a moneylender in 1234, the year in which her first husband, Abraham of Canterbury, was accused of a blood libel and subsequently executed in Winchester. She had three children: Cok, Benedict and Lumbard.[11] In 1240 she married David of Oxford, one of the wealthiest Jews in the Kingdom, who was involved in moneylending and had many clients, including members of the nobility and the King himself. This marriage gave rise to scandals in the Jewish communities from England and France. David divorced his wife Muriel, who was childless, against her wishes and contrary to the decision of the Jewish court of Paris, which Muriel had petitioned. Henry III, the King of England, opposed this French intervention. Licoricia was very active in the joint enterprises she and her new husband operated. She also bore him a son, Asher. Licoricia's role in bringing about this match is not clear; however, it is obvious that it brought together a wealthy widow capable of bearing children and a rich man who had been married to a childless woman.

Four years after their marriage David died, leaving his new bride enormously wealthy. The widow's fortune was so vast that a royal decree was issued for her arrest and she was placed in the Tower of London. David's documents and deeds that were in the *archa*s (a sort of safe where bills and deeds were kept) of Warwick, Berkshire, Buckingham, Northampton and Oxford were sealed and sent to London so that the deceased's property could be estimated before it was turned over and added to his widow's assets. These measures – imprisonment and turning over the *archa*s – were taken so that no one could gain access to David's property and assets before it was all counted and the taxes collected for the King's coffers: one-third of the entire amount. Six people were appointed to carry out this task, and when they finished, Licoricia was freed from prison, wealthier by the remaining two-thirds of her deceased husband's fortune. The sources indicate that she took over the operation of her husband's business enterprises and maintained his connections with the English nobility, members of the Church, and especially King Henry III himself. It appears that every time the King visited his palace in his beloved city of Winchester, he contacted Licoricia. Her name does not appear on the annual tax rolls of the Jews during the reign of Henry III, but reappears in 1272, when his son, Edward I, ascended the throne. In other words, the king exempted her from the poll tax and forced the community to cover the difference. Licoricia took advantage of her access to the King on behalf of her community as well; thus Henry III ordered the tax officials of Winchester to impose reasonable taxes and behave with compassion towards 'my Winchester Jews'. Licoricia, the sources reveal, was a hardhearted and aggressive woman who was not afraid of confronting difficulties or accusations brought against her. In 1251, for example, she was sued by Sir Thomas de Charlecote for circumventing the law by demanding interest on an inheritance; for unlawfully putting a lien against his property and settling on it though she had no right to do so; for her aggressive behaviour when demanding payment of the debt; and for the exorbitant sum she demanded from the debtor. Licoricia claimed in her defence that the inheritance had been obtained by means of a murder. She lost this case, but she paid an insignificant amount because she asked King Henry III to intervene and put pressure on the court.[12]

Licoricia's saga illustrates how the favourable economic status of a Jewish woman in the Middle Ages could also affect her social status in England in general and in the Jewish community in particular. The sources that refer to her indicate that when a woman managed a family enterprise, her sons worked under her, mainly performing tasks a woman could not do. Licoricia's son Cok ran his mother's business together with her, and served as her attorney and legal representative. Officially, women were forbidden by law from signing business documents or from appearing in court; however, the documents prove that women were involved in writing deeds and appeared in court even when they had male representation. In 1275, for instance, Licoricia announced that she could not appear in court because she was ill.[13]

We do not have any Jewish testimony about what transpired in the court when it was realized that David was divorcing his childless wife against her will, and against the ban of Rabbenu Gershom Me'or HaGolah and the ruling of the Rabbinical Court in Paris with the help of the British monarch. Yet, it is clear that Licoricia took advantage of her excellent connections with the nobility and the King to obtain benefits for herself, and to help the community as well. Fortunately for her, the community of Winchester was not put to the same test as that of Blois in 1171, when the nobility were unable come to their aid in matters of theology and blood libel. Nevertheless, the life of Licoricia puts into perspective the saga of Pucinella of Blois 100 years earlier and the hostility towards her revealed in the letters of Ephraim of Bonn. This woman, who conducted herself like a man (who is labelled *gevartanit* and was closely connected with the authorities, could have used her influence for the benefit of her fellow Jews, but she could also have used it to her own advantage, while putting the community at risk. As we have seen, Rabbi Ephraim of Bonn's 'male' attitude led him not only to declare that it was Puchinella's fault that the community was not saved from disaster, but also to downplay the importance of all the martyred women. Ultimately, however, all powerful Jewish women attracted jealousy, and Licoricia herself was found murdered in 1277.

Another Jewish woman, Chera of Winchester, cooperated economically with the Bishop of Winchester, Peter des Roches.[14] The nobility used their land as collateral for the loans they received from her, and when they were unable to pay off their debts, the Bishop stepped in, thus increasing the Church's land holdings at the expense of the nobility. Even though the bishop 'helped' the landowners by providing them with funds, the property reverted to his control. In return, the Bishop gave Chera legal assistance and exempted her from the tallage.[15] In 1266, Almonda, the widow of Jehoshayah ben Elias Cochab, came to the Jewish Court of Norwich to sue for the contents of her *ketubah*, the property of her husband, who had bequeathed it to her in his will. She immediately sold the land holdings to Robert and Donat, the sons of Bartholomew. The deed goes on to say that the deceased's mother sued for her portion of the real estate property and demanded rent from the buyers.[16]

Widows became very desirable potential brides since they brought considerable financial assets to their new marriage. When a rich widow married, the new *ketubah* and the new dowry which she received added even more to her property as a married woman. Mila and her husband, Samuel of Bolum, were at loggerheads, evidently because she was not willing to allow him to make use of the property she had brought with her to this marriage, assets she had received on the basis of her *ketubah* with her deceased husband. Mila claimed that she had married Samuel out of commercial considerations – 'contract and commerce between them' – and the Jewish Court decided that the marriage was not valid.[17]

The sources clearly indicate that these women were trained to function in the economic sphere from a young age. Legal sources show that an unmarried woman would work together with the rest of the family when living in her father's house, while a married woman engaged in business affairs in her husband's absence (due to a journey, imprisonment, or disappearance), and widows took over the business and functioned as proprietors in every sense of the word. It is obvious that from their youth these women were looked upon as partners in the property; moreover, they were trained to enter the realm of finance, moneylending, and pawnbroking, since it is inconceivable that an untrained woman could step into a business and begin to function efficiently immediately upon her husband's arrest or sudden death.[18] The presence of widows in the area of finance and economics proves that they were partners with their husbands in matters of livelihood and the family economy, and shared equally in the decision-making process. While researchers have focused on the activities of the widows, because their presence in the sources is more prominent when they are without their husbands; these women were married beforehand and were without doubt involved in their husbands' financial activities. They also brought substantial *ketubot* and dowries into the marriage, and dealt with their own financial affairs when their husbands were alive and, of course, when they were left on their own as widows. Their proficiency in financial transactions and their ability to understand their rights, matters of property ownership, and the appropriate use of their *ketubot* demonstrates that they were competent in economic matters long before they became widows. As we have seen in earlier chapters, the heirs who sue their mother in court when she took control of the family property, do not wind up with even a small part of the property. The argument put forward by the widow was that the Jewish Court could not return assets she owned to the heirs, because she was entitled to this 'small amount' of property since she had taken possession of it on the basis of her *ketubah*; it had also increased in value thus making her holdings even more substantial. Since women collected debts, bought and sold, lent money, and improved their economic situations, it is decidedly unlikely that they could have learned to perform these tasks only after their husbands' demise.[19]

As well as their prominence in finance, we see exceptional Jewish women celebrated and commemorated for other qualities. Rabbi Eleazar of Worms relates that on 15 November 1196, two noblemen who returned from the Crusades (he called them *mesumanim* (marked) – meaning, it would seem, wearing a cross, the uniform of Crusaders) dealt a mortal blow to his family. His home was attacked and his wife, Dolce, and two of his daughters, Bellette and Hannah, were murdered, while he, his son, and his students were severely injured. His wife was the only one among them who, despite her injuries, had run outside to call for help; but the attackers chased after her and killed her. When they ran out, Rabbi Elazar managed to lock the door and everyone inside raised the alarm and shouted for help until it arrived. An investigation was held and later on the Christian authorities executed one of the attackers. Rabbi Elezar of Worms (died c. 1230) carried on with his life, but suffered great anguish following the event, which he described in prose and in a liturgical poem.[20] From his prose texts it is obvious that he lived in a state of torment and with feelings of extreme remorse. First he described how he himself, along with all the other men, were helpless and, above all, passive, whereas his wife was the only one who ran outside to seek help. His guilt was particularly apparent when he emphasized how, by running outside, wounded and pursued by her attackers, his wife gave him the opportunity to lock the door of the 'winter house', raise the alarm and shout for help until it arrived. Rabbi Eleazar declared that his wife, in effect, had sacrificed herself for him. The detailed description of her injuries – 'They hit her on the head up to her neck and shoulders and from the shoulders to the waist and across her back and face' – is given special emphasis in contrast with his own understated injuries, 'wounded in the head and hands'. And he again repeated 'for my great sins she was killed, she and my daughters'; 'she died before my very eyes'.

In addition to his prose account, Rabbi Eleazar of Worms wrote a liturgical poem in memory of his wife and daughters. As the basis for his poem, he used Proverbs 31, which describes the ideal woman. First, Rabbi Eleazar called his wife a *Hasida* (pious woman). Although we cannot be certain about the exact connotation of this epithet, he meant that his wife performed many pious deeds and performed the Commandments. Following the words of Proverbs, he stressed that she was completely loyal to him, and from his point of view: 'the heart of her husband doth safely trust in her' (cf. Prov. 31:11) allowing him to devote himself completely to his affairs. Dolce was responsible for maintaining the household, although it is not altogether clear how she provided for the family of Rabbi Eleazar of Worms; we know that she ran a *yeshivah* (a talmudic school) for his students[21] as he noted that she was responsible for the students; cooked for them, mended their clothing, served their food, saw to their needs, their books and clothing. She also hired the teachers who helped her husband in the *yeshivah*. She evidently earned money by stitching together the folios of the Torah. Rabbi Eleazar of Worms recounted with pride that Dolce had made forty Torah scrolls. He also revealed that she used the money she earned in this occupation to buy books for him. He reported with satisfaction that his wife knew 'matters permitted and prohibited', i.e., that she was knowledgeable about the practical, day-to-day world of *mitzvot*. From the perspective of religious piety, Dolce was exemplary: she recited all the prayers every day; attended synagogue on the Sabbath, listened to the sermons delivered there by her husband, and recited psalms on a regular basis, leading the other women in all these practices by teaching them to pray. Rabbi Eleazar also recounted the *mitzvot* his wife performed: she was concerned with charity for the poor; visited the sick; spun wool into *tzitziot* (fringes); made the wicks for candles, which were an ongoing and very popular contribution for the synagogue; helped brides; and ministered to the dead. Rabbi Eleazar also related that Dolce considered it her responsibility to teach his female offspring, and pointed out that his murdered daughters had indeed been admirable models of this training. Six-year-old Hannah had already learned to read the *Shemah* prayer and how to separate the dough of the *hallah* and thirteen-year-old Bellette, who had learned the prayers from her mother, took care of her father, made his bed and took off his shoes, and studied Torah with him.

What can we learn from this impassioned and agonized description of the status of women in the patriarchal world in which Rabbi Eleazar of Worms lived? Or is it so idealized that it does not reflect reality?

It is clear that the members of this family were knowledgeable; they were the offspring of learned people, a woman and children who grew up in an intellectual environment and married scholars (Dolce herself was an educated woman, the daughter of a cantor). From the point of view of economic occupations, this study has concluded that women were involved in all areas of finance, commerce, moneylending, pawnbroking, etc. Rabbi Eleazar notes here that his wife's occupation led her to be connected with 'the money of others', that is *commanda* transactions, which implies business on a high level. In a *commanda*, several people deposit money with a representative, who promises them a specific return from his transactions with the funds they have deposited with him; his profit is what remains after he has paid the promised returns. Dolce's involvement in charity is confirmed in other sources, which describe in detail acts of charity by women, communal philanthropic enterprises, as well as aid to individuals. These charitable activities are also reflected in the names given to women in the memorial books and texts that deal with *mitzvot*. We see it in other places, too, where it was hinted that women worked hard at getting their husbands to promise to give money to charity for the poor, philanthropy and the synagogue, when they at first refused to do so.²² *Sefer Hasidim*, which was written by scholars closely associated with Rabbi Eleazar of Worms, tells the story of a husband who returns from a long journey, having previously announced his pending arrival to his wife. She went to the *mikvah* in anticipation of his return and he gives her a gift to show his appreciation of her action, money for a new coat. She exchanged the money in order to buy a book or to fund the writing of a book, which she gave to a Torah scholar. The sources refer to women who make donations without telling their husbands, or against their wishes. There seems to have been a trend among the women of making their immersion in the *mikvah*, and subsequent renewal of marital relations, conditional on their husbands making a donation to charity, especially if they had previously reneged on a promise to make some charitable donation. The author of *Sefer Hasidim* does not hide his positive attitude towards this behaviour, though he does suggest that it is better not to mix matters of sexual intimacy with charity so as not to elicit the wrath of the husband, or out of fear that this might cause him to 'think of sinful behaviour'.²³

The description of Dolce is a woman who knows the rules about 'what is permitted and prohibited', listens to her husband's sermons, and is familiar, in one way or another, with matters of *halakhah*. Yet, from all that we have gathered from the medieval writings, it appears that the male sages were indeed concerned that the women in their households (their wives, mothers-in-law, daughters) would be able to study properly, within the confines of the home; they educated the girls as they grew up into women in the performance of the Commandments; involved the women and girls in family ceremonies (Grace after Meals, the reciting of the *Shema* prayer, etc.), and in essence looked upon the women of the family as the custodians of customs and traditions.²⁴

This is clearly demonstrated in Rashi's family. Before making halakhic decisions, they would often turn to their female relations for clarifications about customs. As we have seen, Rashi's grandson, Rabbenu Tam, who was involved in a dispute with Rabbi Meshulam of Melun over the matter of kindling the Sabbath candles, used his consultation with the women in his immediate environment to substantiate his halakhic explanation.

Unlike Rabbi Meshulam, Rabbenu Tam saw the custom of lighting the candles as having an additional ceremonial value, not just for the purpose of illuminating the home in honour of the Sabbath evening meal. Rabbenu Tam observed that the women extinguished and relit the candles, and recited the blessing over the candles at the designated time for kindling the Sabbath lights. He questioned them about their practice and their response served to substantiate his explanation of the custom. It may be claimed that the male sages used the tradition of the women to support their own halakhic positions, and that they did not rely exclusively on the statements of the women. This is undoubtedly true; however, it is obvious that they did acknowledge the women's power to transmit customs from one generation to the next. Rabbenu Tam called these women 'prophetesses or daughters of prophetesses',[25] borrowing (and feminizing) the expression Hillel the Elder had used in the context of the halakhic conduct of men (Tbab. Tractate Pesahim 61a). In other words, we learn about customs from women; they are the custodians of the custom and its traditions, even when the custom has obvious halakhic repercussions.

Rabbi Simha of Vitry, a favourite student of Rashi's, and who married Rashi's granddaughter (the sister of Rabbenu Tam), adhered to this approach in his home as did his son, Rabbi Isaac, who was married to Rashi's great granddaughter. When he was faced with problems associated with cooking and baking utensils or with meat and dairy dishes, he sought the advice of the women of his family.[26] He consulted with his mother-in-law, the widow of Rabbi Isaac ben Meir (Rashi's grandson) about a question related to a vessel used in baking both dairy and meat items. Normally, the use of the same vessel for diary and meat was strictly forbidden in the *Halakha*. His mother-in-law's response was that since this heavy vessel, that was used only to cover the casseroles, was very expensive and they only had one such utensil, they used it to cover the baking dish whether they were baking dough filled with meat or with cheese; however, they would heat it at a very high temperature beforehand. This heating would *kasher* the vessel making it like new for use with either meat or dairy dishes. This was his mother-in-law's practice; yet she pointed out that she usually heats the vessel a little more than was perhaps necessary to 'allay her guilty conscience'. She had two ceramic baking dishes, she explained, and indicated that she saw herself (and perhaps Rabbi Isaac saw her this way as well) as a link in the chain of women who handed down customs related to cooking and baking. She noted that her first husband (Rabbi Isaac ben Meir) observed her practices and relied upon her; moreover, she followed the same custom in the home of her husband's parents, Yocheved (Rashi's daughter) and Rabbi Meir, her husband. She pointed out that another granddaughter of Rashi, Shlima (the daughter of Rashi's daughter Miriam), followed the same procedure.

Rabbi Isaac attempted to clarify the exact custom because he thought that, of all people, his aunt (the wife of Rabbenu Tam) tended to be somewhat stricter (either using two separate covers or heating the cover at a higher temperature). In essence, he wanted to find out whether she had adopted this practice herself or whether she was following the demands of her husband who sought to be more stringent in this matter. It seems that Rabbenu Tam's opinion would have changed Rabbi Isaac's outlook. In other words, even when men followed the customs practiced by women, they attempted to find out if their husbands had agreed to the practice or not. In any event, Rabbi Isaac showed great respect towards the women of his family, despite that fact that he mentioned only Rashi's granddaughter by name and called his mother-in-law 'Madame, my mother-in-law'. He also repeated the expression 'If they are not prophetesses, they are the daughters of prophetesses', used by his uncle.[27]

The description of Dolce and what she did in the synagogue confirms once again what has emerged throughout this study: women played an important role within Jewish society. They became integrated in certain areas, and where they were still excluded, prayer services, for example, they created a female subgroup where women led prayers for other women. They also took part in male society activities, conducting prayer services alongside them during ceremonies. So we have Richenza, who 'prays for the women', mentioned in a memorial book, and on a tombstone, we read an inscription dedicated to a woman by the name of Urania, who died in 1275 in Worms. The family that mourned her wrote:[28]

> This stone was erected to commemorate the Lady, Madame Urania,
> That eminent, remarkable woman, the daughter of the Haver Rabbi Abraham,
> The distinguished cantor, whose prayers are celebrated and glorious,
> The lavish tones of his magnificent voice singing on behalf of his people.
> And she too sang for the women with such a voice:
> A singer of liturgical poems in notes so rich, they shall always be cherished
> And on the sixth of Adar, Sunday, her soul was fulfilled
> and on the seventh she was buried.
> Heaven shall be her resting place and she will be remembered
> for ever for all the good deeds she has done.

Notes

1   I. Yoval, 'HaHesderim haKaspiyim shel haNissuim beAshkenaz beYemei haBenayim', in *Religion and Economy Connections and Interactions*, ed. M. Ben Sasson, Jerusalem 1995, pp. 191–207; A. Grossman, *Pious and Rebellious: Jewish Women in Europe in the*

Middle Ages, Jerusalem 2001 [Hebrew], pp. 139-159.
2   Isaac ben Moses, *Sefer Or Zarua*, Zhitomir 1862, vol. 1, no. 815.
3   Solomon B. Isaac (Rashi), *Responsa Rashi*, ed. I. Elfenbein, New York 1943, nos 128, 240. He once received a query from a woman who had to travel to the authorities on Thursday, the day on which the fast of Esther was to be observed. (It had been brought forward and Purim was to be celebrated on Sunday.) She had come to Rashi to ask him to permit her to observe the fast on Friday.
4   *Sefer Hassidim*, nos 465, 1265-1266, 309.
5   W. C. Jordan, 'Jews on top: women and availability of consumption loans in northern France in the mid-thirteenth century', *Journal of Jewish Studies* 29 (1978), pp. 43, 47, 51-53; W. C. Jordan, *Women and Credit in Pre-industrial and Developing Societies*, Philadelphia 1993, pp. 20-24, 59-78; M. Adler, *Jews of Medieval England*, ed. E. Goldston for the Jewish Historical Society of England, London 1939, p. 28. Jordan describes the hostility of the Christian women and their children, who would go together to the home of the Jewish woman to obtain money while at the same time handing over all the valuable property they owned.
6   M. D. Davis, *Hebrew Deeds of English Jews*, London 1888; Z. Rokeah, *Medieval English Jews and Royal Officials*, Jerusalem 2000; S. Bartlet, 'Women in the medieval Anglo-Jewish community', in *Jews in Medieval Britain*, ed. P. Skinner, Woodbridge 2003, p. 113; R. R. Mundill, *England's Jewish Solution: Experiment and Expulsion, 1262-1290*, Cambridge 1998, pp. 75-89; Suzanne Bartlet, *Licoricia of Winchester: marriage, motherhood and murder in the medieval Anglo-Jewish community*, London 2009.
7   R. R. Mundill, *England's Jewish Solution: Experiment and Expulsion, 1262-1290*, Cambridge 1998, pp. 45-107; W. Jordan, 'Women and Credit in the Middle Ages: Problems and Directions', *Journal of European Economic History* (Rome) 17 (1988), pp. 34-35.
8   The deeds recording debts to Jews were kept in coffers which were called *archa*, a word meaning chest or archive. S. Bartlet, 'Three Jewish businesswomen in thirteenth-century Winchester', *Jewish Culture and History* 3 (2000), pp. 31-33, 40; W. C. Jordan, 'Women and Credit in the Middle Ages: Problems and Directions', *Journal of European Economic History* (Rome) 17 (1988), p. 53.
9   Bartlet listed forty-one women. S. Bartlet, 'Three Jewish businesswomen in thirteenth-century Winchester', *Jewish Culture and History* 3 (2000).
10 Another female merchant of Winchester, Sarah, was so successful in her business affairs that even her grandson was named after her: Abraham son of Elias son of Sarah. Bartlet, 'Women in the medieval Anglo-Jewish community', in *Jews in Medieval Britain*, ed. P. Skinner, Woodbridge 2003, p. 118; Z. M. Rokeah, *Medieval English Jews and Royal Officials*, Jerusalem 2000, no. 813, p. 220.
11 Cok (Isaac), Benedict (Berachia or Barukh), and Lumbard; apparently there was also a daughter; S. Bartlet, 'Three Jewish businesswomen in thirteenth-century Winchester', *Jewish Culture and History* 3 (2000).
12 S. Bartlet, 'Three Jewish businesswomen in thirteenth-century Winchester', *Jewish Culture and History* 3 (2000), pp. 31-54; S. Bartlet, *Licoricia of Winchester: marriage, motherhood and murder in the medieval Anglo-Jewish community*, London, 2009).
13 S. Bartlet, 'Women in the medieval Anglo-Jewish community', in *Jews in Medieval Britain*, ed. P. Skinner, Woodbridge 2003, p. 119; S. Bartlet, *Licoricia of Winchester: marriage, motherhood and murder in the medieval Anglo-Jewish community*, London,

2009; M. Adler, *Jews of Medieval England*, London 1939, pp. 40-42. The accounts of Licoricia also shed light on the life of Pucellina, also described as a *gevartanit* (a 'virile' tough female), a clever and strong woman who managed her affairs successfully and professionally and had excellent connections with the Christian authorities.

14 Nicholas Vincent, *Peter des Roches, an Alien in English Politics, 1205-1238*, Cambridge 2002.

15 S. Bartlet, 'Three Jewish Businesswomen in Thirteenth Century Winchester', *Jewish Culture and History* 3:2 (2000), pp. 35-38.

16 M. D. Davis, *Hebrew Deeds of English Jews*, London 1888, pp. 136-140.

17 S. Bartlet, 'Women in the Medieval Anglo-Jewish Community', in *Jews in Medieval Britain*, ed. P. Skinner, Woodbridge 2003, p. 124; Z. Rokeah, 'Pietism, Money and Women in Thirteenth Century England', in *Religion and Economy: Connections and Interactions*, ed. M. Ben Sasson, Jerusalem 1995, pp. 179-190.

18 C. Tallan, 'Medieval Jewish widows', *Jewish History* 5 (1991), pp. 63-66; S. Bartlet, 'Women in the Medieval Anglo-Jewish Community', in *Jews in Medieval Britain*, ed. P. Skinner, Woodbridge 2003, pp. 119, 123 n. 14; A. Grossman, *Pious and Rebellious: Jewish Women in Europe in the Middle Ages*, Jerusalem 2001 [Hebrew], pp. 196-198; A. Grossman, *Pious and Rebellious: Jewish Women in Europe in the Middle Ages*, Waltham MA, 2004 [English], pp. 114-116.

19 Meir ben Barukh, *Sheelot u-Teshuvot ha-Maharam*, Prague edition, ed. M. A. Blakh, Budapest 1895, no. 502; Mordekhai on Baba Batra no. 606. This was also the assumption made by Rabbi Samson bar Abraham in response to Rabbi Samuel ben Meir's remarks.

20 J. Baskin, 'Dolce of Worms: Women Saints in Judaism', in *Women Saints in World Religious*, ed. A. Sharma, Albany, NY 2000, pp. 39-69 (esp. pp. 49, 59).

21 Enrolment was not high; Rabbi Meir ben Barukh of Rothenburg apparently had twenty pupils, considered a very large number.

22 Meir ben Barukh, *Sheelot u-Teshuvot ha-Maharam*, Prague edition, ed. M. A. Blakh, Budapest 1895, no. 998; *Sefer Hassidim*, no. 670.

23 *Sefer Hassidim*, nos 670, 844, 1715.

24 L. Bar-Leve, 'Our women have a lovely custom', *Massekhet* 6 (2007), pp. 47-85; Eliezer ben Yoel ha-Levi, *Sefer Raviah*, ed. V. Aptowizer, Jerusalem 1964, vol. 3, no. 841, p. 561; Hayim ben Rabbi Yitzhak, *Responsa*, Leipzig 1860, no. 101.

25 Jacob ben Meir, *Sefer haYashar leRabbenu Tam: Heleq haShe'elot vehaTeshunot (Responsa)*, ed. S. F. Rosental, Berlin 1898, nos 48-49, pp. 92, 99-100; Eliezer ben Yoel ha-Levi, *Sefer Raviah*, ed. V. Aptowizer, Jerusalem 1964, vol. 3, no. 999, esp. p. 264; I. Ta-Shma, *Early Franco-German Ritual and Custom*, Jerusalem 1992, p. 138.

26 Isaac ben Moses, *Sefer Or Zarua*, Zhitomir 1862, vol. 1, no. 442.

27 When he was called upon to deal with matters of *niddah*, he inquired about the practices of the women; however, he also sought support from the world of *halakhah*, and when he did not find such support he qualified his statements or rejected the women's customs. *Teshuvot uPsakim, Responsa et Decisiones*. ed. E. Kupfer, Jerusalem 1973, no. 143, pp. 249-250; *Mahzor Vitry*, ed. S. Horowitz, Nuremberg 1892.

28 S. Salfeld, *Das Martyrlogium des Nürnberger Memorbuches*, Berlin 1938, p. 36; J. Lewyson, *Nephashut Zadikim*, Frankfurt 1855, pp. 85-86.

8

In conclusion

Medieval Jewish society saw itself as being under siege in an ongoing struggle for survival within a Christian population that abounded with threats and temptations, both economic and intellectual. The situation was defined by Jewish society as an emergency situation, and so it recruited all its resources to be able to deal with it.[1] The specific circumstances of the First Crusade may have triggered this stance, but it emanated out to all Jewish communities in northern Europe. In their struggle for survival the Jewish group developed a sophisticated organization (the Jewish community) whose purpose was to keep as many of its members as possible within its confines. This organization saw itself involved in a critical struggle for survival against a majority population that was trying to swallow it up theologically and make it disappear as a religion. In this emergency situation the leadership of the group would in any circumstances and at any price strengthen any factor within the community whose contribution to the matter of survival was not in doubt. The children underwent a unique socialization process, special methods were developed for dealing with those who defected from the normative standards of the group (violent people, people who refused to pay their internal taxes to the Jewish community, and even those who collaborated with the Christian rulers), and there also developed a special attitude towards those who committed the worst moral deviation of all and went over to Christianity, the opposing religion.[2]

In terms of its communal awareness the historical situation changed radically for the Jews in light of the Christian attack on the major Jewish communities along the German Rhine valley at the outset of the First Crusade in 1096. Though this attack was limited to a relatively small number of communities (Speyer, Worms, Mainz, Cologne, Regensburg and Prague) in the German regions, the fact that such an attack was possible at all, the Emperor's inability to prevent it and the Jewish readiness to become martyrs in the Christian cities created the feeling among Jewish groups in Germany and in northern France that they were facing a new and danger-prone situation. The period that follows, the first half of the twelfth century, was one of tense trial for the Jewish communities in the area. The twelfth century was a period in which Christian prestige steadily and demonstratively climbed, as did the self-esteem of individual Christians, and the Jews saw this prestige as a constant threat and challenge. When it became known that the Christians had conquered the Land of Israel, the place that the Jews in Exile cherished a deep yearning for, and had even established a Christian kingdom there with its centre in Jerusalem where the Holy Temple had stood, the Jewish concept of redemption was mortally wounded. The Christian city in Europe undergoes an impressive economic and cultural development during the twelfth century, and Christian society clearly and forcefully manifested its specifically religious characteristics. Tension developed between Christians and Jews against the background of the Christians' desire to understand Jewish writing, past and contemporary, especially the Jewish commentaries on the Bible. Even worse, from the Jewish point of view, were the increasing signs of Jews converting to the rival religion, voluntarily and not from necessity or coercion.[3] Jewish society was led by a group of men who fulfilled all its important leadership roles, as rabbinical judges and teachers, halakhic scholars and communal leaders. This leadership was very aware of the central role played by the women of the community, and it worked towards improving their status as much as possible, partly because of the tradition to do so that dated back to the classical Jewish leadership in the first centuries CE, and partly due to the need to involve the women as much as possible in the preservation of the community at this time and in this specific location. From this perspective, the twelfth century and especially the first half of the twelfth century was a critical period for understanding the changes that Jewish society underwent in general and changes that occurred in the status of women in particular. In all of the sources written by the Jews (all of the writers were men) in the first generation following the attack on the Jewish communities in the year 1096, emphasis was laid on the Jewish woman's readiness to lead religious resistance to the death, together with her unswerving devotion to Jewish values.

The change in the status of the woman manifested itself in at least three significant ways; in her economic-legal status, in her status within the family and in her social standing. It was in this period that, due to the external pressures and due to the social outlook of the male leadership, the first significant change occurred, upon which the other changes were dependent. This change relates to the status of women on their forming a new family unit and the awareness that the wife's cooperation is essential if this unit needs to be dissolved.

The desire to form a new family unit by means of the *Ketubah* document created a mutual financial commitment. The man promised his wife sums of money and property that will be collected in the event of the dissolution of the family cell, and also added sums of money in the light of the actual sums brought into the marriage by the wife (the dowry). Since the *ketubah* was read aloud at the wedding ceremony, it was essential not to embarrass anyone by intimating that different women had different values put on them, which is why the amount of the basic commitment was artificially made equal for all men. This process might be considered artificial because in its legal basis are mutual agreements written for the situation where the family unit might be dissolved in the case of divorce, but in practice it meant that if a woman was widowed she could take control over the common property. In this way, if she formed a new family unit she came into it as a potential owner of significant property. The woman's status changes and strengthens because this change turns her into both a legal entity and an economic entity in her own right. As in the past, the property she brought with her stays hers, but now the 'family property' is also considered potentially hers. This change is accompanied by a real revolution that defines her in an absolute manner as the sole wife in the family unit, and makes any divorce conditional on her agreement.

Even though the first indications of these trends were seen earlier, most sources point to the first half of the twelfth century as the period in which these real changes took place. The definition of a married woman as the only wife of a man, significantly changed the way a woman was viewed even though the Jews were obliged in practice to prohibit bigamy in all places under Christian control. But the more significant change was the empowering of the woman by making divorce conditional on her consent. Instead of being connected passively to a man who forms and dissolves the family unit as he chooses, we now see the wife's power to oppose the totally arbitrary behaviour of a man previously capable of gratuitously dissolving the family unit. The root of this sea change was the preoccupation of the communal and halakhic leadership with the constant state of emergency it perceived the community to be in and the consequent need it felt to recruit women to the cause of communal survival.

Starting in the twelfth century, a woman stepping down from her bridal canopy was a woman of a new and different status. Jewish society around her remained a male society with all its previous pride and prejudice; the house she enters is still defined as 'her husband's house', and all the verbs that define her state are passive verbs. Yet now standing under the canopy is a bride destined to be the sole wife in the new family unit, potentially the owner of much property, someone who has to be taken into consideration because she holds a determining stake in matters of property and, also because she also potentially holds the key in matters concerning the break-up of the family. This is decidedly a totally new situation.

As we are dealing with a dynamic male society, it is obvious that changes working in favour of the woman will lead to a clear male counter action. In a system such as this, a subgroup that perceives itself losing ground to another subgroup will try to regain its lost ground. Indeed, throughout the twelfth century, there were attempts to undermine women's achievements both in terms of their marital and their economic status. This struggle cannot be defined as a 'gender struggle' because the whole struggle took place in a male arena and we cannot know, and can only speculate on, the extent of the female influence. It is important to point out that these attempts to erode the woman's status did not succeed, and we need, therefore, to emphasize once more the feeling of being under siege, and the pressure that the leadership felt which constantly fuelled their efforts to improve women's status, even if in practice these achievements were only partial achievements. We find a sample of this in the male writings that describe the coping with those who converted to Christianity during the twelfth and thirteenth centuries. In the sources written by Jews we hardly find examples of women converting of their own free will, although it would be logical to assume that there were women who converted along with their husbands, and even though we know from Christian sources that some Jewish women did convert.[4] The Jewish sources, however, rarely refer to female apostasy and when there is a mention, it is emphasized that the woman was forced to convert and is waiting for the opportunity to be released from her captivity and return to Judaism. The male writing always focuses on the high standing of the woman and her religious devotion.

In terms of the women's position in the Jewish economic world, more and more sources mention women involved in matters of finance, buying and selling, in giving loans to Christians, in travelling from one place to another to deal with financial matters and to protect their financial interests. This information is culled from several types of source material: from the extensive Jewish correspondence dealing with problems arising in the course of conducting business transactions, from the written documentation of the courts in England, and from property records of purchase and sale by Jews (with many women among them) in German city archives.

From these sources we see that men took the lead in terms of economic activities but in all cases where a man was prevented from doing this, his wife took over the business and ran it until the man could come back on the scene.

The sources written by men also tell us much about the female group itself. The female image that emanates from the study is different from what is usually portrayed. We find an image of a woman who has a great deal of self-confidence, a very developed feminine consciousness, is aware of herself, her femininity, her place in the community, and shows a readiness, whenever the opportunity arises, to disseminate the values of her group. Where they decided that there was a need to express themselves as women in the religious sphere, they worked towards that goal, even if at first the men attempted to impede their participation. (We should bear in mind that most of the women described by the sources come from well educated families.) This is clear from the manner in which women related to observing the *mitzvot*, the Commandments, to prayer and to the synagogue. What was regarded by the Jews as a prestigious lifestyle revolved primarily around keeping the Jewish daily agenda of the Commandments and divine ordinances? This domain had been controlled over the years by men with male religious preferences so that the observance of the Commandments had been placed far more on men's shoulders than on women's, especially in the public domain, the domain of prayer, and the central institution of the Jewish community – the synagogue. Jewish prayer is an event that repeats itself three times every day and during the festivals symbolizes the peak of religious and social activities. Prayer and the synagogue were conceived of as a male realm, partly because public prayer could not take place without a minimum quorum of ten males, and partly because prayer services were regarded as a 'time-related Commandment', from which women were exempt. Female consciousness was such that the women responded in a conspicuously 'feminine' manner towards the world of the Commandments because it is clear that the performance of the Commandments by women was apprehended by them as a given. It seems indeed that the decision on which Commandments to keep was determined by the women themselves through their intuitive grasp of the nature and importance of the Commandments. They kept those Commandments they considered important and adopted Commandments through which they could express their femininity. These Commandments were adopted by the women who observed them without any regard to the male conceptions or to the learned guidance of the male leadership. Usually, the male confirmation for this behaviour was given retroactively, based on the

IN CONCLUSION

sound feeling that confrontation with this genuinely religious approach should be avoided, because the men valued the religious devotion of the women and because of the men's pragmatic understanding that the women would continue to do as they pleased in this matter, no matter what the men might say.

The women also succeeded in bypassing an almost impossible obstacle in regard to study and education. The male attitude regarded study and education as the sole province of men. Since some families educated the women as well, and since the teaching of young boys was done at home, some women were able to acquire the reading skills required for prayer. On reaching maturity, those daughters who had acquired an education took over the female leadership of the community and we find them leading the prayers for the women. This way, even women who did not learn Hebrew at a young age could participate in the prayers when they were led by female cantors. This explains why during the twelfth and thirteenth century, a number of synagogues (in Worms and Speyer, for example) acquire extensions which are in fact synagogues for women. In this I see a decisive proof of the trend that I have mentioned of the male leadership recognizing that much had to be done so that women will form an integral, if separate, part of society, since it is obvious that the planning, financing and construction of these 'women's synagogues' were jobs performed by the men.

What allowed this development? In the Jewish sources we find all the possible male types: the misogynist who is worried that women are enhancing their status at the expense of his own; the caring husband who sees the woman in her role as mother and wife who helps her husband and bears his children; the pious individuals who view women through mystical eyes; and those who value the importance of women as a major factor in unifying the group. The writings that have been left us from the Middle Ages were written by an elite groups of scholars. From these writings we can get the impression that the conscious appreciation of women and girls was common among many men. The misogynist view and the chauvinistic comments are usually based on older sources or as an expression of concern that the women are taking over the world of Commandments and are deviating from their traditional role. In general, the male leadership did not agree with the ubiquitous practice of denying women the opportunity of studying and with the exclusion of women from public worship and other communal events. During the Middle Ages, in the areas I researched, the latter affected the group attitude towards women's status more than anything else. The unique strength of women was recognized and if we ignore sexist comments and the comments of the misogynists, then from most of the sources available to us emanates a male consciousness that associates woman with religious devotion, that values her as a decision maker and that believes in her innate ability to pass on these qualities to her offspring. Analysis of the developments in these centuries shows that a certain historical situation, that combines an aware male leadership with women conscious of their power, can make a difference. From the writings of men we learn that these men identified an exclusively characteristic female consciousness. The men state, sometimes derisively, but for the most part in amazement and esteem, that there is a female consciousness that relates to a wide range of issues, to the world of values and to their worldview. This female consciousness, in my view, is the major new phenomenon of the period and the one that made the difference.

Notes

1. It is, of course, not necessary to prove that the threat from the majority population actually existed, it is enough that the minority group felt threatened and acted accordingly. It is for this reason that this aspect of the Christian–Jewish relationship is not examined in this study, and it is also the reason why the Jewish community living in Spain was not investigated. In Spain the model was different. There the Jewish community lived among a Muslim population and created, in opposition to it, a different system of reactions. Over a period of hundreds of years Christianity triumphed over Islam and conquered ever-increasing territories where Jews were living. In response to the change in sovereignty the Jews were obliged to change their defence mechanisms both internally and towards the outside world. In social terms the communities formed were significantly different from the Jewish communities studied in this work.
2. See S. Goldin, *Uniqueness and Togetherness: The Enigma of the Survival of Jews in the Middle Ages*, Tel Aviv 1997 (in Hebrew), pp. 86–100.
3. Ibid.
4. We know some of their names in thirteenth-century England – those who lodged at 'the Jew's house'. See R. Stacey, 'The Conversion of the Jews to Christianity in Thirteenth Century England', *Speculum* 67 (1992), pp. 263–283.

APPENDIX I

Translated samples of the original source material

Chapter 3

Q. A. often beats his wife. She begged him to promise not to beat her any more, but he refused to make any such promise. Even when she appeared in the Synagogue to demand that A. pay the debts she had contracted in order to pay for her sustenance [probably during a period of separation], A. stubbornly refused to promise that in the future he would refrain from beating her

A. A. must pay for his wife's sustenance, since by his action he has shown that he has not decided to desist from his shameful practice. One deserves greater punishment for striking one's wife than for striking another person, for one is enjoined to respect her. Far be it from a Jew to do such a thing. Had a similar case come before us we should hasten to excommunicate him. Thus, R. Paltoi Gaon rules that a husband who constantly quarrels with his wife must remove the causes of such quarrels, if possible, or divorce her and pay her the *ketubah*; how much more must a husband be punished who not only quarrels but actually beats his wife.

Sources. Meir ben Barukh, *Sefer She'elot uTeshuvot*, Crimona edition, Jerusalem 1986, no. 291; Meir ben Barukh, *Sheelot u-Teshuvot ha-Maharam*, Prague edition, ed. M. A. Blakh, Budapest 1895, no. 780 (p. 319).

Translation. I. A. Agus, *Rabbi Meir of Rothenburg*, New York 1970, No. 298. pp. 326–327.

Isaac left home on the twenty-fifth of the month of Adar (1271) and a year later heard that his wife had given birth to a child. She gave birth in 1272, in the week after the festival of Purim. Isaac quickly came home, tried unsuccessfully to divorce her as an adulteress and to deprive her of her rights under the marriage contract. To do this, he had to go through the rabbinical court. To his surprise, the court that he turned to, three months after the event, refused to hear his case. In his distress, Isaac used what was an accepted technique in those days, the mechanism of the *takana* known as 'Cancelling the daily offering' or 'Holding up the prayer service'. In the case under discussion the *dayanim* stated explicitly that they did not want to meet to hear Isaac's case until he, using the 'Holding up the prayer service' mechanism, created social pressure on the members of the rabbinical court to meet and begin to deal with this case. When the court began its work the protocol allows us to follow the efforts it took and its method of work. The main part of the court's work is to gather evidence and indeed there is information in the protocol on quite a few witnesses.

Sarah claimed that when Isaac left home she was already pregnant, and Isaac claimed 'there was never such a thing' since everyone knew that he was away and that she gave birth twelve months later. According to the protocol three types of witnesses came forward.

The first witnesses were a number of members of the same family, the Shaltiel family, who lived in the township where the incident took place. From the wording we understand the wordings of the court. The court sent emissaries to where the incident took place, and these emissaries required everyone who knew something about the case to come and give testimony, on pain of being banned from the community. It seems that a local court had a mechanism for collecting testimony even from remote places, a mechanism that included making contact with potential witnesses, collecting written testimony, and confirmation of written evidence. These witnesses testified that Isaac had indeed left home in the month of Adar and that his wife had given birth twelve months after he had left.

The second witness was a man who came and witnessed that on the eve of the festival of Shavuot, Pentecost, he was on the way to Sarah's house in order to make *kiddush* for her. Since he knew that there was no man to make *kiddush* for her, he took the trouble to go to her house to do this for her and he saw that she was keeping company with non-Jewish men, and the *dayanim* assumed that it was at this time that Sarah conceived, since from Pentecost to the festival of Purim, when she gave birth, is exactly nine months.

The third witness was the father of the wife who had come to consult the *dayanim* even before Isaac came home, and asked that he be permitted to kill his daughter, to drown her in the river, since he suspected that in the end she would convert to Christianity. The *dayanim* explicitly forbade the father from killing her. They said that the situation described in the Talmud bore no resemblance to the case they had before them and furthermore they emphasized that it was clear that if anyone came to consult a court on whether or not it is permissible to kill someone, the answer must always be that it is forbidden.

Additional testimony that the court heard, that later turned out to be most important testimony, was that on the 7th of the month of Elul, seven months prior to the birth, someone asked Sarah if she was pregnant, and she vehemently denied being pregnant and roundly cursed the enquirer.

Source. Meir ha-Kohen, *Teshubot Maimuniut* in to Moses ben Maimon, *Mishneh Tora,* Ishut No. 25; Meir ben Barukh, *Sheelot u-Teshuvot Maharam bar Barukh,* Lemberg 1860, No. 310; Mordechai ben Hillel *Sefer Mordechai,* Tractat Yebamot, No. 121–122.

Chapter 4

Q. L.'s husband was killed on a day of rioting and massacre. L. lost her *ketubah* document. Is she entitled to collect her *ketubah*?

A. L. is entitled to collect the *ikkar ketubah* (the amount the husband undertakes to pay the wife on the dissolution of the marriage), since no document is required to prove the existence of an obligation classified as *maaseh-beit-din* (a final verdict or decision handed down by a rabbinical court), an obligation imposed by the rabbis on all husbands alike, as a mere verbal claim of having discharged such obligation is of no avail unless one can produce documentary evidence (B.M. 17b). Therefore, if L. can prove through witnesses that her husband married her as a maiden, she will be entitled to collect 200 zuzim as her *ikkar ketubah*; otherwise she will be entitled to collect only 100 zuzzim. As to the £50 of dowry and £50 of additional jointure that we generally include in the *ketubah* of our wives, I am doubtful whether these sums may be considered *maaseh-beit-din.* It seems to me, however, that since we have a firmly established custom throughout our kingdom to write the aforementioned amounts in the *ketubah* of all maidens, the same law should apply to these amounts as to a *maaseh-beit-din.* We should not, therefore, put forth the claim, for the benefit of the heirs, that the widow has already received payment of the dowry and the additional jointure. Moreover since witnesses testify that L. and her husband lived a normal married life when he was killed, we cannot put forth the claim that she has already received payment of the aforementioned amounts, for we have no reason for supposing that the husband deposited valuables with L. to be used in payment of her *ketubah.* Thus Rabbi Simon of Jointville ruled that when a man suddenly dies we need not suppose that he deposited valuables with his wife to be used by her in payment of her *ketubah,* for while he is alive the *ketubah* is not an obligation requiring payment

and as long as he is well he does not think of the possibility of his death.
Sources. Mordecai Hagadol, p. 179 margin. Cf. Asher, *Responsa* 85, 1; *Terumat Hadeshen* 330.
Translation. I. A. Agus, *Rabbi Meir of Rothenburg*, New York 1970, No. 321 pp. 346-347.

Q. L., A's widow, who has had no children with A., gave away his books to religious (or charitable) institutions of two or three communities before she took the required oath regarding her *ketubah*. A's heirs summoned her to court, claiming that she had taken from A. more than was due her according to her *ketubah*. L. appeared in court and was ready to take the required oath regarding her *ketubah* but died before she could do so L.'s trustee asked the judges how to dispose of the books that were entrusted to him, and the judges instructed him to deliver them to the donee institutions. Now A.'s heirs demand the return of these books.

A. This is a highly controversial subject. The courts of Würzburg – and I believe also of Speyer, following a decision by R. Simha – usually follow the decision of R. Eliezer (Shebu. 48a) which in our case would be in favour of the donees. However we follow the ruling of Rav and Samuel (ibid.) that the entire estate belongs to the heirs. According to our opinion, therefore even if the donee has already taken possession of the widow's gift, it should be returned to the heirs; but, if the donee has originally taken possession of the gift at the instruction of a court, we usually uphold the court's decision on the assumption that the court has followed the opinion of R. Eliezer (ibid. 48b). However, you state that the court has also decided that L.'s heirs have no claim on A.'s estate; they followed, therefore the opinion of Rav and Samuel. Thus their decision in favour of the donees can no longer be construed as following the opinion of R. Eliezer, and must be considered a mere error.

Source. Meir ben Barukh, Sefer She`elot uTeshuvot, Crimona edition, Jerusalem 1986, no. 88.
Translation. I. A. Agus, *Rabbi Meir of Rothenburg*, New York 1970, No. 339 pp. 360-361.

Q. While critically ill, A. gave a bill of divorcement to his wife on condition that, should he die from the illness, she should be divorced therewith from the day she received the divorceAfter the bill of divorcement was thus delivered to A.'s wife it was torn up. Subsequently A.'s condition improved; he got up from bed, walked to the synagogue and to the market place without a cane, and even arranged his mother's funeral out of town. Twenty-eight days thereafter, however, he felt ill again and died. During those twenty-eight days he was at times lying in bed, and at other times he was upon his feet. Was the bill of divorcement effective?

A. The bill of divorcement was ineffective. First, according to R. Tam and Ri the stipulated condition, mentioned above, is to be interpreted to mean that A. intended the divorce to become effective an hour before his death. Since on the day of A.'s death the bill of divorcement was already torn up, no divorce took place. A similar query was sent to me from Acco [Aachen?] and l ruled that no divorce took place. I always advise women who receive such conditional divorces to guard their bill of divorcement carefully till their husbands die. Secondly, even according to Rashi, who believes that the divorce becomes effective immediately upon the delivery of the bill of divorcement, if the husband subsequently dies from his illness, the fact that A. was walking thereafter without the support of a cane nullified the bill of divorcement. In any event the advice of a medical authority would be required in order to decide whether or not A. died from his first illness; and nowadays we have no medical authorities on whose expert opinion we can definitely rely in such a vital matter.

R. Meir adds: I do not have available to me the *tosafot* to tractate Gittin, nor the code books from the south (Alfasi and Maimonides). I composed the above with the help of heavenly guidance if you find that the *tosafot* and the codes hold another opinion, my opinion is nullified by theirs; for what does a poor man know, one who dwells in darkness and gloom for three and one half years. [Probably a reference to his being imprisoned at this time.]

This *responsum* was sent to Rabbi Asher from the tower of Ensisheim and was placed in his (R. Meir's) *novellae* in his own handwriting.

Sources. Meir ben Barukh, *Sefer Sharei Teshuvot*, ed. M. A. Blakh, Berlin 1891, no. 108, pp. 199–201; Meir ha-Kohen, Teshubot Maimuniut in to Moses ben Maimon, *Mishneh Tora, Nashim*, no. 30.

Translation. I. A. Agus, *Rabbi Meir of Rothenburg*, New York 1970, No. 378 pp. 385–387.

Chapter 5

Q. A believed that his brother's [childless] widow had retained from her husband's estate more than the amount due her for her *ketubah*, and he refused to go through with the ceremony of *halitzah* unless she paid him some money. They finally agreed on the sum of twenty* marks. Before the ceremony of *halitzah* she gave the money to a trustee in A.'s presence A. said to the trustee: 'After the ceremony, you must give me the twenty* marks.' To this, the trustee replied, 'I shall.' After the ceremony, the widow produced her *ketubah*, swore that she had not received enough to cover same, and demanded the twenty* marks back. The court decided that the twenty* marks belonged to the widow. Is the decision of the court correct?

A. The question is not sufficiently clear for us to express an opinion. If the widow told the trustee, in A.'s presence, to give the money to A. after the ceremony, the money belongs to A., since this money is simply a gift which the trustee received for A.'s benefit. But, if the widow said nothing while she gave the money to the trustee, A.'s words are of no avail, and she can reclaim her money in payment of her *ketubah*.

Sources. Meir ben Barukh, *Sefer She'elot uTeshuvot*, Crimona edition, Jerusalem 1986, no. 65; Meir ben Barukh, *Sheelot u-Teshuvot ha-Maharam*, Prague edition, ed. M. A. Blakh, Budapest 1895, no. 30; Meir ben Barukh, *Sheelot u-Teshuvot Maharam bar Barukh*, Lemberg 1860, no. 339.

Translation. I. A. Agus, *Rabbi Meir of Rothenburg*, New York 1970, No. 384 pp. 390.

I confirm with my signature that Shlomo the son of R. Hananel, a righteous man of blessed memory, on the instruction of my master in Mainz, came before me, because he has been making a protest by disturbing the prayer service and has been complaining about his wife, who was refusing to have sexual relations with him. And her relatives had been saying about him that he is not allowed to be a member of the community since he is *petzua daka* [the term used in Deut. 23:2 to describe a man who has a sexual defect]. And I was asked, not because of any wisdom I might have, and not because of my worth, to give him my humble opinion. I, Avi Ha'ezri [Eliezer ben Yoel haLevi, known as Raviah] examined him and I saw that the orifice of his urethra was out of place and was cut off from the flesh of the glans penis by more than a finger's width and when he urinated he would spray upward towards his eye. And I asked him how his happened to him. And he answered me saying: It was well known in the community that I had been ill and was obliged to walk with the help of a walking stick and in the end my legs gave in and I have not been able to walk at all for more than a year. And I bought a horse and hired a guide and I rode to Barcelona to see the benefactor and esteemed R. Sheshet, the physician. And when I came to see him and he saw my affliction, he said you have a worm in your glans penis which is eating on you and is also pulling towards it the tendons where the tendons come together, since all of them are connected and joined to each other. He said that if I agreed he would cut away the flesh containing the worm, but then it would be uncertain whether or not I would be able to father a child. And I agreed to the operation. And he took a scalpel and he cut in the place closest to the worm. And immediately the tendons of my legs were freed and spread out again as did my other organs. And he took a bandage and a dressing and he cured me, and here I am healthy as you can see for yourself and I have the same sexual desires as any other man. And the place of the cut was almost a finger and a half wide and went as far as the penis duct and beyond, and had damaged and affected to some extent the whole length of the penis, and upwards the cut was the width of the flesh without any damage apart from below where the jet of urine sprays and the sperm duct. And because these two cuts were attached together by the dressing there is now a scar in this place which draws the head of the glans penis upwards so urine sprays upwards. And relating to the subject of his request, I pronounced him fit to be a member of the community. And in the light of these matters his wife returned to him and he took her and a son was born and his father called him Eleazar, after me.

Source. Eliezer ben Joel ha-Levi, *Sefer Ra'aviah*, ed. D. Debelitski. Bnei Brak 2000, No. 983, pp. 74–75.

APPENDIX 2

The main scholars referred to

Asher ben Yehiel, also known as Asheri and Rosh, c. 1250–1327, talmudist. Student of Meir ben Barukh of Rothenburg, lived in Cologne and Coblenz. From there he moved to Worms. Left Germany in 1303, reached Barcelona and settled in Toledo, Spain.

Eleazar ben Judah of Worms, c. 1165–c. 1230, Worms, Germany. Scholar in the fields of *halakhah*, theology, and exegesis. Eleazar was the last major scholar of the Hasidei Ashkenaz. Born in Mainz, he travelled and studied in many of the centres of Jewish learning in Germany and northern France.

Eliezer ben Nathan, known as Raban, 1090–1170, Mainz, Germany. A leading rabbinic authority in Germany in the twelfth century. His major opus is *Sefer Ha-Raban* (the Book of Raban), which he called *Even ha-Ezer* (Stone of Help).

Eliezer Ben Samuel of Metz. c. 1115–c. 1198, tosafist and halakhic authority. Served as an intermediary between the centres of study in France and those in Germany. He was a pupil of Jacob ben Meir Tam (Rabbenu Tam), as well as of Samuel ben Meir, and Hayyim Cohen of Paris. Among his disciples were some of the greatest German rabbis, such as Eliezer ben Yoel HaLevi and Eleazar ben Judah of Worms, author of the *Roke'ah*.

Eliezer ben Yoel haLevi, known as Raviah, c. 1140–1225, Bonn, Germany, rabbinic scholar. His maternal grandfather was Eliezer ben Nathan. Eliezer moved around a great deal, apparently through France and Lombardy, living, *inter alia*, in Bonn, Worms, Würzburg, Mainz, Metz, Cologne, and Regensburg.

Ephraim ben Jacob of Bonn, b. 1132, liturgical poet and commentator. Wrote the *Sefer Zekhirah* (Book of Remembrance) and elegies on the sufferings of the Jews during the Second Crusade.

Gershom ben Judah Meor haGolah, c. 960–1028. One of the first great

THE MAIN SCHOLARS REFERRED TO

German talmudic scholars, born in Metz, lived in Mainz.

Isaac ben Moses of Vienna, *c.* 1180–*c.* 1250, halakhic authority in Germany and France. He is usually referred to as Isaac Or Zarua, i.e., by the title of his important halakhic work. Isaac was born in Bohemia, coming into contact with contemporary German and French scholars, whose teachings had a great influence on him.

Jacob ben Meir, known as Rabbenu Tam, *c.* 1100–1171, Ramerupt, France. Tosafist and leading French scholar of the twelfth century. Rabbenu Tam was the grandson of Rashi and the son of Meir ben Samuel, Rashi's son-in-law.

Judah ben Samuel HaHasid, d. 1217, Speyer and Regensburg. Main mentor and promoter of the Hasidei Ashkenaz movement. Judah was one of the most prominent scholars of the Middle Ages in the fields of ethics and theology.

Maharam, *see* Meir ben Barukh of Rothenburg.

Meir ben Barukh of Rothenburg, *c.* 1220–1293, known as Maharam. Teacher, scholar, tosafist, and supreme arbiter in ritual, legal, and community matters in Germany. He was born in Worms. At the age of twelve Meir joined the well known school of Rabbi Isaac Or Zarua, in Würzburg, where he studied for about six years. Subsequently moved to Mainz, where he studied under his relative Rabbi Judah ben Moses ha-Kohen. Finally, he went to France and studied under the great tosafists Samuel ben Solomon of Falaise and Yehiel of Paris. After 1240 he returned to Germany and within a few years settled in Rothenburg, where he remained for more than forty years, until 1286.

Or Zarua, *see* Isaac ben Moses of Vienna.

Raban, *see* Eliezer ben Nathan.

Rabbenu Tam, *see* Jacob ben Meir.

Rashi, *see* Solomon ben Isaac.

Raviah, *see* Eliezer ben Yoel haLevi.

Rosh, *see* Asher ben Yehiel.

Simhah ben Samuel, Speyer, Germany, second half of the twelfth and beginning of the thirteenth century, German scholar.

Solomon ben Isaac, known as Rashi, 1040–1105, Troyes, France. The leading commentator on the Bible and Talmud.

Glossary of Hebrew terms used

aggada (adj.) *aggadic* That part of the Talmud (cf.) and *Midrash* (cf.) that contains anecdotes, parables, legends, and so forth.

aginut The state of being an *agunah* (cf.).

agunah (pl. *agunot*) A married woman who for whatsoever reason is separated from her husband and cannot remarry, either because she cannot obtain a divorce or because it is unknown whether he is still alive. Here the term is also applied to a 'levirate widow', i.e. a woman who cannot remarry because she cannot obtain *halizah* (cf.) from the levir or if it is unknown whether he is still alive (Tbab. Git. 26b, 33a; Yev. 94a).

al kiddush Hashem In sanctification of the Name of God – the supreme aspiration.

amidah Literally 'standing'; the core and main element of each of the prescribed daily prayer services, must be recited standing.

amora (pl. *amoraim*) Used as a generic term for the rabbis of the post-Mishnaic period, whose activities were centred on the interpretation of the *Mishnah* (cf.) both in Palestine and in Babylonia between the third and sixth centuries.

anusa (pl. *anusot*) A woman forced to convert to Christianity.

Ashkenaz Germany.

Beit Din (pl. *Batei Din*) Rabbinical court.

Beit Hillel, Beit Shammai The two great schools called after Hillel and Shammai (*c.* 50 CE–*c.* 30 CE), the famous pair of the leaders of the Sanhedrin. In general Beit Shammai took a more stringent attitude and Beit Hillel a more lenient one.

beraitah Literally 'outside' (sources) – the writings of *amoraim* (cf.) that were not included in the *Mishnah* (cf.).

bitul tefilah Disruption of public prayers in order to seek redress of a wrong (mainly a judicial or moral one). A form of protest and way of arousing public indignation afforded to an individual who felt that an injustice had been perpetrated upon him by the constituted authorities or by any other individual. This practice was prevalent mainly in the Middle Ages among Ashkenazic Jewry.

brakha God is blessed before the performance of all *mitzvot* (cf.), and the benediction is called a *brakha*.

brakha levatalah (pl. *brakhot levatalah*) A *brakha* (cf.) that is recited inappropriately or incorrectly, so that the name of God in taken in vain, transgressing the Third Commandment of the Decalogue.

chazan Synagogue cantor.

dam hatohar (pl. *damei hatohar*) Literally 'pure blood'; refers to the period (up to forty or eighty days) following childbirth. See Lev. 12: 2–4.

dayan (pl. *dayanim*) Judge – a rabbi sitting on the bench of a rabbinical court.

Eretz Yisrael The Land of Israel.

GLOSSARY OF HEBREW TERMS USED

erusin Engagement prior to marriage at which, originally, the *ketubah* (cf.) was drawn up.
Gaon (pl. *geonim*) The formal title of the heads of the academies of Sura and Pumbedita in Babylonia, recognized by the Jews as the highest religious authority from the end of the sixth century to the middle of the eleventh.
Gemarah Discussions and explanations of the *Mishnah* (cf.), compiled by the *amoraim* (cf.) in Babylonia and Palestine from the fourth century to the sixth.
gematria The assignation of numerical values to Hebrew letters.
geonic period 589 CE–1038 CE.
gett Jewish bill of divorce.
gezerah A rabbinical enactment; usually a preventative measure or ban.
hakhel Meaning 'assemble' and referring to the commandment to assemble all the people before God (Deut. 31:12).
halakhah (general): (adj.) halakhic (adv.) halakhically; *halakhah* (specific) (pl. *halakhot*) As a generic term *halakhah* refers to the whole of the legal system of Judaism, comprising all the details of Jewish law and observance. A specific *halakhah* refers to a specific Jewish law.
halizah A ceremony through which a woman is released from the levirate tie and is free to marry someone else if the levir (her late husband's brother) does not marry her.
hallah A form of bread. The term also applies to the portion of dough set aside and given to the priest (Num. 15:19–20).
hametz Leaven and leavened food.
Hasid (n.), *Hasidic* (adj.) A member of the Hasidei Ashkenaz (cf.) group.
Hasidei Ashkenaz A social and ideological group, with a specific religious outlook, in medieval German Jewry. The first centres of the movement were Regensburg in southern Germany and the communities of Speyer, Worms, and Mainz on the Rhine; from there, its influence spread over most of Germany and, to a certain extent, to France also. Its main literature was composed during the first half of the thirteenth century.
havdalah Literally 'distinction'. The blessing recited at the termination of Sabbaths and festivals, in order to emphasize the distinction between the sacred and the ordinary.
karet Literally 'cutting off' or 'extirpation', a punishment at the hands of Heaven mentioned in the Bible as the penalty for a considerable number of sins committed deliberately, such as: idolatry, desecration of the Sabbath, the eating of leaven on Passover, incest and adultery; and for some forbidden foods.
kasher (v.) To make a vessel 'kosher' or fit for use halakhically (cf.).
ketubah; (pl. *ketubot*) Marriage contract by which a bridegroom obligates himself to provide a settlement for his wife if he divorces her, or through his heir if he predeceases her. *Ketubah* is the name both of the written contract itself and of the amount the husband is obliged to settle on his wife.
kiddush Literally 'sanctification'. The prayer recited over a cup of wine in the home and the synagogue to consecrate the Sabbath or festival in fulfilment

of the biblical commandment to 'Remember the Sabbath day to keep it holy' (Exod. 20:8; Pes. 106a).

kiddush haShem The sanctification in the name of God, referring to the conduct of Jews when among non-Jews that gave Jews and Judaism a good reputation.

kidushin The complete marriage ceremony, which consisted of two parts, the engagement and the wedding. Kidushin is also a tractate of the Talmud.

kitzotah The sum of the three amounts specified in the *ketubah*.

kohen (pl. *kohanim*) Member of the priestly class – traditionally the descendants of the biblical Aaron. The original priests had responsibilities in the Temple in Jerusalem. After the destruction of the Temple they assumed specific ritual functions in the synagogue. They were prohibited from coming into contact with the dead (Lev. 21:1–4), and were restricted as to whom they were permitted to marry (Lev. 21:7).

libun Literally 'whitening' but in fact referring to the additional days following menses and prior to immersion and return to normal cohabitation.

lulav A shoot or young branch of a tree, here referring to the palm branch – one of the components of the Four Species used in the ritual the festival of Sukkot.

ma'akhelet The term for knife used specifically in the story of the binding of Isaac (Gen. 22:10) and so always associated with it.

mamzer (pl. *mamzerim*) A child born from a union prohibited according to the Torah. Though usually translated as 'bastard', it does not refer to a child born out of wedlock.

mamzerut The state of being a *mamzer* (cf.).

maneh One hundred zuz (cf.). The maneh was a weight in gold or silver equal to fifty holy, or 100 common, shekels.

matza (pl. *matzot*) Unleavened bread, eaten on the Passover, when leaven of any sort is forbidden.

Midrash (pl. *Midrashim*) A homiletic method of biblical exegesis and also the whole compilation of homiletic teachings on the Bible. A way of interpreting biblical stories that goes beyond simple distillation of religious, legal or moral teachings. This genre of rabbinic literature contains analogies and compilations of homilies, lore and law, usually forming a running commentary on specific books of the Bible.

mikvah (pl. *mikvaot*) A pool or bath of clear water, immersion in which renders a person who has become ritually unclean through contact with the dead (Num. 19) or any other defiling object, or through an unclean flux from the body (Lev. 15), especially a menstruating or postpartum woman, ritually clean. It is similarly used for vessels (Num. 31:22–23).

milei de-hibah Literally 'words of fondness': the affectionate relationship between husband and wife.

Minhag (pl. *minhagim*) Literally 'custom', and also meaning usage, i.e., customs which have been accepted into practice.

minhah The afternoon prayer service, one of the three daily services of the Jewish liturgy.

Mishnah The redaction by Rabbi Judah the Prince (usually called simply 'Rabbi')

GLOSSARY OF HEBREW TERMS USED

in the late second century of discussions by a group of rabbinic sages known as the *tannaim* (cf.) that attempted to set down the whole of the oral tradition of Jewish law and practice so that it would not be lost following the dispersion of the Jews after the destruction of the Temple.

mitzva (pl. *mitzvot*) Literally 'commandment'. A precept, or religious duty. There are 613 commandments given in the Torah, and the seven rabbinic commandments instituted later make a total of 620.

mohar In biblical times *mohar*, whereby the groom bought his wife from her father (Gen. 24:53; Exod. 22:15–16; Hos. 3:2), was the accepted practice. It was then customary that the groom give the bride gifts, and that she bring certain property to her husband's home upon marriage: slaves, cattle, real estate, etc. (cf. Gen. 24:59–61; 29; Judg. 1:14 ff.; I Kgs 9:16).

moredet Woman who refuses to have conjugal relations with her husband.

movet al kiddush haShem Martyrdom (death by sanctification in the name of God).

nedunyah The dowry that a wife brings to her husband on marriage. The custom of *nedunyah* became clearly defined and institutionalized only in the talmudic period. Evidence of the custom of *nedunyah* is to be found in Tobit (7:14, 8:21) and in the Assuan papyri (Cowley, *Aramaic*, nos 15, 18). This custom gradually superseded that of *mohar* (cf.).

niddah State of ritual impurity, a person in such a state, especially a menstrual woman.

nihbeshet (pl. *nihbashot*) A woman taken prisoner by an enemy in circumstances in which rape or her granting of sexual favours to save her own skin was considered to be very likely.

nikhsei melog Usufructuary property that the woman chooses not to enter into the *ketubah* (cf.), or which she inherits or gains during her marriage. Therefore, the husband does not benefit from any increase in their worth, nor does he accept responsibility for damage, deprecation or loss. His sole benefit from these properties is the right to enjoy their profits.

paytan Writer of liturgical poems.

peru u-revu The Hebrew words for 'Be fruitful and multiply' in Gen. 1:22, the commandment to procreate.

petzua daka The term used in Deut. 23:2 to describe a man who has a defect in his sexual organs: 'No one whose testes are crushed [*petzua daka*] or whose member is cut off shall be admitted into the congregation of the Lord.'

piyyutim Jewish liturgical poetry.

responsa A rabbinic term relating to an exchange of letters in which one party consults another on a halakhic (cf.) matter.

Rosh Hodesh The first day of every month in the Hebrew calendar.

semikhah The ceremony of the laying of hands on an offering brought to the Temple. See Lev. 1:4.

shema One of the basic prayers in Judaism, consisting of three paragraphs from the Pentateuch and starting with the declaration of God's unity: 'Hear, O Israel: The Lord our God, the Lord is One' (Deut. 6:4).

shevuyah (pl. *shevyot*) A woman taken prisoner by an enemy in circumstances in which rape or sexual harm was considered to be unlikely.

shofar The ram's horn, blown at the new year.

sukkah (pl. *sukkot*) During the Festival of Tabernacles, Jews were required (Lev. 23:42) to eat and sleep in a temporary structure with roofing made of natural materials through which sunlight could penetrate. Such a booth is called a *sukkah*.

taharah State of ritual purity.

takanah (pl. *takanot*) A ruling or ordinance agreed upon by the community.

talmidei hakhamim Scholars, especially those erudite in the Talmud.

Talmud The *Mishnah* together with the *Gemarah*. Considered the definitive work on Jewish law and tradition.

tameh A ritually impure person.

tanna (pl. *tanaim*) A teacher of the oral law and in particular one of the sages of the *Mishnah* (cf.) from the time of Beit Hillel and Beit Shammai (cf.) to the period of Rabbi Judah the Prince.

tefillin Phylacteries: two black leather boxes containing scriptural passages (Exod. 13:1–10, 11–16; Deut. 6:4–9, 11:13–21).which are bound by black leather straps on the left hand and on the head and are worn during the morning services on all days of the year except Sabbaths and festivals.

tehinnah (pl. *tehinnot*) A supplemental prayer of supplication.

Tosafists Writers of *tosafot* (cf.).

tosafot Collections of commentaries on the Talmud (cf.) arranged according to the order of the talmudic tractates. The concept of the *tosafot* was originally bound up with the method of study characteristic of the schools of Germany and France in the twelfth to fourteenth centuries.

tumah Ritual impurity.

tzitzit (pl. *tzitziot*) Fringe worn on garments as prescribed in Num. 15:38–39.

tzon barzel Property that is appraised before the marriage and its value entered into the *ketubah* (cf.). The husband undertakes to repay the full value of this property in the event that he dies or they are divorced. On marriage these items are regarded as his property, any increase in their value accrues to him and he is liable for any damage, depreciation or loss.

yeshivah A talmudic academy.

yevamah A married man who died without leaving offspring.

yibbum A levirate marriage – one between a widow whose husband died without offspring and the brother of the deceased (the levir) as prescribed in Deut. 25:5–6.

zav (m.), *zavah* (f.) A person who has involuntary secretions.

zimun Three or ten men who together recite the grace after meals as a group.

zuz (pl. *zuzzim*) An ancient Hebrew silver coin minted during the Roman period, replacing and equivalent in value to the imperial denarii or the Roman provincial drachmas of Vespasian, Titus, Domitian, Trajan, and Hadrian.

Bibliography

Primary sources

Hebrew

Agus, A. (ed.) *Responsa of the Tosaphists*, New York 1954.
Alexander Susslein, *Ha-Aguddah*, Cracow 1571.
Asher ben Yehiel, *Shut haRosh*, ed. S. Yudelov, Jerusalem 1994.
Avot de-Rabbi Nathan, New York and Jerusalem 1997.
Barukh ben Issac, *Sefer ha-Terumah*, Jerusalem 1979.
Davis, M. D., *Hebrew Deeds of English Jews*, London 1888.
Delaborde, H., *Oeuvres de Rigord et de Guillaume le Breton*, vol. I, Paris 1882.
Dinur, B. Z., *A Documentary History of the Jewish People*, second series, 10 vols, Jerusalem 1965.
Eleazar ben Judah of Worms, *Sefer ha-Roqeah*, ed. I. Z. Cahana, Jerusalem 1957–1962.
Eleazar ben Yehudah of Worms, *Shirat Ha-Roke'ah*, ed. I. Meiseles, Jerusalem 1993.
Eliezer ben Joel ha-Levi, *Sefer Ra'aviah*, ed. V. Aptowizer, 4 vols, Jerusalem 1964.
Eliezer ben Nathan, *Sefer Even haEzer, Sefer Ra'avan*, Jerusalem 1984.
Eliezer ben Samuel of Metz, *Sefer Yere'im*, Vilna 1901.
Ephraim of Bonn, *Sefer Zekhirah*, ed. A. Habermann, Jerusalem 1970.
Exodus Rabbah, Midrash Shemot Rabbah, ed. A. Shinan, Jerusalem 1984.
Genesis Rabbah, Midrash Bereshit Rabba, ed. J. Theodor and C. Albeck, Jerusalem 1965.
Gershom ben Judah, *Teshuvot Rabbenu Gershom Me'or haGola*, ed. S. Eidelberg, New York 1956.
Grayzel, S. *The Church and the Jews in the Thirteenth Century*, rev. edition, New York 1966.
Hayim ben Rabbi Yitzhak, *Responsa*, Leipzig 1860.
Issac ben Joseph of Corbeil, *Sefer Amudei Gola hanikra Semak*, Jerusalem 1979.
Issac ben Meir of Duren, *Sefer Sha'arei Dura*, Lublin 1599.
Isaac ben Moses, *Sefer Or Zarua*, 2 vols, Zhitomir 1862.
Jacob of Marvege, *Shelot u-Teshuvot min haShamayim*, Jerusalem.
Jacob ben Judah Hazan from London, *Ez Hayyim*, ed. I. Brodie, 3 vols, Jerusalem 1962–1964.
Jacob ben Meir, *Sefer haYashar leRabbenu Tam: Heleq haShe'elot vehaTeshunot (Responsa)*, ed. S. F. Rosental, Berlin 1898.
Jacob ben Meir, *Sefer haYashar leRabbenu Tam: Heleq haHidushim* (News), ed. S. S. Schlesinger, Jerusalem 1959.
Jacob ben Moses Mulin, *Shut Maharil heHadashot* (new *Responsa*), ed. Y. Satz, Jerusalem 1977.
Jacob Weil, *She'elot u Teshuvot Maharil Weil*, ed. Y. Satz, Jerusalem 1988.
Joseph ben Solomon Colon (Maharik), *Responsa Maharik*, Warsaw 1884.

BIBLIOGRAPHY

Judah ben Samuel, *Sefer Hasidim*, ed. J. Wistinetzki, Frankfurt 1942.
Mahzor Vitry, ed. S. Horowitz, Nuremberg 1892.
Meir ben Barukh, *Sheelot u-Teshuvot Maharam bar Barukh*, Lemberg 1860.
Meir ben Barukh, *Sefer Sharei Teshuvot*, ed. M. A. Blakh, Berlin 1891.
Meir ben Barukh, *Sheelot u-Teshuvot ha-Maharam*, Prague edition, ed. M. A. Blakh, Budapest 1895.
Meir ben Barukh, *Sefer Minhagim deBei Maharam b. Barukh meRotenburg*, ed. Israel Elfenbein, New York 1938.
Meir ben Barukh, *Responsa, Rulings, and Customs*, ed. I. Z. Cahana, 3 vols, Jerusalem 1957–1962.
Meir ben Barukh, *Sefer She'elot uTeshuvot*, Crimona edition, Jerusalem 1986.
Meir ha-Kohen, *Teshubot Maimuniut* to Moses ben Maimon, *Mishneh Tora*.
Meir ha-Kohen, *Haggahot Maimuniuot* to Moses ben Maimon, *Mishneh Tora*.
Midrash Echa Rabbati (Lamentations Rabbah), Vilna 1899.
Midrash Bereshit Rabba, Jerusalem 1965.
Midrash on Psalms (*Midrasch Tehillim*), ed. S. Buber, Vilna 1892 (repr. Jerusalem 1966).
Midrash Devarim Rabbah (on Deuteronomy), ed. S. Liebermann, Jerusalem 1974.
Midrash Sifre on Devarim (Sefre on Deuteronomy), ed. L. Finkelstein, Berlin 1939.
Midrash Tanhuma, ed. S. Buber, Jerusalem 1964.
Mordechai ben Hillel, *Sefer Mordechai*, in editions of the Babylonian Talmud.
Moses Parnas, *Sefer HaParnas*, Vilna 1897.
Moses of Coucy, *Semag. Sefer Mizvot Gadol*, Venice 1807, Iav.
Moses of Zurich, *Sefer haSemak miZurich*, ed. I. J. har-Shosanim, 3 vols (Jerusalem, 1973).
Moses ben Isaac Mintz, *She'elot uTeshuvot Rabbenu Moshe Mintz*, ed. J. S. Domb, 2 vols, Jerusalem 1991.
Nathan ben Yehuda, *Sefer haMachkim*, ed. M. Fridman, Jerusalem 1968.
Pirke deRabi Eliezer, ed. Hayim M. Horowitz, Jerusalem 1973.
Pesiqta Rabbati, Warsaw 1893.
Rokeah, Z. M., *Medieval English Jews and Royal Officials*, Jerusalem 2000.
Salfeld, S., *Das Martyrlogium des Nuremberger Memorbuches*, Berlin 1938.
Sefer Kol Bo, Lemberg 1860.
Barukh ben Issac, *Sefer ha-Terumah*, Jerusalem 1979.
Sefer haDmaut (Book of Crying), ed. S. Barnfeld, 3 vols, Berlin 1924–1926.
Sefer Tosafot haShalem, ed. J. Gellis, vol. 1, Jerusalem 1982.
Sefer ha-Miktso'ot.
Simon ben Zadoc, *Sefer Thazbeth*, Jerusalem 1951.
Solomon B. Isaac (Rashi), *Sefer ha-Ora*, ed. S. Buber, Lemberg 1905.
Solomon B. Isaac (Rashi), *Sefer ha-Pardes*, ed. H. L. Ehrenreich, Budapest 1924.
Solomon B. Isaac (Rashi), *Responsa Rashi*, ed. I. Elfenbein, New York 1943.
Solomon B. Isaac (Rashi), *Siddur Rashi*, ed. J. Freimann and S. Buber, Berlin 1911.
Teshubot Geonim Kadmunim, Berlin 1608.
Teshuvot uPsakim, Responsa et Decisiones. ed. E. Kupfer, Jerusalem 1973.
Yalkut Shimoni, 2 vols, Jerusalem 1968–1973.

Zidkiya ben Abraham, *Sefer Shibolei haLeqet haShalem*, ed. Shlomo Buber, Vilna 1886.

Other

Abrahams I., *Hebrew Ethical Wills*, Philadelphia 1976, pp. 207–209.
Aronius, J., *Regesten zur Geschichte der Juden im fränkischen und deutschen Reiche bis zum Jahre 1273*, Berlin, 1902.

Secondary sources

Hebrew

Aptowizer, V., *Introduction to Sefer Ra`aviah* (Eliezer ben Joel haLevi), Jerusalem 1938.
Baer, I., 'The Religious-Social Tendency of Sepher Hassidim', *Zion* (1938), pp. 1–50.
Bar-Leve, L., 'Our Women have a lovely Custom', *Massekhet* 6 (2007), pp. 47–85.
Blidstein, G. J., 'The Personal Status of Apostate and Ransomed Women in Medieval Jewish Law', *Shenaton haMishpat haIvri* 3–4 (1976–1977), pp. 35–116.
Dinari, Y., 'The Impurity Customs of the Menstruate Woman: Sources and Development' [Hebrew], *Tarbiz* 49 (1980), pp. 302–324.
Dinari, Y., 'The Profanation of the Holy by the Menstruant Woman and "Takanat Ezra"', *Te`uda* 3 (1983), pp. 17–37.
Elias Bar-Levav, L., 'Our Women have a lovely Custom: Halakhic Divisions in Accordance with Women's Practice in the Middle Ages', *Massekhet* 6 (2007), pp. 47–85.
Emanuel, S., 'New Responsum of Meir ben Barukh', *Mayan* 38 (1993), pp. 15–18.
Freiman, A. H., *Seder qidushin wenisu`in*, Jerusalem 1945.
Gilat, Y. D., *Studies in the Development of the Halakha*, Jerusalem 1992.
Grossman, A., *The Early Sages of Ashkenaz*, Jerusalem 1981.
Grossman, A., 'Violence against Women in Medieval Mediterranean Jewish Society', in *A View into the Lives of Women in Jewish Societies*, ed. Y. Azmon, Jerusalem 1995.
Grossman, A., *The Early Sages of France*, Jerusalem 1995.
Grossman, A., *Pious and Rebellious: Jewish Women in Europe in the Middle Ages*, Jerusalem 2001.
Grossman, A., 'Rashi's Teachings concerning Women', *Zion* 70 (2005), pp. 157–190.
Grossman, A., *Rashi*, Jerusalem 2006.
Güdemann, M., *Sefer haTorah veHayim beArzot Askenaz beYemei haBenyim*, 3 vols, Warsaw 1897.
Har-Shefi, B., 'Women and Halakha in the Years 1050–1350 CE: Between Law and Custom', Ph.D thesis submitted to the Hebrew University in Jerusalem, Jerusalem 2002.
Katz, J., 'Levirate Marriage (*Yibbum*) and *Halizah* in Post-talmudic Times', *Tarbiz* 51 (1981–1982), pp. 59–106.

Landau, L., 'Rashi's Stories in the Babelonian Talmud', *Eshel Beer-Sheva* 3 (1986), pp. 101–117.
Lewyson, J., *Nephashut Zadikim*, Frankfurt 1855.
Rokeah, Z. M, 'Pietism, Money and Women in Thirteenth Century England', in *Religion and Economy Connections and Interactions*, ed. M. Ben Sasson, Jerusalem 1995, pp. 179–190.
Schapiro, M., 'Divorce on Grounds of Revulsion', *Dine Israel* 2 (1970), pp. 117–153.
Shiloh, S., 'Impotence as a Ground for Divorce', *Fifth World Congress of Jewish Studies* (1969), vol. 3, pp. 353–367.
Sperber, D., *Customs of Israel*, 7 vols, Jerusalem 1989–1998.
Ta-Shma, I., 'On the History of Polish Jewry in the Twelfth–Thirteenth Centuries', *Zion* 53 (1988), pp. 347–70.
Ta-Shma, I., *Early Franco-German Ritual and Custom*, Jerusalem 1992.
Ta-Shma, I., *Ritual, Custom and Reality in Franco-Germany, 1000–1350*, Jerusalem 1996.
Urbach, E. E., *Abraham ben Azriel, Sefer Arugat Habosem: Prolegomenon*, Jerusalem 1963.
Urbach, E. E., 'The Responsa of R. Asher b. Yehiel in Manuscripts and Printed Editions', *Shenaton Ha-Mishpat Ha-Ivri* 2 (1975), pp. 1–154.
Urbach, E. E., *Ba'alei ha-Tosafot* [Hebrew], 4th edition, Jerusalem 1980.
Valler, S., *Women in Jewish Society in the Talmudic Period*, Ramat Gan 2000.
Weinroth, J., 'The Law of the Rebellious Wife', doctoral thesis submitted to Tel-Aviv University, 1981.
Westreich, E., *Transitions in the Legal Status of the Wife in Jewish Law*, Jerusalem 2002.
Wieder, N., *The Formation of Jewish Liturgy in the East and the West*, 2 vols, Jerusalem 1998, vol. 1, pp. 323–351.
Zimmer, E., *Society and its Customs*, Jerusalem 1996.
Yasif, E., 'The Body Never Lies: The Body in Medieval Jewish Folk Narratives', *People of the Body: Jews and Judaism from an Embodied Perspective*, ed. H. Eilberg-Schwartz, New York 1992, pp. 203–221.
Yoval, I., 'HaHesderim haKaspiyim shel haNissuim beAshkenaz beYemei haBenayim', in *Religion and Economy: Connections and Interactions*, ed. M. Ben Sasson, Jerusalem 1995, pp. 191–207.

Other

Abulafia, A. S., 'The Interrelationship between the Hebrew Chronicles on the First Crusade', *Journal of Semitic Studies* 27 (1982), pp. 221–239.
Adler, M., *Jews of Medieval England*, ed. E. Goldston for the Jewish Historical Society of England, London 1939, pp. 17–42.
Agus, A., *The Binding of Isaac and Messiah*, New York 1988.
Anderson, G., 'The Garden of Eden and Sexuality in Early Judaism', in *People of the Body; Jews and Judaism from an Embodied Perspective*, ed. H. Eilberg-Schwartz, New York 1992, pp. 47–68.
Baron, S., *A Social and Religious History of the Jews*, vol. 6, Philadelphia 1958.

Bartlet, S., *Licoricia of Winchester: Marriage, Motherhood and Murder in the Medieval Anglo-Jewish Community*, London 2009.
Bartlet, S., 'Women in the Medieval Anglo-Jewish Community', in *Jews in Medieval Britain*, ed. P. Skinner, Woodbridge 2003, pp. 113–127.
Bartlet, S., 'Three Jewish Businesswomen in Thirteenth Century Winchester', *Jewish Culture and History* 3:2 (2000), pp. 31–54.
Baskin, J., 'Some Parallels in the Education of Medieval Jewish and Christian Women', *Jewish History* 5 (1991), pp. 41–51.
Baskin, J., 'Jewish Women in the Middle Ages', in *Jewish Women in Historical Perspective*, ed. J. Baskin, Detroit 1991, pp. 94–114.
Baskin, J., 'From Separation to Displacement: The Problem of Women in Sefer Hasidim', *AJS Review* 19 (1994), pp. 1–18.
Baskin, J., 'Dolce of Worms: Women Saints in Judaism', in *Women Saints in World Religious*, ed. A. Sharma, Albany, NY 2000, pp. 39–69.
Baumgarten, E., *Mothers and Children: Jewish Family Life in Medieval Europe*, Princeton, NJ 2004.
Berger, D., *The Jewish-Christian Debate in the High Middle Ages*, Philadelphia 1979.
Biale, D., *Eros and the Jews*, Berkeley, CA 1997.
Biale, R., *Women and Jewish Law*, New York 1984.
Blumenkranz, B., *Les Auteurs chrétiens latins du Moyen-Ages sur les Juifs e le Judaisme*, Paris 1963.
Bonfil, R., 'The Cultural and Religious Traditions of French Jewry in the Ninth Century, as reflected in the Writings of Agobard of Lyons', in *Studies in Jewish Mysticism, Philosophy and Ethical Literature*, Jerusalem 1986, pp. 327–348.
Borchers, S., *Jüdisches frauenleben im Mittelalter*, Frankfurt am Main 1998.
Boshof, E., *Erzbischof Agobard von Lion. Leben und Werk*, Vienna 1969.
Boshof, E., *Königtum und Königschersschaft im 10. und 11. Jahrhundert*, Munich 1993.
Brooke, C., *The Medieval Idea of Marriage*, Oxford 1994.
Brundage, J. A., *Law, Sex, and Christian Society in Medieval Europe*, Chicago 1987.
Buckley, T., and Gottlieb, A., 'A Critical Appraisal of Theories of Menstrual Symbolism', in *Blood Magic: The Anthropology of Menstruation*, ed. T. Buckley and A. Gottlieb, Berkeley, CA 1988.
Bynum, C. W., *Jesus as Mother*, Berkeley, CA and Los Angeles 1984.
Cadden, J., *Meaning of Sex Difference in the Middle Ages*, Cambridge 1995.
Chazan, R., 'The Blois Incident of 1171: A Study in Jewish Intercommunal Organization', *PAAJR (Proceedings of the American Academy for Jewish Research)* 36 (1968), pp. 13–31.
Chazan, R., *European Jewry and the First Crusade*, Los Angeles 1987.
Chazan, R., 'The Timebound and the Timeless Jewish Narration of Events', *History and Memory* 6 (1994), pp. 5–34.
Chazan, R., 'Ephraim ben Jacob`s Compilation of Twelfth Century Persecutions', *Jewish Quarterly Review* 84 (1994), pp. 397–416.
Chazan, R., *The Jews of Medieval Western Christendom, 1000–1500*, Cambridge 2006.

Cohen, J., *Living Letters of the Law: Ideas of the Jews in Medieval Christianity*, Berkeley, CA 1999.

Cohen, S. J. D., 'Menstruants and the Sacred in Judaism and Christianity', in *Women's History and Ancient History*, ed. S. Pomeroy, London 1991, pp. 273-299.

Cohen, S. J. D., 'Purity and Piety: The Separation of Menstruants from the Sancta', in *Daugters of the King: Women and Synagogue*, ed. S. Grossman and R. Haut, Philadelphia 1992, pp. 103-116.

Cohen, S. J. D. 'Purity, Piety, and Polemic: Medieval Rabbinic Denunciations of "Incorrect" Purification Practices', in *Women and Water: Menstruation in Jewish Life and Law*, ed. R. R. Wasserfall, Hanover, NH and London 1999, pp. 82-100.

Cook, L. A., 'Body Language: Women's Rituals of Purification in the Bible and Mishna', in *Women and Water: Menstruation in Jewish Life and Law*, ed. R. R. Wasserfall, Hanover, NH and London 1999, pp. 40-59.

Dalarun, J., 'The Clerical Gaze', in *A History of Women: Silences of the Middle Ages*, ed. C. Klapisch-Zuber, Cambridge, MA 1992, pp. 15-42.

Davis, M. D., *Hebrew Deeds of English Jews*, London 1888.

Douglass, M., *Purity and Danger: An Analysis of Concepts of Pollution and Taboo*, London 1966.

Douglass, M., *Implicit Meanings*, London 1975.

Eidelberg S. (ed. and trans.), *The Jews and the Crusaders: The Hebrew Chronicles of the First and Second Crusades*, Madison, WI 1977.

Eilberg-Schwartz, H., *The Savage in Judaism*, Bloomington, IN 1990.

Einbinder, S. L., 'Pucellina of Blois: Romantic Myths and Narrative Conventions', *Jewish History* 12 (1998), pp. 29-46.

Einbinder, S. L., 'Jewish Women Martyrs: Changing Models of Representation', *Exemplaria*, 12 (2000), pp. 105-127.

Einbinder, S. L., *Beautiful Death*, Princeton, NJ 2002.

Ennen, E., *Frauen im Mittelalter*, Munich 1984.

Epstein, L. M., *Marriage Laws in the Bible and the Talmud*, Cambridge, MA 1942.

Falk, Z. W., *Jewish Matrimonial Law in the Middle Ages*, Oxford 1966.

Fentress J., and Wickham, C., *Social Memory*, Oxford 1994.

Finkelstein, L., *Jewish Self-government in the Middle Ages*, New York 1924.

Fonrobert, C. E., 'Yalta's Ruse: Resistance against Rabbinic Menstrual Authority in Talmudic Literature', in *Women and Water: Menstruation in Jewish Life and Law*, ed. R. R. Wasserfall, Hanover, NH and London 1999, pp. 60-81.

Friedman, M. A., *Jewish Polygamy in the Middle Ages* [Hebrew], Jerusalem 1986.

Geisel, Christof, *Die Juden im Frankenreich. Von den Merowingern bis zum Tode Ludwigs des Frommen*, Frankfurt am Main 1998.

Geller, S., 'Blood Cult: Towards a Literary Theology of the Priestly Work of the Pentateuch', *Prooftext* 12 (1992), pp. 97-124.

Germania Judaica, Tübingen 1963.

Goldin, S., '"Companies of Disciples" and "Companies of Colleagues": Communication in Jewish Intellectual Circles', *Vox Iudaica: Communication in the Jewish Diaspora in the Pre-modern period*, ed. S. Menache, Leiden 1996, pp. 127-139.

Goldin, S., 'The Role of Ceremonies in the Socialization Process: The Case of Jewish Communities of Northern France and Germany in the Middle Ages', *Archives de sciences sociales des religions* 95 (1996), pp. 163-178.

Goldin, S., 'The Socialisation for *Kidush ha-Shem* among Medieval Jews', *Journal of Medieval History* 23 (1997), pp. 117-138.

Goldin, S., 'Juifs et juifs convertis au Moyen-Age "Es-tu encore mon frére?"', *Annales, Histoire, sciences sociales* 54 (1999), pp. 851-874.

Goldin, S., 'Jewish Society under Pressure: The Concept of Childhood', in *Youth in the Meddle Ages*, ed. P. J. Goldberg and F. Riddy, York 2004, pp. 25-43.

Goldin, S., *The Ways of Jewish Martyrdom*, Turnhout 2008.

Goldy, C. N., 'A Thirteenth Century Anglo-Jewish Woman crossing Boundaries, Visible and Invisible', *Journal of Medieval History* 34 (2008), pp. 130-145.

Graetz, N., *Silence is Deadly: Judaism confronts Wifebeating*, Northvale, NJ 1998.

Grayzel, S., *The Church and the Jews in the Thirteenth Century*, rev. edition, New York 1966.

Gregg, J. Y., *Devils, Women and Jews*, New York 1997.

Grossman, A., 'Medieval Rabbinic Views on Wife-beating, 800-1300', *Jewish History* 5 (1991), pp. 53-63.

Grossman, A., 'The Status of Jewish Women in Germany, Tenth to Twelfth Centuries', in *Zur Geschichte der jüdischen Frau in Deutschland*, ed. J. Carlebach, Berlin 1993, pp. 17-35.

Harris, M., 'The Concept of Love in Sepher Hassidim', *JQR* [*Jewish Quarterly Review*] 50 (1949), pp. 13-44.

Hauptman, J., *Rereading the Rabbis: A Woman's Voice*, Boulder, CO 1998.

Heill, J., 'Agobard, Amolo, Das Kirchengut und die Juden von Lyon', *Francia* 25 (1998), 39-76.

Herlihy, D., and Klapisch-Zuber, C., *Tuscans and their Families: A Study of the Florentine Catasto of 1427*, New Haven, CT 1985.

Hoffman, L., *Covenant of Blood: Circumcision and Gender in Rabbinic Judaism*, Chicago 1996.

Johanek, P., 'Merchants, Markets and Towns', in *The New Cambridge Medieval History*, vol. 3, ed. T. Reuter, Cambridge 1999, pp. 64-94.

Jordan, William C., 'Women and Credit in the Middle Ages: Problems and Directions', *Journal of European Economic History* (Rome) 17 (1988), pp. 33-62.

Jordan, William C., 'Jews on Top: Women and Availability of Consumption Loans in Northern France in the Mid-thirteenth Century', *Journal of Jewish Studies* 29:1 (1978), pp. 39-57.

Jordan, W. C., *The French Monarchy and the Jews*, Philadelphia 1989.

Jordan, W. C., *Women and Credit in Pre-industrial and Developing Societies*, Philadelphia, 1993.

Kanarfogel, E., *Jewish Education and Society in the High Middle Ages*, Detroit 1992.

Krautheimer, R., *Mittelalterliche Synagogen*, Berlin 1927.

Liberman, S., 'The Martyrs of Caesarea', *Annuaire de l'Institut de philologie et d'histoire orientales et slaves* 7 (1939-1944), pp. 395-446.

Linder, A., *The Jews in Roman Imperial Legislation*, Jerusalem 1987.

Loudon, I., *Death in Childbirth: An International Study of Maternal Care and Maternal Mortality, 1800-1950*, Oxford 1992.

Marcus, I. G., *Piety and Society: The Jewish Pietists of Medieval Germany*, Leiden 1981.

Marcus, I. G., 'Mothers, Martyrs and Moneymakers: Some Jewish Women in Medieval Europe', *Conservative Judaism*, 38 (1985), pp. 34-46.

Marienberg, E., *Niddah: lorsque les juifs conceptualisent la menstruation*, Paris 2003.

McCulloh, J. M., 'Jewish Ritual Murder: William of Norwich, Thomas of Monmouth, and the Early Dissemination of the Myth', *Speculum* 72:3 (1997), pp. 698-740.

Meacham, T., 'An Abbreviated History of the Development of the Jewish Menstrual Laws', in *Women and Water: Menstruation in Jewish Life and Law*, ed. R. R. Wasserfall, Hanover, NH and London 1999, pp. 23-39.

Meens, R., 'Ritual Purity and the Influence of Gregory the Great in the early Middle Ages', in *Unity and Diversity in the Church*, ed. R. N. Swanson, Oxford 1996, pp. 31-43.

Meens, R., 'Questioning Ritual Purity: The Influence of Gregory the Great's Answers to Augustine's Queries about Childbirth, Menstruation and Sexuality', in *St Augustine and the Conversion of England*, ed. R. Gameson, Stroud 1999, pp. 174-186.

Meens, R., '"A Relic of Superstition": Bodily Impurity and the Church from Gregory the Great to the Twelfth Century Decretists', in *Purity and Holiness: The Heritage of Leviticus*, ed. M. J. H. M. Poorthuis and J. Schwartz, Leiden 2000, pp. 281-293.

Meens, R., 'Sacred Space and the Right of Sancturity in the early Middle Ages', paper presented at the University of Exeter, 10 April 2003.

Morrell, S., 'An Equal or a Ward: How Independent is a Married Woman according to Rabbinic Law?' *Jewish Social Studies* 44 (1982), pp. 189-210.

Müller-Mertens, E., 'The Ottonians as Kings and Emperors', in the *New Cambridge Medieval History*, vol. 3, ed. T. Reuter, Cambridge 1999, pp. 233-266.

Mundill, R. R., *England's Jewish Solution: Experiment and Expulsion, 1262-1290*, Cambridge 1998.

Noble, S., 'The Jewish Woman in Medieval martyrology', *Studies in Jewish Bibliography, History and Literature in honor of I. E. Kiev*, ed. C. Berlin, New York 1971, pp. 347-355. See also this article in *Proceedings of the Fifth World Congress of the Jewish Studies*, vol. 2 (1972), pp. 133-140.

Ozick, C., 'Notes towards Finding the Right Question', in *On Being a Jewish Feminist*, ed. S. Heschel, New York 1983, pp. 120-151 (repr. from *Lilith Magazine*, no. 6 (1979).

Porsche, M., 'Speyer: The Medieval Synagogue', in *The Jews of Europe in the Middle Ages, Tenth to Fifteenth Centuries*, ed. C. Cluse, Turnhout 2004, pp. 435-488.

Power, E., *Medieval Women*, Cambridge 1975.

Prawer, J., *Histoire du Royaume Latin de Jérusalem*, Paris 1969.
Riley-Smith, J., 'Crusading as an Act of Love', *History* 65 (1980), pp. 177–192.
Riley-Smith, J., 'The First Crusade and the Persecution of the Jews', *Persecution and Toleration, SCH* 21, ed. W. J. Sheils, Oxford 1984, pp. 51–72.
Riley-Smith, J., *The First Crusade and the Idea of Crusading*, London 1986 (1993).
Riley-Smith, J., *The First Crusade, 1096–1131*, Cambridge 1997.
Rokeah, Z. M., *Medieval English Jews and Royal Officials*, Jerusalem 2000.
Ross, T., *Expanding the Palace of Torah*, London 2004.
Runciman, S., *A History of the Crusades*, vol. 1 Cambridge 1968.
Shatzmiller, J., 'Doctors and Medical Practices in Germany around the Year 1200: The Evidence of Sefer Hasidim', *Journal of Jewish Studies* 33 (1983), pp. 583–93.
Shatzmiller, J., *Jews, Medicine and Medieval Society*, Berkeley, CA 1994.
Shaye, J. D., 'Menstruants and the Sacred in Judaism and Christianity', in *Women's History and Ancient History*, ed. S. Pomeroy, Chapel Hill, NC 1991, pp. 273–299.
Simonsohn, S., *The Apostolic See and the Jews: Documents, 492–1404*, Toronto 1988.
Simonsohn, S., *The Apostolic See and the Jews: History*, Toronto 1991.
Soloveitchik, H., 'Three Themes in the 'Sefer Hasidim', *AJS Review* 1 (1976), pp. 311–357.
Soloveitchik, H., 'Concerning the Date of the Composition of Sefer Hasidim', in *Culture and Society in Medieval Jewry: Studies dedicated to the Memory of Haim Hillel Ben-Sasson*, ed. M. Ben-Sasson, R. Bonfil, and H. J. Hacker (Jerusalem 1989), pp. 383–388.
Spiegel, S., *The Last Trail: On the Legends and Lore of the Command to Abraham to Offer Isaac as a Sacrifice*, trans. J. Goldin, Philadelphia 1967.
Stacey, R. C., 'The Conversion of Jews to Christianity in Thirteenth Century England', *Speculum* 67 (1992), pp. 263–283.
Taitz, E., 'Kol Ishah, the Voice of Woman: Where was it Heard in Medieval Europe?' *Conservative Judaism* 38 (1985), pp. 46–62.
Taitz, E., 'Women's Voices, Women's Prayers: Women in the European Synagogues of the Middle Ages', in *Daughters of the King, Women and the Synagogue*, ed. S. Grossman and R. Haut, Philadelphia 1992, pp. 59–67.
Tallan, Cheryl, 'Medieval Jewish Widows: their Control of Resources', *Jewish History* 5 (1991), pp. 63–74.
Ta Shma, I., 'Niddah', *Encyclopedia Judaica*, vol. 12 (1972), pp. 1141–1148.
Toch, M., 'Die jüdische Frau im Erwerbsleben des Spätmittelalters', in *Zur Geschichte der jüdischen Frau in Deutschland*, ed. J. Carlebach, Berlin 1993, pp. 37–48.
Toch, M., *Dunkle Jahrhunderte. Gab es ein jüdisches Frühmittelalter?* Kleine Schriften des Arye-Maimon Instituts, vol. 4, Trier 2001, 29.
Toch, M., *The Jews in Europe, 500–1050*, The New Cambridge Medieval History, ed. P. Fouracre, vol. 1, Cambridge 2001.
Udovitch, A., 'At the Origins of the Western Commenda: Islam, Israel, Byzantium', *Speculum* 37 (1962), pp. 198–207.

Wallace-Hadrill, J. M., *The Frankish Church*, Oxford 1983.
Wasserfall, R., 'Menstruation and Identity: The Meaning of *Niddah* for Moroccan Women Immigrants to Israel', *People of the Body: Jews and Judaism from an Embodied Perspective*, ed. H. Eilberg-Schwartz, New York 1992, pp. 309–327.
Wasserfall, R., 'Introduction', in *Women and Water: Menstruation in Jewish Life and Law*, ed. R. R. Wasserfall, Hanover, NH and London 1999, pp. 1–18.
Wegner, J. R., *Chattel or Person?* New York 1988.
Weissler, C., '*Mizvot* built into the Body: *Tkhines* for *Niddah*, Pregnancy, and Childbirth', *People of the Body: Jews and Judaism from an Embodied Perspective*, ed. H. Eilberg-Schwartz, New York 1992, pp. 101–115.
Woolf, Jeffrey Robert, 'Medieval Models of Purity and Sanctity: Ashkenazic Women in the Synagogue', in *Purity and Holiness: The Heritage of Leviticus*, ed. M. J. H. M. Poorthuis and J. Schwartz, Leiden 2000, pp. 263–280.

Index

Abba Saul 135, 136, 146
Abbaye 20, 45
aginut 148, 252
Agobard 6, 9, 24, 261, 263
Alexander Zuslin HaCohen 214
Amidah 174
Ammi 100, 106, 108, 126, 127
amora, amoraim 20, 21, 45, 56, 100,
    107, 136, 140, 142, 150, 151, 179,
    196, 200, 203, 252
Anjou 113
anusa 252
Asher ben Yehiel (Rosh) 53, 67, 84, 114
Ashkenaz 24, 68, 69, 70, 71, 72, 73, 78,
    108, 109, 126, 146, 149, 154, 161,
    166, 167, 184, 209, 212, 224, 250,
    251, 252, 253, 259
Augustine 8, 9, 264
Avigdor ben Elijah haCohen 146, 166

Babylonia 14, 118, 136, 151, 152, 188, 189,
    202, 252, 253
Barukh ben David HaCohen 66
Beit Hillel 91, 252, 256
Beit Shammai 91, 252, 256
Ben Azai 21
Beraitah 202
Bernard of Clairvaux 11
bigamy 40, 41, 102, 103, 104, 110, 113,
    119, 124, 146, 154, 238
Bitul tefilah 117
Bordeaux 7

brakha 179, 180, 185, 219, 252
brakha levatalah 180, 185, 252
Burchard of Worms 102

Charles II the Bald 6
Chazan 25, 47, 48, 49, 86, 261
Cologne 6, 7, 33, 109, 214, 236, 250

damei hatohar 213, 252
David ben Kalonymus of Minzburg
    147
David ben Rabbenu Shealtiel 40, 41
Dayan 54, 56, 60, 61
Divorce 165, 167, 260

Eleazar of Worms 17, 63, 69, 174, 177,
    207, 229, 230
Eliezer ben Nathan (Raban) 75, 76, 77,
    88, 93, 94, 96, 98, 99, 103, 106,
    107, 108, 109, 112, 117, 118, 119,
    140, 147, 154, 158, 159, 181, 167,
    198, 200, 201, 209, 210, 217, 218,
    220, 221, 222, 250, 251, 257
Eliezer ben Samuel of Metz 109, 143,
    218, 219, 221, 257
Eliezer ben Simon 130
Eliezer Ben Yoel haLevi of Bonn,
    Raviah 80, 111, 112, 117, 119, 120,
    125, 130, 131, 141, 147, 166, 191,
    201, 202, 207, 216, 219, 220, 221,
    222, 235, 248, 250, 251
Elijah of Paris 214

INDEX

Ephraim ben Jacob of Bonn 36, 53, 63, 64, 65, 66, 67, 86, 119, 227, 257
Eretz Yisrael 100, 107, 108, 112, 118, 252
erusin 95, 252
Evrard 9

Family Purity *see Niddah*
First Crusade 7, 11, 23, 25, 32, 35, 36, 37, 47, 48, 64, 75, 76, 103, 109, 216, 236, 260, 261, 265

Gaon 118 152, 189, 243, 253
Gershom Me'or Ha-Golah 22, 47, 67, 98, 104, 105, 109, 112, 113, 114, 152, 153, 157, 159, 161, 227, 250
gett 22, 37, 46, 67, 77, 78, 79, 88, 100, 101, 104, 110, 113, 114, 120, 124, 125, 126, 127, 128, 130, 131, 132, 133, 148, 149, 150, 151, 152, 153, 155, 156, 157, 159, 160, 161, 162, 163, 164, 253
Gregory I, 9

Hakhel 217
halakhah 4, 10, 13, 15, 17, 21, 39, 41, 58, 67, 78, 82, 83, 100, 115, 121, 134, 144, 148, 169, 170, 172, 176, 183, 184, 189, 190, 197, 198, 203, 206, 208, 210, 211, 213, 220, 231, 235, 250, 253
Halizah 79, 88, 259
Hallah 186
Hametz 56
Hasid 69, 70, 73, 87, 253
Hasidei Ashkenaz 72, 73, 224
Havdalah 178
Hayim Paltiel 132, 165
Hayim, the son of Rabbi Isaac 40, 47
Huna 196

Ile de France 113
Innocent III 9
Isaac bar Sheshet 103, 118
Isaac ben Abraham (Rizba) 95, 127, 128, 129

Isaac ben Elijah 146
Isaac ben Moses Or Zarua 39, 40, 41, 42, 43, 47, 50, 79, 85, 88, 113, 114, 120, 134, 145, 146, 158, 163, 165, 166, 189, 202, 203, 214, 215, 216, 217, 218, 219, 221, 222, 223, 234, 235, 251, 257
Isaac ben Samuel 145
Isaac ben Todros 144
Isaac haLavan 145

Jacob ben Meir (Rabbenu Tam) 17, 37, 46, 49, 50, 64, 75, 124, 125, 126, 140, 141, 144, 145, 147, 148, 155, 156, 157, 158, 161, 168, 181, 182, 190, 191, 194, 205, 206, 209, 211, 214, 217, 219, 220, 222, 231, 232, 233, 235, 247, 250, 251, 257
Jacob ben Moses 163, 168, 185, 218, 257
Jacob of Marvege 182, 183, 218, 257
Jonah Girondi of Provence 192
Joseph the Blind 181
Judah HaCohen 137

karet 59, 164, 187, 195, 197, 207, 253
ketubah 19, 20, 22, 44, 45, 60, 76, 77, 81, 82, 84, 88, 89, 91, 92, 93, 94, 95, 96, 97, 99, 100, 104, 105, 106, 111, 113, 114, 115, 116, 117, 119, 122, 123, 127, 128, 129, 130, 131, 132, 133, 134, 137, 138, 139, 140, 141, 143, 148, 150, 151, 152, 153, 155, 156, 157, 159, 164, 165, 167, 227, 228, 238, 243, 245, 246, 247, 248, 253, 254, 255, 256
Kiddush, blessing 33, 81, 178, 188, 244
Kiddush haShem 27, 28, 29, 30, 33, 35, 36, 42, 43, 44, 45, 46, 252, 254
see also martyrdom
kiddushin, (marriage) 95, 115, 179, 254
Kiddushin, (Tractate) 20, 25, 54, 120, 178, 217
kitzotah 77, 93, 94, 96, 117, 254
Kohen 88, 89, 117, 120, 122, 165, 215, 216, 217, 218, 221, 245, 247, 251, 258

INDEX

Levirate Marriage 124
libun 196, 197, 198, 205, 206, 207, 208, 211, 254
Limoges 7
Lotharingia 6
Louis the Pious 5, 6, 9
Louis VII 11, 12, 66
lulav 88, 180, 181, 183, 254
Lyons 6, 9, 24, 261

Mainz 6, 7, 28, 54, 75, 103, 109, 114, 147, 163, 200, 236, 248, 250, 251, 253
mamzer 77, 79, 81, 136, 164, 254
mamzerut 82, 89, 124, 157, 161, 254
Maneh 117
Marital relations 121
Martyrdom 25, 47, 48, 86, 88, 255, 263
Mar Zutra 151
Meaux 7
Meir ben Barukh 25, 39, 49, 53, 67, 75, 80, 81, 82, 83, 84, 88, 89, 95, 97, 98, 116, 117, 118, 120, 131, 133, 134, 147, 149, 158, 160, 161, 162, 163, 164, 165, 166, 167, 168, 174, 176, 177, 214, 215, 216, 217, 218, 219, 222, 235, 243, 245, 246, 247, 248, 250, 251, 258, 259
Menstruation *see Niddah*
Meshulam ben David 40, 41
Meshullam ben Nathan 190
Metz 28, 144, 202, 250, 251
Midrash 21, 25, 33, 34, 35, 42, 48, 49, 50, 85, 86, 188, 216, 218, 252, 254, 257, 258
mikvah 45, 195, 196, 197, 209, 210, 211, 212, 231, 254
milei de-hibah 198, 254
Minhagim 215, 217, 258
Minhah 189, 192
Mishnah 3, 13, 14, 19, 20, 21, 22, 24, 25, 38, 67, 83, 85, 93, 110, 115, 117, 118, 120, 121, 122, 123, 126, 128, 131, 135, 139, 150, 151, 159, 164, 167, 173, 179, 181, 184, 185, 187, 193, 195, 196, 215, 218, 219, 252, 253, 254, 256

mitzvah 171
Mosel 7

Nathan ben Isaac 130
Nathan ben Maqir 54
nedunyah 22, 92, 128, 255
Nethanel of Chinon 144
niddah (Menstruation and Family Purity) 110, 116, 160, 172, 186, 187, 193, 194, 195, 196, 197, 198, 199, 200, 201, 202, 203, 204, 205, 206, 207, 208, 209, 210, 211, 212, 213, 214, 219, 220, 221, 222, 235, 255, 265, 266
nihbeshet 39, 40, 41, 42, 45, 255
nikhsei melog 148, 255
Normandie 113
Nürnberg 28, 120, 215, 217, 235, 258

Oppenheim 114
Organization of Jewish Life 13
Orleans 7, 208

Paris 7, 11, 12, 14, 24, 25, 47, 144, 155, 156, 219, 225, 227, 250, 251, 257, 261, 264, 265
Paul 9, 102
paytan 63, 255
Perez ben Elijah 146
Peter the Venerable 11
petzua daka 125, 164, 248, 255
Philip II 11
piyyutim 3, 27, 30, 36, 48, 54, 166, 178, 255
Poitiers 7
Prayer 173, 240, 244
Privilegium 6
Prominent Jewish Women 223

Raban *see* Eliezer ben Nathan
Rabbenu Tam *see* Jacob ben Meir
Rami bar Hama 136
Rashi *see* Solomon ben Isaac
Rav 140, 166, 200, 246
Rava 20, 45, 100, 105, 106

269

INDEX

Raviah *see* Eliezer Ben Yoel haLevi of Bonn
Regensburg 6, 28, 159, 166, 207, 236, 250, 251, 253
Reims 7
Responsa 24, 25, 49, 50, 84, 85, 86, 117, 118, 165, 166, 167, 168, 215, 216, 217, 218, 219, 220, 222, 234, 235, 246, 257, 258, 260
Rosh Hodesh 170, 215
Rudiger 6

Samson ben Abraham 147
Samuel ben Azriel 111
Samuel of Chappes 156
Samuel the Hasid 69
semikhah 180, 255
Shalom of Neustadt 214
Shema 173, 231
Sherira ben Hanina 152
shevuyah 39, 40, 41, 256
Shlomo son of Hananel 125
Shmuel bar Avraham 40, 41
Shofar 217, 218
Simha of Vitry 232
Simhah ben Samuel 77, 110, 112, 142, 147, 251
Solomon ben Isaac, Rashi 24, 42, 52, 54, 55, 56, 57, 58, 59, 60, 61, 62, 63, 106, 139, 140, 142, 145, 147, 148, 151, 153, 180, 181, 182, 187, 198, 199, 200, 201, 204, 206, 207, 223, 224, 231, 232, 233, 247, 251, 258
Source Materials 243
Speyer 6, 27, 28, 29, 77, 83, 86, 88, 112, 114, 142, 147, 163, 166, 185, 217, 236, 241, 246, 251, 253, 264
St Richard 11
sukkah 178, 180, 181, 185, 188, 256
Synagogue and Prayer 173

taharah 116, 196, 199, 204, 210, 212, 256
takanah 15, 256
Talmidei Hakhamim 14

Talmud 3, 4, 13, 14, 15, 18, 19, 20, 22, 33, 34, 42, 45, 51, 52, 54, 56, 62, 68, 73, 76, 79, 82, 83, 84, 85, 86, 91, 93, 99, 100, 101, 106, 107, 108, 110, 115, 124, 125, 126, 129, 136, 137, 145, 148, 150, 151, 153, 155, 157, 165, 169, 173, 174, 175, 178, 179, 181, 184, 189, 190, 192, 196, 198, 199, 200, 204, 208, 210, 211, 212, 213, 214, 215, 217, 218, 223, 244, 251, 252, 254, 256, 258, 260, 262
Talmudic Scholars 259
tameh 194, 195, 204, 256
Tam Rabbenu *see* Jacob ben Meir
Tanna 218
tefillin 173, 179, 256
tehinnah 192, 256
Theodosius 101, 102
The Rebellious Wife 149
Tosafists, Tosafot 49, 85, 87, 88, 120, 125, 164, 165, 166, 168, 215, 216, 217, 219, 220, 221, 222, 247, 256, 258, 260
Toulouse 7
Trier 7, 24, 30, 265
Troyes 7, 16, 54, 144, 251
tumah 194, 195, 196, 197, 198, 199, 200, 202, 203, 208, 210, 212, 256
Tzitzit 218
tzon barzel 152, 256

Verdun 7
Vienna 97, 113, 145, 166, 251

Weisselburg 28
Women's special commandments 185
Women's Status 16
    Change in 90
    Economic Status 90
    Social Standing 121
    Status within the family 99
Worms 28, 54, 87, 109, 114, 147, 163, 178, 214, 215, 216, 217, 218, 221, 222, 229, 230, 231, 233, 235, 236, 241, 250, 251, 253, 257, 261

Würzburg 28, 39, 40, 81, 246

Yedidiyah bar Yisrael 46
Yehiel HaKohen 66
Yekutiel the son of Rabbi Judah 66
Yeshivah 136
yevamah, 126, 256
Yibbum 88, 165, 166, 259

Yom Tov ben Isaac 109
Yosé 94, 180, 181

zav 195, 196, 256
Zera 196
zimun 88, 175, 256
Zuz 117, 254

EU authorised representative for GPSR:
Easy Access System Europe, Mustamäe tee 50,
10621 Tallinn, Estonia
gpsr.requests@easproject.com

www.ingramcontent.com/pod-product-compliance
Lightning Source LLC
Chambersburg PA
CBHW020122240426
43673CB00038B/557